The Turquoise Conspiracy

To my loving husband and children, each of you a beacon
whose light guided me throught the stormy seas.

The Turquoise Conspiracy

Asil Nadir,
the Collapse of Polly Peck and
the Persecution of a Family

Bilge Nevzat

with Gill Fraser

NOBLE HOUSE

Copyright © Bilge Nevzat 1999
First published in 1999 by Noble House
50 The Drive
South Woodford
London E18 2BJ

Distributed by Gazelle Book Services Limited
Falcon House Queen Square Lancaster
England LA1 1RN

British Library Cataloguing in Publication Data
A catalogue record for this book is available from the British Library

ISBN 0-9535096-0-5

Typeset by Amolibros, Watchet, Somerset
Publication of this title has been managed by Amolibros
Printed and bound by T J International, Padstow, Cornwall

CONTENTS

Prologue		1
Chapter One	*Beginnings*	7
Chapter Two	*From Rag Trade…*	29
Chapter Three	*…to Riches*	55
Chapter Four	*Polly Peck*	75
Chapter Five	*Noble Raredon*	101
Chapter Six	*Polly Peck Goes Public*	131
Chapter Seven	*The Taxman Cometh*	151
Chapter Eight	*The Turquoise Conspiracy*	185
Chapter Nine	*Beware of Strangers*	209
Chapter Ten	*End of a Dream*	239
Chapter Eleven	*The Great Escape*	261
Chapter Twelve	*British Justice*	297
Epilogue		321

LIST OF ILLUSTRATIONS

Facing page 166

1   The Nadir family, Cyprus, 1948

2   1953: a birthday party for Asil and Bilge

3   1951: Asil and his mother in front of the Europa Grocery Shop, Cyprus

4   1973: Wearwell goes public — Asil Nadir, Irfan Nadir, Fehim Nevzat, Güner Kasif, Johnny Holder & Jean Thomas

5   1983: Asil and Levent in St Tropez

6   1988: Bilge with Asil at Tijen & Rifat's wedding

7   1987: Asil with President Denktas in Cyprus

8   1988: At home after the wedding of Tijen & Rifat — Bilge and Asil 's mother with seven of her grandchildren

9   1988: A reception in Loch Manor in Cyprus to celebrate the marriage along with Bilge's & Fehim's twenty-fifth wedding anniversary

10   September 1989 — "Del Monte"

11   1984: Asil with Princess Anne

12   1992: Michael Mates — his gift of a watch to Asil was grossly distorted by the media

13   1990: After the opening of the Antalya Sheraton, from left to right — Tijen, Bilge, Asil, Safiye & Meral

14   1990: Lonely days in London — Bilge and Sunny

15   1992: Elizabeth Forsyth, the former head of South Audley Management — conviction for handling stolen funds quashed

16   1993: Bilge & Fehim in Cyprus

17   10th May, 1993: Asil back in Cyprus — "the big bird is back!"

ACKNOWLEDGEMENTS

A special thanks to Gill Fraser, without whose help asnd encouragement this book would not have been written.

Photograph of Elizabeth Forsyth courtsey of Carlton Television, copyright Carlton Television.

Photograph of Michael Mates courtesy opf Michael Mates, copyright Michael Mates.

PROLOGUE

The aeroplane door thudded shut in front of me as we prepared to taxi to the runway...and for a chilling instant I thought I heard once more the slam as I was locked in the police cell. Although it was only February, outside the aircraft window the London sky was the cornflower blue of a summer's day and the sun gleamed with the promise of an early spring. Inside, I was untouched by the warmth. In my head was the cold turmoil of self-doubt, loss and fear.

For the second time in my life, I was making an escape, leaving the tatters of my former existence behind me. More than thirty-one years earlier, I had sat on another aircraft willing the pilot onwards to let me embark on a glorious future. Then, I was with my family fleeing the cruelty and danger of 1960s Cyprus - freshly independent and locked in the suspicion, fear and political intrigue which were soon to erupt into violence, eventually into bloody warfare. On that night in August 1961, I had been full of excitement and hope for the new and prosperous life my family was planning to build in Britain. And I had been eager to see at last this nation which had for so long been held aloft as an ideal during my upbringing in colonial Cyprus.

Now it was 1993 and this time, it was from Britain that I was making my escape, hounded out by persecution and injustice which had wrecked my business, shattered my dreams and almost destroyed my family. Three decades of work, hope and ambition - not a trace left behind. As the jet hurtled into the sky taking me back to the eastern Mediterranean, I felt my last ties to Britain finally and painfully snap. Locked in a dark world of my own, my thoughts were inexorably drawn to that day, just a few weeks earlier, when the heavy door had clanged shut behind me, leaving me suddenly, frighteningly, alone in the police cell. In my mind, I was there again. The 5th November...

...For a few seconds, I remained quite still, taking in the scene around me - the grimy walls closing in on me; the wooden bench with its plastic mattress; the open box in the corner which I knew was a makeshift toilet; the thickly-glazed grille which let in only the barest glimmer of light. A shiver of revulsion passed through me. How could an ordinary day have led me to a place such as this? How long would it be before I was back with my family? Could it be that I would have to stay overnight?

1

That I would have to sleep on that grubby mattress and even use that stinking latrine? Fear and mounting horror mingled. My heart pounded faster and the stale atmosphere seemed to press down on me, the thick, dusty air choking in my throat...

Just a few feet away, locked in a nearby cell, sat my brother Asil - once the powerful head of Polly Peck and the tenth richest man in England, now bankrupted and charged with a string of thefts. I heard the muffled sound of his coughing from somewhere along the row of blank doors. Knowing he was so close brought a tiny scrap of comfort, yet it hurt to know that worry about me would be added to his own burden. The events of the previous few hours - when I had been torn from my family in the early morning, had seen my home turned upside down, had been bombarded with bewildering questions and now locked up in London's Holborn police station like a criminal - still seemed somehow unreal. The police line of questioning had been bizarre, but even through my mental numbness, I was dimly aware of some interlinking thread in the background which as yet eluded my grasp, and sensed a more sinister motivation beneath the surface...

A tremor of horror wrenched me back to the present - a present in which I was still in shock, barely half aware of what I had gone through and of how the experience would cloud my life for years to come. Had I known what I would learn during the next few months - known of the sordid machinations which could have seen me jailed for life for a fictitious bribery plot related to my brother's case - my faint sense of disquiet would have been magnified a thousandfold. As it was, I reflected, now belted into a front-row seat on the Cyprus-bound aircraft, that day in 1992 had shattered my faith in British justice; it had killed the fighting spirit which had driven me against the odds to try to save my business and keep our family together; it had deadened my natural optimism and trusting nature, introducing depths of black despair I could never have imagined before and which came close to destroying my marriage. For only the second time in my life, I had had to concede that there was nothing I could do to fight back.

Hot tears stung my eyes as I thought now of Asil, left behind in London that morning. Since childhood, we had shared a unique closeness, bonded first by our upbringing and then by our business aspirations. How ironic that we had shared, too, that grim incarceration. Once so full of hope, dreams and confidence, now all that lay virtually in tatters around us. How had we come to this?

Just two and a half years earlier, Asil had been chairman of Polly Peck International, the Stock Exchange miracle of the 1980s, turned by him from a rag-trade loser to the multi-million-pound conglomerate that he had envisaged, spanning half the world. For decades before, I had looked on as Asil groomed himself for the role of international entrepreneur; I had seen him develop from an ambitious young immigrant into a suave, charismatic tycoon with lavish offices. In recent years, though, I had seen disillusionment creeping up on him - disillusionment with his status in the City; with the City's demands as to how he should run his business and who should operate it alongside him; and with sycophants who would tell him only what they thought he wanted to hear. And I had seen, too, his sadness that business and financial success had never been able to help him secure the prize he valued most - happiness in his private life. Finally, I had seen him ousted from the firm he had loved and brought to riches; incarcerated and stripped of his dignity; laden with debt; publicly damned as a suspected thief and a liar, and facing a legal battle to clear his name. Since 1990 I had done my best to support him through the difficult times, to let him know he was not facing the crisis alone. Every day during those two years, I had seen him or spoken to him by telephone. For every court appearance, I had been there in the public gallery, listening to the legal argument and waiting for the day when he would be able to defend himself and the charges against him would be overturned. With a growing sense of disbelief - a sense of being caught up in a nightmarish real-life *Alice in Wonderland* - I had seen more charges brought, only to be dropped again, and then reinstated. At first, I had been certain that the whole charade would soon be over. But the passage of weeks, then months, then years, had proved me wrong and now I worried for Asil's health under the unrelenting strain. Behind the sleek exterior which had become his public facade was my generous, loving, sensitive brother, who was deeply wounded by each fresh blow - the brother whose private tears and disappointments few but me had ever seen. Guilty or innocent, I felt that if others knew him as I did, they could not have vilified him as they had. For Asil, too, that 5th November would prove to have been a turning-point, launching a puzzling train of events which would convince him he could never have a fair trial in Britain...and culminating in his dramatic flight to North Cyprus.

Asil's downfall had proved the catalyst for my own business undoing. For more than four years, I had headed my own firm, Noble Raredon, and was one of the few women to chair a public limited company in Britain. From modest beginnings, my husband Fehim and I had laid the foundations to make Noble Raredon the global chain of businesses of which we had dreamed. Just as it had been poised to reap the rewards, though, it had been dealt a deadly blow, starved by the banks of the vital finances it needed to grow. For twenty-five months since then, I had devoted my life to the business, struggling for ways to escape the faceless forces driving it inexorably, slowly, into a corner. Spurned by the City's financial institutions simply because I was a member of the Nadir family, I had spent each new day of those twenty-five months hoping to find the answer to our problems, as with each asset sale, with each staff lay-off, I had been pushed further against the wall. Fighting spirit alone - the stubborn refusal to be beaten - had kept my hopes alive, and with them the shell of Noble Raredon, its shares frozen on the Stock Exchange. But that determination was now extinguished.

Already my family and I had paid a high price for the battle to save the company. Far from being the strong mother I wanted to be for my children, I felt I had become a liability. With each new blow that had befallen the business, with each new disappointment I had received in my quest for financial survival, and finally, now, with the force of the law turning on me, I had seen my own pain reflected on the children's faces. My husband, too, had suffered. For months, Fehim had counselled me to sell my shares while I still could, to cut my losses and start a new life by severing all ties with Noble Raredon and handing it over to someone who might be able to save it. But I, furious at the injustice meted out at every turn, refusing to give up because it would look to others like an admission of wrongdoing, blindly certain for so long that some solution would emerge, had insisted on doing things my own way. A man who shrank from upset and unpleasantness, Fehim had been devastated to witness first my brother's arrest and then, two years later, my own, as our home was raided. Already, we had lived apart for eighteen months - Fehim in North Cyprus and me in London with the children - while he wrestled with the depression and fears that had followed. Now he was unable to face life in the Britain he had once admired and considered home, and had returned to the island. I knew that if I wanted to be with him, I must make my life there too.

As the plane sped onwards across Europe, the tears which had been constantly in my eyes for days before my departure - for weeks, even, as I saw my world crumbling - began anew, flowing harder as I thought, too, of my widowed mother. Seventy years old, living alone in North Cyprus, she had been made ill by the worry about her children's ordeal and the stress of trying to cope with the family's businesses over there. I thought, too, of my father, whose blessing as he lay dying six years before had set me on the path to buying my own company. My business troubles and the let-down to Noble Raredon shareholders hurt badly - but far more wounding was the shameful feeling that I had also failed my father. I remembered the day, just before he died, when he had told me of the trust fund he was setting up which would provide for me and my children's future. That money I had used to establish Noble Raredon; I had seen it virtually tripled in two years and seen it wiped out in a matter of days as the company's share price tumbled and was suspended. Now there was nothing left. With the thought came a sense of self-reproach and nagging doubt which were totally new to me. Though logic told me I had done all I could to try to save the company, I could not ward off the thought that there might have been some other avenue I should have explored. In almost the same moment, I was overwhelmed by anger - not simply for the business and the fortune I had lost, but for the way it had all happened. For once, though, it was not an anger which inspired me to fight back.

Suddenly, the memories crowded unbidden into my mind - from the nightmare of the 1990s, back in time to the happier decades when we were building businesses and families; to the night we left Cyprus for Britain, fleeing from violence and persecution to a society we thought then was the epitome of justice; to the innocent days of childhood in Famagusta, where our story began; even back to the day I was born - a moment I have heard so much about I almost feel I can remember it myself.

CHAPTER ONE

Beginnings

Young Asilkan Nadir's eyes glowed with anticipation as he surveyed the feast set out on the living room table. Plates piled high with sandwiches nestled among a treasure trove of delicious-looking cakes, brightly-coloured jellies towering shakily above the china plates and fresh lace tablecloth. Today was a very special day - one which Asilkan had been living in his dreams for several weeks. Today was his fifth birthday and he would be the centre of attention. The table in the living room had been laid ready for the birthday tea party, at which his friends and the family's neighbours would help him celebrate the important occasion. Asilkan knew his sister, Meral, three years his senior, must have got him a present since he had caught her several times during the last few days quickly hide something whenever he walked into the room. And his mother and father were bound to have a surprise gift for him, as well as laying on the party.

At the thought of his mother and father, a worried expression crossed Asilkan's face. The events of the last few hours had left him slightly bewildered. He had been told to expect the arrival, some time during early May, of a baby brother or sister. But he had still felt a little taken aback when his mother, Safiye, had retired to bed at lunch-time. He gathered from the short snatches of conversation he overheard that the baby would soon be here. Now his mother had been in the bedroom for several hours and Asilkan was anxious that she should not miss the birthday tea.

Outside on the covered terrace which ran along the rear of the house, his father Irfan paced distractedly. Asilkan walked out of the back door and fell into step, skipping occasionally to keep up and placing both hands firmly behind his back, just like his father had. They had been striding out for only a few minutes when there was a sudden commotion inside the house. Asilkan heard a child's shrill cry from his parents' bedroom and seconds later a plump woman, whom he recognised as a local nurse, appeared in the doorway and beckoned to his father. Within moments, it seemed to Asilkan, the house began to fill with neighbours who shook his beaming father by the hand and trooped in and out of the now open bedroom door. As each guest came and went, his father served up generous portions of cake and sandwiches.

Within an hour, the birthday tea had been reduced to little more than crumbs and crusts. Asilkan was surveying the devastated table when his father reappeared and led him by the hand into the bedroom. There, propped up on three pillows, lay his mother, cradling a blanket-wrapped bundle. As he peered cautiously over the edge of the wool, he glimpsed the tightly screwed-up face of his new sister. He was not impressed by her sense of timing.

––––––––––

That new arrival, on 1st May 1946, was me. Even now, my brother Asil jokes about how I came along just in time to ruin his birthday party - and how I have been the "thorn in his flesh" ever since, always stealing the limelight from him! Whether or not because of that shared birth-date, five years apart, the two of us forged a lasting bond during our childhood in Cyprus. And it is this tie which, binding us closer to each other than to almost anyone else, has enabled us to help each other through the dark days of the 1990s.

By the time I made my appearance in the world, our family was already setting out on the road to business prosperity - and ultimately to the heady success and the nightmare that was to be Polly Peck. In May 1946, we lived in a cramped residential street just within the walled town of Famagusta on Cyprus's eastern coast, but by the end of that year we had moved into a newly-built modern house in Herod of Attica Street, part of a developing suburb between the old town and the flourishing Greek Cypriot-dominated resort area of Varosha. The new house cost the princely sum of £700, from which my parents were later able to recoup a proportion by selling off part of the large plot. There were five rooms and a large glass sun-room leading on to the garden. There, showing the love of grapes typical of people from the south-western harbour town of Paphos, my father planted a vine which soon came to cover most of the garden on an overhead trellis and provided the cool shade under which we ate our meals in the summer. He also planted a fig tree which quickly grew to be enormous, a pomegranate tree and several almond trees. So many of my youthful memories are decorated by the delicate, white almond blossom. As children, we used to think of this house as a virtual palace and we would sit in state on the balcony overlooking the street. When I returned there once, after we had been living in Britain for many years, I had to laugh at our delusions of grandeur - everything seemed so small compared to the huge buildings I had grown used to seeing all around me in London.

Nevertheless, that 1946 move was a bold one for my parents and a major stride forward as they then tentatively laid the foundations of a minor business empire in and around Famagusta. Just three years earlier, they had moved from Lefke, on the opposite side of the island, where my father, Irfan, worked as an interpreter for the Cyprus Mines Corporation - a government-owned concern exploiting the region's rich copper reserves. In 1943, it had become known that all interpreters working for the colonial authorities would have to sign up as part of the military. My father feared this could mean him being sent off to fight anywhere in the world so, thinking of his wife and two young children - my sister Meral was then five and Asil just two - he decided to quit his job with the corporation. My father had been born in Paphos in 1917 and my mother, Safiye, three years later in Nicosia. They had met in Famagusta in 1936 and married a year later, settling immediately in Lefke. When they decided to move on, they chose to return to the east coast. My father already harboured ambitions to have his own business and they both saw Famagusta as a promising place for such a venture. They would also be close to my mother's widowed father, who still lived there.

In 1943, then, Irfan, Safiye, Meral and Asil had moved to the tiny old-fashioned Turkish house in Mustafa Pasa Yolu where I would be born. Soon afterwards, my father had opened his first shop in the main street of the old town, selling new and old books, stationery and gifts. It was the first bookshop in Famagusta and, because my parents did not have the capital to buy in a large stock, it became the town's first library as they lent out volumes for a small fee. Spurred on by the success of the bookshop, my father opened a second shop called Europa Novelty on Princess Elizabeth Street in Varosha in 1950. Nearby, he launched a patisserie of similar name - Europa Patisserie. Looking back, I see the choice of those names as a hint that my father was already looking beyond the narrow boundaries of Cyprus.

When a British army camp opened up near our house during the early fifties, my father quickly realised he could do profitable business with the newcomers because he spoke such good English. He secured the agency for such British staples as Heinz and Crosse & Blackwell and ensured a roaring trade. My father's idea was that we should live "above the shop". He converted the front two rooms of our house into a supermarket stocking British foodstuffs, newspapers and magazines and extended the living accommodation out to one side. In later years, the shop would expand to take over the whole of the original house. At around the same time - in 1954 - he won a tender to take over the management of a new tourist complex in Varosha, called Alasia - the only Turkish Cypriot in the area to attain such a position. His other big venture in Famagusta began in 1953 when he imported six second-hand single-decker red London Transport buses and launched the island's first public bus service.

Throughout my childhood, the family businesses dominated our lives in many ways. By the time I was a toddler, my parents were so busy with the first shop that I started at nursery school about two years earlier than most children, when I was two and a half. One of my earliest memories is of Asil pushing me to Nahide Hanim's kindergarten in my pushchair. Because we had moved away from the old town, my father used to drive us to the shop in his Ford car - one of the few privately-owned cars in Famagusta at the time. Asil would then take me to the nursery on his way to elementary school and he would collect me again at the end of the day. Later, when I progressed to elementary school, I was expected to help in the shop at our house alongside my brother each night, either serving customers or stacking shelves.

My mother and father worked well together. My father conceived the business ideas and it was my mother who made them work. With the long hours she spent serving in the shops, then coming home for an evening darning stockings and tights for the local women to bring in a few extra pennies, and sewing all our clothes, my mother sacrificed her own life for the sake of her husband and children.

———————

My father was very strict with us and could be a demanding task-master. A man always bursting with energy, who could get by on as little as an hour's sleep or a ten-minute cat nap, he taught us never to waste a moment of our lives. My father had been born into a once-wealthy merchant shipping family who had lost everything in a shipwreck and he reacted against the hardships of his own impoverished childhood by making sure we had everything we needed - yet he always made it plain to us that we had to earn any little extras we wanted. When I was six, I asked my father for a bicycle. He told me I could either wait until the end of the school year, when I would receive my bike as a reward if I came top of the class, or I could "pay" for it by helping in the shop and doing chores around the house. I chose the latter.

These lessons in living life to the full and working hard rubbed off on all of us but, I think, most of all on Asil and me. To this day, we both find it almost impossible to simply "switch off" and relax and we are often at our happiest when working - something I did not realise for years was part of the legacy from my father.

Another important element of that legacy was a sense of family pride and common purpose. As we grew up, we accepted it as quite natural that we should work alongside our parents, helping in the family business. We also grew up feeling proud to be part of a family which was well known and respected within the community for its entrepreneurial zeal and sheer hard work.

As well as being one of the town's few families to own their own car - and my father quickly progressed from the elderly Ford to a much-admired Opel saloon - we were also the talk of Famagusta when we acquired the first television set. The day in 1955 when we arrived home from school to find this mysterious, magical box was a day of high excitement. We children could scarcely contain ourselves until it came time for a transmission and we could switch the set on. The picture was not very clear, but we thought it was fantastic. Our neighbours were similarly enthusiastic. The television set stood in the glass sun-room and whenever there was a film being shown, a few of the neighbours would bring their chairs and range themselves in the garden in a row, where they could see the screen.

———————

Deep inside, a small part of me feels we missed out on our youth, always helping in the shop after school and often having little or no time for play. And yet my overwhelming memory is of a very happy childhood. I was my father's favourite child and the certainty of his love and approval instilled in me an enormous confidence in myself and my own abilities. He used to call me his "lucky charm" because, he said, the family had begun to prosper after my birth. My brother and sister both knew I was favoured and saw me get away with misdemeanours for which they would be punished. They often sent me as the messenger to ask my father for permission if we wanted some special treat.

Even my name, Bilge, in some way brought me closer to my father - meaning "clever" or "learned", it is virtually a modern Turkish equivalent of his own old Turkish name, Irfan. My mother chose all our names carefully - mine came from a novel about two sisters. Meral, meaning "gazelle", was named after one of Turkey's first female pilots; Asilkan, meaning "noble blood", was drawn from a rousing appeal to Turkish youth by Mustafa Kemal Atatürk. My brother would drop the "kan" when he left Cyprus as a teenager, believing the name "Asil Nadir" had a better ring to it.

Although my father was a great disciplinarian, he was also great fun and had a fine sense of humour. He often related stories about how he and my mother had met, poking gentle fun at my mother and telling us how it had been "love at first sight". My father had joined the police force as a teenager and met my mother after he was posted to Famagusta, into the unit commanded by my mother's father, Mustafa Sevki. My

11

father used to tell us how, one day, he had been sent round to his boss's house on an errand and my mother - then only fifteen - had answered the door. Confused by his Paphos accent, she had shouted out to her father that there was a "Greek gentleman" to see him. My father would tell us, too, that my mother was so keen on him that she would race to the window to catch a glimpse of him as he went by - and that one day she was too eager and banged her head on the glass.

The truth was that my mother turned him down when he first asked for her hand in marriage, vowing that she would never marry a policeman because the job entailed travelling to different postings around the island every two or three years. After learning of her refusal, my father asked his boss for permission to speak to my mother. He pledged to her that he would leave the police force instantly if she would agree to marry him. At this second time of asking, she did consent - hence the move to the Cyprus Mines Corporation and Lefke.

Our family routine during childhood meant weekdays of hard work, with little time for relaxation...but weekends often packed with fun and outings.

Every day except Sunday, my father would get up at five in the morning and drive to the open-air municipal market in Varosha to buy fresh produce for the shops. Sometimes he took Asil with him and I remember going to the market once or twice, standing there breathing in the aroma of fresh fruit and vegetables and listening to the shouts of the traders. My father would deliver the goods to the shops before returning to Herod of Attica Street for the family breakfast. Afterwards, Asil and I would clamber into the back of the car for the drive to the old town and our walk to school.

During our early years, my father sold Turkish newspapers at the bookshop in the old town - later he would go on to sell British newspapers, magazines and comics in the supermarket at our house. As a young boy, Asil would go out early every morning to sell the Turkish papers around Famagusta - then a busy hub for the island's international trade and the best pitch in town for an ambitious paper-boy like my brother, who was paid commission on each copy he sold. Later, when he was in his mid-teens, Asil would help with the customs formalities on the products my father imported for the shops. One morning, I remember, he had to sit an exam at school, but he got back late from the customs office and found the school doors locked. Asil was so afraid he might miss the test that he climbed in through a window to get to his desk.

In my early days at kindergarten, Asil used to come and collect me every day on his way home from school. Later, we both attended the

Gazi Ilkokulu elementary school together for one year - Asil in his final year and me in my first - so we would walk back together through the lanes and fields to Herod of Attica Street. We used to get home at about four o'clock. My mother would be busy serving in the shop but our housekeeper, Saime Hanim, would be at home to greet us. Straight after school, Asil and I would settle down to do our homework before going into the shop to help our mother. I always tease Asil that, even then, he made sure I did all the hard work - when we replenished the stacks of tins, he used to stand on the shelf while I had to do all the bending and lifting, stooping to pick up the tins and then reaching to hand them up to him. When we had finished the stacking, we would avidly read all the English comics in the shop before replacing them on the shelves.

We also all had our own chores to do at home. My job was to go round the house as dusk fell, closing all the shutters for the night. Meral's duty was to help prepare the evening's dinner. Asil's, which he loathed, was to polish every pair of shoes in the house. This was no small task, since my father alone had some forty pairs of shoes ranged in his cupboard. This obsession with footwear, I put down to a reaction to his childhood when, he told us, he used to walk in a certain way so that no-one could see the holes in the soles of his shoes. Shoe-cleaning came to be a source of dread for my brother. Particularly hated were several pairs of brogues crafted in contrasting cream and brown leather - the very worst to polish, so Asil would complain.

Dinner in the evening was always an occasion when the whole family sat down together. Even so, customers would frequently come round to our back door in Famagusta and summon my mother to come and serve them in the shop. Some winter nights, after dinner, we would sit round the fire for a family sing-along. Meral played the piano and Asil the violin, while I played the piano-accordion. My mother would sing and my father was the conductor who kept us all in time. On other evenings, my father would go out to the local men's club to play cards and have a drink. Whenever the men went out, it was customary for the women to keep each other company, and an elderly Greek neighbour would often come and sit for the evening talking to my mother. But I never saw my mother simply sit and do nothing. Even when she had a visitor, she would always be busy mending customers' stockings or stitching clothes for us.

On the long, warm summer evenings, all the children in our street would play together. One regular game, especially favoured by Asil because he often won, was the "almond game". The players would dig a small hole near the garden wall and each would then throw his or her almonds into the hole. However many nuts they succeeded in getting on target, their opponent would have to "pay" them the same number. By the time the game was finished, Asil had almost always collected up all his opponents' almonds. I think my mother enjoyed this game too, since the almonds had all been bought in her shop in the first place and Asil would hand all his victor's spoils over to her to sell again the next day! Football was another childhood passion - for me as well as for my brother. On those hot evenings, we would gather for a knockabout on an empty field opposite our house. I was the only girl and I did not always get a game. If Asil was the oldest boy there, I was allowed to play because he would insist. But I was not so lucky on nights when our neighbour, Yiorgios Iacovou, was there. He was a couple of years older than Asil and he refused to let a girl join in the game. That same Yiorgios grew up to become Greek Cypriot Foreign Minister more than two decades later. In a true-life Cain and Abel story, he would become the self-confessed bitter enemy of his one-time playmate, Asilkan Nadir.

After an evening's fun, we were always ready for an early bed. My brother and I shared a room for about four years once my father had converted part of our house into the supermarket and Asil would often disappear to bed long before me, even though I was five years his junior. By the time I came to bed, he would be fast asleep and I would sometimes hear him dreaming of football, shouting "Shoot!" and "Goal!" in his sleep. Even now, he maintains the early-to-bed, early-to-rise habit. We can go round to his house at nine o'clock in the evening and find him just about to retire for the night, in preparation for his routine six o'clock start the next morning. Asil's early bedtimes have long been a standing family joke. My mother tells how, when I was a baby, Asil used to disappear to bed from the dinner table frequently without eating his evening meal. Then, when it was time for my ten o'clock feed, he would wake up complaining of hunger and ask my mother for something to eat. One night, she warned him that the next time he did this, he would get a smack instead of food. Sure enough, a few nights later, Asil woke up while I was being fed. But instead of asking for a snack, he asked my mother cautiously: "Did we have dinner tonight or not?" My mother thought she must be bringing up a diplomat-in-the-making.

Asil would often confide his already-firm ambitions to me as we lay in bed at night. Many a time, stretched out in his bed next to the window, he would tell me how he was going to become a very wealthy man. An inspirational talker even then, Asil would drift off to sleep, leaving me to dream of a wonderful future in which he would realise his aims. In fact, spurred on by my father's example, the young Asil nurtured many very lofty hopes for his future. In the early 1950s, Greek tycoon Aristotle Onassis's yacht was anchored off the coast of Varosha for several days.

British Prime Minister Winston Churchill was on board. Asil used to row out every morning to the yacht and paddle around it, admiring the huge boat. One morning, he told us he had caught sight of Churchill on deck, sitting at an easel, painting. He did not stop talking about this for days and told us repeatedly, "I'm going to have a boat like that one day." If ever I disturbed Asil when he was doing his homework, he used to warn me: "Just you wait, Bilge. When I'm older I am going to have a huge office and you will have to get past two secretaries to reach me." I remembered his words. When the day came that he did indeed have two secretaries and a receptionist outside his office, I deliberately walked in through the back door, announcing as I stepped inside, "There you are! I'm still going to get in!"

Even as a young boy, Asil demonstrated a flair for commerce. My mother tells a story about how four year old Asil's kindergarten teacher wanted some moisturising cream and asked my brother to bring some from the shop. My mother gave Asil two pots of Pond's cream to take to the teacher the next morning and impressed upon him that he should put the money safely in his pocket and bring it home to her. Asil duly handed the jars to his teacher. When home-time came, she dismissed the class without a thought. A few minutes later, though, as she tidied the classroom, she heard a cough and turned to see Asil still standing in the doorway. Wondering why he was there long after the other children had left, the teacher asked him what he was waiting for. "I want the money," came the fearless reply. So well had my mother drummed into him the need to be careful with the money that he dared not go home without it.

Childhood weekends were always a source of great excitement. Saturday was the day we would go down to one of the cinemas in Varosha, where all the good English films were screened. Asil loved going to the pictures. His silver screen favourites then were Errol Flynn and Gary Cooper and he never missed a cowboys and Indians picture. If he had particularly enjoyed a film, he would make a point of trying to catch it again the following weekend. My own favourite was Audrey Hepburn, whose elfin grace and beauty I revered. Asil's regular film-going partner was Mustafa Salih, a school-friend who lived in the old town. Mustafa would cycle over to our house and then he and Asil would ride out to Varosha together on their bikes to see the matinee performance. Asil would encourage me to ask our father if I might be allowed to go to the cinema, since that meant he would have to take me. If I was allowed to go along, however, poor Mustafa - who continued to be a staunch friend and later worked at Polly Peck - would be instructed to carry me

15

on the seat on the back of his bike. Extremely dapper even then, Asil liked to get dressed up for his cinema outings and did not want a little sister in tow to spoil his image. If ever I was unable to go to the cinema, I still did not miss out. Asil would come home full of breathless enthusiasm to regale me with the entire story of whatever film he had seen, complete with songs and actions.

Sundays were the one day of the week my mother kept the shop shut. On Sunday mornings, particularly in winter when the weather was bad, we three children would cluster around my father in bed to hear him tell the latest instalment in the adventure stories he made up for us. Whenever he got to a really exciting part, he would take a look at our eager faces and then announce, "OK - that's it. Come back next week for another chapter!" We could hardly wait seven days to discover what happened next. On sunny winter days, we would go to Kantara - a mountainous forest expanse where there was a picnic area and an ancient castle. Often, we would travel there with family friends and my father would light a fire and barbecue kebabs. During the spring and autumn, my mother would tack a notice to the front door, "Gone to the races", and we would all pile into the car and spend the afternoon at Nicosia race course. In the summer, we would spend the day at the beach outside Famagusta, learning to swim as we splashed around with friends in the cool, clear water.

Racing was one of my father's hobbies and for much of my childhood he had one or two racehorses. He sold them in about 1958, when the island's political troubles were worsening, because he felt uneasy at being one of only three or four Turkish Cypriot racehorse owners. During race seasons, the horses would be liveried with a trainer in Nicosia, but out of season they would stay in the field behind our house, where my father had built two stables. The first horse was Alev (Flame), then came Bora (Storm) and finally Arriverderci. Asil used to groom them every day and often we both rode them. On race season mornings, my father and Asil would drive over to Nicosia very early to see the horses being put through their paces at trials. The trials were staged at four in the morning, so they had usually been out and come home by the time the rest of us got up. On race day itself, my father would give us a few shillings each to place our bets. We used to stand around the enclosure looking at the competition before making our choice. Our horses often did well and they won several prizes - this was fortunate, because if one of the horses lost my sister used to sob uncontrollably all the way back to Famagusta. If one of the horses won, my father would treat us all to dinner in a restaurant on the way home, by way of celebration.

Growing up in the Cyprus of the 1940s and fifties meant adhering to some very strict codes of behaviour - particularly so for Turkish Cypriots brought up in the Muslim faith. Young people were not allowed to go out with each other on "dates" unless they were engaged to be married, and even then they had to be chaperoned by a member of the family. My parents made no exceptions to that rule. When Meral became engaged to her future husband, Güner Kasif, either I or Asil would be detailed to shadow the young couple whenever they met. I used to hate this because I could tell Güner resented it - he felt three was definitely a crowd. Far from relaxing these strictures when we later emigrated to London, and I was of an age for boyfriends, my father became even stricter. Maybe he feared that the temptations of metropolitan life might prove too great for a small-town Cypriot like me. I remember clearly the two-hour lecture on morals that he gave me on our second morning in London.

As for Asil, his first taste of romance brought the severest of punishments down on his head. It was in 1955 that my brother acquired his first girlfriend - an English girl of about the same age called Yvonne. She came from an army family who lived quite near us. Because of Asil's commitments, he did not have a lot of time to see Yvonne, so one day the two of them skipped school and spent the afternoon sitting together, talking, at the edge of a small wood close to our home. Inevitably, one of the neighbours spotted them and reported back to my father, who was furious, mostly because his son had played truant. Asil had his pocket money stopped and was also forbidden temporarily from going to the cinema - the worst penalty of all, as far as he was concerned. Asil never again skipped school, but his friendship with Yvonne continued until she and her family returned to London at the end of the 1950s. They exchanged a couple of letters after that, but distance quickly killed that young relationship.

It was Yvonne who introduced us to rock 'n' roll - and, ironically, set Asil on a musical track which would eventually lead him to meet Aysegül, the woman who twice became his wife. Yvonne had brought her collection of records from England and she used to bring them round to our house in the evenings because we had a gramophone. Our early pop heroes were Cliff Richard, Tommy Steele and, of course, Elvis Presley. When we got together, Asil would strum his guitar and the three of us would dance around and sing along to tunes like *Living Doll*. Meral, who was then almost eighteen, felt a bit too grown up to join us in our rock 'n' roll sessions, preferring to hum some of the romantic ballads which were popular at the time.

If my father was a typically strict Turkish Cypriot parent when it came to dating, he was remarkably liberal in other respects - probably, at least in part, because he lived and worked outside the predominantly Turkish old town. In our street, we were one of only four Turkish Cypriot families; there were around six British service families and the remainder of the twenty households were Greek Cypriot. I think my father must have noticed the relatively relaxed way in which the other children were treated, and some of it rubbed off on him. While the other girls among my Turkish Cypriot classmates would be expected to stay at home with their mothers much of the time, and would be escorted everywhere on the odd occasions they were allowed to go out, I had the freedom to be with Asil and his friends. I believe I was the only Turkish Cypriot girl in Famagusta who was allowed to play football with the lads - and certainly the only one to help make grocery deliveries across town, even venturing into the later-risky areas inhabited by the Greeks.

Unlike other Turkish Cypriot men of his generation, my father saw no reason why women should not work and run businesses. He happily let my mother run his shops and later his London clothing business. Yet I could not say he viewed women as equals. In our household, when we were growing up, it was my father who always had the final say. In later life and business, it was Asil who he expected, as his son, to assume the mantle of decision-maker. Those of my old school-friends who did go on to higher education or to work mostly chose the teaching profession. For me - perhaps because I was influenced by the aspirations of our Greek Cypriot and British neighbours; perhaps because my father had such big ambitions that he needed all of us to help - it seemed natural that I would follow him into business. But I know his assumption was that he or Asil would be running a family firm and that I would simply be involved in some supporting role. Although he nicknamed me his "rebel", my father never thought I might head my own company - let alone become one of few women to lead a publicly-quoted British firm - and it was not until shortly before his death, in 1986, that I revealed to him my aspirations to go solo and won his blessing.

Although my parents were intensely proud of their Muslim heritage, theirs was not a strong religious influence as we grew up. Neither my mother nor my father attended the mosque regularly or took part in the annual Ramadan fasting. Religion did not play the major role in our youthful lives that it did for many of our friends. My father's creed was more concerned with morals and "doing the right thing". He often told us: "If you help the poor; if you do good—that is religion. God doesn't need our prayers, it is the people who need our help." He practised what he preached by quietly helping dozens of needy people over the decades - so quietly that it was only after his death that we discovered the enormous extent of his charitable works, when those he had aided came to give us their condolences. While we still lived in Cyprus, my father always made a point of employing the poor in his businesses. Once we had moved to England and his own financial situation was vastly improved, his assistance knew no bounds. He would give money to Turkish Cypriot students who were finding it hard to make ends meet in London; he paid for people to have vital medical treatment in the UK; he gave hard-up families a helping hand if they were struggling to build a home of their own; he financed the construction of an orphanage in Famagusta. Asil inherited our father's philanthropic spirit although, inevitably, because he became a public figure, his generosity would be far more widely known.

For many years, our neighbourhood was a happy mixture of nationalities and Asil, Meral and I grew up naturally able to slip easily between the Turkish, Greek and English languages, depending on our playmates at the time. But in 1955 a single bomb blast forced us to appreciate the complex political undercurrents which were to rip our tranquil world apart - turning each day into a constant vigil, each night into a dark world of fear; sending many small traders to the wall and culminating in the bloody, Greek-inspired coup and Turkish intervention of 1974 which resulted in the island's partition. From an early age, I remember hearing my grandfather tell tales of the first stirrings of anti-British feeling among the Greek Cypriot community, expressed in the nationalist movement of the 1930s. I never associated his accounts, however, with our friends. To us, there was no distinction between the sons and daughters of any of our neighbours, whatever their nationality. We children were continually in and out of each other's houses and everybody was always very friendly to us. As Muslims, our family did not celebrate Christmas, yet every year Asil and I would join our Greek Cypriot pals singing Greek carols around the local houses, Asil accompanying on his violin. At each house we visited, we would be given gifts of sweets.

On the first of April 1955, all that changed. A wave of bombs went off and a Greek Cypriot terrorist group - Ethniki Organosis Kypriou Agoniston (National Organisation of Cypriot Fighters) - claimed responsibility. The group, known as EOKA for short, advocated "Enosis" - union between Cyprus and Greece. It was led by Colonel George Grivas, later to become General Grivas. Initially aimed against the British colonial administration - in force since 1878 after just over three centuries of Ottoman rule - the extremists' campaign of violence would quickly turn into an intercommunal battle against the Turkish Cypriots too. In June 1955, a letterbox bomb planted inside the central police

19

station in the Turkish Cypriot quarter of Nicosia injured thirteen people and brought home to us the vulnerability of the minority Turkish Cypriot community. The bombing would be followed, over the years, by a mass campaign to wipe out all traces of Turkish culture - street names and monuments were eradicated - and by moves which ended most official contact between the two communities. Turkish Cypriots, fearful for their safety, looked to the British for protection, many joining up as auxiliaries in the police and security forces, but this simply fuelled the fanatics' allegations that the Turks were "colluding" with the colonial regime. At first, the British seemed to take a tough stance against the terrorists, deporting Greek Cypriot leader Archbishop Makarios and other high-ranking clergymen in the pro-Enosis Greek Orthodox Church to the Seychelles and hanging several EOKA terrorists. When the Suez debacle of 1956 reduced the need for a strategic British presence in the region, however, the hard-line attitude would evaporate and attempts to negotiate a Cyprus settlement would be stepped up.

That April 1955 was the first time EOKA had been heard of and as news of the attack spread through the island it brought in its wake a climate of unease. The chill wind of suspicion swept through Herod of Attica Street almost instantly. Some of our Greek Cypriot neighbours stopped speaking to us and banned their children from playing with us. In the supermarket, trade was hit badly as Greek families complied with an EOKA instruction not to trade with Turks or Britons. We kept ourselves very much to ourselves, aware that our Greek neighbours suspected we might pass information to our British friends. Our carefree existence died virtually overnight.

Although the initial thrust of EOKA was then against the British, my father quickly came to realise that, as a prominent supplier to them, he and his family might also become targets. One day in 1955, two British women were shot dead as they walked in Princess Elizabeth Street, just yards from my father's patisserie. When my father rushed to see what had happened, he found Nicos Sampson - a young Greek photojournalist who frequently ate at the patisserie - taking photographs. That night my father came home white-faced and told us sadly, "I think this country is not going to be a nice place to live in." It was the first inkling we had that someone we knew might be involved in the violence. Shortly afterwards, Nicos Sampson called on my father at his shop and warned him, in a friendly way, that he would be well advised to think of leaving Varosha. Sampson would later be revealed as a prominent EOKA man who headed up a terrorist cell called the Assassination Squad. He would be installed briefly as the "President" of Cyprus in the aftermath of the 1974 Greek coup. In 1955, though, he was just a lad from a poor background who my father felt sorry for and allowed to eat at the patisserie for free. In the decades since then, I have often thought how lucky we were that my father had made a friend of Nicos Sampson, otherwise his warning may have come in the form of a bomb or bullets.

The following year, the patisserie again brought us some good luck. We were sitting in the front garden at home one summer's evening when two car-loads of machine-gun-toting EOKA men pulled up in the road. The first few jumped out and ran into our garden. One of the last to get out, we recognised as a Greek Cypriot who had worked for my father as a waiter in the patisserie. In a typical display of courage, my mother stood up and called "Hello" to him in a friendly tone. He did not answer her, but simply turned to the other men and shouted to them: "Come on! Let's go! Leave this house, let's go." It was clear the group had been sent either to frighten us or to shoot us. Maybe they had picked on us because our home was one of the first Turkish houses outside Varosha - there were many random shootings at the time. Whatever the reason for the visit, it seemed that we were spared either because the young terrorist knew us...or simply because, if murder was their plan, he knew he would be identified if the attack went wrong and any of us survived.

The spreading violence was initially the cause of many arguments between my parents. My mother saw Cyprus standing on the brink of civil war and was enraged when my father would still come up with ideas for starting new businesses. Although they never discussed their fears in front of us children, I would often lie in bed at night then, listening to the sound of them rowing in another room. That was one of my worst memories. It was ironic that, some years later, it was my father who realised we had little future in Cyprus, while my mother was desperate to stay.

As the troubles grew worse following Nicos Sampson's warning, several incidents made my father increasingly aware of the dangers we faced. Once, I went with him to a warehouse owned by a wealthy Greek Cypriot merchant with whom he used to do business - the merchant used to buy the goods my father imported from Britain to sell in his shops. That day, we were walking up to the back door of the warehouse when my father heard voices raised inside and pulled me back. As we listened, we heard two EOKA men pushing the businessman around and hitting him. "This is the last warning you will get," they told him. "You're not to trade with Irfan Nadir and you are not to buy English produce. Next time, it will not be a warning - you will be punished." The merchant told us afterwards the two men had been brandishing guns. This incident revealed to us that we had "spies" in our midst. We had a store at the back of the house and the Greek businessman used to send a lorry to collect his goods under cover of darkness at about two in the morning. It was one of our neighbours who had reported this to EOKA. Later, one of Yiorgios Iacovou's sisters, Elli, was arrested by the colonial authorities for heading an anti-British march. When their house was searched, a printing press for producing EOKA leaflets was discovered in the basement. Elli was taken to a Turkish police house in the old town and I remember my mother running all the way there when she heard of the arrest and exhorting the authorities to take good care of her neighbour's daughter.

On another occasion, my parents had a run-in of their own with EOKA. While my father was running the Alasia tourist complex in the mid-fifties, British MP Barbara Castle came to Cyprus. The Mayor of Famagusta invited her to be guest of honour at a dinner at Alasia - a request which incensed the Greek Cypriot extremists. They did not want a British politician visiting at all and were even more enraged to learn that the dinner was being held at a Turkish-run restaurant. Pressure was put on the Greek staff working at Alasia to strike that night and when my father got there to oversee this dinner for more than 100 guests, he found he had virtually no waiters or kitchen hands. My mother was wearing a lace evening dress made specially for the occasion, but when she realised the predicament, she took a clean tablecloth, wrapped it around her, and set to working in the kitchen for the night, cooking and dishing up the meal. At the end of the night, after all the guests had left, my parents were in the kitchen when they heard noises outside on the restaurant terrace. They looked out and saw several young men snatching the crockery from the tables and smashing it on the floor, and hurling the cutlery into the sea. My mother was furious and made to go and stop them, but my father persuaded her that it was best for them to stay indoors.

The last straw came when my father received a message warning him that Meral and I would be kidnapped if he did not call a halt to his businesses in Varosha. To have called the terrorists' bluff would have been too big a risk. I was not aware of the threat at the time, but learned later that my father had taken it seriously enough to call in local resistance fighters for protection. One by one, he began shutting down all the businesses in Varosha. He gave up the lease on Alasia and sold the shops in the area. He also stopped his public transport service and sold the buses after EOKA threatened to put bombs on the vehicles because they were widely used by the British. The buses used to be parked on some waste ground close to our house. When we woke one morning to find that every tyre on all six buses had been slashed, we knew this was no idle warning.

———

The years following 1957 were the worst. The tensions between the country's different national communities could virtually be cut with a knife and - although we did not consciously register it at the time - we were plunged beneath the pall of almost constant terror. At the end of 1956, a new idea had been thrown into the Cyprus melting pot when British colonial secretary Alan Lennox-Boyd had suggested that the island might be partitioned between Greece and Turkey. The proposal was welcomed among the Turkish Cypriots, who took up the slogan "Partition or death" as their rallying cry. In Ankara, too, the idea was received as a means to pressurise the Greeks and Greek Cypriots into abandoning Enosis, so that a compromise solution of an independent Cyprus might be reached. Alarmed by a rapid rise in Greek military assistance to the EOKA bandits, Turkey took a closer involvement in the Cyprus conflict, threatening military action to prevent Enosis. The Turkish Cypriots had already formed their own self-defence group, Volkan (meaning Volcano), but it was poorly equipped. In 1957, Turkey began to provide weapons and advice to Volkan, which they regrouped into a new anti-terrorist force, the Turkish Resistance Organisation, or TMT.

Fear began to shape our daily and nightly routines. We nailed protective wire screens in front of all our windows as the bombings and shootings went on, the ubiquitous leaflets called for a Greek Cyprus and Archbishop Makarios preached politics from the pulpit. We still had the shop in Herod of Attica Street and knew that, while British soldiers and their families were its main customers, we were always in the terrorists' sights. Many of our Turkish friends were moving back into the old town for safety, but my parents were loath to leave their home and supermarket. They did, however, bar us children from wandering off alone into Varosha and we soon grew very cautious about straying beyond our own neighbourhood. Somehow, we cherished the notion that the Greeks we had grown up with would not harm us, even if some of them were part of EOKA. By this stage, any Turkish Cypriot who had helped the British or done business with them could expect retribution. If a Turkish policeman had been instrumental in capturing a terrorist, the colonial authorities would pay for his family to be sent to Britain, where they might escape EOKA's revenge. Stories were rife of how Turkish Cypriots travelling between Famagusta and Nicosia were liable to be stopped and searched at EOKA checkpoints; one tale was told of a lorry driver with a full cargo of melons who was ordered to unload every single piece of fruit and then put them all back on the vehicle again. On our way to Nicosia, we had to drive through the village of Lisi, which was known EOKA territory. Whenever we went there, my father used to put his foot down hard so that we passed through Lisi as quickly as possible.

23

Every night when we went to bed, I used to pray that we would all wake up in the morning without having been attacked or bombed in the night. In retrospect, it amazes me how, with childish resilience, I simply accepted this state of high anxiety as normal and only recognised after my first night in London the sheer relief of being able to sleep without fear. In some way, I believe we became inured to our terror, perhaps through a streak of mental self-preservation. Once, in 1959, my father was confined to bed with an asthma attack. Asil and I had to help out with the deliveries to keep the supermarket going. Sometimes I would go on the delivery bike, cycling deep into Greek Cypriot areas where our Turkish Cypriot staff refused to venture. On other days, we would both go out in the shop van - Asil had no licence, but he had been taught to drive at the age of twelve, practising on a long, empty field beside the beach at Salamis. Neither of us would admit to being frightened, but I remember the bone-deep chill which seemed to hang about us as we crossed through known EOKA strongholds. I do not think we saw our adventures as demonstrations of bravery. Rather, we made those journeys out of young foolhardiness...and out of business necessity.

Even as children, we were acutely aware of the deteriorating political situation, although our parents did their best to keep it from us. Famagusta in those days was a small town where all the Turkish Cypriots knew each other and news of any incidents spread rapidly. Living close to a British army camp, we became conscious of signs that an attack had happened somewhere; six or seven jeeps piled with soldiers would speed noisily out of the gates. When somebody tried to force his way into the camp at night, we would be woken by the blaze of floodlights and the jangling alarms. Many a night, we would hear a bomb go off as we lay in bed. If a fire was started, we would hear the sirens blaring from the station near our house.

In 1958 the British, tired of the incessant terrorist campaign, the shooting and bombings which had cost so many lives, launched talks aimed at giving Cyprus its independence. Turkish Cypriot leader Dr Fazil Küçük and Rauf Denktas - later to become the president of the post-1974 Turkish Cypriot state - set out the Turkish side's arguments for partition, under which they sought a third of the island for self-rule. The Greek Cypriots were represented by their leader, Archbishop Makarios, newly-returned from exile and putting his Enosis ambitions on ice to come to the negotiating table.

At the outset of the talks, we had high hopes of success. Each evening, our family would rush to switch on the radio and learn of the latest position. That nightly bulletin became of vital importance to us all - we desperately wanted to know what would become of us. Eventually, a year of talks culminated in conferences in London and Zurich at which Dr Küçük and Mr Denktas had no option but to agree to an independent bi-communal republic in Cyprus. It was to be a partnership republic with two official languages - Greek and Turkish - and a Greek Cypriot president and Turkish Cypriot president elected by their own communities. The Council of Ministers and fifty-seat House of Representatives would comprise seventy per cent Greek Cypriots and thirty per cent Turkish Cypriots. The new republic's constitution would be safeguarded by a Treaty of Guarantee which installed Britain, Greece and Turkey as joint guardians and gave each of the powers the right to intervene in Cyprus jointly or individually. The three countries were also allowed to station their own troops on the island.

While some Turkish Cypriots welcomed the new regime, believing this Treaty of Guarantee would protect their rights and their lives, the announcement came as a body blow to many. For me, the deal was a major disappointment and the first real knock to the ideal of Britain and British justice with which I had grown up. In our colonial society, Britain was often upheld as an example of fairness and good faith. Now, although we made excuses for the British, telling each other they had to recognise that their empire was diminishing in a rapidly-changing world, all many of us saw was that the loyal Turkish Cypriot community had been sold short by a colonial power desperate to wash its hands of a very tiresome situation. In later years, my discontent over Britain's handling of EOKA and the independence talks would crystallise further. I would come to be certain that the British could have crushed EOKA if they had acted quickly. In Turkish, we have a saying: "You kill a snake while it is young." In the case of the EOKA serpent, the British failed to act decisively and allowed the movement to grow and grow, until it reached a point where the authorities just could not cope. It was to be almost exactly three decades later that my belief in British justice would finally be shattered for good.

For us, the day the Cyprus independence deal was struck we knew our lives must change. We could no longer live in continual fear for our safety and yet the option of moving to the comparative security of Famagusta's mainly Turkish old town was unpalatable. Neither of my parents wanted to quit their home and their business and both felt that effectively to be enclaved in their own country was not enough of a life - and certainly not enough to sustain a healthy business. It was a solemn moment when my father summoned us all to a family meeting. Sitting at the big kitchen table, my father explained our position: he did not believe we could stay once the British had left, partly because the lion's share of our businesses had depended upon British custom, and partly because he felt sure that the Greeks aimed to secure Cyprus for themselves. After they had despatched the British, he feared they would turn their attentions to getting rid of the Turkish Cypriots. Subsequent events would prove him right. It was not a question of whether we should leave Cyprus, said my father, but when and how. A visit by my mother's brother in 1959 provided an answer. He had set up a clothing business in London eleven years earlier and he suggested that my father should go to Britain and look for opportunities there. My father took him up on the offer and spent several weeks exploring various possibilities. By the time he returned, he had decided that we should wind up our remaining ties in Cyprus and emigrate to the UK.

On the 16th of August 1960, the constitution was signed and the fledgling Republic of Cyprus was born. We all celebrated independence and there was great excitement among the Turkish Cypriots as we crowded into Famagusta harbour to welcome the first Turkish troops in living memory to come to the island. A band played and flags flew as their ship sailed into the port, the men all lined up on deck.

A few weeks earlier, my father had moved to London in advance of the rest of the family to try to carve out a new life for us all. Asil started his first year studying economics at Istanbul University that autumn. I was fourteen, and in my final year at middle school and Meral, who had been studying English literature at Ankara University, had graduated and returned to teach at my school. My father was away for a year and it was to prove a sad and difficult twelve months. I missed my father terribly. My mother was running the shop and at the same time trying to sell off whatever other assets we had left.

In the run-up to the new republic, Archbishop Makarios had made it plain he had not abandoned the struggle for Enosis, but merely saw the Republic of Cyprus as a tactical manoeuvre towards that aim. He did not alter his stance when, soon after independence, he was elected president, with Dr Küçük vice-president. He named two of the most fanatical EOKA men as cabinet ministers. Immediately, the government dismissed hundreds of Turkish Cypriot auxiliary policemen and replaced them with Greek Cypriots, many of them ex-terrorists. At public appearances, Makarios would go on to champion the cause of Enosis, urging in an August 1962 sermon that Greek Cypriots, "must continue to march forward to complete the work begun by the EOKA heroes," and adding that, "the struggle is continuing in a new form, and will go on until we achieve our goal." In a speech at his home village of Panayia, he would proclaim: "Unless this small Turkish community forming a part of the

Turkish race which has been the terrible enemy of Hellenism is expelled, the duty of the heroes of EOKA can never be considered as terminated."

In our Famagusta neighbourhood, the whole atmosphere changed after 1960. All our old British service friends moved out and their places were taken by sometimes hostile Greek Cypriot families. With my father and Asil gone, my mother, Meral and I felt very vulnerable and the three of us would often sleep together in the same room for safety. On nights when trouble was expected, one or two men from the TMT would be sent to guard the house. The only high spots were my father's frequent trips home - probably between eight and ten during the year. He never told us when he was coming. He would just jump into a taxi when he arrived in Cyprus late on a Friday night and the first we knew of his visit would be when he turned up at the house and I would wake to hear his special whistle outside my window. Delighted, I would race to wake the others and let him in so that all four of us could hug each other in the hallway. The year was a struggle for my father too. He was staying with my uncle and each time he visited he would give us a progress report on his efforts to launch his own small clothing manufacturing firm. Using virtually all the money from the assets we had sold in Cyprus, he took the lease on a building in the East End of London and had just enough cash left over to buy some industrial sewing machines. In the summer of 1961, he told us it was time for us to join him in Britain.

In August that year, the whole family was together again in Cyprus. Meral married Güner Kasif in Famagusta on the 6th and flew the next day to Istanbul, where Güner was in his final year of studying to be a civil engineer. Two days after the wedding, we closed up our house for the last time. The house and shop were to be rented out because my mother, very reluctant to leave her homeland, had every intention of returning soon. She left some of our personal possessions locked up in one bedroom - we would never see any of them again because the room would be broken into and looted during the troubled years which followed.

We took an overnight flight from Nicosia to London. My mother wept quietly most of the way, while my father tried to comfort her, assuring her that Britain was a land of opportunity for us. Asil, confident that England would give us the chance to build the life we hoped for, spent the journey laying before me the thrills of London - the shops, the cinemas, the television. He had spent a few weeks there with my father and I bombarded him with questions about the city. Too excited to sleep, we could feel no sense of loss for Cyprus. Peering through the scratched windows into the inky black beyond, I willed the plane to speed us faster to this fantastic land of film stars, sophistication, hope and plenty. It was the gateway to a brand new world.

CHAPTER TWO

From Rag Trade...

My first impressions of London were dull, grey and disappointing. We landed at Heathrow on a typical British summer's day - overcast, cool and with a persistent drizzle which soaked everything within seconds. My heart sank as I surveyed the pale crowds huddled under the low clouds as we waited outside the terminal for a taxi, our luggage piled about us on the pavement. The journey through London to our temporary new home did little to revive my flagging spirits. Everywhere I looked I saw grey-faced people hurrying blankly through the streets; women swathed in bulky overcoats and head-scarves; bowler-hatted businessmen with regulation-issue pin-striped suits and black umbrellas. Fresh from a colourful, heat-drenched Cyprus August, that first drive through the city made me realise with dismay just how different my new life was going to be - and that dismay was confirmed during the following few days. Used to an outdoor life and a close-knit home neighbourhood, I found both the weather and my surroundings gloomy. The cheerful smile I had always been used to directing at passers-by was never returned. Instead, people would look away or stare fixedly at the pavement as they walked. Everyone seemed to be in a continual rush, going virtually everywhere on the run. To make my early impressions even worse, my Aunt Nevin, married to my mother's brother Kemal, died giving birth to her fourth child, casting a heavy black pall over the household.

Determined to like England, though, I swallowed my initial sense of disappointment and set about getting acquainted with my new surroundings. And there was one major change which I was able to appreciate immediately - from the very first night I lay in the tiny spare bedroom in east London, the knowledge that we could go to sleep, free of fear for our safety and liberated from the early-hours panic engendered by any unexpected noise gave me an overwhelming, light-headed sense of joy. I had not known how much we had been living in the shadow of terror until - just as the recognition of a chronic pain may come only when the agony subsides - that inner darkness was lifted.

Within days of our arrival, it became plain that the easy-going lifestyle I had enjoyed in Cyprus was also at an end. After a series of Turkish Cypriot neighbours came calling, inviting me and Asil to join them for trips to the cinema or the coffee bar, my father took me to one side and delivered a stern two-hour lecture. No matter where we were, he warned, I was never to forget my Turkish and Muslim background. "We may build our business here, but we will live our private lives in accordance with the way our culture dictates," he cautioned. "You are not to accept any invitations unless I know who you are going with and where you are going. Maybe I will also have to take you and pick you up." The severity of these new regulations came as a surprise from the lips of my father who, always a liberal, had been particularly lenient towards me. Perhaps he spoke out of fear that I was at an especially vulnerable age - but that lecture brought it home to me that I was now to live under a far stricter regime than ever before. I suddenly found myself living the rather sheltered life of many a Turkish Cypriot girl in London.

We spent our first months living with my uncle Selçuk and his family at their house in Whitechapel, east London - a rather drab property which was certainly not the stuff that had filled my young dreams of Britain. While I had nurtured visions of a mansion, this was a typical three-storey terraced town house. For several weeks after our arrival, almost all of our spare time was taken up with the hunt for a home of our own. At first, the search seemed destined to be fruitless. Whenever my father discovered an affordable house close to the East End premises where he had started his business, the four of us would pile into the car to go and view it. Asil and I would nudge each other with excitement as we entered unknown neighbourhoods, looking over the area and the building with a critical and important air, mentally planning how we would adapt this or that property. My mother would clamber slowly from the passenger seat, take one look, shake her head sorrowfully and announce: "I can't live here." She wanted, she told my father, a house with a garden - but we all knew there was little chance of coming across an inner-city house with a garden. I suspect what she was really hoping was that my father would decide to transport us all back to the Mediterranean instead. Determined both to please her and settle his family, however, my father cast his house-hunting net much wider and eventually landed a large suburban three-bedroomed semi in Pettits Boulevard, Romford. It was a forty-minute drive from my father's work but it came complete with the vital garden. We moved in during November 1961.

Throughout this protracted house-hunting, both my parents were extremely busy building upon the foundations of the clothing manufacturing firm my father had launched the year before. Its name - which we all thought rather trendy at the time - was Nadir Modes. At that stage it was housed in part of a three-storey corner building at 21 New Road, in east London, but it would soon expand to take over the entire premises. Initially, my father had twelve people working for him there, cutting and making up orders for customers. In the gloomy red-brick factory, my father maintained a tiny office, with just a desk and telephone, on the first floor next to the six machinists and downstairs from the cutting tables and pressing units. When orders came in, the factory machinists would make up samples to show to customers and also to give as guidance to my father's "outworkers", who would make up the garments at home before they were returned to New Road for finishing and pressing. Many of the "outworkers" were women from families like ours, who had come in the hopes of starting a new life and who made badly-needed extra money by buying a sewing machine and working from home. During the time we stayed with my uncle, I had the distinct impression that my Aunt Serif never left her sewing machine. Some days she would be bent over her table for as long as eighteen hours at a stretch. Every day I would get up and go to bed accompanied by the sound of her whirring sewing machine.

My mother, who had trained in dressmaking as a teenager, soon established herself in charge of production at Nadir Modes, leaving my father free to travel round the capital, seeking out potential customers and making deliveries. My parents were at the factory from Monday morning until Saturday lunch-time, keeping long and punishing hours at work. Often during weekends, the whole family would gather upstairs at home to experiment with laying out different patterns and fabrics on a cutting table my father had put up there. I helped where I could and Asil pitched in for about six weeks after we came to England, until the time came for him to return to his university studies.

In September that year, Asil packed his belongings into a brand new car and drove off to begin his second year at Istanbul University. Hidden behind the seat underneath some clothes was another cherished new possession which had to be kept from my father's eyes - a burnished wooden electric guitar. Asil and I had journeyed secretly to Berry's music shop in Whitechapel High Street one Saturday and had sneaked home with the instrument. Asil and some of his friends at the university had got together and formed their own band - named Asiller, or The Nobles, a play on the name of my brother, their lead singer and guitarist. They planned to use their musical talents to earn a little extra spending money in Istanbul by playing at a high-class restaurant, Çati. Asil knew my father would disapprove of such frivolity and would ask him whether he intended to do any work while he was at college. But my mother, who could deny her much-loved only son nothing, was in on the secret. Unknown to my father, every Saturday for eight months she would slip me £1-10s and, on the pretext of running errands, I would take the bus to Berry's to pay off the hire purchase.

Asil's new car was a sleek, turquoise MG which my father, ever true to his practice of rewarding our efforts and achievements, had presented to Asil for performing well in his first-year exams and for spending much of his holiday helping out in the fledgling London business. My parents and I waved from the doorway of my uncle's house as Asil gingerly manoeuvred the MG out into the London traffic to begin a three-day journey to Turkey, happily unaware of the way that sports car and the electric guitar inside it were to change his life for ever. My father, proud to see his son working hard and doing well, had been happy to use money left over from the sale of the Famagusta businesses to give Asil this vehicle which would make him the envy of his fellow students. But the car and guitar would quickly combine to attract the attention of one young lady - Ayşegül Tecimer - who became the first real love of my brother's life. It was an unforeseen consequence which made my father later rue the day he ever set eyes on the turquoise MG.

———————

While my brother set off for university, I was destined for the Pitman's College in London. I had very much wanted to follow Asil and Meral into higher education, but I soon realised that the move to Britain at the age of fifteen had effectively put paid to that ambition. Although not impossible, aiming for a university place would have meant me spending at least three years at school in the capital, working for "O" and "A" levels and bringing my English up to scratch. For an uncertain teenager in a strange city, it seemed far too daunting a prospect, so I readily agreed to my father's suggestion that I should study commerce with the ultimate intention of entering the family business—enrolling in "the Nadir University", as he put it. Later, I would come to regret abandoning my education, but now I realise that my lack of paper qualifications has simply meant having to work twice as hard as many other people to secure the same achievements. Where others learned their business skills from books, I picked mine up from hard graft and experience and I believe now this "hands on" approach was invaluable.

In September 1961, I embarked on a year's course at the college in Southampton Row, Holborn, having been shown which buses to catch by my father during several "dummy runs" over the previous days. For that academic year, I studied English, shorthand, typing and book-keeping. It was not what I dreamt of, but my decision to attend the college was to prove fortuitous. One miserable Friday lunch-time in February 1962 I went to the canteen as usual for my meal. As I stood in the queue for the servery, absently banging the metal tray against one knee, I noticed a young man I had never seen before sitting nearby and talking to a Turkish Cypriot friend of mine, also an emigré from Famagusta. I was intrigued. I could not tell whether this well-dressed newcomer was Turkish or British. His slicked-back hair was Mediterranean dark, yet his eyes were blue. I collected my tray of food and crossed to their table to investigate. My friend introduced his other pal as Fehim Nevzat, a fellow-Cypriot from the northern coastal resort town of Kyrenia who was in London to study law at university. We chatted for a few minutes and, when I left the canteen, I remember thinking how nice this Fehim Nevzat was. He seemed gentle and considerate.

Fehim's recollection of our first meeting is rather different to mine. His story has it that I, so stunned at the sight of him as I turned from the canteen servery, dropped my tray and had to pick everything up off the floor. Naturally, I dispute this version of events, but in the years which followed he has recounted this tale so many times that, regardless of its foundation in truth, it has become something of a family legend.

Fehim and I began to meet quite often. He started visiting our canteen several times a week and I grew to like him more and more. I could see he was different from the other young men I knew. He was quiet and polite - a real gentleman, I remember thinking. As the weeks passed, I noticed that Fehim seemed to be paying more attention to me than to any of our other friends. Many an evening, I would look out of the third-floor college window and see him standing on the pavement far below, waiting to walk me to the bus station. Once or twice he even took me out to lunch at an Italian restaurant in Holborn. Years later he confessed that, as a hard-up student trying to impress, he had gallantly bought me lunch—only to be forced to survive on bread and jam for the rest of the week until his next allowance arrived.

True to the "rebel" nickname given to me by my father, I began to be a little more daring. I was expected home straight from college every evening and had always had to say "no" if anyone suggested staying behind to chat. Now, I began to join the others occasionally at an Italian coffee bar round the corner from the college where they all used to meet after classes. I would stay for half an hour and then dash to catch the next bus. At home, when my father would quiz me about where I had been, I would tell him I had had to stay late for an extra lesson...all the while crossing my fingers behind my back and hoping he would not catch me out in this white lie.

In the spring of 1962, a letter from Istanbul arrived in Romford which instantly deflected attention from me. It was from Meral, announcing to my parents that Asil had met a girl and wanted to marry her. The news sent shockwaves through our household. My parents were furious. My father feared this new interest would distract Asil from his studies and had visions of the high hopes he nurtured for his son's future in the family business going to waste. He was so distraught that we called in the doctor the following day and he diagnosed him as having suffered a very mild heart attack. Both my parents were distressed that the object of their son's affections was a teenager from Istanbul, since they felt the most suitable partner for him would have been a Cypriot girl from the same kind of background as ours. I was shocked but excited by the development.

A series of emotional letters and telephone calls between Romford and Istanbul revealed the full story. In December, The Nobles had been invited to play for a Christmas party and show at the French lycée in the city, Notre Dame de Sion. After the show, one of Asil's fellow band-members had introduced him to the compère, sixteen-year-old Aysegül Tecimer, who was a pupil at the school. They chatted for a while and Aysegül was with the band when they left at the end of the evening. She was highly impressed to see the gleaming MG parked outside - the first car of its kind she had glimpsed in Istanbul. The MG provided an instant talking-point and Aysegül, more pushy than the other lycée girls admiring the vehicle, walked straight up to a bemused Asil to announce: "I just love the smell of sports cars." The friendship developed from there.

Asil was lodging that year with our sister, who was teaching at the British Council, her civil engineering student husband and two university friends who were also from Cyprus - Tahsin Bilginer, who is now a doctor in London, and Zeka Alsancak, later to join us on the board of our first public company, Wearwell. The first Meral knew of Asil's blossoming relationship was when Aysegül discovered where he lived and began to come visiting - a very bold step for a teenage Turkish girl. Concerned to try and halt this liaison which she, like my parents, deemed unsuitable, Meral sometimes lied to Aysegül, saying that Asil was out if she called while he was studying in his room. But there was no thwarting Aysegül - a very persistent young lady, as my sister later reported to us - and the relationship soon began to get more serious. Asil would invite Aysegül out for a drive and the two of them would cruise alongside the Bosphorus in the turquoise MG, happily turning heads wherever they went. They would stop for tea overlooking the water before heading back home through the city.

A few weeks after they had started seeing each other, Aysegül invited Asil to her parents' apartment. Her family had a summer home on Büyükada, one of the small islands in the Bosphorus off the Istanbul shore, but they were living in the centre of town, not far from trendy Taksim. As a child, Aysegül had enjoyed little attention from her socialite parents. Her mother was usually still asleep in bed when the family maid got Aysegül off to school in the mornings and would be out playing cards in a club by the time she returned, going on later to dine and dance the night away. Days often went by without the family even getting together for a meal or a chat. As Aysegül began to approach marriageable age, however, the Tecimers began to take their parental responsibilities more seriously. They took on the swish parquet-floored flat in one of Istanbul's smartest areas, considering it a better base from which to find their daughter a suitably well-off husband.

Asil was not what Hasan and Nuran Tecimer had in mind. They saw in him simply a student little more than four years older than their daughter - a far cry from the wealthy professional they had hoped for. Asil, in his turn, was impressed by the kind of lavish lifestyle he aspired to and by the polished Istanbul Turkish spoken by the Tecimer family - a speech much more concerned with linguistic niceties than the more rough-and-ready Turkish of Cyprus. He was completely captivated by the tall, striking Aysegül, flattered that she should be so keen on him - and determined to provide her with the same level of luxury she had apparently been used to all her life.

Once Asil had made up his mind, his next step was to ask my parents' permission to approach Aysegül's parents and request their daughter's hand in marriage. Anticipating the reaction back in Romford, he thought the news would be better received if it came from his elder sister, so he pressed a reluctant Meral into penning the difficult letter. The debate raged in our house for several days before any reply was made. Eventually my mother, mindful of Asil's special place in her affections, pronounced her final judgement. "If our son has chosen this girl," she told my father one evening as we sat in the living room, "maybe we should not say no. Maybe we should wait and meet her, get to know her, and time will tell." At that stage, my parents assumed the prospective wedding was bound to be some way off - delayed two and a half years, at least, until after Asil's graduation - and I think they secretly hoped the young couple would come to realise their differences and part before they ever set foot in the registry office. They did not bargain for the alacrity with which Asil, duly informed of my parents' sanction, began to prepare for marriage.

In May 1962, Meral and Güner, as the heads of the Nadir household in Turkey, called on the Tecimer family in accordance with Turkish custom and declared Asil's intentions over tea. Hasan and Nuran Tecimer, already expecting the approach and warned by the headstrong Ayşegül not to try and stand in her way, agreed to the marriage. They quickly arranged a small engagement dinner party at the Hilton Hotel. Meral and Güner, and Tahsin Bilginer and his fiancée, Samime, were the only guests from our side to attend the party with Ayşegül's family and friends. It was a showy occasion, with the Tecimers seemingly keen to demonstrate their considerable means—and at pains to show that Ayşegül had attached herself to a family of similar standing. My sister was told that she was expected to bring the young couple an engagement gift, but since she was a teacher and her husband a student, Mrs Tecimer was clearly concerned that the gift they chose might not be suitable. To ensure no hitches, she brought an enormous and expensive silver fruit bowl round to my sister beforehand and told her she should present it to Asil and Ayşegül in front of the guests, pretending it was her gift. Güner was outraged at the suggestion. He told my sister that they should refuse to go along with the pretence and, moreover, should boycott the engagement party. But Meral was anxious not to rock the boat and persuaded him to do what Mrs Tecimer wanted. In the years that followed, we have often joked that it might have been better if she had bowed to her husband's wishes on that occasion.

The wedding took place on the 15th September 1962 and provoked another Nadir family disagreement. Asil travelled back to London briefly in July to buy his bride-to-be's wedding dress and my mother and father followed him back to Istanbul two months later to attend the registry office ceremony. My sister and husband were not there because they had returned to London after Güner's graduation. The reception was to be held in the Tecimers' apartment and on the evening before the wedding my mother and father went there to meet their future daughter-in-law and her parents for the first time. The encounter was not a success. At one point, my father even suggested that he and my mother should return to London without attending the wedding. My father predicted then that the marriage would never work - he did not think they were suited. Despite his determination to leave, however, my father softened in the face of my mother's obvious distress and he reluctantly agreed to stay. The wedding passed off politely and my parents flew home to London with their misgivings the next morning.

Amid all the turmoil of Asil's wedding plans, my parents also had to contend with another engagement in the family - mine and Fehim's. While the family's attention had been focused on Istanbul, we had quietly grown more and more attached. By the early summer of 1962, we were seeing each other virtually every day at lunch-time or after college although the traditions of our culture did not permit us, as an unengaged couple, to spend any time alone together. That June, unexpected visitors to Romford proved the catalyst which cemented our relationship.

The callers were family friends from Cyprus. I was at home when they came round on a Saturday afternoon and soon realised, from the snatches of conversation I caught as I served them tea in the living room, that I was the prime reason for the visit. The family had a son some years older than me and they wanted to sound out my father's opinion as to whether - in keeping with Turkish Cypriot tradition - a marriage might be arranged between us. The idea filled me with alarm. At that moment, I became convinced that Fehim was the only man I wanted to marry. Although I was a naïve young girl, just turned sixteen and with no idea of love, I knew he was the only man I had ever felt so strongly about. In my panic, I could scarcely sleep until Monday came and I saw Fehim after college. When I spilled out the story, I was relieved to see that he reacted with the same concern. That night, Fehim called on his elder brother, Ilker, who was also living in London at the time, confided in him and asked his advice. Ilker and Fehim consulted an uncle in the city and the three of them asked my father if they could visit him.

Throughout this process, which took only a few days but seemed to last an eternity, I acted at home as if I was aware of nothing unusual going on - although Fehim kept me fully up-to-date with progress each time we met. My father duly received the three new visitors, heard Fehim's application for my hand in marriage, and then announced that he would weigh up the matter for a short time before letting them know his decision. I was in the kitchen, keeping out of the way and trying to act calmly. My father came through and explained what had been said and asked if I would like to marry Fehim. My heart was leaping with glee, but I did my best to adopt a cool air and mumbled some noncommittal answer, afraid of arousing my father's suspicions that I had had some part in prompting this approach. Meral, who was visiting at the time and to whom I had confessed my feelings, did me proud. She was standing at the sink pretending to be busy and when she heard my silence turned to my father and said, "In my experience, when a person says nothing to a question like that, they really mean 'yes'." My father looked at me closely and said, "Is that right? Will you be happy marrying this boy?" I seemed to have lost my voice and could only nod my head dumbly.

My father's deliberations went on for a few weeks while he recruited friends and relatives in Cyprus to make inquiries about the Nevzat family and report their findings. Fehim's maternal grandfather - Fehim Efendi (Master Fehim) - had been the biggest landowner among the Turkish community and a major olive oil and carob exporter, my father discovered. He was clearly satisfied with what he learned and called Fehim, Ilker and their uncle back to Romford to tell them he agreed to the proposal. He also took me to one side and informed me of his decision. While he gave his blessing to our marriage, he also warned me of his reservations: I was too young for marriage, he said; I had only just left college and Fehim was still a student, struggling to support himself on his father's allowance, let alone support a wife. Nonetheless, I think my father had approved of Fehim from the first moment they met, as he came from an honest and respected family. It was my father's biggest fear that the British way of life might have had some adverse effect on me at such a formative age, so he was relieved to think of me settling down with a young man he liked, who was also a Turkish Cypriot. Our engagement took place quietly on 5th August 1962, just over a month before Asil's wedding in Istanbul. The few relatives in England at the time joined us for a dinner party and during the evening an elderly member of the Turkish Cypriot community ceremoniously placed the rings on our fingers, blessing them with a prayer that our union would last a lifetime.

At the outset, I promised my father that Fehim and I would not marry for two or three years, when he had graduated from university, but that soon proved an impossible pledge to fulfil. At the time of our engagement, Fehim was still going on with his law studies and I had just begun work at the Solicitors' Law Stationery Society, where I would remain for some months - at my father's instigation - learning how to put into practice what I had been taught in college before joining Nadir Modes. Fehim's father, Hasan, then boarding master at the prestigious English School in Nicosia, had been sending him money regularly to keep him during his student days, but when he heard he was planning to marry, he stopped the allowance, saying his son would have to take on the responsibility of keeping a wife and family.

This left Fehim with a difficult choice. My father offered to support him while he finished the remaining two years of his course, but he would not hear of it, although he agreed to my father's suggestion that he might save money by moving out of his Finchley digs during his holidays and coming to live with us in Romford. By the time I left my first job and began work at Nadir Modes early in 1963, Fehim was still

38

finding it a struggle to survive financially and he readily accepted my father's next suggestion - that he, too, might join the company. He decided to work part-time in the factory so that he could earn enough money to live while he continued his law studies. In the meantime, I had come to the conclusion that the two of us could live together virtually as cheaply as one person on their own - but to do that, we would have to marry first. So we set about looking for a home of our own and decided to go ahead with the wedding. We chose the 3rd August - almost exactly a year after our engagement - as our wedding date.

As soon as Asil heard of our marriage plans, he announced that he and Aysegül would drive the MG over to Britain for a holiday and to attend the wedding. With preparations in full swing and then the news that there would be two extra live-in guests, the house seemed in a state of constant uproar. As the date of Asil's arrival drew closer, I grew more and more excited, almost forgetting about my own imminent wedding. I had not seen Asil for a year and was missing him badly. At the same time, I was eager to meet my new sister-in-law. Of course, I had heard my parents give their not entirely complimentary impressions of Aysegül during the previous few months, but I put those thoughts to one side, determined to make up my own mind and looking forward to the companionship of another girl of my own age. To me, just seventeen and from a relatively sheltered background, this metropolitan creature sounded exciting and glamorous.

On the late July night when Asil and Aysegül were expected to arrive by ferry in Dover, there was torrential rain and gale-force winds. Their car broke down and by the time my mother and father were able to bring them home it was early morning. While we waited, Fehim and I prepared a big family breakfast. After what seemed an eternity, I heard a key in the lock and we both raced to the front door. What I saw there sent my high spirits plummeting.

Aysegül stepped through the door and, glancing first to right and then to left, appeared to look the place thoroughly up and down in a disdainful manner. She half-turned to Asil, who was hovering behind her with an anxious smile, and said loudly, as if they were alone: "Is *this* really your house? I thought it would be much bigger."

I was shocked, but we all tried to brush over the remark with a warm flurry of greetings. Meanwhile, I tried discreetly to take stock of my new sister-in-law. She was tall and, though well-rounded rather than slim, she struck me as a very sophisticated creature from a different world. She had naturally curly, dark hair and probably her best feature was her eyes, which were beautiful, large and almost honey-coloured. Breakfast did little to thaw the rather strained atmosphere in the house. Ayşegül announced that she did not like the butter we had - not the unsalted type she had been used to - nor were our British eggs to her liking. By the time she rose from the table and announced that she wanted to sleep, I had already made up my mind that if I wanted to get on with my sister-in-law I would have to try and ignore some of her more supercilious remarks.

Fehim and I were married in a noon service at Romford Registry Office. I wore a full white bridal outfit and, that being unusual for a civil ceremony in those days, the event was recorded for posterity with a picture and story in the local newspaper, under the headline "Turkish delight stops traffic". It rained off and on most of the day, but the weather could not dampen our spirits - in fact, when I saw the grey skies, it brought to mind only a Turkish saying that if it rains on your wedding day, you will be blessed with children. We honeymooned for a week in the Isle of Wight before settling into our married home in the Camberwell Green area of London. The two-storey house had cost us £1,700 and we had done all the decorating ourselves. To help pay the mortgage, we had rented the lower floor to a Turkish family who worked for my father, so even as newly-weds we had little time completely alone.

In Romford, meanwhile, my parents had received a shock. Asil had one year left at university before he could graduate, but within days of my wedding he took my father to one side and told him he had decided not to go back to Istanbul, but to stay in London and work at Nadir Modes. His announcement sparked off days of argument. My mother and father - seeing their worst fears realised - both tried to insist that he should return to Turkey and finish his degree, but Asil was not to be moved. He had been examining my father's young business, could see the immense difficulties under which he was operating, and had come up with ideas as to how he could help. He persuaded my father to let him stay and he and Ayşegül settled permanently in the house in Pettits Boulevard.

It was not an easy time for any of them. Ayşegül was not an accommodating house guest; my parents felt she made no attempt to fit in with the busy family routine and Asil was often on edge, aware of the lack of warmth between his wife and his own family. No words of criticism were ever spoken to her face or to Asil, but seeing Ayşegül within his home surroundings, away from the rarified atmosphere of Istanbul city life, made my brother keenly aware of the very great gulf between them. Ayşegül came from entirely different stock to us - from the wealthy Istanbul society which did not consider employment to be the "done thing" - and she made no secret of the fact that she could not understand the work ethic that permeated the family. Her attitude was clearly quite alien to my parents. Asil made no effort to try and get Aysegül out to work and obviously intended to take it upon himself to provide for her the lifestyle she demanded. My father was very worried by what he observed over the months. There were never any rows, but he told me privately that the Aysegül he had got to know simply confirmed his initial fears that the marriage would not last. Worse still, he was certain his son would be the one to suffer.

Aysegül was always distant. We tried to make excuses for her at first, telling ourselves she was shy and still trying to adapt to a new environment where she spoke little of the language, but we could see no sign of change during the year she and Asil lived with my parents. Where we had always been a warm, demonstrative family, Aysegül was cool in the extreme and never showed emotion. One frightening incident at the end of 1963 served to bring that difference home to me. Meral and Güner by now had a baby of a few months, Tolga. Güner was working for the government in Cyprus and they lived in a mixed suburb of the capital, Nicosia. My mother, who still yearned for her homeland, decided that she would go and spend Christmas and New Year with them. We were all aware of escalating tension on the island, but in spite of that - or even because of it, in case she could be of some help to my sister - my mother insisted on making the journey. We waved her off on the 20th December, unaware that the island was on the brink of a conflict which would go on for nearly eleven years.

In the two years since we had left Cyprus, the political situation had been deteriorating steadily - now it was reaching crisis point. In November 1963, the Turkish Cypriot MPs who constitutionally made up thirty-five per cent of the new republic's Parliament had been expelled after refusing to vote away their own rights. There were sporadic attacks on isolated Turkish villages and in Turkish areas. Roadblocks were set up by armed Greek Cypriot civilians hired as "special constables" and Turkish Cypriot motorists were stopped, searched and summonsed.

That December came an all-out Greek attack on the Turkish Cypriot community. The steadily rising tensions of the previous three years came to a head in Nicosia in the early hours of Saturday the 21st December 1963, when Greek Cypriot "special constables" attempted to search a woman in the Turkish sector of Nicosia. As an angry crowd gathered, the constables fired, killing the woman and her male

41

companion. The crisis quickly escalated. Greek Cypriot "constables" took pot-shots at passing vehicles from the street corners and civilians joined in, shooting from car windows as they raced through the Turkish Cypriot area. Meanwhile, there were attempts to round up and hold all Turkish Cypriot policemen by Greek Cypriot forces split into three groups, one led by Nicos Sampson.

Fearing for their lives, Turkish Cypriots living outside the Turkish Cypriot quarter or mostly Turkish suburbs fled their homes in search of safety. All lines of communication with the outside world were severed as terrorism raged for days in Nicosia and rapidly spread island-wide. The mainly Turkish Nicosia suburb of Omorphita (today's Küçük Kaymakli) came under attack twice in one day but held out until dark, when 3,000 of the Turkish Cypriot residents were escorted to safety during the night. The next day, the defenders having run out of ammunition, Nicos Sampson and his men finally seized Omorphita, bundling 550 remaining Turkish Cypriots off to Kykkos School as hostages. Sampson acquired the nickname "The Butcher of Omorphita" from his exploits that day.

As foreign journalists arrived on the island and news of the massacres emerged, Turkey, Greece and Britain stepped in to restore peace. Turkish Prime Minister, Ismet Inönü, sent three air force jets to buzz Nicosia as a warning to the Greek Cypriots. He also ordered the 650-strong mainland army contingent to take up strategic positions along the Kyrenia road. On Boxing Day, Makarios, fearing Turkish intervention, accepted the offer of a peacekeeping force, led by British troops supported by soldiers from Greece and Turkey, to be sent to the island. By the 30th of December, British troops - later to be replaced by a mixed United Nations force - had taken up positions along the cease-fire line through Nicosia - known as the "Green Line" because it had been marked on a wall chart in green pen. The fighting finally ended in January 1964 after the United Nations Security Council in New York called for an immediate cease-fire. By that time, according to official records, 364 Turkish Cypriots and 174 Greek Cypriots had lost their lives. More than 25,000 Turkish Cypriots from 103 villages had fled their homes. In effect, the crisis had almost completely separated the two communities - beginning a process which would be brought to a conclusion ten and a half years later.

The conflict had broken out within hours of my mother reaching Cyprus and by the first morning of her visit Turkish Cypriot homes throughout the island were abuzz with news of the hostilities. Meral's house lay outside relatively protected Omorphita, in a newly-developed mixed suburb called Yeni Sehir. My mother, Meral, Güner and the baby sheltered inside for days as gunfire and bombings raged outside. An old school-friend of Güner's was also with them - he had come that morning to warn Meral and Güner of the troubles and had found himself unable to leave. Roads into the Turkish quarter were blocked and gangs of armed Greek terrorists roamed the streets. Trapped and terrified, they all slept together in the hallway and strained to listen to the tinny news broadcasts of Turkish Cypriot Bayrak (Flag) Radio, which had been born out of necessity in the early moments of the conflict and was being transmitted illicitly from a stable using home-made equipment powered by car batteries. After three days, food supplies were low and the baby's milk was all but finished. An attempt to venture out to the tangerine trees in the garden under cover of darkness almost ended in tragedy as bullets cracked through the night sky.

On the ninth day there was a knock at the door. My sister opened it to two armed Greek Cypriots and two from the Greek mainland. The men stormed into the house brandishing machine guns and made them all stand against the wall while they searched the building for weapons. Of course they found none. One of the men turned to my sister and poked at Tolga, who was in her arms, with the muzzle of his gun. He glanced at his friends and spat: "Why don't we kill this one before it gets old enough to attack us." He looked coldly at Meral for a moment then strode out of the front door. The others stepped forward and marched them all out of the house at gun-point.

In the road outside stood a dusty coach. Inside, my sister recognised her Turkish neighbours. They all stared blankly through the grimy windows. The atmosphere was one of shock. Nobody shouted; nobody screamed; no voices were raised in protest. One woman, taken from her kitchen where she had been preparing dinner, nursed a huge turkey in her lap. "I spent hours plucking this turkey - I'm not going to leave it behind for the Greeks to eat," she told my mother.

As the bus pulled away and began to weave through the narrow streets of Nicosia, my mother spoke out. Never one to sit back and wait for her fate, she challenged the armed Greek riding with them: "Where are you taking us? Wherever it is, we are not going. We want to be taken to the airport. We are British subjects and we demand to be allowed to go home." As soon as the trouble had started several days earlier, my mother had made a point of keeping her passport in her pocket and had made sure Meral and Güner - both also British passport holders - did the same. Now she produced her passport and waved it in the bewildered man's face, gesturing to my sister and Güner, who both tried to look away. Güner, who was sitting next to her, kept treading on her foot and hissing at her under his breath to "keep quiet" as she kept up this monologue throughout the journey. He and Meral feared they would all be the first to be killed because of my mother's tirade.

The drive took them through scenes of virtual anarchy. My sister tried not to look, but busied herself with her son as the bus skirted round the bodies of people who had been shot and left lying in the street to die. Everywhere, the wreckage of bombings and fires was evident. Heavily armed men patrolled the city as United Nations troops, unable to halt the carnage, stood around helplessly. My mother described the scenes later as those of a nightmare. After about half an hour, the coach reached its destination - the remote Greek monastery and school at Kykkos, south of Nicosia, where residents of Omorphita were already being held hostage. The driver and guard began to order all the Turkish Cypriots off at gun-point. My mother dug her heels in and refused to get off the vehicle, insisting that Meral, Güner and Tolga stay with her. I dread to think what might have happened then, but with a stroke of luck, just at that moment a carload of foreign journalists pulled up. They parked nearby and began taking notes and photographs.

Seeing this and apparently not wanting their actions witnessed, the Greeks made all those Turks still left on the bus stay where they were— my mother, of course, decided then that she would get off the bus. She went over to the monastery window and peered through the glass. Inside were dozens, even hundreds, of people - men, women and young children - lying and sitting on the stone floor. The chilling sight convinced my mother that she should create a scene and take the chance of being able to save herself and her family. She marched up to the guard, showed her passport again, and told him: "We are British subjects; we are only here on holiday; is this how you treat your tourists? We refuse to go in there and we want to be taken to the airport." Gesturing towards the journalists, she added, "Unless you agree to take us there, I will go over there and tell them all exactly what you are doing." The guard, looking at the reporters to see if they had overheard this exchange and with a wary eye on my mother whom he clearly considered crazy, sidled over to consult with his colleague. A few moments later, he returned to tell my mother that, as long as they had money for tickets, she, Meral, Güner and the baby could go free and would be taken to the airport. Güner's school-friend, Necati Ayhan, was not allowed to leave with them because he did not have a British passport, but he survived the ordeal and was later able to tell my family what a miraculous escape the four of them had had. During the hours that the rest of the Turkish Cypriots were held in the monastery, several of the men were taken outside into the gardens and cold-bloodedly killed, sometimes in front of their wives and children.

44

Another armed Greek took my mother, Meral, Güner and Tolga to the airport. It was a nerve-wracking journey. The three adults sat in silence, acutely aware that their driver could, at any moment, decide to "lose" them en route. When they got to the airport safely, the suspense was to continue - they were told there was no plane out for the rest of that day and they would have to wait until the next morning to escape. The driver then took them on to a hotel near the airport. This proved to be another lucky break, since the Greek Cypriot who ran the establishment recognised my mother from childhood days and remembered that her father had once or twice done him a good turn. This man was very careful to ensure the family's safety that night. He asked them all to stay in one room, told them not to open their door, not to speak in Turkish and not to eat any food unless he had given it to them himself. The four of them spent a sleepless night in the dingy hotel room and the next morning the hotel owner took them to the airport to catch the flight to London.

Back in England, meanwhile, we had all been frantic with worry. Radio and television news bulletins gave us no comfort as they broadcast scenes of murder and destruction. In the chaos, we made desperate telephone calls round the Turkish Cypriot community in London and to everyone we could think of in Cyprus, but they were unable to give us any news because my sister did not have a phone and the troubles meant they could not reach her house. We felt helpless and frustrated. We had no idea what had happened and passed several sleepless nights and tearful days imagining them all killed or held as hostages. Often, my father, Asil, Fehim and I would cling to each other for comfort. Aysegül, however, seemed genuinely perplexed by our concern and we often caught her looking at us as if we had gone quite mad. She was very calm and would tell us coolly, "There's nothing to get so upset about. We'll hear something soon."

It was about one o'clock on the afternoon of the 30th December that we got the call we had longed for. Totally out of the blue, my mother rang from the airport to say they had landed safely in Britain and were just about to set off for home in a taxi. Tears of relief poured down our faces as we hugged each other in greeting when the taxi eventually pulled up in Pettits Boulevard; but there were also tears of sorrow - sorrow for the nine-day nightmare through which we had lived, and sorrow for Cyprus and for our fellow-Cypriots whose sufferings had not ended so happily. The dishevelled and exhausted travellers who arrived home that day without a single piece of baggage were scarcely the same people they had been when we last saw them. They were all deeply disturbed by their experience and could do nothing that first night but sit and discuss what had happened, endlessly reliving the terror. My sister seemed the worst affected. Only days before, she had been full of hope and living happily in Cyprus. Now that life lay in ruins around her as she sat, rocking Tolga, in the slippers and dress which were the only clothes she had left - having seen her infant son threatened at gun-point by a man apparently no different to our one-time Greek Cypriot playmates. In her distress, Meral there and then abandoned any idea of life in Cyprus and settled alongside our parents in north-east London.

There was little sleep in the Nadir household that night and we were all still bleary-eyed when we got up the next day - New Year's Eve and also my mother's birthday. In the living room we found propped up on the mantelpiece a note which my father, who considered we should put the ordeal behind us, had left when he went off to the factory. It instructed us all: "Discussion of Cyprus is forbidden in this house." We had to laugh when we saw this and it injected just the note of light-heartedness we needed. Although the brush with disaster remained in the back of our minds for a long time, it was with happier expectations that we raised our glasses that midnight in a toast to 1964.

The new year was to prove a turning point for our business fortunes. While my father had been labouring solidly for more than two years, it was the vision of my brother, newly-returned from Istanbul and eager to make his way in the commercial world, which steered us from hard-working obscurity and into the limelight of eventual stock market success.

At the beginning of 1963, I had left my job at the Solicitors' Law Stationery Society, fully grounded in office practice, and had joined the staff of Nadir Modes. My father had devised a training programme for me in the factory, but my first lesson began before I got into the building, when my father instructed me that I was to come in through a side door, instead of walking right past the benches, so that I did not distract the machinists. "If all of them lift their heads for just thirty seconds to look at you when you come in, it means that we will lose several minutes' production time," he warned. I forget the total amount of time he reckoned would be lost, but I certainly realised he had it all worked out! Far from starting off with clerical tasks at New Road, he set me to work on the factory floor, ensuring that I learned every inch of the production line, learned how to operate every piece of machinery, before I could move on to the next stage. I spent several months picking up the intricacies of how to organise and control production before I began to realise that I had a flair for the design side.

By then, Asil had joined us, making Nadir Modes a real family business. Fehim too had succumbed to the excitement of business and had given up his legal studies after a difficult few months of trying to combine the two. All of us would join in and do whatever tasks were needed to get the orders finished on time, and I am sure the fact that we were prepared to roll our sleeves up inspired the factory's staff to work even harder alongside us - it was real teamwork. Many an evening we would stay on at the factory for hours after the staff had gone home, coming in on weekends, too, if there was an urgent delivery to be made. In those early days, my father could not afford to pay the staff overtime, so we would tackle whatever jobs needed to be done. By then, I had learned to turn my hand to any of the machines, so my mother and I would sit sewing in the empty factory. Upstairs, Fehim and Asil would operate the pressing machines - often, to while away the time, they would have some fun by turning the task into a race to see who could press the most garments in a certain time. When the clothes were all packed up and ready for the customer, Asil and my father would make the deliveries. As well as serving his apprenticeship in the garments industry during this time, Asil also made one lasting acquaintance - Anil Doshi, an accountant of Indian origin, came to the factory every Friday to help my father do the books and prepare the pay-roll. He and Asil became firm friends and their business relationship would endure for more than a quarter of a century, during the high-flying and turbulent years to come.

Fresh from his economics studies, Asil was soon busy devising ways to increase profits. He persuaded my father that the only way to make good money in the clothing trade was not to stick cautiously to the practice of CMT - cutting and making garments to order for other people - but to break into the riskier business of manufacturing and selling our own designs. This was a gamble because it meant paying to manufacture garments without any guarantee that they would ever sell, but it was where the serious profits lay, Asil argued. My father decided to give the idea a try, so my mother and I began designing and making up patterns for a range of our own styles, based on the lines which were in fashion that season. Asil took on the job of selling the clothes and he opened his own showroom opposite Nadir Modes in New Road. By 1964, the family had control of a complete production line.

In a way, that year was a fulfilment of my father's dreams. Although he had started off his London business making clothes for other firms, he had always nurtured plans for expansion and had hoped his children would work alongside him to help bring those plans to fruition. Nadir Modes was already showing steady growth and had blossomed to take

47

over the entire New Road premises in 1963. Asil's input and ideas, however, were to prove the catalyst for a phenomenal business take-off. His showroom, Wearwell Limited, began modestly enough in a rented shop at Number 20 New Road. There, the garments designed by my mother and made up across the road in my father's factory would be displayed on racks. Asil would welcome retailer customers and take orders for the styles on show. So successful was this idea that within a year and a half the showroom had grown to fill first the neighbouring shop unit and had then expanded into a third until it became the biggest clothing showroom in London. The showroom triumph sowed the seed of another novel idea in my brother's mind. He suggested to my father that he should launch a clothing cash-and-carry - bulk quantities of various styles would be made up at Nadir Modes and by "outworkers" operating from home, and retailers would be able to drop in and simply pick up whole new lines for their shops. My father gave his blessing to the scheme and in 1967 Asil launched the cash-and-carry at his showroom. Wearwell was the first enterprise of its kind in the London rag trade and it quickly became a stunning success. In later years, it would spawn a series of similar showrooms around Britain, in Manchester, Newcastle and Glasgow. In the late 1960s, Wearwell already showed signs of being the vehicle through which our family would gain real prosperity. By the early seventies, it had taken over as the main Nadir business, becoming the stepping stone to Polly Peck.

Asil was not the only member of the family team to branch out. By 1967, I was beginning to feel a certain discontent. I had served my apprenticeship at Nadir Modes and now I was finding it increasingly difficult simply to work for someone else, even if it was for my father. I wanted to have some control, some say in running the business. It was a trait of mine which was to surface again more than a decade later and crystallise in my running my own public company. Luckily for me, Fehim has always been happy to lend his support, letting me take the lead. In 1967, Asil suggested that Fehim and I might consider starting up our own factory. We spent several months looking at premises and eventually settled on a block not far from Asil's showroom. It was rather shabby, but we repainted the building ourselves and opened early in 1968 with just five staff, under the name Fame Models. Asil helped us with ideas, my father gave us the cash to start up and we began turning out our own range of designs - styles I had adapted from current fashion trends to turn them into more commercial garments.

Although by then our first child had just been born, Fehim and I were not shy of hard work and long hours and Fame Models soon began to earn as much in profits as my father's business. Within six months, we were finding our original factory too cramped and moved to more spacious premises further down New Road. My brother-in-law, Güner, although a civil engineer by profession, had been observing our businesses for some time and could see the potential of the clothing trade. In late 1968, he moved into the premises vacated by Fame Models and started up his own garments factory, Celebrity Fashions.

Suddenly, just seven years after arriving in total obscurity, we had become well-known figures in the East End rag trade and were earning more money than we had ever dreamed of. I began to feel we had really "arrived" in Britain. The sense of excitement and achievement became self-perpetuating. As we began to realise what could be done through good ideas and hard graft, we came up with new ideas to expand the businesses. In 1969, just a year after the launch of Fame Models, Asil unveiled a scheme which surpassed all others in the scale of its ambitions. Calling us all together in Romford one evening, his eyes gleamed with enthusiasm as he explained how we should gather all the family firms under one roof and merge them under a single name. Then, he said, we should take that single company public, giving us the capital to do much more, to invest in new, complementary businesses. Maybe we might even consider weaving our own fabrics, so that we could control the entire production process from start to finish. It was a giddy sensation, eyeing the vision Asil laid out before us—but we knew it was within reach and the determination to achieve that progress took root in all of us.

If the Nadir star was in the ascendant in the realm of business during those years, our family's personal fortunes were more mixed. Meral, getting over the remembered horrors of the December days in Cyprus, was settling happily into London life. She found a job in teaching and in 1966 gave birth to her second son, Tunç.

For Fehim and myself, the 1960s were a time of hard work, self-discovery and personal fulfilment. The house we bought when we were first married in 1963 remained our home for three years. In 1966, we moved to a bigger house in Hackney, east London, which was closer to town and also closer to my parents in Romford. Now a rather swish area near Victoria Park, the location of that house was then very run-down. It was an old building with no central heating and to help us with the mortgage we had a family lodging in the basement and rented two rooms out to students. It didn't take long for us to get fed up with the lack of privacy in this cold and draughty house, and it was just one year later that we moved to South Woodford, into a small flat which was also the first home we had entirely to ourselves. We were to remain in South Woodford for the next twenty-five years.

The year we moved into the flat also brought us our first child. The baby arrived at a particularly hectic moment. In January 1968, Fehim and I opened Fame Models and our daughter was born just a month later. On Sunday, the 11th February, I realised the baby was on its way. I knew Fehim would be very short of help while I was off work after the birth, so I made him take me in to New Road so I could get some extra work done in advance. All that day, I sewed and sewed, stopping only when the contractions were at their worst, and carrying on until I had overlocked and button-holed every single garment in the factory. The baby was born in Wanstead Hospital at seven o'clock the next morning and we named her Tijen. Tijen means "Carcassian princess" and she was every inch our princess.

Four weeks after Tijen's birth, I went back to work at Fame Models taking her with me. I turned the office next door to mine into a nursery and tried to get back into the swing of my old job - a difficult task when I had to fend off gently all the admirers who wanted to look at the baby. After a few months of this, I was able to take on a nanny who stayed with Tijen during the day while I was at work. This nanny was a South Woodford widow of Irish descent who had raised four sons and a daughter and nursed her husband through the throes of Parkinson's disease which finally killed him. I had no idea then how the nanny - Mrs Finney, or Auntie Finney as my children called her - would become part of the family, looking on my three children almost as her own.

While my parents were undoubtedly happy to have all three of their children near them in London and working closely together, there were many moments of concern for all of us as we witnessed the gradual deterioration of Asil's marriage. It gave my father no pleasure to watch his early fears slowly come true. Late in 1963, shortly after my marriage to Fehim, Aysegül had discovered she was pregnant. She was developing an interest in art and antiques, so had already decided that life in suburbia was not for her - the pregnancy confirmed for her the urgent need to leave Romford before she was stranded there with a baby to look after. She pressured Asil into taking on a rented flat in Bayswater and that was where they were living when baby Birol Nadir entered the world in June 1964. The West End flat was well beyond Asil's then limited means, however, and by Birol's first birthday they had been forced to move back out of town and into a South Woodford flat. Every summer, Aysegül would pack her bags and take herself and the baby off to stay with her parents in Istanbul for two months. She would return home full of tales about the rich and handsome suitors who had apparently come to Büyükada to try and woo her away.

As Asil's fortunes began to take a sharp upturn towards the end of the 1960s, so Aysegül's interest in spending his new-found wealth grew keener. He tried very hard to please her, but because he worked such long hours, he could not take her out on the town as much as she would have liked. They were just so different - she was a night-time party animal who liked to get dressed up and go out, while Asil preferred an early night in bed after a hard day at the office. There were rows and cold silences if Asil ever told her he could not afford whatever it was she wanted and that she would have to be patient. For her birthday one year, Asil bought her an E-type Jaguar and had it filled to the brim with red roses - not just romantic but particularly apt since the *gül* part of her name means "rose" in Turkish. Any other woman would have been very impressed.

It came as little surprise when Asil confessed to me in 1969 that Aysegül disliked their flat in South Woodford and was house-hunting again. She soon found what she was looking for - a house in The Bishop's Avenue, Hampstead, with a squash court and swimming pool. It may not have been the central location Aysegül truly sought, but as a status symbol it would do well enough and it was a very desirable address, being known in the area as "Millionaires' Row". The house cost £30,000 and when they moved in 1969 Asil named it "Turquoise" - a recurrent theme incorporating a hint of things Turkish and his favourite colour.

The year of Asil and Aysegül's upmarket house move saw a change of address for the family businesses. Nadir Modes, Fame Models and Celebrity Fashions joined Asil's showroom and cash-and-carry operations under the name Wearwell. The new integrated company moved to swish premises at 191 Commercial Road, the main road out of the City. The new building was called Nadir House and it was big enough to house all the family firms in comfort. Nadir Modes' seventy staff, Celebrity Fashions and Fame Models, which by then had fifty staff and more than 150 "outworkers" sewing at home, each occupied one floor. On the top floor was Asil's Wearwell. The move was the beginning of the big business future Asil envisaged. If we were to "go public", it was necessary for the integrated company, Wearwell, to have records showing four or five years of solid commercial performance. Asil was keen to pursue new opportunities and he was the driving force behind our joining of assets. He would sit with my father for hours, discussing other companies in the clothing trade and expounding the benefits of operating as a united front.

I had my reservations about the merger. I was enjoying being in control of my own company, along with Fehim, and being able to make my own decisions. At that time, though, the call of my Turkish Cypriot upbringing was louder than the inner urgings spurring me towards freedom. As a young woman of just twenty-three, the respect I held for my father and brother was such that I would never have gone against their wishes - it mattered less to me then that I would lose the element of control than that the family would be made stronger by our decision. For the next seventeen years, though, the feeling of being left out of the decision-making process would gnaw away at my mind until the moment came when I could hide it no longer.

As the merger with Wearwell took place, however, and in the years which followed, I found plenty to keep me occupied—and not just in the office. In September 1969, shortly after Auntie Finney joined our household, Fehim and I were overjoyed to find out that I was pregnant with our second child. With another baby on the way and our financial fortunes looking up, we decided the time was ripe to move from the flat where we had lived for the past two years and buy a place with a garden. We decided to stay in South Woodford and eventually ended up in a detached house with a big garden in a pretty, tree-lined street called The Drive, which overlooked a stretch of green, moving in during January 1970. By the time the spring came, when the baby was due, I felt tired but determined to carry on working again until the last day. The 25th May was Whitsun Bank Holiday Monday and I went to the factory that morning in the throes of labour. There was a lot of work on, so the factory was open that day. I stayed upstairs while Fehim gave his instructions to the staff and then we drove straight to hospital - this time around to the much more prosperous surroundings of the private Avenue Clinic in St John's Wood. Our first son was born late that afternoon. We called him Levent, which means tall and handsome and was the name given to young soldiers in Ottoman times. Two days after the birth, I was sitting up in bed in my room at the clinic when I received a surprise visitor - it was Cilla Black, who was being shown round before having her first baby there about a month later.

After Levent's birth, Fehim and I had decided that, with a boy and a girl, we would stop at just two children. But it struck me later that none of the five grandchildren born so far had been named after either of my parents - a mark of respect very common in Cypriot culture. I spoke to Fehim and he agreed that we should try for one more child. If it was a girl, she would be named Safiye after her grandmother. If it was a boy, we would give him the name Irfan. Our new son arrived on the 5th March, 1973 and I could see tears of delight in both my parents' eyes as my father first held the baby we had named in his honour. From that day, young Irfan became my father's favourite grandchild and he used to spend every spare moment with him, telling of the great plans he had for him. Even when our son was still a baby in a high chair, I would often catch my father talking seriously to him as he spoon fed him, explaining how, in years to come, the second Irfan would achieve far more than the first one ever had! Years afterwards, when my father lay dying, I changed both of my sons' surnames by deed poll to "Nadir-Nevzat" so my father's name would live on.

While my own marriage was blissfully happy, Asil's home life was quickly turning into a nightmare. The rows had begun in earnest soon after he and Ayşegül moved into The Bishop's Avenue. Ayşegül would wait for Asil to come home from work and then demand to be taken out on the town. My brother had been up with the lark and at his desk since half past seven in the morning, but if he refused to go out, she would sulk for hours. On Saturdays, he would always make the effort to take her out, often to a favourite jazz club off Regents Street, but it never seemed to be enough. Sundays were our traditional day for getting all the family together, but many weekends Ayşegül would not allow Asil to join us because she did not wish to come. The only times we could be sure of having his company was on birthdays or religious holidays. Since we saw him every day at work, the loss did not seem so great, but it saddened me to have little chance of seeing my brother on occasions when he had the time to relax. A single look at Asil's face when he arrived at Nadir House would be enough to tell me whether there was a problem at home - and during the early 1970s there was many a morning when he arrived for work clearly unhappy. Often, Asil would pour his heart out to me and seeing him so hurt turned me more and more against the woman I held responsible for his distress.

As the years went by, the wedge created by their vastly different characters was driven further and further between them. Asil, preparing eagerly for the eventual flotation of Wearwell, was working extremely hard. Ayşegül, on the other hand, had no interest in the business and was more and more dissatisfied with her life in London. The marriage had got to a point where they just argued all the time they were together. Frequently, they were apart. Ayşegül had got into the habit of spending two or three months at a time with her parents in Turkey. Then she took up with a group of "arty" friends who raved about travel. She began dressing in way-out clothes and wearing her hair long and frizzy. In the spring of 1972, Ayşegül took off for South America with these friends, leaving eight-year-old Birol behind and saying she was unhappy and needed to "find herself". She was away for several weeks, during which time Birol stayed with his grandparents and with us.

Soon after Ayşegül returned, in May 1972, Asil arrived at Commercial Road uncharacteristically unshaven and strode straight into his top-floor office. I knew instantly that something was very wrong and followed him into the room. He asked me to call the rest of the family because he had something to tell us. When we were all together, a grey-faced Asil told us bluntly: "I can't take this any longer. I have decided to divorce Aysegül." Although deeply upset by Asil's patent sadness, the news came as something of a relief to us all - he and Aysegül were two totally different personalities; their union was not happy and at least a divorce meant they could both do what they wanted. We believed this would be the close of the unhappy chapter in Asil's life. In 1973, Aysegül and Asil agreed after several months of negotiation on a divorce settlement of £110,000, which gave joint custody of Birol.

It was a year which promised fresh beginnings. Within weeks of Asil's divorce coming through, we saw our plans for Wearwell come to fruition at last. The day of the company's flotation was set for July 1973. Asil was to be managing director of the newly public Wearwell and my father chairman. Asil had appointed the other board members - Fehim was sales director and Güner production director. Asil's former Istanbul flatmate, Zeka Alsancak, became marketing director and Anil Doshi was finance director. Also on the board were Johnny Holder, who was in charge of the leather division, and Adrian Huggins, a lawyer friend and neighbour of ours. I was not on the board. At first I was too caught up in the excitement of being part of a public company to be conscious of the disappointment at that omission, though it was to surface later.

On the morning of the flotation, Asil, my father and Adrian went down to the Stock Exchange to see the company's name listed for the first time. That first day, the shares rose to fifty-one pence from the launch figure of forty-six pence. The three returned in jubilant mood and we popped the champagne corks over a celebratory lunch. Afterwards, we threw a party for the 200-plus staff at Nadir House and our several hundred outworkers. For the management team at Commercial Road, though, there was little time for self-congratulation. If hard labour had been important before, we knew it was even more so now we were in the public eye. As a company quoted on the Stock Exchange, our share price would depend on our perceived performance. It was more crucial now than ever that we produce the financial goods.

Chapter Three

...to Riches

The flotation of Wearwell heralded some of the best years of my life. Fehim and I were working hard, earning well and bringing up our children. I could see my parents at last reaping the reward of all their years of toil, and even Asil seemed at first to be finding a measure of personal happiness to go with his blossoming business success.

It was at the 1971 Wearwell Christmas party that I first met Lesley Ellwood. She was very young - just eighteen or nineteen - and very pretty, and she had just started working for the company as an assistant to Asil's secretary, Jean Thomas. Lesley seemed a very nice young woman, but I thought little more of her until I began to become aware during the following year that her relationship with Asil involved more than just business. My brother was, like all of us, home-loving and family-orientated and he did not set out to embark on an affair with Lesley. But with Aysegül more and more often absent from England and Asil, becoming more depressed about his home life, spending ever-longer hours at the office preparing for the flotation, the two of them began to grow closer. When Asil and Aysegül agreed to separate in early 1972 and began divorce negotiations, the way was clear for Asil to make a new start. Frequently when he and Lesley worked late, they would be alone in the office because Jean would go home to her family. Asil fell into the habit of taking Lesley out to dinner after they had finished those late working sessions and their relationship developed from there. After several months, I questioned Asil about his friendship with Lesley, but he grew embarrassed and would only talk jokily, only admitting she was a "very nice girl". I was happy to see the friendship blossoming and felt the time was ripe for Asil to find some belated personal happiness. Although, at thirty-two, my brother was much older than Lesley, I saw in her a good partner for him. She was soft-natured and seemed quiet and introverted. As I got to know her better, I thought her one of the kindest people I had ever met.

In 1973, after Aysegül and Asil had agreed on their divorce settlement, Lesley moved into the house in The Bishop's Avenue. By this time, she had left Wearwell, since Asil felt that it would no longer be right for them to work together. Although Asil had employed a nanny and a cook, Lesley brought a wifely touch to caring for the house and looking after Asil's son, Birol. Then just nine, Birol seemed to get on with Lesley, but later he would turn against her, regarding her as the obstacle which stood in the way of his mother and father's reunion.

One day that year, my father was upstairs talking to Asil in his top-floor office in Commercial Road when my brother confided in him that he wished to marry Lesley. Within minutes, the telephone on my desk rang. It was my father, who told me: "Fetch your mother. All of you come upstairs for a family discussion." In a state of excitement, wondering what this discussion was to be about, we all trooped up to the top floor. The moment my father informed us of Asil's intentions, my mother started sobbing. An alarmed Asil - who can never see someone cry without trying to help - asked my mother why she was so upset. Through her tears she told him: "After all you've been through, I don't want to see you hurt again and I don't think this marriage would succeed either. You married someone from Turkey, someone with the same language, the same religion, and it didn't work because you had different family backgrounds. Now you are planning to marry a girl with a different religion, a different language and it definitely is not going to work out."

The rest of us tried to persuade my mother that marriage to Lesley would give Asil a chance for happiness after all the miserable years he had been through. Even my father, who would have preferred his son to find a Cypriot wife, spoke in favour of Lesley. We all wanted Asil to be married to someone who would look after him, appreciate his hard-working lifestyle and make him happy. My mother, though, was inconsolable. For her, it was not a personal objection to Lesley, whom she hardly knew, but almost an article of faith that her only son should take a wife from his own culture. Eventually, after half an hour of tearful debate, Asil took my mother's hand and said: "OK, if it is what you want, I will not marry her." That decision was one of the greatest demonstrations of Asil's enormous respect for our mother - and his recognition of the numerous sacrifices she had made for us throughout the years of our youth. Asil and Lesley still went on living together - an arrangement that mildly scandalised my mother, but she conceded that it was better than the alternative. While the two of them remained unwed, she could still nurture her hope that one day Asil would marry someone from North Cyprus.

If all did not go according to Asil's plan on the personal front, at work things initially went very smoothly. Within a year of the flotation, Wearwell had built up a countrywide network of cash-and-carry showrooms and in our second year the company showed a pre-tax profit of £1 million. In 1974, as Asil became more and more successful in business and Wearwell's shares hit new heights, taking him towards millionaire status, a fresh twist entered his tangled love life. Aysegül returned to London, having apparently decided she had made a mistake in divorcing Asil, and began a campaign to win him back. She was living in a flat in Chelsea and would call Asil, asking to see Birol. At first, Asil would simply send the boy round to her flat with his chauffeur, but then he agreed they should meet occasionally for lunch, for Birol's sake.

Since her arrival in London, Aysegül had conceived a big grudge against Lesley and held her responsible for her marriage break-up. She discovered that Asil had met Lesley before he was divorced - although the relationship had not progressed until the marriage was over - and she convinced herself that she and Asil would still be together if Lesley was not on the scene. She started working at getting Lesley removed from The Bishop's Avenue house and recruited Birol to her cause, turning him against Lesley. In June 1974, Aysegül and her mother came to The Bishop's Avenue to help Birol celebrate his tenth birthday and decided that they would stay. Lesley was very upset. Asil was unhappy and confused and totally at a loss as to how to handle the situation. Aysegül and her mother remained in The Bishop's Avenue for several weeks, while a miserable Lesley lived at her flat in Little Venice. It was during this time that events began to unfold in Cyprus which not only involved our family but would also have an enormous effect on our commercial future.

Cyprus's strategic position at the eastern end of the Mediterranean has long made it a temptation to foreign powers wishing to exploit the island's location and intercommunal tensions in pursuit of their own ends, giving little thought to the needs of its people. Near the end of British rule, the colonial authorities had sought to whip up ill-feeling between the two native communities in a policy of "divide and rule". Post-independence, both Greek and Turkish governments had put money and weapons into extremist forces after their own goals, Athens sponsoring the terrorists of General Grivas, Ankara the Turkish Cypriot TMT resistance group in response, and both nations sending their own troops. Nor had interference in Cyprus been confined to the immediate supporting players, Greece, Turkey and Britain. The United States, too, recognised Cyprus's role in maintaining the balance of power in the eastern Mediterranean and in relations between NATO members Greece and Turkey. The US was also aware of its importance as a potential base and listening post from which it could monitor the troublesome Middle East.

During the months after the intercommunal crisis of 1963-4, the Americans had sought to bring about the kind of solution in Cyprus which suited them. At the request of President Lyndon B Johnson, former US Secretary of State Dean Acheson had come up with a proposal for an orderly division of Cyprus - a partial Enosis - designed to appease both Athens and Ankara. When then-Cypriot President Archbishop Makarios had turned it down, he had sown the seed for the vehement dislike of him which the US would come to share with the "Colonels Junta" in Athens. As British journalist Christopher Hitchens pointed out in his book on Cyprus, the Americans had distrusted Makarios because of his insistence upon independence and, more importantly, because of his leanings towards the USSR and the Non-Aligned Movement. Hot on the heels of the Bay of Pigs fiasco, they had feared this could turn Cyprus into a Mediterranean Cuba. Later, capitalising on friction reported by US intelligence sources between Makarios and EOKA leader General Grivas, Washington had established secret contacts with the Athens-backed terrorist chief. When Greece had told the US that it could not accept Acheson's 1964 plan, according to Hitchens, President Johnson had told the Greek Ambassador in far-from-diplomatic terms: "Fuck your parliament and your constitution. America is an elephant, Cyprus is a flea, Greece is a flea. If these two fellows continue itching the elephant, they may just get whacked by the elephant's trunk, whacked good." If America was to get its way over Cyprus, it had seemed that the Greek government headed by Prime Minister George Papandreou would have to go. And go it had, in an April 1967 military coup which showed signs of heavy American involvement despite denials from Washington. The coup installed a "Colonels' junta" in power in Athens, led by Colonel George Papadopoulos, who, according to Hitchens, had been on the pay-roll of the American secret service, the CIA, since 1952.

In Cyprus, the decade following the crisis of Christmas 1963 had seen Greek Cypriot extremists led by Grivas engaged in sporadic activity. Most seriously, in November 1967 two Turkish Cypriot villages had come under attack and Greece had admitted it was behind the actions. Turkey had threatened to invade but had held off after a brusque letter to Turkish President Ismet Inönü from Lyndon Johnson. The confrontation had eased with a US-negotiated withdrawal of 12,000 extra Greek troops stationed on the island, and the removal of Grivas himself.

Intercommunal relations, though frequently good on a personal level, had in official terms been strained - sometimes non-existent. The Greek Cypriots had remained in charge of the republic's administration, while the Turkish Cypriots had found themselves economically underprivileged, taking second place to the Greeks when it came to job opportunities or financial aid. The continuing violence had meant Turkish Cypriots were being gradually pushed into protective enclaves, frequently unable to travel from one town to another for fear of attack or being stopped at Greek Cypriot roadblocks. Many Turkish Cypriots had, like us, decided there was no future for them in Cyprus. They had been emigrating by the score to London, America, even as far as Australia. Many had given up hope as they had seen the three guarantor powers of the 1960 Cypriot constitution - Britain, Greece and Turkey - apparently standing idly by while injustice and atrocities ruled.

Politically, Makarios had been winning considerable support for his policy of an independent Cyprus, although he was creating enemies of those who preferred Enosis as their goal. His resolute independence had made him no friends among the dictators in Athens who - more and more impatient with the Archbishop, contemptuously referred to by opponents as the "red priest" - had taken every opportunity to infiltrate the Cypriot authorities. The tensions between the Archbishop and Athens had begun to come to a head in November 1973 with the overthrow of Greek junta leader Papadopoulos by his own military police chief, a former major with the Cyprus National Guard and associate of Nicos Sampson. Two months later, Grivas had died of a heart attack, dealing a blow to EOKA-B and giving Makarios new strength to go on the offensive. During spring 1974, Makarios had rallied against the terrorists, outlawing EOKA-B and rounding up suspected members and their weapons. Crisis point came in early July 1974, when Makarios made public a letter which he had sent to the Greek head of state, accusing Greek officers of the National Guard of planning a coup against him and demanding the immediate recall of the officers involved. It was the first time Makarios had voiced his opposition to the junta and it spurred the Athens regime into action.

Our family had followed the course of events in Cyprus with growing concern - concern for the island as a whole and for our friends and relatives still living there. By the early 1970s, from our vantage point 3,000 miles away, we had become sure something would have to happen. But we were unaware quite how rapidly that "something" was about to happen when Lesley flew out for her first visit to Cyprus in July 1974. Fed up with waiting for Aysegül to decide she was leaving The Bishop's

Avenue, Lesley concluded that she might as well take a holiday. She was keen to learn Turkish, since she often spent time with our family and would have liked to understand some of the conversations and banter that broke out around her. Asil arranged for her to go and spend a few weeks with our uncle, Izzet Bolkan, who had a farm at Bogaz, between Nicosia and Kyrenia. He saw her off from Heathrow on the 13th July and returned to Commercial Road relieved that a potential flashpoint between Lesley and Aysegül had at least temporarily been averted. His relief was to be short-lived and would be replaced by a far greater worry.

Two days later, on Monday the 15th July 1974, the world woke to learn of an early-morning coup in Cyprus. Tanks and heavy artillery commanded by Greek mainland officers rumbled through the streets of the capital.

Fehim and Güner were listening to the radio news at work when they heard that Makarios had been overthrown and was missing, possibly assassinated. My father's former patisserie customer, Nicos Sampson, had been installed as the new President. The elevation of Sampson - a hastily-chosen last resort following the death of Grivas - sent shock-waves through the Turkish Cypriot and British communities and horrified us that day at Wearwell. Sampson was a well-known Turk-hater who claimed to have killed one person for every year of his life, Britons included, during the pre-independence civil war of the 1950s. In 1969, he had been voted into the House of Representatives with the slogan "Death to the Turks". I was in Asil's office when Fehim and Güner rushed in to tell us what they had learnt. Asil turned white when he heard the news. The situation on the island was far from clear, but with a known terrorist ruling from the presidential palace and right-wing extremists in control, we were all afraid for Lesley and for our fellow Turkish Cypriots. It seemed the Greek terrorists' goal of Enosis might not be far away.

The next few days passed in a whirl of worry and international diplomacy. At Wearwell and South Woodford, we were glued to every news bulletin. In The Bishop's Avenue, Asil had to fake an air of calm, not giving away his concerns for Lesley for fear of arousing Aysegül's wrath. Soon we heard that Makarios was alive - he had been spirited out of Nicosia to Paphos and then on to safety in Malta on a British RAF plane. There, he spoke on the radio to declare the new regime in Cyprus illegal.

As events unfolded, governments around the world moved to condemn the Greek junta's clear interference in Cyprus's internal affairs. Washington, though, remained neutral, adopting a policy described by one State Department official as "constructive ambiguity".

In Nicosia, US Ambassador, Rodger Davies, was the only foreign envoy to receive Sampson's "Foreign Minister". The State Department refused to accept that the coup had been the work of Athens, despite the evidence of Greek command and the fact that Secretary of State, Henry Kissinger, had already acknowledged that Athens was readying a strike against Makarios.

In Ankara, news of the coup and the muted American response was greeted with alarm. Prime Minister Bülent Ecevit, believing the putsch to be tantamount to Enosis, saw a Greek-aligned Cyprus as a grave threat to Turkey's own security, as well as being a danger to the Turkish Cypriot population. He ordered immediate preparations for military intervention, believing swift action was vital before the Americans took the unilateral step of recognising the Sampson regime. According to Turkish journalist Mehmet Ali Birand, Ecevit was certain the coup bore the stamp of CIA involvement. He was not alone in his worries. Former Premier Nihat Erim, too, thought the US could be behind the events and suspected that Sampson might enjoy some sympathy in Washington.

As the Turkish military laid plans for intervention, Ecevit flew to London and appealed to his British counterpart, Harold Wilson, and Foreign Secretary James Callaghan for joint military action by Britain and Turkey, under the terms of the 1960 Treaty of Guarantee. His request fell on deaf ears. Wilson said Britain disagreed that the Treaty of Guarantee gave it the right to intervene militarily. Though the Greek government never acknowledged that the Turkish intervention was legal, almost five years later in March 1979, the Athens Court of Appeals would rule that: "The Turkish military intervention in Cyprus, which was carried out in accordance with the Zurich and London Accords, was legal. Turkey, as one of the Guarantor Powers, had the right to fulfil her obligations. The real culprits...are the Greek officers who engineered and staged a coup and prepared the conditions for this intervention."

Washington sent an envoy to urge Turkey to attempt negotiation before resorting to force. Ecevit countered with Turkey's demands to the Greek government: the resignation of Sampson, the withdrawal of the Greek National Guard officers and pledges that the island would remain independent. The Greeks, believing the Turks would not intervene militarily, did not give way. On Thursday, the 18th July, Archbishop Makarios addressed the UN Security Council and confirmed the world's worst fears: "The Greeks from the mainland have invaded Cyprus and bloody clashes are taking place in the island...Tanks are roaring through the streets, casualties are being continually rushed to hospitals and the Greek flag is hoisted on all important buildings...The Turkish Cypriot community too is, today, in danger..."

On the island, EOKA-B terrorists and supporters of the Athens junta rampaged, attacking Makarios supporters and the Greek Cypriot National Guard. Turkish Cypriots, fearing they would soon become targets of aggression, sought shelter in enclaves and monitored the situation through the broadcasts of Turkish and local Bayrak radio. There were many reported instances of Greek and Turkish Cypriot neighbours who, far from acting as warring enemies, came to each other's assistance, protecting, providing food and water or passing on messages.

Turkey launched its military action on Friday, the 19th July when five destroyers carrying 3,000 troops and thirty-one landing craft set off from the southern coast. At five o'clock the next morning - Saturday, the 20th July - bombardment of selected targets in the northern half of Cyprus began in preparation for the subsequent landings. At the same time, jets took off from Turkey and headed south for Cyprus. At ten past six that morning, a weary Ecevit broadcast to the world the Turkish intervention. "We are…going to Cyprus not to wage war but to bring peace, not only to the Turks but to the Greeks on the island," he said, adding: "I…hope that this operation will prove a blessing to our nation, to all Cypriots and to the rest of the world. May God protect our nation and all mankind against calamity." Turkish Cypriot leader, Rauf Denktas, announced over Radio Bayrak: "Our century-old aspirations are bearing fruit and our day of salvation is at hand. The Turkish army has landed in Cyprus. This is a limited action against the Greek junta and is not directed against the Greek Cypriot community, our fellow guardians of the independence of this island. There must be no hostility against them. Stay peacefully at home and thank God for allowing us to witness this day." Afterwards, an alarmed Denktas realised that, confused by the time difference between Turkey and Cyprus in those days, he had inadvertently given an hour's warning of the impending attack. Luckily, it seemed the coup leaders were not listening in to the Turkish station that early morning.

It was about half past eight in the morning when Turkish troops set foot on the sandy beach below the whitewashed village of Karavas, now renamed Alsancak. Meanwhile, paratroopers and a commando brigade were dropped in at Bogaz, a small, closely knit mixed village perched half-way up the stony slopes on the southern flank of the Kyrenia range, overlooking the wide Mesaoria plain. Our Uncle Izzet was a former police superintendent and an organiser of the Turkish Cypriot underground movement, TMT, responsible for the Bogaz area. In the middle of the night on July 19th, he was called to the local police station and took a telephone call from a senior government figure, telling him the intervention was on for the following morning. It was his job to inform Turkish Cypriots in Bogaz and the neighbouring hamlet of Agirdag - these were mixed villages and the Turks needed to be on their guard in case of attack from the Greeks once the intervention began. At dawn on the 20th July, Uncle Izzet, his wife Emine Teyze and Lesley watched as the first paratroopers began to land at Bogaz. Dummies were parachuted down in advance to draw the Greek Cypriot fire and Turkish jets pinpointed and bombarded their positions while many of the men were able to land safely. Battle raged around the village as the Greek Cypriots tried to fight back against the Turkish paratroopers. Lesley joined my uncle and aunt giving water and first aid where needed to the paratroopers, dodging crossfire which killed about twenty of my uncle's cows. That night, and for the next four nights, the whole family took refuge together under the stairs.

At six o'clock on the morning of the 20th July, Asil had woken us with a telephone call to South Woodford. "Have you heard the news?" he asked. "The Turkish army has landed in Cyprus." We raced downstairs and sat clutching cups of tea while we listened to the radio and saw dozens of news-flashes on the television. We were jubilant - at last, Turkey was going to the aid of the Turkish Cypriots, for so long at the mercy of the Greek terrorists. But we were also afraid for the safety of all the people we knew on the island, particularly Lesley, and Fehim's parents too, who were by then living in a hillside village called Kasaphani (now Ozanköy), about two miles east of Kyrenia and about two miles inland on the lower slopes of the mountain range. It was to be several days before we had news of any of them.

In all, some 6,000 troops were landed in Cyprus on the 20th July. All that first day, the Turkish troops pressed on in their mission to establish a bridgehead linking Bogaz and Karavas - on opposite sides of the mountain range, some fifteen miles apart. As night fell, the skies were illuminated by the glow of the blazing mountainsides, the forests set alight by the day-long jet strikes. As soon as dark fell and the Turkish jets pulled out, the Greek and Greek Cypriot troops attacked, waging a four-pronged assault on the Turkish forces which lasted until dawn. At the same time, armed men surrounded the Turkish Cypriot communities in several towns and villages. As the battles, hostage-taking and reported massacres went on, members of the United Nations peacekeeping force stood by, powerless to intervene.

For three days, the US envoy and UN conducted frantic diplomatic efforts to avert a Greco-Turkish war and bring about a cease-fire. Finally, Kissinger, Ecevit and the Greek junta leader agreed on a cease-fire to take effect at five o'clock on the evening of the 22nd July. By that time, further troops and weapons had been landed, Kyrenia had been taken and a fragile link established between the resort town, Bogaz and the north of Nicosia. Turkish casualties totalled 111 dead, 242 missing and more than 184 wounded. In mainland Greece, the biggest casualty was the military junta, which cracked under international pressure and collapsed. Constantine Karamanlis agreed to step in as Prime Minister and form a government.

Two tension-filled international conferences took place in Geneva as representatives of Britain, Greece and Turkey sought a diplomatic solution for Cyprus. On the island itself, Turkey continued to reinforce and extend its bridgehead, mopping up pockets of resistance in sporadic clashes. Under international pressure, Nicos Sampson stepped down to be replaced by the more moderate Glafcos Clerides. In Ankara, Bülent Ecevit grew more and more concerned at the continued siege conditions under which many Turkish Cypriots were being held across Cyprus, while the Turkish troops were hemmed into a limited area. Some 22,000 Greek Cypriots and 20,000 Turkish Cypriots - out of relative populations of 500,000 and 120,000 - had become refugees. While the talking went on in Geneva, Ecevit secretly ordered preparations for the second stage he had envisaged in the "Peace Operation".

Fehim's parents were the only household in their village to have a telephone, but contact was difficult enough in normal conditions at that time - in the heat of war, it became impossible. On the British news, contact numbers were given out for people trying to get information about relatives caught up in the fighting. We tried to call but could not get through. Finally, while we were going frantic for news, we had a call from a British soldier. He had been asked by Fehim's father to pass a message on to us and, true to his word, he rang to give us the information - Fehim's parents were both safe and told us not to worry about them. A couple of days later, telephone connections to Cyprus were restored and we were able to speak to Fehim's father. He told us that on the first day of the intervention, not a shot had been fired in Ozanköy. He had been called upon to act as an interpreter for the Turkish troops because he spoke good English and Greek. For much of that day, Fehim's mother had sat on the balcony at their house, watching the action all around through a pair of binoculars we had bought them.

It was July 26th when we got the first word about Lesley. She called to say she was back in Britain and came to our house in a taxi. The moment she arrived, Fehim telephoned Asil in The Bishop's Avenue to let him know she was safe. It was a difficult conversation. Asil was guarded because Aysegül was with him and when Fehim gave him the message he simply said, "I will be with you soon," and put the receiver down. Within an hour, he and Lesley were reunited. That evening, Lesley told us all that had happened. The British navy had come to

Kyrenia and, after her nights sleeping under the stairs at Bogaz, Lesley had been taken to the Dome Hotel at Kyrenia, where many of the other British citizens and holidaymakers had been rounded up. It was a hair-raising journey - climbing into the farm cart which was to take her from Bogaz, Lesley had come face to face with the first corpse she had ever seen. And she clung on, terrified, as her drivers charged along at breakneck speed to try and avoid sniper-fire from the shrub-covered hills on either side of the hairpin bends. From Kyrenia, Lesley and the others were shipped around the coast to the British RAF base at Akrotiri, in the far South, where they were loaded on to a Hercules transport plane for an eight and a half hour journey back to the UK - an uncomfortable ride, with only rope seats to sit on, but Lesley said she had never been so relieved to climb on board an aeroplane. I do not know how Asil explained it to Aysegül, but he spent the next four nights with Lesley, reluctant to be parted from her again. The following month, Aysegül and her mother decided to go to Istanbul for a summer holiday and Lesley moved back into The Bishop's Avenue. When Aysegül returned from Turkey, she would live at her flat in Chelsea and Asil would see her from time to time. So the situation was to remain until December 1974.

By the time a second international conference on Cyprus was convened in Geneva on the 8th August, Ecevit had little hope of achieving what Turkey wanted - a federal state on the island, based on geographical separation and giving the Turkish Cypriots access to the sea. During the night of the 13th August, Ankara's General Staff HQ issued an order that the second operation would begin at three o'clock the next morning.

At dawn on the 14th August, the Turkish troops began their advance to secure the town of Famagusta, where some 1,000 Turkish Cypriots had taken refuge within the ancient walls, and vulnerable towns and villages to the west. More than 180,000 Greek Cypriot civilians abandoned their homes as the army approached. Others, of the National Guard and EOKA-B, embarked on a final orgy of killing. That morning, armed men rounded up the inhabitants of three Turkish Cypriot villages near Famagusta - Atlilar, Murataga and Sandallar - shot them and bulldozed their bodies into mass graves. More than 140 mutilated corpses were later unearthed. The same day, eighty-four Turkish Cypriot men from three villages near the southern coast were taken from their villages and shot. Only one survived to tell the tale.

By the 16th August, with the Turkish forces occupying thirty-four per cent of the island's territory, Ecevit agreed to a cease-fire. The Americans must have been monitoring the situation closely - as the fighting still continued, Kissinger told Ecevit that he understood the

Turkish forces needed one more hour to achieve what they wanted, and added: "You've got it." Precisely one hour later, the battle ended - with the Turks having reached their intended goal. Six days later, Rauf Denktas announced that an autonomous Turkish Cypriot administration had been set up. The return of Archbishop Makarios that December set the seal on separatism; mass population exchange, with thousands of Greek Cypriots moving to the South and thousands of Turkish Cypriots travelling North, would complete the *de facto* partition. In the space of a few weeks, turmoil sparked off by externally-inspired meddling had turned Cyprus upside down and set the stage for the independent Turkish Cypriot state which exists today in the North of the island - unrecognised and ostracised by the world.

There was family turmoil, too, in 1974, with Asil's private life taking a shock turn at the end of the year. On the 2nd December, our whole family attended the wedding of Johnny Holder, an elderly member of the Wearwell board. In the middle of the evening reception came a telephone call to say that Aysegül had been rushed to hospital, having apparently taken an overdose of tablets. The call was taken by Dr Wootliffe, our family and company doctor. Asil stayed on at the reception for a while but, clearly concerned, left within an hour of the telephone call. I never found out what conversation passed between the two of them that night, but the next time we saw him, he gave us the shock news that Aysegül was expecting another baby.

Asil's second son, Serhan, was born in June 1975. The baby's name, which I suggested for him one evening before the birth when a few of us were sitting together, means "leader of leaders". Throughout her pregnancy, Aysegül had been an exemplary daughter-in-law and sister-in-law, moving back into The Bishop's Avenue. Lesley went back to her flat in Little Venice and Asil still saw her frequently. She had been devastated by Aysegül's reinstatement and new baby, but could not bear to turn Asil away. She still loved him in spite of what had happened and she was more concerned for his happiness than for her own personal welfare. Such was the three-cornered life that my brother had created for himself and was to live for the next decade.

While the 1974 conflict in Cyprus was eventually to open up new business opportunities for us, the mid 1970s also saw upheaval at home which similarly paved the way to Wearwell seeking fresh trading horizons. During 1975, we began to feel the effects of the general economic malaise which had hit Britain as a whole. Cash-and-carry orders began to drop off as Wearwell's customers tightened their belts and with huge increases in fuel prices as a result of the 1973 Arab-Israeli war, retailers became more reluctant to travel to buy their stocks. In addition, rag trade rivals became wise to our success and began to offer up tough competition by importing labour from India and Pakistan which was far cheaper than even the lowest-paid London "outworkers" could be.

Over a fairly grim two years, we thought long and hard how to drum up fresh business. The first venture, suggested by Asil, was to go into the mail order field. With customers unwilling to travel to our showrooms, it seemed like a good idea. But it had its drawbacks: it meant we had to build up more stocks than before and also that we would have to give credit to buyers - something we had avoided by means of the cash-and-carry concept. The mail order operation was not a success. By the second half of 1975, Wearwell was showing a loss and there were more difficulties as the banks began to demand repayment of company loans. In a bid to improve the situation, Asil halted the mail order business and stopped all credit to customers. We also had to cut our staff by half, to around 150. In 1976, two things came to Wearwell's rescue - one was a cash injection of £2.5 million from another company. Our other salvation, which was to bring long-term prosperity to Wearwell, was an excursion into the export market.

The export business, which culminated in Wearwell receiving two Queen's Awards a few years later, began almost by chance. A major Libyan merchant - one Mr Guernazi - walked into the Commercial Road showroom and placed a huge order for some of the garments on show. Asil dealt with that order himself and in the course of their conversation that day, the Libyan gentleman planted the seed of an idea in my brother's head - perhaps, Asil thought, looking abroad for sales might be the best way to ride out the current bad times at home. Because of the importance of the Libyan order, Asil decided to keep in personal contact with Mr Guernazi. Shortly afterwards, he flew out to Tripoli and Fehim, Wearwell's sales director, followed on. The two of them quickly realised that Wearwell had one major advantage over other rag trade competitors in dealings with the Middle East - it was a firm with a strong Muslim background, and that could count for a lot. With that first fortuitous Libyan order in 1976, we set our sights firmly on the Middle Eastern market, selling children's wear, adult clothing and school uniforms. Soon, Saudi Arabia and the United Arab Emirates were also on our list of customers. Iraq would follow by the end of the decade.

The team spirit engendered in Wearwell as we fought to build up our export trade made business worthwhile for me. For a time, after our first year's trading following the flotation, I had been disillusioned by the new climate which surrounded us as a public company. Excited to be a part of this new venture, I had looked forward eagerly to the reaction to our first year's results in 1974 and was deflated when some of the financial press casually dismissed all our hard work as "disappointing". It was only then that I realised just how crucial a word of praise or damnation in the right place could be in determining the public's attitude towards a business. Now, with exports as a new focus, I felt all my old enthusiasm bubbling up again.

The venture kept Fehim and myself very busy and we learnt to put up with frequent separations. As Wearwell's product planner, I was in charge of the buying and design department. I would choose and buy in the fabrics for our garments, having attended the twice-yearly *pret à porter* shows in Paris to pick up ideas of what styles would be in fashion for the coming season. I would also travel to the fabric producers in the north of England and as our exports flourished and the size of the orders grew, I found myself able to strike ever-harder bargains as I haggled over cloth prices. In the meantime, I would also have translated the Paris fashion ideas into a series of more commercially attractive garments for our seasonal range, helped by a small team of designers. Asil would pick out samples from the range and then Fehim would tour the Middle East with our samples, scouting around for new customers and new orders. Sometimes he was away for only a couple of days; on other occasions he might be out of the country for a week or more. He became a frequent visitor to Libya, Saudi Arabia, the United Arab Emirates, Kuwait and the Yemen, returning with orders for garments by the hundred thousand.

While work gave me a focus outside South Woodford, I was in my element at home. My children were growing up and I was intrigued to see each of them beginning to show signs of the characters they would later become. It was a wonderful and fascinating time - although I adored being in business, my children were my biggest love. Multi-million-pound orders or not, I felt the family was my biggest responsibility. Sometimes, when the children were small, I would feel guilty at being so involved in my work and spending so much time away from them. I remembered then how, growing up in Cyprus, there had been days when I had envied my friends because their mother would be waiting for them when they got home from school, not serving in a shop until early evening. Now I found myself repeating the same pattern with my own family and the realisation came as something of a shock. Determined to do our best as parents, we set aside all our spare hours as family time. I reasoned too that, as a mother, I could do better for my children by being happy and fulfilled in the time we did spend together than by playing the housewife and resenting them because of it.

While Fehim and I were away at work, I had no fears for the children. In the redoubtable Auntie Finney we had the perfect nanny. She was kind and loving, yet she was also strict on good behaviour - even with Levent, who was her favourite - and would stand for no nonsense. When Irfan turned one and a half, she was also joined by another helper, Jill Phelps, who became our housekeeper. Having Auntie Finney and Jill in the house helped me in my one major ambition for the children - for them to acquire the best of both worlds, both British and Turkish. Already, I had come across occasions when, not being fully British and not having a university degree, I had felt myself at a disadvantage. I was determined that my children would not have that experience, but would enjoy the best that the British system could offer, as well as having the support of a close-knit Turkish Cypriot-style family life as Asil, Meral and I had had. In matters of religion, too, I tried to give the children a dual outlook on the world. Even while they were young and beginning to learn about Christianity at school, I also explained to them the guiding principles of Islam and the Muslim way of life our family led. I passed on to them my own belief that - regardless of individual creed - there was only one God. In later years, I read the Bible as the children studied it at school and we would sit and discuss the differences between its teachings and those of the Koran. Because they all attended Christian schools and had largely Christian friends, Fehim and I made a point of celebrating Christmas so our children would not feel left out. As a counter-balance, I also explained to them all about Muslim religious holidays - with the result that, when they were feeling cheeky, they would occasionally argue for a day off school when it came to an important Islamic festival.

When Tijen and Levent started school in the 1970s, it was natural that the British influence should predominate. My attempts to bring the three children up speaking Turkish as well as English appeared doomed - they hardly spoke Turkish at all, except to my mother whose English was still quite limited, and we would have these odd bilingual conversations where I would doggedly speak in Turkish and the children would answer me back in English. Even when I brought a Turkish Cypriot girl, Meryem, over to London as an au pair for four years, the children still would not speak Turkish to her - she ended up perfecting her English. It was not until they reached the age of about ten or twelve that they began to pick up the language. In subtle ways, however, the children did absorb, unawares, aspects of the Turkish Cypriot lifestyle. They grew up knowing only the strongest of family ties and aware of the importance of family unity. While the children were still small, South Woodford had become something of a Nadir and Nevzat family "enclave". Wishing to be nearer to us, my mother and father had moved

69

to the house next door to ours in The Drive. Meral, Güner and their children lived round the corner. Their property backed on to ours and Meral had had a gate made in the fence between the two gardens. On the other side of our house lived Fehim's elder brother, Ilker, and his wife, Rezzan. Fehim's sister Sidika and her family also had their home nearby. Unlike so many British families, our children all grew up - as we had in 1950s Cyprus - accepting it as the norm to have grandparents, aunts, uncles and cousins living side-by-side and in and out of each other's houses. Sundays were our big family day, just as they had been years earlier in the eastern Mediterranean. Each weekend, about twenty of us would gather for the day at my mother's house. My father loved Turkish entertainment and often organised some ethnic musicians to come to the house and play for us all. We would get up and dance or sing along, vying with each other to get hold of the microphone. My mother laid on a big lunch - for most of us the only Turkish meal we had in the week. Many a time, Fehim's brother or my father would round off the day telling stories about other relatives and the old days in Cyprus. The children would sit, round-eyed, lapping up the crumbs of tradition and history they handed out.

It was during those years too that we started taking the odd weekend off for the first time in our lives. In 1974, Asil had bought a country mansion with several acres of land, tennis courts, squash courts and a swimming pool at East Grinstead, about one and a half hours from South Woodford. He followed this acquisition with the purchase of a stud farm nearby, where he became involved in breeding horses. Cynics claimed he was attempting to become an English "country gent", but to Asil - and to the rest of the family - the moves were simply a natural return to something like the rural life we had lived as children. Every month for several years, we would pack the children into the car and drive off to East Grinstead on a Friday night or Saturday morning, staying until after tea on Sunday. There, we would be joined by my parents and my sister and her family. Sometimes Asil would join us and my parents' faces would light up to look round the huge sunny morning room and see the whole family together. We would rarely know, however, who Asil was going to bring with him - Lesley or Aysegül. Often, Asil would tell us to go on ahead to East Grinstead and he would follow later - and sometimes he never made it, spending the weekend working instead.

Even our annual holidays were a family occasion. There were several French holidays, as well as visits to Majorca and Spain, still very undeveloped. At that time, Asil had a boat moored at St Tropez, and we would meet up with him there whenever he managed to snatch a couple of days off. Later, Asil replaced the boat for a larger one and sent it along the coast to Cannes. There, he discovered a tiny island outside the town which boasted just a monastery and a no-frills fish restaurant called Frederic's where we were all serenaded by a mandolin player and dined on the best lobster we had ever tasted. We used to feel rather proud that we alone had unearthed this restaurant jewel - until one year we all went there and found Roger Moore and Rex Harrison sitting at the next table.

While everything else in life seemed so perfect, inside my heart was aching for my "workaholic" brother, who seemed so much in control of the business, yet so mixed-up in his personal life. He had been brought up the same way as me, to have the same high regard for the family, so I knew how much it hurt him that he did not have the kind of loving, supportive home background that the rest of us had secured. He had two young children with the woman he had already divorced after a stormy nine-year marriage and now lived with on a part-time basis - and he had had to abandon plans to marry the other woman in his life, for fear of upsetting the mother he revered. Asil was becoming a very wealthy man, yet at times I would look at him, apparently on top of the world, and catch the sadness in his eyes. When we were children, like all Turkish Cypriot mothers, my mother used to pray for Meral and me, asking God to "give my daughters husbands who will look after them". Remembering this, Asil would remark - only half-jokingly, I felt sure - that maybe she ought to have included him in that prayer. The traditional wish for sons was "success and wealth". It was partly his natural application, partly this lack of personal satisfaction, which drove him to work harder and harder as the seventies wore on. He seemed to find less and less time for relaxation. There were occasional snatched weekends, but many weeks he would be working seven days, either in the showroom or the Commercial Road offices. His one regular way of winding down was to play squash at home in The Bishop's Avenue, usually with Fehim or Adrian Huggins. Even those games, though, were hard-fought contests. Once, Asil came off court with blood pouring from a cut eyebrow where he had been accidentally struck by Adrian's racket in the heat of the action.

It was clear by the latter part of the 1970s that all our efforts and Asil's unremitting toil were paying dividends. In 1977, as the export drive was just beginning to take off, our profits were £322,000. The following year they were more than doubled at £751,000 and exports accounted for ninety per cent of our sales. It was a bad time generally for the British textile industry, and ours was the only factory which was busy all the time. We were all working tremendously hard and often felt exhausted, but the patent success of what we were doing gave us an enormous sense of satisfaction and an incentive to do even more. I was still spending much of my time buying fabrics and because of the quantity of the orders we received - sometimes as many as half a million items per style for Libyan children's school uniforms - we were able to command the lowest prices for the cloth we bought. Fehim was away a great deal. In 1978, we worked out that he spent 156 days of that year abroad.

In the summer of 1978, my father and mother flew out to Cyprus for their first visit since the winter of 1974, shortly after the war. What they saw in the north of the island - since February 1975 the Turkish Federated State of Cyprus, unrecognised by any country outside Turkey - shocked them, but also gave my father the germ of an idea which would shape the progress of Wearwell in years to come. My father found the Turkish Cypriot state still reeling from the effects of war and the international cold shoulder it was receiving. Without diplomatic or political recognition, the Turkish Cypriots had no official line of communication with the outside world, while the Greek Cypriots still claimed to represent the now-defunct Republic of Cyprus at every forum - a political ruse which persists to this day. Unemployment was rife and production at a virtual standstill. Factories everywhere stood idle and decaying, exports were non-existent because of crippling embargoes and the tiny state's sole source of foreign income was Turkey. Even direct international airline flights were not allowed to North Cyprus because it was not a recognised destination. Every aeroplane had to land first in Turkey, where it was then registered as a domestic flight for the onward journey to Geçitkale, a remote military airfield - built before 1974 with aid from the US - between Famagusta and Nicosia.

My father saw how desperately the country needed an economic lifeline - and how the situation could be exploited for the benefit of all. He was full of the potential of North Cyprus when he returned to London. The day after he got home, he called us all together in Commercial Road and excitedly outlined his plans. The vast Middle Eastern orders that Wearwell was now receiving meant it was a constant struggle to keep down our costs while producing in Britain and we were coming more and more under threat from countries like Morocco, Jordan and Yugoslavia which could knock out the garments with considerably less overheads than us. If we set up a factory in North Cyprus, my father urged us, we too would be able to produce the goods far more cheaply and, at the same time, help the Turkish Cypriot state by creating jobs and bringing income from abroad. His suggestion was that he and my mother should return to live in Cyprus, where they would be able to set up and run the Wearwell factory and train its staff. There was no arguing against the idea. My father was quite determined to take up what he saw as a wonderful opportunity. My mother, who

72

had never really liked being away from her homeland, jumped at the chance. Her only sorrow was that she would be leaving behind her children and grandchildren. In keeping with the Cypriot tradition of daughters setting up home next to their parents, my mother and father put aside their home in The Drive for Tijen. It would remain empty for nine years until she moved in after her marriage.

That year of 1979 was to prove a turning point for us in many ways. Just after New Year, my father flew out to North Cyprus to set the wheels of his venture in motion. On the 12th February, my mother joined him and they settled in a house in a quiet residential suburb of Nicosia. By this time, my father had leased from the government two empty factories in the industrial area of Haspolat, about six miles from the capital on the way to the airport. As soon as my mother arrived, she got down to the task of training Turkish Cypriot staff in the skills needed for mass production. She took on about sixty machinists at the factory and also trained up scores more "outworkers" who would sew garments at their homes all over the country. A fleet of drivers was employed to deliver work to far-flung areas once or twice a week. Distribution points were also set up in Kyrenia and Famagusta, and machinists would go there to pick up the cut fabric and hand in the finished articles. Completed garments were returned to London, where they were checked for quality and then repackaged for export to their final destination.

It was an exciting time for my parents and the new venture also injected a fresh impetus into our operations in London. It was at that time that we realised our performance was also being recognised by others. That spring, we gathered for the grand opening of Wearwell's first purpose-built showroom and office suite, at 101 Commercial Road. The guest of honour was the local Tower Hamlets MP, Peter Shore, who was also Secretary of State for Trade and Industry in the then-dying Labour government. When he stood up to speak, I was amazed to hear him say he was also there to announce that Wearwell had won the Queen's Award for Export Achievement. And it was with an even greater sense of disbelief that I then heard Asil, as he stood up amid applause to reply, tell the assembled crowd: "This should be presented to my sister, Bilge Nevzat. A big part of this success is down to her and I think she deserves it." I was in a daze as I stepped forward to receive the certificate from the minister. For the last sixteen years, I had put my hard work in behind the scenes and this was my first taste of the limelight which had largely been focused on Asil. It was a taste I would not easily forget.

The next Wearwell board meeting that year brought me further public praise from my brother - and the prize I had long been hoping for. As the only member of the family who was not on the board, I had grown to feel very left out of the decision-making process. If I was helping this company attain its great success, I argued to Asil, I should be accorded a say in the way it was run. I attended every board meeting, but could only sit in as an observer. This time, though, I heard Asil announce to the other directors that the time had come for me to be appointed to the board. At last, I thought, I was joining the leaders, instead of being kept forever in the background.

While I had achieved one of my goals, I was aware of a growing restlessness about Asil. He always relished a challenge and I could see by then that Wearwell was no longer enough for him. The business was running smoothly and had reached a point where it could make little more progress in the clothing industry. On top of that, he was aware of unease in the City over the extent of Wearwell's dependence on the Middle East for its trade. He knew he must come up with some new idea to bolster City confidence and hit upon the plan of buying a brand name company in order to diversify back into the British market. He began looking in earnest for a suitable acquisition late in 1979. It was shortly before that Christmas, during one of our customary morning chats over coffee in Asil's office, that my brother leaned forward eagerly and said, "It's early days yet, but I think I may have found just what we're looking for - a company called Polly Peck."

CHAPTER FOUR

Polly Peck

Polly Peck was indeed a brand-name - a twenty-year-old company known throughout Britain for its fashionable womenswear - but by 1979 it had fallen on hard times. It was heavily in debt and husband-and-wife founders Raymond and Sybil Zelker knew they needed outside backing if Polly Peck was to survive.

Asil's interest in Polly Peck was its household familiarity, along with its many department store franchises - including one in Harrods - and its established mail order business. He felt the company was commercially way behind the times, yet saw the chance of turning it into a highly profitable concern by making use of the existing outlets and injecting some new ideas and the buying power and cheap manufacturing capability of Wearwell. At the back of his mind, Asil also harboured ambitions beyond the rag trade. In Polly Peck he saw a potential vehicle for expansion into other fields of business and even visualised the global trading entity it was eventually to become. His approach to the Zelkers could not have come at a better moment. Over dinner at The Bishop's Avenue in February 1980, a deal was struck which - supported by the Zelkers and a third director - would give Asil fifty-seven per cent of the business for £270,000. On 13th February 1980, Asil asked his secretary, Jean Thomas, to telephone Messel's, the stockbrokers who acted for Wearwell. The rather cryptic message he asked her to deliver was that, "Mr Nadir would like you to call us when there is a Stock Exchange announcement about a company called Polly Peck." We all sat in Asil's office, waiting for the telephone to ring. Sure enough, half an hour later, there was a call from Messel's to say that Restro Investments of Jersey was offering ninepence a share for Polly Peck. Restro was an offshore trust of which Asil was the main beneficiary.

The instant the announcement came through, the share price started to rise. Having secured more than thirty per cent of Polly Peck, Asil was obliged to make an offer for the rest of the company. Several shareholders took advantage of the ninepence-a-share offer - which looked very attractive compared to the fivepence level at which Polly

Peck had been languishing shortly before - giving Asil an ultimate sixty per cent controlling stake.

As Polly Peck's share price carried on rising that spring, one of the purposes for which Asil had bought it began to emerge. My mother and father had been in Cyprus for just over a year and my father had been looking around for potential new ventures in a country which, struggling to survive economically, was wide open for investment. The family could not just limit itself to the clothing business when there were so many other things crying out to be done in the then-Turkish Federated State of Cyprus, he would urge us in his letters and telephone calls. My father often travelled around the country and when he visited the lush citrus-growing areas around Güzelyurt, in the West, it grieved him to see much of the orange crop left unharvested on the trees and lying, rotting, on the ground, because the Turkish Cypriots had no proper mechanism for exporting it to Europe. The state-owned Cyprus Fruit and Vegetable Export corporation, known as Cypfruvex, was managing a limited amount of exports, but because it had a monopoly at that stage it was in a position to dictate to growers the prices it would pay for their fruit. The growers, in their turn, calculated that the level of payment they received was not enough to cover the costs of employing staff to look after their trees and to pick the fruit. As a result, the citrus industry had declined into a state of apathy - but my father was sure he and Asil could kick-start it back into life if they could give growers fresh incentive to look after their groves. To do this, however, another problem needed to be tackled: in 1980, every single carton in which Turkish Cypriot citrus fruit was packed for export had to be imported into the country. In conjunction with the citrus exports, my father suggested that it would be a wise move to establish a cardboard box factory in North Cyprus.

From these suggestions were born Sunzest, the fruit export firm, and the packaging production plant Uni-Pac, both of which were launched under the Cypriot flag of Nadir Holdings. Given the green light by Asil, my father located a warehouse on the docks at Famagusta - disused since being damaged during the 1974 war - which he felt was an ideal position for Uni-Pac. He secured the building at a peppercorn rent and negotiated with the Turkish Cypriot authorities, who were keen to encourage outside investment and the opportunity to bring in hard currency, an eight-year tax "holiday". In July 1980, Asil announced a £1.56 million Polly Peck rights issue to purchase Uni-Pac and install the machinery needed to manufacture packaging. The plan was that Uni-Pac would be in production in time to produce the packaging needed for that autumn's citrus harvest. In the event, it did not begin operations until the following February and would not work at full capacity for several months after that. At the same time, Sunzest was established in premises in the heart of citrus-growing country. Again, my father struck the same deal with the authorities for an eight-year tax exemption to help him get the infant company off the ground.

Asil, meanwhile, was equally eager for new investments back home in Britain. In September 1980, rumours began to circulate that he was involved in a take-over of another ailing clothing business - Cornell Dresses, a thirty-four-year-old East End firm which had gone public in 1964. News of the approach sent Cornell's shares soaring and by the time the £570,000 purchase was finally effected by Polly Peck at the end of that year, Cornell was valued at £3.2 million. Asil was well on the way to fulfilling his ambitions of becoming an international tycoon. Though we did not know it then, his was to be a giddy success story running in tandem with the premiership of Margaret Thatcher. Her espousal of private industry, hard work and entrepreneurial spirit; her abolition of foreign exchange controls, which focused the City's sights beyond Britain's shores - all this would ensure that Asil was every inch the man for the high-flying eighties. As writer Tim Hindle would later remark: "...had Asil Nadir not existed, [the City] might have had to invent him. He suited them perfectly."

On the personal front, Asil's life was far from rosy. Although he tried to put up a good front, there were many occasions when I detected a sadness in him. Far from enjoying a high-living lifestyle, he was becoming more and more caught up in his increasingly complex business world and his home circumstances appeared to grow more bizarre by the year. Earlier in 1980, Aysegül had persuaded Asil to move closer to the hub of high society and they had sold the house in The Bishop's Avenue. For a year, they rented a house in Knightsbridge. In 1981, Asil bought the lease on a flat in Eaton Square - a magnificent property on the first floor in which the chief attraction was a spectacular veranda-style balcony, some eight feet wide and thirty feet long, which Asil went on to fill with an exotic assortment of the plants and flowers he loved, including even an olive tree growing in a huge terracotta pot.

Lesley, meanwhile, was still living in Little Venice and Asil was a frequent visitor there - suspicion of which on Aysegül's part sparked off many rows between her and my brother. One night much later on, when she suspected Asil and Lesley were together, Aysegül even went round to Lesley's flat and started smashing the earthenware flowerpots on her windowsill in the street outside. The police were called, but Lesley decided not to press charges. In 1979, just before the take-over of Polly Peck, Lesley had given birth to a son, Giles. Asil was not the most involved of fathers - Lesley can only remember one occasion when he changed Giles's nappy. When the baby was born, Asil announced that he wanted to give him a Turkish name, but Lesley waited in vain for him to come up with one. Finally, after three weeks during which the child was known simply as "Baby Boy" from the words on his hospital wrist tag, Lesley decided she would have to register the baby's name herself. Giles was the name she picked. Two years later, she would produce another son for Asil, Eren. I chose that name - it means manliness and wisdom and I also thought it would be easy for Eren's English friends to pronounce. Although their often stormy relationship was to endure for another seven years, Asil and Lesley would never set up home together. They often stayed at each other's flats. They would have their ups and downs, sometimes not seeing each other for months after a particularly big disagreement, but would always get back together. If ever I asked Lesley how she could be so forgiving towards my brother, she would say, "But he's just so irresistible - I have to take him back." Regardless of the state of Asil and Lesley's relationship, Giles and Eren were accepted from birth as part of our family and we have always looked on them with as much love as Asil's other children.

For me, the 1980s dawned as a time of achievement and great personal satisfaction. In February 1980, Wearwell was invited to send three representatives to a cocktail party at Buckingham Palace to mark the company winning the Queen's Award for Export Achievement. Asil decided that I should attend the event, along with Jean, his secretary, and my mother, who flew to London specially. I remember being overcome by a sense of unreality when the Queen finally shook my hand and congratulated us all on our achievements. Prince Charles, who was with his mother, commented on the fact that all three Wearwell representatives were women. "Are there no men in your company?" he joked with me, adding, "I didn't realise you ladies were so liberated in Cyprus!" The word in the press was that Prince Charles was preparing to marry, but he good-humouredly side-stepped a question about that from the guest standing beside me. A week later, the prince announced his engagement to Lady Diana Spencer. When the afternoon drew to a close, I felt myself almost float out of Buckingham Palace on a cloud of warmth. At last, all the years of hard work had been recognised—even by the Queen herself. And through our efforts, we had been able to contribute something worthwhile - in our own small way - to the prosperity of the land which had become our home. I glowed with the pride that, twenty years after arriving as a teenage immigrant, I had gained the ultimate acceptance into the British society I had long wanted to be a part of. We had a thriving business and I had a comfortable home in suburbia, plus three beautiful children destined for the best I could give them. I had never felt so very thoroughly British in all my life, and it was a feeling I loved.

That afternoon at Buckingham Palace gave me a renewed spring in my step. At Wearwell, I found my energy for buying and design redoubled as the orders poured in. At home, I continued to devote all my spare time to Tijen, Levent and Irfan as they approached their teenage years. After my parents' return to Cyprus, we had carried on our traditional family Sundays in their absence, now all gathering in our house instead of my mother's. Asil was not there every week, but when he could make it he would arrive on the doorstep with armfuls of roses, carnations, freesias or sweet peas. The next morning, Auntie Finney would take one glance round the house as she arrived for work and comment dryly, "I see the florist's been again."

In April 1981, I walked into Asil's office to find him brandishing a newspaper cutting. He waved it towards me and said, with a wry smile: "Read this." I had to laugh with him when I read the *Daily Mail* story. It was by one Michael Walters and told how, on a visit to North Cyprus, he had supposedly discovered that Uni-Pac was nothing more than "a bullet-scarred shed". Until then, none of us had known about this journalist's trip to Cyprus. True enough, there were about six bullet-holes in the whitewashed brickwork - a legacy of the 1974 war, when buildings island-wide caught the crossfire - but this was at that time so commonplace in Cyprus that it went virtually unnoticed by those who knew the island. To a London city-dweller like Michael Walters, though, on his first trip to Cyprus, the factory's external appearance must have begged the immediate question: "Is *this* really what all those shareholders are paying for?" That article was the first "knocking story" to be printed about Polly Peck, but far from being angry, Asil found the whole thing rather amusing. He leaned over the desk and told me, "One day, I'm going to prove to this man how wrong he is." Then he picked up his telephone and asked Jean Thomas to send someone out to get hold of one of the newspaper stand billboards which, bearing the slogan "Polly Peck's bullet-scarred shed", had been used to publicise that issue. By the next day, Asil had had the billboard framed and it hung on his wall for several years until one of his office moves. It was the first time any of us had heard of Michael Walters and little did we realise then he would later become a close friend. At the end of the first AGM following his article, Michael went up to Asil and the two of them spoke for the first time. Michael would become one of Polly Peck's biggest supporters in the press, but would good-humouredly put up with a lot of teasing from us about that "bullet-scarred shed".

The immediate spin-off from the *Daily Mail* article was that Asil decided it was time to take the Polly Peck investors and stockbrokers over to North Cyprus to calm any fears they might have - to introduce them to the country and let them see for themselves the businesses that were being built up in their name. If there were any doubts in the minds of any members of the party which journeyed out in May 1981, they were wiped out by the time they returned. The trip was Asil's first visit to North Cyprus for almost exactly twenty years and he received a rapturous welcome. There was a welcoming party in the VIP lounge at the airport and dozens more crowded into the terminal to welcome him home. There was a special hug, too, from my mother and my father who, so busy setting up the Cypriot businesses, had only been able to visit England for a few days at a time during the previous two years. In the days that followed, the head of state, President Rauf Denktas, gave a dinner in Asil's honour. Like all Turkish Cypriots, Asil had always felt very close to the country of his birth, even though his few snatched holidays over the previous two decades had never brought him closer than Istanbul. He was very moved to be greeted almost as a conquering hero by his compatriots who, although downtrodden and internationally ignored, were at last taking charge of their own destiny.

During that visit, the British bankers, brokers and investors quickly came to know the high regard in which Asil and my father were held in their native land - and also saw the enormous potential there waiting to be tapped. Already, Nadir Holdings was on the way to becoming the country's biggest single employer. By the middle of the decade, the firm would give direct employment to some 10,000 Turkish Cypriots - a staggering twenty-five per cent of the working population. In all, about 40,000 people would eventually benefit from the Nadir operations, either directly or indirectly. Asil and my father, as the engineers of a budding upturn in the Turkish Cypriot economy, were fêted wherever they went.

Across the United Nations-patrolled Green Line in the South, meanwhile, the Greek Cypriots were eyeing with growing alarm this resurgence of Turkish Cypriot fortunes...and the part played in it by Asil Nadir.

For two years after Asil bought into Polly Peck, the Greek Cypriots looked on as the company turned around its loss-making status to record a group pre-tax profit of £9.04 million in late 1982. In August that year, Asil announced a scheme to make Cornell Dresses into the part-owner of a mineral water-bottling plant at Niksar, near to the Turkish Black Sea coast, taking advantage of incentives being offered to new investors by the economically-floundering Turkish government. Three months later, he revealed plans to break into the protected Turkish electronics market to manufacture televisions under the brand name Vestel. Keen to give something back to his adopted homeland, he decided on a partnership with British firm Thorn-EMI. That December, Asil also announced his intentions to merge Wearwell and Cornell with Polly Peck, creating a diverse group with a joint market capitalisation of £225 million. Wearwell had won its second Queen's Award for Export Achievement.

Enough was enough for the Greek Cypriots. Until then, they had succeeded in maintaining the Turkish Federated State of Cyprus in the role of international pariah, denied an equal say in political and diplomatic negotiations on the future of Cyprus. They believed that the economic hardship into which the Turkish Cypriots had fallen would drive them into accepting a political settlement on Greek Cypriot terms. In Asil and his expanding Turkish Cypriot business activities they saw someone who was undermining that aim, helping the Turkish Cypriots towards a state of economic self-sufficiency. Not only that, but the Turkish Cypriot fruit exports were a direct threat to Greek Cypriot agricultural trade. In Greek Cypriot South Nicosia it was decided that the onward march could no longer go unchallenged. Early in 1983, despite a warning to the Greek Cypriots from the then-United Nations Secretary-General not to interfere in the affairs of Asil or Polly Peck, an Anti-Nadir Committee was formed which would operate out of their High Commission in London. Its members included figures from the Greek Cypriot intelligence service and a number of high-ranking politicians, among them, ironically, Greek Cypriot Foreign Minister-to-be Yiorgios Iacovou, our old Famagusta neighbour, who vowed to bring his one-time playmate down.

In late January 1983, a story appeared in the *Financial Times* which revealed that the tax holiday given to Polly Peck's operations had never received cast-iron status from the authorities. This much was true - unbeknown to Asil, my father had struck that deal with the authorities in time-honoured Cypriot style, orally and without receiving any written confirmation. The *FT* story, written by Ankara-based Turkish Cypriot correspondent Metin Münir, said there was little danger that the tax exemption might not materialise and that the Turkish Cypriot government was preparing legislation which would give similar tax-exempt status to all activities - like Uni-Pac - in the Famagusta Free Port area. The story had little impact at first, but the stormy month which it took for the Turkish Cypriot government to confirm the tax holiday - with rumour piled upon rumour and outright attack by the Greek Cypriots - almost proved the undoing of Polly Peck. Gossip that was probably Greek-orchestrated swept an increasingly nervous City during the first three weeks of February. There were rumours of a disagreement between Asil and Rothschilds bank; mutterings of a rift between him and the government in North Cyprus; suggestions that a tax bill for several hundred thousand pounds had already landed on Asil's desk.

It was amid such jitters that the Greek Cypriots struck on Thursday, 24th February. The South Cyprus government announced that it might ask Britain to investigate Polly Peck; that it was thinking of citing the firm in a case against the Turks being brought at the European Commission on Human Rights; that it was beginning a civil suit against Polly Peck and Wearwell in the British courts. The Greek Cypriots claimed properties exploited by the firms in North Cyprus - including the citrus groves and the Uni-Pac factory - had been Greek Cypriot-owned prior to 1974. Therefore they deemed them to be stolen property and were keen to test out amendments to Britain's trespass laws, effected in 1982, which could extend the UK courts' jurisdiction to overseas property. In addition to the legal assault, the Greek Cypriots also launched an attack on the commercial viability of Polly Peck and Wearwell.

As the aftershocks of the political propaganda bombshells resounded the next day, the Turkish Cypriot Council of Ministers met to confirm the tax holiday for Polly Peck. At the end of the day, it emerged that the matter was still being considered and a decision was expected by the following Monday - 28th February. The delay, sparking doubts in the minds of many shareholders, proved almost fatal for Polly Peck. Confirmation of the tax exemption - in the end to run for six years and ten months - did indeed reach London that Monday morning, but by then Polly Peck's share price was plummeting in the early rush to sell. The first twenty minutes of trading on the Stock Exchange saw more than £48 million demolished from the firm's market value. At the end of the day, the share price, which had peaked at £34, stood at £23.50 having touched bottom at £16 a few hours earlier.

Backed by its brokers, who stood by their glowing profits forecasts, Polly Peck lived on, but Asil was more distressed by what had happened than he cared to admit. Although the British government announced quickly that it did not intend to pursue any investigation against Polly Peck, the Greek Cypriots still did not let up their campaign. Two bulky dossiers alleging regulations breaches were handed to the authorities from the Greek Cypriots' London High Commission. A series of press allegations also followed from the pen of Michael Gillard, an *Observer* journalist, and later in the satirical magazine, *Private Eye*. Asil was unable to take the reports with his earlier equanimity. He began, too, to be unsettled by an ever-increasing number of threats from the Greek

Cypriot community. The more they realised they were losing their "war", the more it seemed they stepped up the battle against the man declared "public enemy number one" by South Cyprus. Several times, I was in his office when he took a threatening telephone call. Having been brought up among Greeks, Asil recognised the very thick accent and unique pronunciation of English instantly. His face would change as he listened to the caller for a few seconds, then he would shout, "You just try it," into the receiver before putting it down.

When the threats first began, he refused to take them seriously, convinced that the Greeks would never try to harm him for fear of Turkish reprisals. As noises from Cyprus that spring of 1983 began to indicate the imminent proclamation of a wholly-independent Turkish Cypriot state, however, the verbal assaults became more frequent and more alarming. Eventually, in 1989, he would employ a team of bodyguards on the advice of the anti-terrorist squad at New Scotland Yard.

After the hiccup of February 1983, developments at Polly Peck began to gather pace again. Shaken by the ferocity of the Greek Cypriot onslaught, Asil diverted his attentions to mainland Turkey where there were prospects of a return to civilian government after three years of military rule. He forged ahead with the proposed Vestel plant, having recruited as Polly Peck commercial director a top Thorn-EMI man, Brian Handicott, who would oversee the electronic firm's launch. Preparations were moving on, too, for the launch of the Niksar bottling plant, which would open in August 1984. Asil also considered other Turkish ventures, one with Racal Electronics and another with Daihatsu, which ultimately failed to bear fruit. At that time, he forged a friendship with senior Turkish politician, Turgut Özal, whom he met at a party in London. Özal would go on to become Turkey's Prime Minister and then President and would be Asil's most powerful ally on the mainland.

In Cyprus meanwhile, my father was still the driving force behind new venture ideas - and he found in Asil a partner who was not scared to take risks and to go after a new challenge if it looked likely to reap long-term rewards. My father's aim was to secure a vertically integrated business, with each division servicing the others. With citrus growing already secured, the packaging side received a major fillip in November 1983 with the opening of a second-stage plant at Famagusta, Uni-Pac-2, boosting the factory's production capacity. My father also turned his attention to the method of transporting the fruit to its European destination. At that time, all such exports had to use Turkey as a stepping stone and the natural development, my father concluded, was to launch

83

Polly Peck's own shipping line. By the middle of the decade, Polly Peck would launch a fleet of two cargo ships, ironically headed by a Greek captain. Asil perpetuated a long-standing family joke by christening one of the launch ships the *Safiye Sultan* - a nickname we used to call my mother, which translates roughly as "Safiye, her Majesty". My mother, who went to Famagusta for the official launch ceremony, was delighted to see this tribute from her son emblazoned across the vessel's hull.

The 15th November 1983 was an important day in the history of Turkish Cypriots - the day their leadership declared North Cyprus the independent Turkish Republic of Northern Cyprus (the TRNC). Since 1975, the country had been the Turkish Federated State of Cyprus - in name, therefore, the Turkish Cypriot wing of a new federal republic which it was hoped would be formed in Cyprus. For the eight years since then, though, intercommunal talks between the Turkish and Greek Cypriots had made little progress, with the Greek side - backed by Athens - refusing to acknowledge the Turkish Cypriots' right to self-determination. By that autumn, with a general election looming in Turkey to replace the military government with an unpredictable civilian administration, Turkish Cypriot President Rauf Denktas decided the time was right for independence. A crowd of 10,000 greeted his historic announcement to Parliament with thunderous applause as his words were relayed live on radio and television. Though there were fears that the independence declaration would provoke international anger, we thought it was high time for such a move. After all, there was virtually nothing the international community could do to make the country's situation any worse than it had been since 1974. We welcomed the birth of the new TRNC because it made more permanent the land of physical safety Turkish Cypriots had enjoyed for almost a decade.

Polly Peck's growth continued with a flurry of activity in 1984. In January, the company took a twenty-five per cent stake in Northampton leather and tanning firm Strong and Fisher. June saw the first production of video cassette recorders begin at the high-tech Vestel plant at Manisa, outside Turkey's "second city" Izmir. Manufacture of colour television sets began in October, just after the start of colour broadcasting in Turkey. By the end of the year, the plant had 240 staff. In Cyprus, the businesses were growing so big that Fehim's brother, Ilker, agreed to move back to the island from London to help my father run them. A few hundred miles away, in north-east Turkey, the Niksar bottling plant was officially opened by Turkish Minister of State, Sudi Turel. In August and Asil and my mother flew out for the lavish ceremony. A party of British journalists and Polly Peck investors was also there, and when Asil got off the coach taking them all to the Niksar plant, he was confronted by a man in a white coat, brandishing a huge knife in bloody hands, setting about the slaughter of a row of sheep. Though Asil knew it to be a traditional honour, aimed at bringing good fortune to the new business venture, he realised the visitors from Britain would be shocked and passed an urgent message to the man to stop what he was doing. It was too late, though - one sheep had already been sacrificed and as Asil turned back to the coach he saw each member of the foreign party turn pale as they came face to face with the sight. Though he tried to explain the tradition to them later, telling them the meat would be sent to help poor families, he sensed there was nothing he could say which would shift the impression of horror fixed in their minds. The memory of that day would send shivers down his spine whenever he recalled it in years to come.

By the end of that year, when Asil reported record pre-tax profits of £50.55 million, Polly Peck had moved out of the offices it shared with Wearwell at 101 Commercial Road and into luxury purpose-built premises on a former synagogue site just two doors away at number 97. The smart smoked-glass edifice was sold to Barclays Bank on a "sale and lease back" agreement under which Barclays occupied the ground floor and Polly Peck the upper four floors. Spread over the first, second and third floors were a massive board room, two reception areas, directors' and secretaries' offices and a grand dining room. On the fourth, Asil had his luxurious offices.

The year had also seen another major Polly Peck acquisition - this time much closer to home. On the 9th July, the long-awaited merger with Wearwell took place at a cost to Polly Peck of £32.44 million. As part of the deal came Inter-City Investments, a loss-making Commercial Road textiles company in which Wearwell had acquired a fifty-one per cent stake a year earlier.

For Asil, the Wearwell merger was hugely important. It gave him solid UK assets and profits to counter continuing City unease over Polly Peck's very extensive foreign trading. It also, through Inter-City, gave him manufacturing links with the Far East. As 1984 gave way to 1985, Asil was living and working in the style of an international entrepreneur. He had already moved to safeguard Polly Peck from the dangers of concentrating on any single industry or country and was setting his sights on his dream of becoming a truly global industrialist. He was also looking ahead and planning to reflect this aspiration in a change of title for his newly-expanded corporation - in 1985, it would be renamed Polly Peck International, or PPI for short.

For Fehim and me, the Wearwell merger was a turning point of a different kind. At the time, the personal significance of the take-over was not immediately apparent. But the move quietly ushered in a period of dissatisfaction which would ultimately prompt our departure from

Polly Peck. While the merger was still in the pipeline, Asil told me there would be a new board at Polly Peck to reflect the larger company. There would also be a management reorganisation, he said, with Polly Peck's different activities being ranged into separate divisions, each with its own director. Wearwell and Inter-City would form the textiles division, and Fehim and I understood from Asil that one or even both of us would be appointed to the board as its director.

In the event, as the next AGM drew closer, it emerged that our hopes were misplaced. Joe Harris, who was the chairman of Wearwell's Inter-City subsidiary, was named the new director in charge of the textiles division. We were bitterly disappointed. Asil explained to us that he could not put either of us on the board at that moment because he had been advised that the City would frown upon it. As a Stock Exchange-listed multinational conglomerate, the City did not consider it appropriate for Polly Peck to have a board on which family was heavily represented. He told us to be patient, though, and he would try and win the City round. "I know you deserve to be on the board," he reassured me. I knew the rather xenophobic City institutions had always viewed Asil with a certain amount of suspicion. Now that he was becoming more and more successful, there was a large measure of jealousy too. Those in the City who were friends admitted that the biggest hurdles standing in the way of his acceptance into its very close-knit world were that he was Turkish and a Muslim. Aware then that he had started out at a disadvantage through not having the right background or the "old school tie", Asil was determined to play everything else by the book in order to win the approval of the "right" people. If the City disapproved of family directors at Polly Peck, so be it; Asil would remain the only Nadir on the board. I understood his position, but I could not help feeling badly let down.

The months following the merger were to prove very traumatic. Fehim and I carried on working as normal at Wearwell, just down the road from Polly Peck's smart offices, but even there we were no longer fully in charge since Joe Harris's appointment. He never tried to rub in his superior status and was, I am sure, prosaic about the reasons for his elevation to board level. But having been used largely to running our own ship for several years, it was very difficult for me and for Fehim simply to plug away in the business without having any say in the directions it took.

In the early days following Polly Peck's move, we used to walk from number 101 every day for lunch in the new executive dining room. Over those lunches, we would swap notes about the businesses and would be kept up-to-date with any new developments at Polly Peck. As Polly Peck grew, though, absorbed Wearwell and began to take on more and more new faces, these friendly lunch parties began to break up. The atmosphere shifted subtly too. I felt that some of the new directors, however, well-qualified they may be in the world of business or finance, had no feel for the way we had founded our companies and made them successful. To these newcomers, Polly Peck was just another job, and a very good one at that. It was an attitude with which I could not come to terms.

Asil, meanwhile, was looking to the future and brimming with new ideas. That spring, he announced a plan to build a 300-bedroom hotel at Antalya, on the south coast of Turkey. In May, he headed a whistle-stop tour taking stockbrokers and institutional investors to see the Polly Peck operations in Turkey and North Cyprus. The following month, he announced the merger of Cornell - now owner of the Niksar plant - with Polly Peck. Two months later, Polly Peck acquired three fruit and vegetable packaging plants in Turkey for £12.2 million.

That August Fehim and I, feeling slightly jaded, took the children to Cyprus for our annual holiday. There, we found ourselves plunged into a positive hive of activity. Far from slowing down at the ages of sixty-seven and sixty-four, my father and mother seemed busier than ever. Running the Cyprus businesses gave my father an enormous thrill. It took him back to the days when he was setting up his chain of shops in old Famagusta - but this time everything was on a far grander scale. Those were the happiest days of his life. He always liked to check on everything personally, and was working sometimes as many as eighteen hours a day, shuttling hundreds of miles a week between home in Nicosia, the citrus groves of Güzelyurt and the packaging factory in Famagusta. He was talking of buying a helicopter for the company so that he would not waste so much time on the road. On a typical day, he would be up by three in the morning to go to Güzelyurt and check that the citrus trees were being watered properly before dawn. Then he would return to Nicosia for breakfast and take my mother to the Wearwell factory where she spent her day. From Wearwell, he would visit Uni-Pac and might then go to Sunzest and to the Niksar and Vestel distribution centres in Famagusta, Nicosia, Güzelyurt or Kyrenia. There was the shipping side to oversee - PPI Lines and its agent, Özari Shipping - and another new Polly Peck enterprise, Inter-Channel Pharmaceuticals. There was also the cash-flow of the businesses to manage, giving advances to citrus growers so that they could care for the trees and harvest the fruit. In addition, scenting the likelihood of a foray into the tourist industry and the world of finance, he had already established a car hire firm, Travel-Oz, and the Özari Tourism travel agents, along with the Kibris Endüstri Bankasi - Cyprus Industrial Bank.

My father was working extremely hard - but he also knew how to enjoy himself. Even at the end of such an exhausting day, he would still be raring to socialise and my parents spent many nights of the week out with friends. He mixed easily on many levels - a keen sports fan, he sponsored chess and football tournaments in Cyprus. One evening, he might enjoy a lively dinner with the growers, sitting at tables set out among the citrus trees in Güzelyurt. The next, he might be hobnobbing with the President or members of the government. His best friend, Dr Ali Atun, was then Minister of Health and my father and Asil had earned the acquaintance and respect of other politicians through their unparalleled investments in the Turkish Cypriot state. On the nights my parents did not go out visiting, they would sometimes have friends round to play cards. At other times, my father would stroll out after dinner to the Doctors' Union Club near their house. There he would play backgammon or cards. He was a mean poker player and excelled at the game's bluffing because he could sit at the card-table with a perfectly deadpan expression, giving nothing away. As youngsters, he had taught us all how to play poker, but he always knew how to psyche us out at the start of a game by remarking casually: "Did I ever tell you that I used to play poker and backgammon with King Farouk?"

One day during our visit that August, my mother came with us to the beach and my father said he would join us all there later. As we sat round a table in the beach bar that lunch-time, I saw him walking towards us carrying a newspaper. I waved, but as he got closer, I could tell from his face that he was very upset about something. Instantly worried, as soon as he reached us, I asked him: "What's wrong?" He dropped the newspaper on to the table and replied: "Asil has just made the biggest mistake of his life." None of us knew what he was talking about. I picked up the paper. It was the Turkish daily, *Hürriyet*, dated the 10th August. There on the front page was a photograph of a smiling Asil and Aysegül outside Chelsea Register Office in London, with a brief story saying they had remarried the day before. I could not believe what I was seeing. We all spent the rest of that day in a state of shock and dismay. My mother was in floods of tears, my father shook his head in disbelief. Over and over, we asked ourselves the same two questions. Why marry Aysegül again? It had not worked the first time and was unlikely to be any better the second. And why not tell us about it, instead of sneaking to the Registry Office and letting us find out from the newspapers? No matter how many times we repeated the questions, we came no closer to finding the answers.

By the time we flew back to England a few days later - accompanied by my mother, who was coming for a holiday - I was furious and very hurt that he could just go out and get married without letting any of us know. It was Saturday evening when we got home and we heard nothing from Asil that night or throughout the next day. He was obviously lying low. The next day, Lesley came round to our house. She was distraught but could shed no further light on what had gone on. As we sat there, my mother and I discussed angrily what we would say to Asil when we saw him next. I was amazed to hear Lesley - one person who, as mother of two of Asil's sons, had the most right to be furious with him - plead selflessly: "Please don't get upset with him. He must have had his reasons. I'm angry with him and I'm not talking to him now, so if you don't talk to him either, it will break his heart."

The next morning, I marched straight to Asil's office and was very surprised to find it empty. I quizzed Jean Thomas about what had happened. She told me that the first she knew was when Asil came to her on the morning of the 9th and said, "Jean, I'm going out now. I'm going to the Registry Office to get married."

"Why didn't you telephone me? Couldn't you stop him? You should have tied him to the chair to stop him going," I told her.

Jean just shook her head: "I was so shocked, I didn't know what to do."

It was a very sheepish Asil whom my mother and I finally confronted in his office later that morning. The press had portrayed his remarriage as a Wuthering Heights-style grand passion, with Asil and Aysegül unable to live with each other…yet unable to live apart. The truth which he revealed to us that day was far less exciting. His and Aysegul's younger son, Serhan, was ten years old and was in the preparatory school at Eton College. Asil and Aysegül no longer made any pretence of living together - she was at the flat in Eaton Square and he had a flat of his own overlooking the Ritz hotel, where Lesley and their two children often stayed. During one of their sporadic meetings, Aysegül had reported to him that Serhan was being teased by his classmates about the fact that his parents were not married. Never one to stand by and see somebody unhappy, the problem - and the obvious solution - niggled at Asil's mind. Shortly afterwards, it was Birol's twenty-first birthday and when he asked his eldest son what he would like as a birthday present, Birol replied, "For the four of us all to have dinner together as a family." The birthday dinner took place at Aysegül's favourite restaurant outside Cannes in June. It was an agreeable evening which left Asil thinking that he and Aysegül could give marriage another go, if only for Serhan's sake. The two of them made their arrangements, but Asil was careful to keep the news from us. He knew my mother would have been very upset if she had known about his plan - and if he had known she was unhappy, he would not have been able to go through with it.

89

On the day of the wedding, Asil and Aysegül met at the Registry Office. When the brief ceremony was over, Aysegül went to Eaton Square and Asil went back to the flat near the Ritz and Lesley. As far as Asil was concerned, this was a marriage purely for appearances' sake - a "technical marriage", he explained to me. Aysegül took the continued estrangement with barely a murmur. I suspected that she had achieved what she wanted - she had proved to Lesley that, even though Lesley had two children by Asil, she, Aysegül, had the stronger hold over him. Though Asil would have other girlfriends in the future, it was his relationship with Lesley that always rankled with her. "I think the reason she hated us being together was that Asil once admitted to her that he loved me," Lesley would say later. By this time, too, Aysegül was in her element socially. She lived in the right area, moved in the right circles, could indulge her passion for antiques, and had built up a network of influential friends, including the Queen's sister, Princess Margaret. Asil had met the princess through his charitable work and they had become friendly. My brother had dinner with her once at her home and Princess Margaret had spent a holiday at his *yali* (summer house) on the Bosphorus in Istanbul.

When Asil suggested later that they should divorce, however, Aysegül was not so easy-going. Asil had grown tired of the continuing media coverage in Turkey of Aysegül's social life and he was concerned that the name Nadir should not feature so prominently in the mass circulation gossip columns. But Aysegül would not hear of a second divorce and insisted that any proceedings would have to take place in Turkey, where they had first married. In the end, the situation would remain unresolved for years. When the Polly Peck troubles were at their height and Aysegül had left Britain, she suddenly decided that divorce might be the best policy after all - possibly fearing that, as Asil's legal wife, she might become embroiled in the situation. The signed divorce papers would arrive in Asil's office by fax from Turkey the day he was declared bankrupt, in November 1991.

Our visit to Cyprus in the summer of 1985 had made me even more discontented with my role at Polly Peck. Listening to the excitement in my father's voice as he told of this plan or that project, touring the island with him and watching him point out the strides being made, I came to realise just how left out of things we were in Wearwell. Our operations - which had also taken on Polly Peck's textile concerns with the 1984 merger - were still doing well, but they were simply rather dull. The excitement and glamour of Polly Peck lay elsewhere, in all the new ventures, and were passing us by. Like Asil, I was keen to diversify. Unlike him, I had no way of realising that ambition. I was particularly eager for Polly Peck to tap the enormous potential I could see for tourism in North Cyprus. My father said he agreed, but Asil merely seemed to pay lip-service to the idea, showing little interest in action. Without a seat on the board, I had no chance to put my desires into practice.

By the end of 1985, even the profitability of the textiles operations was being called into question. For almost a decade, Wearwell's business had relied on bulk exports - mostly from the Middle East, although we had also dipped into the Polish market. That autumn, Fehim returned from visiting Iraq - our biggest customers - with bad news. The Iraqis wanted to place more huge orders, but because of financial difficulties arising from the country's political situation, they wanted two years' credit. Reluctantly, we agreed we must turn the business down. The loss of the Iraqi orders left us with only a minimal amount of business from Poland and the smaller Gulf states. It was clear we could not afford to keep all our staff on with such a small order book. We moved from one of the three East End buildings then occupied by Wearwell and were forced to cut our workforce by half. There were tears all round as we said goodbye to staff who had been with us since 1961.

As Christmas and the New Year loomed, it seemed all the signs were pointing in one direction. Polly Peck's star was in the ascendant, but the textiles business was clearly fading. It had lost its charm for me and I suspected Asil was only keeping it going for old time's sake. It was frustrating to feel that our contribution was no longer really needed. Meanwhile, Fehim was bursting with ideas for exploiting the opportunities in newly-liberated Poland, where he had forged some interesting contacts. I was certain that there was a tourism potential in Turkey and North Cyprus, just waiting to be unleashed. We began to talk of striking out alone.

That December, though, we received shock news which wiped all thoughts of business from our minds. Three months earlier, my father had gone down with apparent jaundice. He seemed to recover, but doctors in Cyprus suspected he had a gallstone. In November we had a telephone call from his secretary, Mine, who warned: "Your father does not look at all well." We insisted that he come to London - backed by my father's friend, Dr Ali Atun, who I think suspected something seriously wrong - and Asil sent his private plane over at the end of that month to collect the two men and my mother and bring them to England. At that time, Dr Atun's son, Rifat, was newly graduated from Guy's Hospital Medical School and working his houseman's year in the hospital. Rifat knew all the specialists at Guy's and as soon as my father arrived in London he was whisked in for a check-up. The gallstone suspicion was confirmed and my father was told he would need surgery.

The operation was fixed for Christmas Eve. I took my father to Guy's first thing in the morning and spent a few hours shopping for the children's presents, trying to take my mind off everything. When I got back to the hospital that afternoon to see how the surgery had gone, I bumped into Rifat. I remember thinking he seemed strangely slimmer-looking than usual and rather pale. Rifat took me by the arm and said, "Come on, let's go for a walk." He led me out of the hospital and into a garden outside. We sat down on a wooden bench. Rifat turned sideways and looked at me for a few seconds, as if weighing his words. "I'm afraid it's terminal," he told me quietly. For a few moments I did not know what to do, what to say. Then the tears came. Rifat put his arm round me. Suddenly, as I leaned against him, the world seemed at a standstill. It was just not possible that this man, so full of life, was on the verge of death. His favourite as a child, I had grown even closer to him over the years that we worked together. We understood each other implicitly and shared the same business hopes. Even during the six years that we had lived 3,000 miles apart, we still spoke to each other almost every day on the telephone. If my father had a business problem or a point of disagreement with Asil, I was the one he would turn to for advice. Now came the shock understanding that there were times in this life when problems could not simply be overcome through hard work and determination. My father might be dying and there was absolutely nothing I could do.

The first concrete thought that crossed my mind was Asil. I had to ring him. I dried my tears and Rifat guided me to the nearest telephone. "I'm afraid it's not very good news," were the shaky words I managed before Asil said: "Stay where you are. I'm coming." Within ten minutes he was at the hospital. For a few moments we held on to each other in the hallway, trying desperately to cling to something solid in a world which suddenly seemed far from certain. We agreed then to keep the news to ourselves, at least for the time being. That evening, Asil and I visited my father, who was coming round from the anaesthetic. As well as detecting the cancer, the surgeon had also removed a large stone from my father's gall-bladder and this stood in a jar at the side of the bed. Fighting back tears and determined to be cheerful, I pointed to this and told him, "Look at this huge stone they've removed." Sleepily, without even opening his eyes, he replied: "Take that stone and hit Koreli on the head with it." His words took us by surprise. Ibrahim Koreli was the leader of the citrus growers' union in Cyprus - later to become an MP - and my father had had a lot of argument with him over the past six years. My father had clearly recovered from the operation with his sense of humour intact, yet it was distressing to see that Koreli was the first thing on his mind while he was half awake, half asleep. Several months later, when Koreli tried to attend my father's funeral, Asil would turn him away at the cemetery gate.

We left my father dozing and joined the specialist in his office. In his despair, Asil was clutching at straws. There had to be something we could do; some treatment we could try; a trip to America perhaps? But the specialist just shook his head slowly and told us, "I'm sorry, there's nothing. The kind of cancer we found is one in a million and it is one type for which there is no cure, it develops so fast. In my opinion, your father has three months to live."

We broke the news to Fehim that night. Between us, we made a pact that we would tell no-one else. Rifat and his father already knew, but we asked them not to let my father know the truth. If the rest of the family knew, we reasoned among ourselves, he would be sure to find out sooner or later. Our fear was that if my father had no hope, he might die even sooner. In the back of our minds, too, I think we secretly hoped that once he returned to Cyprus his health might improve. That knowledge proved a difficult burden to bear...and I am sure now, looking back, that my father guessed the truth for himself without being told. He was not a stupid man. When he was strong enough to leave hospital, Asil took him to convalesce in the flat overlooking the Ritz that he then shared with Lesley. He and my mother stayed there for a month and my heart bled when we went to visit them to see my father losing weight almost daily, becoming weaker and weaker.

I recalled how, nearly eighteen years ago when Tijen was born, my father had said half-jokingly to his old friend Dr Atun, over one of their many card-playing sessions, that it would be ideal if one day his granddaughter were to marry Dr Atun's son, Rifat. The two pals kept this scheme to themselves for a long time, but when my father eventually confessed it to me, it did not seem such a ridiculous idea - Rifat had grown up a kind, intelligent boy. He was a nephew of my sister's husband, Güner, and often came to stay with them, so he and Tijen knew each other well. I sensed in Tijen an attraction towards Rifat and had noticed, whenever Rifat visited, that he showed a keen interest in her. I had been reminded of the two friends' plan that summer of 1984, before my father was ill, when Dr Atun had come to London for a few days on his return from Brussels. While he was in Britain, he came to see us and tell us formally, as is traditional in Turkish Cypriot families, that Rifat would like to marry Tijen. Rifat had asked his father to make the approach to ask our permission. At the time, I told Dr Atun that it was really too soon to think of marriage for Tijen - she was still studying for her "O" Levels that year - and we should wait and see what the future held. Thinking about it again eighteen months on, I realised that an engagement between Tijen and Rifat would be perhaps one thing above all which would really make my father happy.

One night, just after New Year, Fehim and I sat down alone with Tijen and told her of Rifat's intentions. She did not seem surprised and admitted her own feelings towards Rifat, but she felt she did not wish to rush things, telling us she wanted to study, to go on to university and did not want to consider marriage at that stage. She would rather wait until the next summer before making a decision. I was sure that Tijen would feel differently if she knew the truth about my father's condition, so I confided in her that he would almost certainly be gone by the summer and that it would give him so much pleasure to see his dearest wish fulfilled before he died. It was a difficult decision for me to make, to confide in Tijen, but I felt sure that if I did not, she might later blame me for depriving her of the chance to give her dying grandfather a moment of happiness. A stunned Tijen discussed the matter with Rifat and the two of them agreed that they would get engaged, but would wait a year or two before contemplating a wedding. The engagement was announced and a formal ceremony was arranged for two days later.

My father was delighted to hear the news. Asil was a member of a famous old club, The Ambassadors, just round the corner from his flat and he suggested holding the engagement party - a dinner for the immediate family - in a private room there. My father was to perform the ceremonial duty of placing the engagement rings on Tijen's and Rifat's fingers and I asked him if he felt strong enough to go to the club for the occasion, or whether he would prefer us to hold the party in Asil's flat. "This is such a special occasion that, even if I were hundreds of miles away, I would still make sure I got there," was his firm reply. The night of the engagement ceremony - 20th January 1986 - was an occasion of very mixed feelings. We were all wishing Tijen and Rifat well for their future together, yet I knew my father might not live to see it. As I watched him putting the engagement rings on in the elegant wood-panelled room, I just did not want to accept the awful truth. I prayed fervently for a miracle to save him, but in my heart of hearts I knew he was fading rapidly. I could see by then that he had not only lost a lot of weight, but even seemed to be shrinking in height too. Physically, he was a shadow of the energetic, fun-loving man I had known.

My father was itching to get back to his beloved North Cyprus. We all wanted him to stay longer in London, but we knew how much it would mean to him to go home and catch up with his friends and businesses there, so we arranged the journey back. I tried to prepare my mother for the end, telling her that my father's illness could be serious - that it would take him a long time to get over it and that it was touch-and-go whether he would recover at all. Nothing I said got through to her. It seemed as if she had put up a mental barrier against my words and just refused to accept them. They left for Cyprus at the end of January. By then, my father was a very changed figure from the Irfan Nadir who had left the island just two months before. Friends would come up to him in the street and enquire anxiously after his health. One even asked whether it was true that he had terminal cancer and I remember my mother telling me that my father turned to her and commented, "How evil people are to say things like that."

As soon as he got to Cyprus, my father went back to work. He was too weak to spend very long in the office, but he would go there for a couple of hours every day and insisted on remaining in control of the companies. Even the week before he died, he would be extolling the virtues of this scheme or that plan, fretting over whether the cargo ships were keeping to the sailing schedule he had pinned to the wall beside his bed. Until two days before he died, he was still signing the cheques for Nadir Holdings.

By the last few days of his life, it became plain that my father realised he was dying. When I told him that Asil would be with us in a day or two, he answered, "I hope I am still here when he comes." On one of those last days, the sadness got too much for me and I spent a few minutes weeping in the garden. When I came back into the room, red-eyed, my father asked me what was wrong. I told him there was nothing - I had been standing next to the lemon tree blossom and it had brought on my hay fever. He looked at me and smiled. I could see from that smile that he knew I had been crying...and knew the end was near. Then he told me softly, "I'm ill now, but, even if something happens to me, don't worry. How old am I? Sixty-eight? Well, I've lived my life as if I had 108 years. I've lived my life to the full. You, all of you, must see that you too live your lives the way you want." When the children came to see him a few days before his death, Levent moved towards the bed to give him a customary kiss and cuddle, but my father spoke up: "It's all right, Levent. No more kisses for granddad."

It was during those final days that I had the chance to tell my father how I felt about Polly Peck. He wanted to know all about London and how the businesses were doing, so I would sit beside his bed for hours answering all his questions. If I was to leave Polly Peck and go it alone, I wanted to hear my father's opinion first - to get his blessing. I did not tell him how unhappy I had become working at the company. I explained only how I wanted to expand into tourism but that Asil seemed too busy to pay any attention to my ideas. "When he makes decisions now," I told my father, "he's not the old Asil - he makes decisions according to what the City wants and how it will react. He has so many things on his plate now." At first my father urged me not to leave Asil and to embark on the tourism projects together. But when I persisted, asking, "What if Asil doesn't want to go into tourism?" he said, "I will talk to Asil when he gets here - I'm sure he will listen to me. Give him a year, and if by this time next year he still hasn't agreed to do it, then I give you my blessing to go your own way and I will see that you have enough money to do what you want."

My father kept his word within the next few days. Asil had arrived and the three of us were together in my father's bedroom. My father was urging Asil to go and look at the Cyprus businesses. Then he went on: "I know you've become a well-known company with a big board of directors and you are busy rushing here and there, but I still feel it is important for you to have your family around you. You should have your sister with you - why don't you change the office next to yours and put Bilge in there? Sometimes you may be wasting your time seeing people you don't have to see and you could let Bilge cope with some of the burden - I'm sure she would be invaluable to you. She has good ideas too and you could work on those together."

Without hesitation, Asil replied, "Yes, you're right, father. Maybe I have been too busy, rushing from one side of the world to another." Later, when Asil had left the room, I thanked my father for what he had said. I told him I would do what he wished and give Asil another year's grace.

On the evening of the 31st March, three months and one week since his cancer was diagnosed, we could see he was deteriorating rapidly. Afraid that he would not last the night, we sent Levent and Irfan to spend the night with Fehim's brother, Ilker, and decided to stay at the house in Nicosia and take it in turns to sit with him. We also asked Rifat to stay. At five o'clock in the morning - the 1st April - Fehim, Asil and I went upstairs and found my mother trying to nurse my father and clearly exhausted. Fehim told her, "Mama, you're tired. I'll sit with him."

We could see from my father's face that the pain was very bad, so we persuaded him to take some morphine. As the drug took effect, he was speaking to us while Fehim and Asil rubbed his arms and legs and he grew gradually calmer. After a few minutes, as Asil and I made to leave the room, my father opened one eye and said urgently, "Where's Fehim? I want him to stay." Then he looked at my mother and told her, "You look very tired. Why don't you go to sleep? Fehim is here if I need anything."

My mother lay down beside him on the double bed. She had not slept properly for days and quickly fell into a doze. For the next two hours, my father lay half-awake and holding Fehim's hand while my mother slept alongside. The clock opposite the bed showed eight minutes to eight when Fehim noticed a dramatic change. Suddenly my father began taking huge breaths and Fehim could see his heart beating violently, battling for life in a fading body. As he looked, the pounding heart simply stopped. Fehim did not know what to do. He could not move from the bedside because my father's hand still gripped his tightly. He could not shout to us because he did not want to wake my mother. As he sat thinking for a few moments, he caught sight of Mustafa, my father's driver, who had arrived from his own house to spend the day with us. As Mustafa peered round the door, Fehim whispered to him, "Mustafa, please call Rifat and Asil and ask them to come up."

I awoke from a fitful doze to hear Rifat and Asil taking the stairs two at a time and knew something must have happened. Upstairs, Rifat was able to catch the last pulse beats, as my father's life ebbed away. They covered him with the blanket and left my mother to carry on sleeping a while longer. Then they came back downstairs and broke the news to us. The reality of his death hit me like a stinging blow. I walked out into the garden without a word. I did not want to believe it. As I stood for a while in the fresh air, I remembered something my father had said the previous week. I had thought little of the words at the time, but now they flooded back to me and it was as if my father had had a premonition. The day after Asil had arrived in Cyprus, my father had seemed to regain some strength and had been able to sit up in bed and talk to us. At one point, he had looked at us all and commented that it was unfair on us all to be spending our whole holiday in Nicosia. Then he added, "Never mind. Next Tuesday everything will be all right. Next Tuesday we'll go to Kyrenia and we'll all have a good rest." It was that Tuesday when he died.

I gathered my thoughts and walked back into the house. We all cried together quietly for a few minutes, holding on to each other in our grief. Then Asil, assuming his new role as head of the family, took charge. He took care of the formalities, informing the hospital of the death and calling for the *hodja* - a religious man who would come and say prayers for the deceased. Then he gave us a solemn lecture, telling us that we must all maintain our composure in the face of this tragedy and try and help my mother through. "If we all collapse, how will she be able to cope?" he said. "We have to show our dignity in public and we have to see it through to the end of the funeral. Then after that we will shut the door and we will all cry as much as we want."

When eventually my mother showed signs of waking, Fehim whispered to her that my father was sleeping and she should come downstairs with us. When she came down, we gave her some tea and a tranquilliser, saying it would help her relax. Then we told her that my father had died. She was devastated. For more than an hour, she sobbed ceaselessly. She was inconsolable; angry with herself for going to sleep, upset with us for not waking her. All I could do was hold her in my arms. "Maybe God wanted you to sleep so that you would not see it," I told her.

As news of my father's death filtered out, the telephone rang virtually non-stop. If the day of his death had seemed significant to me, the date itself - the 1st April - would not have been lost on my father. He had had a great sense of humour and would have considered it particularly amusing that he would now always be remembered on April Fools' Day. North Cyprus radio and television first reported his death and the word quickly spread to the Turkish Cypriot community in London. Several people who knew my father's wit rang us in confusion, uncertain whether to believe what they had heard or whether it was just one of my father's pranks. Fehim took a call from one middle-aged man who burst into tears on the other end of the line the instant Fehim had to tell him, "No, I'm afraid it is not a joke."

We arranged the funeral for the following afternoon. Burials traditionally take place very quickly in Cyprus, but we wanted to give the many people in Britain and Turkey who knew my father the chance to attend. In the event, hundreds flew in from both places. Asil even had to send his private jet over to Istanbul to pick up mourners who could not get a seat on any of the normal flights. When we drove from the house to the centre of Nicosia to attend the ceremony at the main Selimiye Mosque, we were moved to see the crowds who turned out to pay their respects. From the mosque to Atatürk Square - a distance of more than half a mile - the streets were a sea of people, packed shoulder to shoulder, who somehow parted to let us through behind the coffin as it was carried on its way. Many people said afterwards they could not remember seeing so many mourners at any funeral in North Cyprus before. At the cemetery, the ground was awash with flowers. Florists in North Cyprus were sold out and many wreaths had been flown in from Istanbul. President Rauf Denktas and the Speaker of Parliament, Hakki Atun, made glowing speeches.

It was a fitting finale to a life which had had so much impact in so many different ways. What a great honour for my father - a man born into poverty - that he had achieved a position where almost the entire country wanted to be at his funeral; where tributes flowed from the highest authorities. In his quiet, unassuming way, he had played an enormous role in North Cyprus life, helping so many people through his businesses and through his charitable works. In Britain too, there were many who - if they did but know it - owed much to my father's commercial acumen and his hard work on behalf of Polly Peck and Wearwell. Greatest of all, though, was the impact he had on us, his family. With his death, we suffered our first big loss, and it affected us all immensely - far deeper than we realised at first. We had mixed emotions. Having watched the life simply drain away from such an active, vital man, it was a relief to us to know his suffering was over. Yet we knew also that we had lost in him the person who was the driving force within our ranks. We used to think of him as the solid central support to whom we were all bound, keeping the family together. Now that support was gone and we were cast loose in uncharted territory.

CHAPTER FIVE

Noble Raredon

My father's death was a watershed for all of us. My mother's world was turned upside down, and yet she seemed to find more strength than Asil, Meral or me to cope with her loss. Straight after the funeral, she flew back with us all to London, but spent only about a month there before returning to Cyprus for the traditional prayers said at the mosque forty days after a death. Back on the island, she threw herself into work with a vengeance to take her mind off her loss. During the day, her iron willpower kept her thoughts from straying to my father. But it was at night that the cold feelings of bereavement would creep up on her as she lay in bed. Then, in the dark, accustomed for so many years to dozing lightly until my father came home from an evening out playing cards, she would find herself listening out for the sound of his key in the front door.

My children were knocked sideways by the loss of their beloved "*dede*" (grandfather). They all cried for weeks. Tijen tried to control her own grief so that she could help to console me. Levent, who had spent a holiday in North Cyprus on his own for the first time the year before and had been shown round the businesses by my father, felt as if his "dede" had been taken away from him just as he was beginning to get to know him as an adult. He had been looking forward to the time when he might come to work alongside my father and learn from him, and he felt he had been deprived of that chance. Irfan missed the grandfather in whose honour he had been named so much that he would often dream of him. One night, he came into my bedroom and told me he had woken to see my father standing near his bed, smiling down at him, before rising gently and disappearing through the window. I, too, believed for years that my father was still there in spirit - I would often dream that he was with me, talking about my business problems, and at those times I had the strong feeling that he was sitting right there on the edge of the bed.

Asil was devastated. For forty-five years, our father had been the centre of Asil's life, the major force he respected and his greatest

101

influence. He had been the sounding board for his business ideas and the one to whom Asil looked as a judge. If Asil and he had ever disagreed on business matters, my father had been the only one who could persuade him. Asil trusted his judgement implicitly and even when they did not see eye to eye, Asil would readily listen to his opinion. Ultimately, what he had always wanted was our father's approval. He was shocked, hurt and even angry at his passing. In taking over his role as head of the family, Asil shouldered the weight of the family and its grief along with the ever more enormous burden of Polly Peck. As he set about a life without his father in the background to guide, he reacted to his deep-seated grief by turning away from the past. He seemed to want to shrug off the old, and with it the sadness, and move on to on an entirely new outlook. He seemed deliberately to forge a new life in which there was no link to the world his father had inhabited, thinking perhaps that that way he could somehow escape the pain he felt.

One of the first casualties of this sudden life-change was Asil's relationship with Lesley. Still distraught, Asil became increasingly irritable and impatient. Inevitably, Lesley, Giles and Eren bore the brunt of his moodiness. For weeks, he stayed away as much as possible, as if throwing himself into exhausting business travel would somehow deaden the pain. Instead, he would find himself back home with the demon still intact. When he was home, there were frequent rows. Preoccupied with my own sadness, I could see the gulf between them widening but was powerless to help either of them. Finally, by the early summer, the quarrels reached such a stage that Lesley - generally the mildest, most forgiving of people but pushed over the brink by this perplexing new Asil - announced that she had had enough. That day, she packed her bags and moved out with the children, then just seven and five. She would never again return to live with Asil, although they remained on good terms and my brother often saw his younger sons while he was still in London. Later, Lesley would stand by him when he hit troubled waters during the Polly Peck crisis and beyond.

As fate would have it, the bad patch in Asil and Lesley's relationship coincided with the appointment of a new designer at Inter-City. On one of his visits to the subsidiary, Asil was introduced to the newcomer, Joanne Mackey - a tall, vivacious, wisecracking blonde. He was instantly smitten by this exciting stranger with the model-girl looks and the quirky sense of humour. The contrast between this bubbly personality and the more reserved and serious Lesley could not have been greater - and for Asil, with his entire life and emotions in turmoil, Joanne swept in like a gust of fresh air. Joanne was equally interested in Asil and the two of them began going on regular dinner dates. My mother did not take to Joanne and was instantly disapproving of the budding

102

relationship. She was growing gradually more upset about the unsteady nature of her only son's private life and told him it was about time he settled down with someone who would create a stable and respectable home life for him. I, like the rest of the family, could not understand the attraction Joanne appeared to hold for Asil. I felt certain the relationship would not last, but I would come to realise how much Joanne tried to fit in with Asil's lifestyle and interests - taking an antiques course at Sotheby's and brushing up her speech and appearance. Asil never liked to live alone and - although he maintained his own flat - he always liked to set up home with his current love. In Joanne's case, I urged him not to invite her to stay with him, otherwise she would end up moving in and he would get used to having her around - making the inevitable break-up all the more painful.

Asil paid little attention. He agreed with me that this would not be a permanent relationship and that he and Joanne were really just very good friends. But he was firm that he would go on seeing her. She was funny and made him laugh, he said, and that was something he needed badly after the sadness of the last year. Soon afterwards, when I visited him at the flat one Saturday, it was plain that Joanne had taken up residence. In fact, Asil and Joanne's relationship would continue for five years and would drive a barely perceptible wedge between my brother and the rest of the family, of whose disapproval he was keenly aware. While Joanne was a pleasant person, she had nothing in common with the rest of us and somehow never fitted in. Though she and Asil might call on us once a month, he would rarely bring her to family occasions.

At work, too, Asil seemed determined to shake off the past during that gloomy 1986. He severed all ties with the old days, transferring Polly Peck's headquarters out of the East End that October into far more fashionable premises at Number 42 Berkeley Square. The upmarket move, carried out on the advice of the public relations people, took Polly Peck into the Mayfair district, populated by most of the capital's multinational companies.

For several months, boardroom friction had been bubbling up between the Polly Peck old hands and some of the newcomers. In the spring of 1986 it boiled over. While our father was ill, commercial director Brian Handicott had taken advantage of Asil's absence to lead a boardroom revolt, enlisting the support of some other directors to back a plan to restructure the company, a move which would have reduced the power of the chairman and chief executive - Asil. In the event, the rebellion had simply melted away on Asil's return from North Cyprus, with Handicott resigning from the board, to be replaced by Tahsin Karan in charge of the Turkish operations. Though the ringleader was gone, however, there remained an atmosphere of resentment against those who had backed him. Nemesis arrived in the form of PPI's move to the sumptuous new Berkeley Square offices, furnished with lavish good taste. There, the ground floor and first floor of the white-painted Georgian building, where Asil had his office, were exquisitely furnished with antiques, plush Turkish and Persian carpets and rugs and beautiful paintings. In every room were plants and bowls of fruit. Those of the old directors who had supported Handicott's attempted boardroom coup - Mark Ellis, Anil Doshi and Radar Reshad - were left behind in Commercial Road while Asil and his selected personnel moved on. Number 97 Commercial Road remained as the group's European Regional Head Office, while the chosen few at Berkeley Square operated the group headquarters. Regional head offices were also established in Istanbul, in Hong Kong and New York, reflecting the increasingly cosmopolitan flavour of the company.

Relegated to Commercial Road, Anil Doshi soon parted company with the firm, leaving to pursue his own interests, although the link would never be completely severed and Asil would often look to him for financial advice, even after Doshi's role as finance director was assumed by David Fawcus, an accepted City figure. Fawcus's appointment was a move that pleased Asil's brokers and bankers, who had long been hinting that Polly Peck's shares might be viewed more favourably if there were fewer "foreign" faces on the board. Another stalwart to leave at this point - emphasising the break with the past - was Jean Thomas, who had been Asil's secretary for seventeen years but did not wish to make the move to Mayfair. For all those years, Jean had been a real part of our family and business lives - and I felt her departure was a great loss to Asil and the company. It also marked the beginning of a new image and atmosphere for Polly Peck and my brother. Her position was filled by Dublin-born Aisling Daly, who joined Polly Peck after being PA to the chairman of a firm distributing Louis Ferraud ladies' wear.

The textile division stayed where it was in Commercial Road and I felt more acutely than ever the distance which I sensed opening up even between myself and Asil. Suddenly, the easy lines of communication which had existed when we all worked cheek-by-jowl in Commercial Road were frayed. For the first few months after my father's death, Asil and I had been able to exorcise some of our sorrow during our morning chats. As soon as I reached Commercial Road, I would stop only to look at the post and pick up any messages before walking down the road to Asil's fourth-floor office. There, over a private cup of coffee, we would talk for ten or fifteen minutes about how we felt. We spoke often about our father, his business hopes and dreams and about how we could go about carrying on his ambitions. Often, one of us would have dreamt about my father and we would talk about what we had seen in our sleep. Often, I would cry. Sometimes Asil would break down in tears. These were the only times I saw him weep for our father. During those meetings - the two of us alone, behind closed doors - we could drop the masks we wore in public and let our inner grief show.

When Asil moved to Berkeley Square that autumn, it marked the beginning of some of the most miserable months I had ever experienced. Personally, it was as if I had been struck by two blows in quick succession. First, with my father's death, I had lost the person who had been the major force in my life from earliest recollection. As the weeks wore on, slowly Asil began to play for me the role my father had always fulfilled. In my dreams, I would see my father and would be discussing some business matter with him, when gradually his face would fade out and be replaced by Asil's. Now, just as I was beginning to seek in my brother the guidance my father had provided, I felt that he too was slipping away from me in both physical and emotional distance. He spent his working hours in the West End, far from Commercial Road, and his social life revolved around Joanne. At a time when, emotionally, I needed him most, I was only just realising that he was a public figure and there were many other people besides myself who had a claim to his attention. Increasingly, I began to feel the very special intimacy we had always shared diminishing. The partition of reserve which had sprung up between us after Asil's remarriage seemed to grow slowly. Where we had always been completely open with each other, now there were areas of conversation which we steered around. Knowing how I disapproved of recent turns in his private life, he told me less and less about his feelings and problems. He avoided, too, discussing board-room matters because he knew I felt left out. For my part, I stopped relating some of the more trivial incidents which went on within the family, thinking that he no doubt had far better things to consider. To the outside world, we were as close as any sister and brother, yet during the coming years we would be emotionally more distant from each other than we had ever been. It would take the crisis of 1990 to bring back to me the brother I had known.

At work, I felt as if I had been shunted into a siding - while all the fast trains roared past to Mayfair without me. Polly Peck was doing well and was clearly commanding respect with its plush new headquarters, but the textiles division was plainly not the parent company's favourite child and it was where I seemed destined to remain. When I met Asil for lunch some days, he would keep me up-to-date with his exciting new projects and hopes, yet he could come up with only well-meaning but vague promises for the future whenever I raised my own proposals.

Several times, he assured me that Fehim and I would be appointed to the Polly Peck board, even inviting us as observers to the odd board meeting and announcing his intentions to the other directors. Yet he always had to seek the City's approval before making a move, and the promised board appointments never took place.

Fehim and I spent the year after my father's death marking time and winding down the textiles division's activities. I had passed a subdued fortieth birthday in May and was more anxious than ever to begin exploring new opportunities - me looking to tourism and Fehim to Eastern Europe, where *glasnost* was rapidly breaking down decades-old barriers and opening up vast and exciting new markets. We were still determined, though, to fulfil the deathbed promise I had made my father to give Asil a year's grace. It was a soul-destroying and long drawn-out twelve months, since there was no longer the buzz of healthy trading to keep us occupied. That year's figures sealed my gloom. In textiles, our turnover was £34.6 million - up from the previous year's £33.9 million - but pre-tax profits took a dive from £4.2 million in 1985 to just £1.3 million in the year to September. As if to emphasise our status as "country cousins", the group's performance elsewhere that year remained buoyant. Ironically, Asil was even considering the prospect of developing a hotel in North Cyprus. A year or two earlier, the idea of entering the tourism field would have excited me - now, though, I knew I would not be involved in the way I wanted. I would still not be given a role at board level. The company was making more money than ever before, but life within our little backwater was no longer much fun and, distressingly, I was losing all the old enthusiasm for my work.

From our vantage point on the fringe of Polly Peck that year, we could see a gradual change in the company's image and atmosphere being completed. Where it had once, like Wearwell, been a small and intensely focused production company, it was spreading into a hugely diverse body with no clear core operation, absorbing all the smaller companies which had come within its reach. At the same time, it was beginning to acquire a quite different character. Asil had taken on Polly Peck as his own, becoming its brain and the visionary who would take it in new directions - able to launch new ventures without getting involved in the minutiae of their management. Though I admired him for that vision, for his courage to take risks, I could see that his isolation from everyday matters distanced him from the hands-on approach which had always been the key to success for all our family businesses. As I watched him looking constantly forward to the next idea - and never back to check on the last one - I caught echoes of my father as he set up business after business during our childhood. My father had been fortunate to have my mother behind him, tackling the nitty-gritty to make sure each new project succeeded. It seemed there was no-one like that behind Asil to take care of the detail. In his preoccupation with expansion, he was no longer aware of everything going on within an empire which had grown too big.

And there was plenty going on which I felt he should have known about. Extravagance abounded. Some departments were becoming top-heavy with over-staffing. New key staff were taken on at inflated salaries because advisers said they brought with them the sort of image favoured by the City. Directors who had no understanding of the frugal principles from which our family's success had grown would refuse to travel any other way except first or club class. It was difficult to forge an instant bond of trust with the new arrivals when we simply did not know them. Because they had no idea of the years of hard work behind Polly Peck, it did not hurt some of the newcomers to see time and money going to waste. It hurt me to see that, unlike the old days when staff had wanted to work for our family, now so many of them were interested in Polly Peck largely for the good salary it paid. There were those, too, who resented people like me and Fehim because they could see we had a closeness to Asil which they felt should rightly be theirs. Scornfully, they considered that we only had a position in the company because we were related to the chairman - never thinking that we had earned our position through decades of commitment. Worse still, I could see that many of the people surrounding Asil were "yes men", willing to tell him only the things they believed he wanted to hear and reluctant to risk an argument with him. Much information which would have been genuinely useful never reached his ears from those quarters.

We were not alone in our concerns. There were several people, involved in the company from the earliest days, who confided their own worries and observations to us, thinking that we would be able to communicate them to Asil. Having seen that Asil was unlikely to get a frank opinion elsewhere, I was happy to speak openly to him about the problems within the business. But it proved an embarrassing and frustrating exercise - embarrassing because, even though we were family, we could not seem to get through to him; frustrating because as non-board members it was impossible to mount an effective challenge to the abuses which were going on before our eyes. Whenever we tried to raise the subject with Asil, he would brush it aside, telling us we should not be bothered with such small issues. Sights set firmly on the creation of a world-wide corporation - as publicity photos of the time testify, Asil leaning with one hand resting casually on a metal globe - my brother would exhort us to "think big". He dismissed the matters we raised as too minor to hurt the company in any way. With the benefit of hindsight, he would come to realise that it had been a mistake to allow family authority over the business to be usurped.

————————

The 1st April 1987 could not come soon enough for me. As the first anniversary of my father's death, it was a black date to be looking forward to...yet it was also the end of my year-long obligation to stay with Asil at Polly Peck. Fehim and I took the children to Cyprus to join my mother at the traditional Muslim *mevlit* - memorial prayers said every year on the date of a person's death. We flew back to London in determined mood, no longer prepared to be overlooked at Polly Peck as mere family "hangers-on". We were eager to launch a business venture of our own before the passing years meant it was too late. I felt I had played the supporting role for too long. Had Polly Peck been a family company, I would have been content with that. But with the company the way it was - with cosmetic appointments being made over my head - it was a humiliation I could no longer stomach.

The day we got back, I went round to see Asil in Berkeley Square and told him of our decision, explaining how we had held off for a year in accordance with my father's wishes, but now wanted our own business. Asil was taken aback, but when he asked me to think again, I told him, "I have made up my mind. Please—if you care for me and you want me to be happy, don't object. Just let me go." That was when Asil realised just how determined I was. It was agreed that we should leave officially at the end of April, but would take a holiday for the rest of the month. I left with the promise that I would keep him closely informed of whatever we decided to do.

At that stage, in fact, Fehim and I just wanted out of Polly Peck and had little in the way of clear plans for our business future. What we were certain of, though, was that we wanted to build up a company of our own and recapture some of the old family feeling that we had watched drain away from Wearwell and the mighty Polly Peck. First, free at last to do what we wanted, we whisked the children and my mother off on an eighteen-day Easter holiday to the Far East, sightseeing all the way from Singapore to Hong Kong, Bali and Bangkok with Fehim's cousin, Ziya Özkan, and his wife and some close friends. On the exotic island of Bali we all relaxed for a few days, glad to have shaken off the cares which seemed to have hung over us for so long. We flew back to London refreshed and eager for the new challenge ahead - and also armed with one idea which we would put into practice three years later. It was my ambition to build a hotel in North Cyprus and I was impressed by the way the Bali Hyatt Hotel where we stayed was seated around the fringe of a spectacular square turquoise swimming pool with a bar in the centre, creating an intimate and friendly atmosphere. As we sat over drinks one night, I turned to Ziya - an architect - and told him: "Look at this very carefully because one day this is how I want to build a hotel in Cyprus." Smiling, Ziya took a paper napkin from the table and made a ball-point pen sketch of the hotel's layout. That rough drawing would later be part of the inspiration for the hotel we opened in north Cyprus in spring 1990 - the Olive Tree, nestling in the foothills of the Kyrenia mountains overlooking the Mediterranean.

Our first task when we returned from the Far East was to set up a business which would tide us over until we could find the vehicle we needed to carry us on our new ventures. We planned either to launch or buy into a public company and clearly this would take some time to organise. Since textiles were what we knew best, we decided to begin with a clothing enterprise and came up with Tri-Sun Textiles. The name referred to Tijen, Levent and Irfan, the three "suns" on my horizon. When we had announced our intention to leave Polly Peck, Asil had decided to shut the textiles division in London - confirming my suspicion that he had really only kept it going for our sake. Güner, going back to his civil engineering training, moved to PPI's building development department. In Cyprus, my mother refused to lay off her Wearwell staff, so instead she took over the factory and changed its name to Saftex, keeping on her workforce and taking on CMT orders from other customers - a business she still runs today, at the age of seventy-six. In London, meanwhile, several of our textiles division staff - some of them long-serving employees dating back to the early Wearwell days - found themselves out of work. Fehim and I saw our new Tri-Sun Textiles as a means of helping some of them out of unemployment. We took on a handful, including Canan, by then eight months pregnant with her first child, who was so determined to be part of the action that she worked right up to the day before the baby was born. We had some of the garments machined in London and sent others out to Cyprus. We dealt only with customers in Poland, Fehim keeping up business links with the Eastern Bloc customers he had known from Wearwell. It was never intended to be a huge money-maker, but it was a useful stop-gap for all of us.

Meanwhile, I set out on the road which would eventually lead to Noble Raredon. Number one on my agenda was to find us a suitable base. Asil and Polly Peck had seemed able to command far greater attention and respect since the move to Berkeley Square, so I could see the importance of finding the right office in the right location from which to view potential companies to buy. I set my sights on Mayfair and started looking around. After three months of searching, I found just what I was looking for - a five-storey Edwardian building complete with basement and attic, once a family house, at number 73 South Audley Street, just round the corner from Berkeley Square. I was immediately taken with the classically-styled stone frontage, the attractive wrought-iron railings and the three broad stone steps leading to the high, arched wooden front door. Inside were airy rooms with high ceilings and a beautiful staircase. The building badly needed decorating and there was only a short lease of five years available, but this meant the rent would be relatively cheap - £25,000 a year. Fehim agreed that it would be the perfect base and we signed the lease in July 1987.

We had the building painted throughout, polished up the wooden floors and put up attractive curtains at the high sash windows. I furnished the main offices with antiques, some of which were given by my mother, and made sure there were always plenty of fresh flowers in vases around the building. I tried to maintain a comfortable, homely atmosphere and, apart from in the accounts department, there were few computers to be seen. Many of the people who came to visit us there during the next five and a half years would comment that it felt rather like stepping into a genteel drawing room. My instinct about the importance of the office image would also be proved right - I would glimpse from the faces of merchant bankers and brokers that they were suitably impressed by what they saw. A month after we signed the lease, the building was ready for us to move in. Tri-Sun Textiles occupied the basement, but the whole building was clearly too big for our needs in those initial days.

At that time, we had recently been advised to set up family trusts for the money which my father had left - he had died a rich man after all his years of hard work and had been one of the original investors in Polly Peck when it was a penny share. Before he died, my father had sold his personal Polly Peck shareholding because he had wanted some portion of the family's money to be spread over a wider range of investments. He did not leave his money direct to family members - he always worried that some might prove spendthrifts in the future and I believe he had a premonition that times might not always be so good - so he had asked for the money to be put in trust. For this purpose, Asil was setting up a company to administer the investments of the private trusts. Elizabeth Forsyth - previously his personal banker at Citibank - was employed by the company. Elizabeth's job and the management company had no connection with Polly Peck, and I can only recall one occasion when Asil went to visit her at her office.

The trust administration company would come to be called South Audley Management - a name which I helped to provide. In its early days, Elizabeth and the three staff she had taken on to help her had nowhere to work, since Asil considered it inappropriate for them to be at Polly Peck. Our offices were too big for our needs at the time, so I offered to let Elizabeth's team operate for the time being out of the empty ground floor at 73 South Audley Street, leaving the remaining upper storeys for Fehim and me. They moved in during August 1987, beginning a temporary residence which inspired the choice of name. A year later, when Fehim and I bought into our own public company, we felt it would no longer be right for us to share our headquarters with South Audley Management, so they moved out into their own premises at 24 Berkeley Square, just across the way from Polly Peck. I had no idea that my brief "cohabitation" with South Audley Management would come back to haunt me three years later when SAM - as it was known for short - became the focus of intense media speculation and allegations of illegal share trading.

The months which followed sped past in a haze. Fehim travelled regularly to Poland pursuing new orders, while I oversaw Tri-Sun's operations and kept up the quest for a company. We had enlisted merchant banker, Panton Corbett, and the bank where he worked, Singer & Friedlander who had been Wearwell's merchant bankers, to find us a suitable business to buy into. It had to be a firm with a good core business, on the foundations of which we would be able to build an international corporation. We were also looking to acquire a minimum fifty per cent of the shares. Just waiting for word from them kept me in a state of perpetual excitement, knowing that this time we would be in the driving seat. I was also sure that this time, having learned our lessons from Polly Peck, we would be in a position to accomplish quickly what we wanted to do. I had quite recovered from the gloom which had settled upon me during the last year at Polly Peck. I was back to my old self, happy to leap out of bed every morning and rush into the office, which to me felt like a home-from-home.

It was April 1988 when word came of a company we might be interested in. I had to smile when I saw the information sent over to South Audley Street. The company was called Gnome Photographic Products PLC - an unlikely-sounding business to become the basis for the giant international entity I was intending. Still, when I looked closer, it certainly had potential. And it was a family company, which instantly attracted me. Based in Cardiff, Gnome had been founded in 1938 by the grandfather of the current majority shareholder, Karin Brass. It manufactured and sold a range of photographic and visual aid equipment, principally overhead projectors, of which it was Britain's sole maker. The latest accounts, for the half-year to the end of November 1987, showed a turnover of £1.2 million and pre-tax profits of £247,640.

There were also assets amounting to £1.77 million. Mrs Brass had inherited control of the company from her mother, who had run the firm until her death in 1986, but she wanted to sell her shareholding.

The more I thought about Gnome Photographic Products, the more sure I became that this was the right company for us. I told Panton Corbett to set up a meeting between us, Karin Brass and Gnome's managing director, James Hallsworth, who had been running the firm for several years. I had not seen the Gnome factory, but I had such a good "gut feeling" about the firm that I felt we should go after it. We had already asked Arseven Gümüs - a Turkish Cypriot friend and accountant who had recently returned to the UK after being Polly Peck's senior executive in Turkey - to study the books of any firm we considered and give his opinion as a finance expert. But I made a snap decision not to show him the details about Gnome straight away, unwilling to let anything put a damper on my enthusiasm. Nor did Fehim see the papers immediately. He was in Poland at the time and, without consulting him, I asked for the meeting to be on the day after he was due back. When I picked him up from the airport, I told him everything. Fehim often teased me about my habit of making major changes at home while he was away. This time, still tired from the journey, he put his head back, closed his eyes and said calmly, "So this time it wasn't knocking down a wall or changing the furniture, but going out to buy a company."

That first meeting took place in early May at Singer & Friedlander's offices in Bishopsgate, east London. I carried my brand new "lucky briefcase" - a fortieth birthday present from Fehim to mark the new beginning in my business life. As someone who had always worked behind the scenes, this was my first official engagement in the City and I was bursting with excitement, although I tried to calm down by reminding myself that there were three or four other rivals interested in buying Gnome. Mrs Brass and Mr Hallsworth were joined at the meeting by Peter Dunscombe, representing the Imperial Trust Fund, who had the second biggest shareholding after Mrs Brass. Mrs Brass was anxious to sound me out so that she could choose from among the rival bidders the one who would do the best for Gnome, its employees and shareholders.

Karin Brass and I hit it off straight away and James Hallsworth gave me the impression that he liked me. I admitted I was not interested in overhead projectors, but as Gnome was the only manufacturer in Britain I would stand by that side of the business and would try to develop it further. As a major shareholder, Peter Dunscombe's opinion was of crucial importance because we would need to win the support of the big institutional shareholders if we were to have successful rights issues to raise capital for expansion. I knew, too, that his verdict would have a major influence on Karin Brass's decision. I must have convinced him, because at the end of the meeting he announced that he would be willing to retain his stake if we took over. The next day, I went to Asil's office to tell him I had found a company I wanted to buy. He listened to all the information about the factory, the product, the business and its track record and then told me, "Go for it. I think you're right - it's perfect." I was relieved to get his approval; it inspired me with more confidence. To this day I'm not sure, though, what I would have done if he had advised me not to go ahead.

During the next fortnight, we went to two more meetings about Gnome. Having secured approval for our plans with the adviser to Fairweather Investments, the family trust which was going to buy the shares for us, on the 18th of May, we signed contracts to buy 64.9 per cent of Gnome's issued share capital from Karin Brass - 1,632,384 shares - at a total cost of £4.489 million. She was to retain a one per cent shareholding and remain on the board temporarily to allow a smooth transition. We paid 275p for each share, which then stood at 250p. Having acquired more than thirty per cent of the company, we were obliged by the City's rules on take-overs to make a cash offer - also at 275p - for the rest of the shares we did not already own. The offer valued the company at £6.9 million.

Details of our purchase and the share offer were made public in a press statement from Singer & Friedlander later that day, in which it was said that the existing board of Gnome and its advisers believed our acquisition of the company would introduce the experience and skills needed to develop the business. The news was greeted with excitement in the City, where it was quickly noted that I was Asil's sister. The *Investors' Chronicle* nine days later tipped shareholders that it was "worth staying on for the ride," adding, "There's always a chance Gnome could turn into another Polly Peck." By then, the shares had soared to 400p.

Soon after we signed the contracts, Fehim and I took the train from London to Cardiff to go and view our new business premises for the first time. Until then, we had only seen photographs of the factory, because Karin Brass and James Hallsworth feared a tour of inspection by potential buyers might further upset the staff, who were already feeling a little insecure at the prospect of a take-over. It was the first time we had ever been to Wales and we were both keen to see our new purchase. My first impression as we pulled up outside the factory was favourable. There was a small lawned area with flower beds outside the two-storey brick building and it had obviously been tended carefully. When we walked inside, though, I got quite a shock - the interior of the factory was like something out of the Victorian era. Not only was the factory very aged; so too were a lot of the staff. Of the 120 men and women working there, some had been with Gnome for thirty to forty years, joining the company as fifteen-year-old school leavers. I had to hide a smile when James Hallsworth, seventy-three years old himself, would introduce us to a fifty-odd-year-old as "young so-and-so". Our reception by the staff was mixed. There were some friendly looks, some suspicious and others downright hostile. There we were, this couple who were not just from London, but foreigners to boot; no-one was sure what we had planned for the firm, but they knew their future now depended on us and they did not know what to think. Sensing this fearful reserve, Fehim and I wrote out an announcement telling the employees we wanted to keep the factory going, to modernise it and build upon the existing business. The announcement was pinned to the notice-board when we left and after that we received a far better welcome whenever we visited. We used to travel to Cardiff every month for a board meeting and it struck me there how warm and friendly everyone was in Wales, compared to reserved Londoners.

After that initial visit, we began to lay our plans. I was appointed company chairman and Fehim became chief executive, responsible for supervising our planned Polish investment programme and overseeing the trading side. Arseven Gümüs was still with us, taking on the preparation of feasibility studies and the roles of company secretary and internal auditor, and at the annual meeting he would be named our corporate development director. One of our first tasks was to headhunt suitable key staff to lead us into the leisure and tourism market. The man we chose was Trevor Davies, the former international director of travel giants, Thomas Cook, who would advise us on all our leisure investments and would be managing director at Tri-Sun Travel. The shares would leap 50p to 485p on the day, in August, when we announced his appointment to the board as an executive director in charge of the leisure division. Trevor also brought to us Dennis Barrett, another former Thomas Cook man, who became the general manager of our travel business. For the first few months, Arseven Gümüs, assisted by an old family friend Mehmet Yilmaz, would run the finance department. Later, in December 1988, the board would be completed by the appointment of David Heaton, former finance chief of a firm called Sintrom, as finance director, controlling the company's purse-strings and liaising with the financial institutions.

Before we could get down to business in earnest, I had to deal with another very important "merger" - Tijen's wedding to Rifat. There were to be two weddings, one in London and another to follow in North

Cyprus. The first wedding was set for the 16th July, soon after Tijen was to graduate with a business law degree, and Asil - keeping a promise he had made to me when Tijen was just a baby - arranged a lavish party at his house in Cyprus for the 3rd August. The planning went on for months, and while I spared no expense on the physical preparations, equally there was no effort shirked in trying to ensure that the day went smoothly. Asil's already complicated love life meant it was a nightmare trying to juggle the invitations and plan the seating so as to avoid offending anyone - and avoid any embarrassing confrontations. Tijen wanted her young cousins, Lesley's sons, Giles and Eren, to be among her pageboys for the evening celebrations at The Dorchester, so I told Asil that we would like to invite Lesley along too. Of the women in Asil's life, Lesley had always been closest to Tijen and seemed somehow more a part of the family. By then, of course, he was living with Joanne, so she too would be invited, but I told Asil he could not sit beside her because it would upset Lesley. By way of an excuse, I asked him to be our mother's escort at the top table. Aysegül would not be in the country on the day, which was fortunate because it would have been impossible to think of bringing her together in a room with Lesley. I told Asil, though, that I would like to invite his and Aysegül's sons, Birol and Serhan - although they had always refused to have anything to do with their father's younger sons by Lesley.

At that time, twenty-four-year-old Birol had dropped out of Kent University and was working in the City as a stockbroker. Serhan was thirteen and a pupil at Eton College. Giles and Eren were only nine and seven and lived with their mother. One day, when Birol visited me at my office, I steered the conversation round to the family. I told him how sad we had all been for him and Serhan when their father and mother had divorced, but we all had to accept the situation. I said he was now old enough to appreciate that his father had had relationships with other women - and to accept the fact that Asil had two more sons. I knew the younger boys were anxious to get to know their elder half-brothers, of whom Lesley always spoke kindly. "I am sure your father would be much happier knowing that his four sons could at least be friends," I urged Birol. "I know it is difficult and you resent them, but you should give them a chance—the other two are still very young and they could look up to you."

At first, I thought I was getting through to Birol, but when I suggested arranging a meeting between the four of them, he refused point-blank, saying, "I never want to meet them."

Having failed in my attempt at reconciliation, I then had to broach the subject of the wedding arrangements. He said he and Serhan would not come if Lesley was there, so we finally settled on a compromise -

Lesley would attend the evening reception and Birol and Serhan would come to the registry office in the morning and the buffet lunch in our garden at home, to neither of which we would invite Lesley. Lesley, in turn, agreed to the plan.

As I tried to iron out the family difficulties, I was also keeping a discreet but close eye on Tijen. Because of the way their engagement had taken place, I was anxious to ensure that she and Rifat did not feel pressurised into tying the knot. Had I not observed their childhood friendship turn into a deeper bond, I would have been very reluctant to let the wedding take place, but my worries were assuaged when Tijen reassured me one night that they were both very happy and in love.

Only close family members were at Ilford Registry Office for the noon wedding ceremony, at which the witnesses were Asil and Güner, who was uncle to both bride and groom. The evening reception for 350 proved an event which combined both a Turkish flavour through the festivities themselves, which included a singer and musicians, and an old English grandeur, created by the dark wooden panelling and ornate gilded decor. The newly-weds spent the night at The Dorchester, before being flown out in Asil's private jet the next morning for a week-long honeymoon in Marbella. A week after the new Mr and Mrs Atun returned from honeymoon to my parents' old house next door to ours, it was time to fly out to North Cyprus for the party which Asil had organised - a joint event to celebrate their marriage and Fehim's and my twenty-fifth wedding anniversary earlier that year. Asil had invited some 750 guests to the garden party and buffet dinner at Loch Manor - an old stone house belonging to the family, set in magnificent gardens at Çatalköy, five miles east of Kyrenia. As we turned through the wrought iron gates into the gravelled driveway, hidden from the road by the traditional yellow stone wall, it was like entering a fairy-tale realm. Asil had insisted on making all the preparations for the night himself, and I was stunned by the transformation he had effected. I hardly recognised the place as I looked at the trees glowing with tiny lights, violinists played from the balconies, the candle-lit tables groaning with food being served by scurrying waiters, huge decorative stands of flowers imported from Turkey, and the garden's own blooming shrubs which cast their exotic scent into the night air. It was a truly magical event which was the talk of North Cyprus for months afterwards.

After that fantasy night, we all came back down to earth with a bump. It was straight back to business for me and Fehim and we were joined by Tijen, who came to work as the assistant to the company secretary and to run the personnel department. Our next move was to change the name of the company from Gnome Photographic Products, which did not create the right aura for the company we planned to develop. We racked our brains to try and think of a suitable title but it was only when I was driving home from South Audley Street one day that I had a sudden idea. I decided to name the firm in tribute to my father and brother, who had been my business mentors. *Asil* meant "noble" in Turkish and our family name from my father, *Nadir*, translated into English as "rare". I played around with the combination of words and came up with "Noble Raredon". That night, I asked Fehim what he thought. He repeated the name a few times and then said: "Yes, it has a good ring to it." I did not realise then that even Fehim - along with the rest of the family and many other people - had not caught on to the family reference. Only afterwards did I discover that Fehim thought the word "Raredon" was a play on the name of well-known snooker player Ray Reardon!

Noble Raredon it was, and the name change was announced in August, though it did not take effect until after the annual general meeting two months later. August was also the month when we announced our intention to restructure the company into three divisions - engineering, leisure and trading. The engineering division would comprise the existing photographic products business, to be renamed Elite Optics and to remain under the stewardship of James Hallsworth, as a non-executive director. The trading division would consist of Tri-Sun Textiles and the proposed new ventures into Poland. Leisure was to be the umbrella division for the travel and hotels operations.

I knew we had to work fast if we were to be able to launch our travel business in time to catch bookings for the 1989 summer season, when we aimed to take 25,000 British tourists to mainland Turkey and North Cyprus. By August, we had already formed a company, Tri-Sun Travel, to handle the business within the leisure division, and were busy seeking out hotels in Turkey and Cyprus, chartering flights for the following year and making preparations for our first brochure. We decided to base Tri-Sun in Peterborough, which had good transport links and was close to our proposed departure airport, Stansted. We also set up a firm called Tri-Sun Tourism Industries in North Cyprus, headed by former TRNC Tourism Ministry under-secretary, Mehmet Ziya Berkman, to act as the general manager for our North Cyprus operations, including being handling agent for our holidaymakers once they arrived on the island. Trevor advised us that another name would be needed for the tour operator itself, saying Tri-Sun was not catchy enough to command the public's attention. For days, we sat around trying to dream up a name. Between us, we arrived at the name "Mosaic". It was an inspired choice. It conveyed the historic flavour of Turkey and also carried the same meaning in other languages - a must, since I wanted to branch out into the French and German travel industries, where we realised we could sell holidays at a higher price than in the UK. The launch later that year of Mosaic Holidays in the UK would be followed by the establishment of sister operators, Mosaic Reisen in Bremen, Germany.

By the time our first annual general meeting took place on Wednesday the 12th October, we were working flat-out and attracting considerable interest in the City and the newspapers. I was amused and rather flattered to be described as a "Bond Street siren" in the *Mail on Sunday's* money page. Many of the reports focused on the fact that I was Asil's sister and there was clearly widespread hope that, as the *Daily Express* put it, the "family magic" would rub off on our business too. I often had to point out, though, that while Asil and I were very close and he was available to give brotherly advice, he had no stake in our company at all.

Investors were obviously happy with what they saw, too. On the day of the annual meeting, our share price stood at 695p - well over twice what it was when we had taken over just five months earlier. Later, we would take advice and reduce the share price by splitting the existing shares. Following our take-over of Gnome, much of my time would be taken up, as chairman, giving presentations to woo potential institutional shareholders such as pension funds, whose considerable financial backing was vital if we were to be able to raise the cash for the developments we had in mind. Centre stage for the first time, as the head of my own company, I found it an ordeal at first to face these rooms full of pinstripe-suited City gentlemen. At my first presentation to the Friends Provident life assurance group, I remember being struck by sheer terror as I sat there at the head of the table, trying to look confident with my navy suit and carefully prepared information pack, and realising that they were all quietly waiting for me to speak. I felt sure I had lost my voice, but when I glanced across to see Sally White - our account manager at merchant bankers, Paribas - nod encouragingly towards me, I knew I had no option but to take the plunge and begin my talk. Soon, I shook off the tremble in my voice and gained in confidence as I warmed to the theme. I never got rid of those initial butterflies, but after a couple of presentations I came to realise that, serious as my audience appeared, I could win them over with my enthusiasm for the company. After all, these were investors seeking innovative and unusual firms which offered a chance of good profits - and our venture fitted the bill. Within two years of our take-over, the company's list of shareholders would include the twelve most impressive institutions, who were recognised as investment leaders in the City.

We emerged from the October 1988 annual meeting having been officially renamed Noble Raredon, and having revealed that our tourism business would not only take travellers to Turkey, but would also deal with holidays in North Cyprus. I expected this announcement to provoke a response from the Greek Cypriots, who had always vociferously opposed any schemes to bring new trade to the North, which they considered an illegal regime. There was little negative comment at first, though. In November 1988, we launched the first Mosaic Holidays brochure with something of a fanfare. I travelled to Peterborough for a special ribbon-cutting ceremony with Peterborough Mayor, Connie Gray. The event received wide coverage, including a major article with photograph in the *Travel Trade Gazette* and another story in *Travel News*. A week later, the Greek Cypriots hit back with a letter and story in *Travel News* claiming Mosaic was "immoral" in promoting holidays to North Cyprus. The accusation came as no surprise to us and we shook it off easily. But there was far worse to come.

We worked hard behind the scenes to ensure that Mosaic would be well promoted throughout January, February and March - the crucial time for holiday bookings in the UK. Trevor had persuaded Thomas Cook to sell our holidays across the country and we also devised a massive advertising campaign which included large, colourful posters in London underground stations urging commuters to "Discover Northern Cyprus". The ads were launched after New Year 1989 and on the first day we were inundated with calls at South Audley Street telling us how attractive they were. It was the first time North Cyprus had been placed in the public spotlight in Britain in a professionally marketed way. Two days later, the threatening telephone calls and letters started coming to the office and to our home in South Woodford. The advertising agency which had prepared the posters also received more than twenty calls. One letter warned me that unless I stopped marketing North Cyprus, I would be in "big trouble". One caller, a university lecturer, said she wished to "remind" me that I was trying to "sell stolen property". I had had enough experience of the Greek Cypriot attacks on Asil to be able to shrug off the approaches, but two days later came a development which was impossible to ignore. That day, we learned that the Mosaic posters in the underground stations had all been blacked out.

I was livid. We had paid about £100,000 for a three-month contract with London Transport to display our adverts. Trevor Davies went straight round to London Transport and reported back that the posters had been withdrawn after the underground authorities received four telephone calls from Greek Cypriots. The callers had complained that the posters were offensive to Greeks and had threatened to bomb the train stations where the posters were on show. We could not comprehend how threats of violence had had so much influence. Every promotion would be bound to upset someone, we argued, but that did not mean they should be allowed to get their own way by making bomb threats. After several meetings, telephone calls and legal advice, London Transport agreed to reinstate the posters in April - but by then we knew it would be too late for most of the holiday trade. We only managed to get some of the £100,000 back.

And so it went on. Sometimes adverts which we wanted to place in certain publications would be withdrawn at the last minute. Travel agents would refuse to carry our brochure or sell our holidays because they feared losing their business with the lucrative Greek and Greek Cypriot holiday trade. We learned that many agents had been told they would be blacklisted by the Greek and South Cyprus tourist industries. As the threatening telephone calls continued to come in, we warned our sales staff - all of whom we had taken out to North Cyprus to see for themselves the place they were selling - to expect some unpleasantness but not to be alarmed.

There was no time to relax that January. Just as we emerged, battered but unbeaten, from the problems over the adverts, a fresh crisis struck. Our first passengers to North Cyprus were due to fly out with Toros Air on the 19th March, and with seven and a half weeks to go before their departure, we had a visit from the airline's owner, who offered us a half share in Toros Air for £3 million. We had no intention of going into the risky airline business during our first year's trading, but said we would think about it. Shortly afterwards, we had a call from a creditor Swiss bank looking for confirmation that we were going to be partners in Toros Air. Trevor and Arseven flew out to Switzerland to look at the accounts. What they saw filled us all with horror. Toros Air needed $12.5 million if it was to survive the summer. By then, we had thousands of bookings, all due to travel with Toros Air, and the first flight was already full. I had recurrent nightmares about hundreds of passengers turning up at Stansted to find there was no plane and the thought of the bad publicity gave me cold shivers.

The day we heard the news about Toros, I went to Asil for advice for the first time since quitting Polly Peck. "We're in trouble," I told him as I sat down across the desk from him. At the time, Polly Peck had just started up its own leisure division and had brought in someone to head up the new operations. I suggested that if Polly Peck was going into the leisure and hotel fields in Turkey and North Cyprus, it would be useful

120

to the company to have its own airline. Asil started off by saying he did not think it was the right time for PPI to start up an airline, but when he saw how my face fell at his answer, he sat back looking thoughtful. When I told him just how desperate the situation was, he said: "OK - I'll finance it myself, but you have to do all the hard work of setting it up and running it yourselves." My relief on hearing those words was enormous, but I still knew what a massive job we faced. I had never heard of anyone setting up an airline from scratch in seven and a half weeks, but I was determined to give it my best shot.

The task in hand was to establish a charter company based in Turkey - the only way we could carry passengers to North Cyprus without breaching the rules of the international air travel body IATA. Under Turkish law, no foreigner may own more than forty-nine per cent of a Turkish airline, but this would be no problem for us, since Asil, who would be the owner, had dual Turkish and British nationality. We knew the situation demanded the leadership of someone familiar with the airline industry, so we immediately set about finding the right person. By chance, Yalim Tilev, the general manager of Toros Air's European division, who also had experience with Turkish Airlines and SwissAir, came to sound out Trevor Davies about the possibility of Noble Raredon going into partnership in Toros and agreed to join us.

With Yalim in charge, the airline project began moving quickly. He carried out a feasibility study and recruited a technical expert who inspected different planes available for lease. The feasibility study showed us that it would be a very profitable project which, despite the initial outlay, would quickly become self-financing. Meanwhile, we had a logo designed for the airline - to be called Noble Air - and had uniforms designed to team in with the airline's colours of navy blue and gold. Then we signed a forty-two-month lease on two ex-Air France Boeing 727-200s and had them painted up in the Noble Air livery. I could see Asil was impressed by the speed and care with which we got down to work. We, in turn, were impressed by his contacts in Turkey, who on a few occasions managed to cut through the swathes of red tape. On a number of occasions, he spoke to government ministers in Ankara himself to get the formalities speeded up. With just a few days to spare before the inaugural flight, Noble Air was signed and sealed. Our planes were still not quite ready, but we had chartered other aircraft to tide us over the first two flights. We congratulated ourselves on a job well done and took a well-earned breather for a day or two before the flight went out. Just as we thought everything was finally under control, though, a disaster struck which it took all Asil's high-level influence to solve.

The first Noble Air flight, carrying 160 travel agents, was due out of Stansted on a Saturday morning and the arrangements had all been made. On the Friday morning, less than twenty-four hours before take-off, we received a fax message in the office from the Civil Aviation Authority telling us our flight slot had been cancelled because it was understood our destination was North Cyprus and that was an unrecognised country. The fax was signed by a man called Kakoullis - we later learned he was Greek - who was in charge of the eastern Mediterranean region at the CAA. I held the fax in my hand in total disbelief. What business was it of theirs, where we were going after we landed in Turkey? The information that related to them was that we were flying to Istanbul, a legitimate international destination. From that point on, the flight was to become an internal Turkish flight and its route was the concern only of the Turkish and Turkish Cypriot authorities. The entire office went frantic trying to salvage the situation. Trevor rang some of his travel business contacts then went to the CAA and told the officials there that they had no right to stop the flight. The CAA refused to budge.

By about one o'clock that afternoon it was clear we were getting nowhere and in desperation I rang Asil, who was on a business trip to Istanbul. By a huge stroke of luck, I managed to catch him on his car phone. I tried to explain to him what was wrong, but I was so worked up I kept gabbling and tripping over the words. "Slow down, stay calm and tell me what the problem is," he soothed over the line. On the third try, I managed to explain properly what had happened. "OK," said Asil, "I'm on my way to have lunch with the British Ambassador and I'll talk to him about it. I'll call you later." As I put the receiver down, I knew there was nothing more we could do. We would just have to wait for Asil to ring back.

For three interminable hours we stayed in the office, pacing around nervously, making pots of tea and jumping every time the phones went. As the time wore on, I began to lose all hope. I knew that if we could not sort anything out before the CAA offices closed for the weekend at five o'clock, we would not be able to save the flight. It was about four o'clock when Asil called from Istanbul with news I hardly dared to believe. He said he had been assured by the ambassador that the Foreign Office in London had instructed Kakoullis to let the flight leave as scheduled. Sure enough, a few minutes later, Kakoullis sent us a second fax saying the flight had been reinstated and giving the precise details and departure time. Then he telephoned personally to check we had received the message, chiding Trevor that there had been no need for "diplomatic pressure" to sort the problem out. From that day, we never had any more trouble with the CAA.

The next morning, Fehim, Trevor and I drove to Stansted to see our first passengers off before going back to the office to crack open a bottle of vintage champagne I had bought for the occasion. At the airport too, it was like a carnival. We gave champagne and free drinks to everyone travelling on the first few flights and the first flight was greeted by a display of Turkish folk dancing when it got to Ercan, the airport serving North Cyprus. Throughout that season there was fresh orange juice and posies of sweet-scented jasmine and fluffy yellow mimosa flowers for all the ladies as they arrived in Cyprus - posies which my mother got all her neighbours to make up. The newly-painted Noble Air planes made their debut in time for the third flight and again we went to Stansted to see them - we had all seen the blue and gold design on a model plane in the office, but it was like witnessing a dream come true to see the huge aircraft taxiing across the tarmac. Ours was the first Turkish airline to use Stansted and we were accorded one of the best gates nearest to the terminal building. Watching the passengers walk on and off that gleaming jet for the first time, it felt as if I had given birth to a fourth baby - exhausted, yet triumphant. It had been the most heart-stoppingly exciting two months of my life and as I looked in the mirror later I was sure I caught sight of the first few grey hairs.

For the rest of the summer, as a total of 7,500 people flew between western Europe, Turkey and North Cyprus on Noble Air, the excitement continued. A nervous flyer, I insisted that Noble Air's ground crew kept me informed about every flight. They would ring me whenever a plane took off and then there would be a call from the other end to say it had arrived safely. Every night I offered a silent prayer that nothing should go wrong. In fact, it was only through travelling by Noble Air and talking to the pilots in the cockpit that I was able to gain some confidence in flying. By the end of that summer, Noble Air had already recouped the start-up costs and was in the black. The two original planes had been used to the full - when they were not flying Mosaic passengers, they shuttled backwards and forwards carrying Turkish "guest workers" living in Germany. Demand was already so great that we had to lease two more aircraft in preparation for the 1990 season, doubling the fleet. Noble Raredon already had the sole agency for ticket sales in the UK and mainland Europe. Asil awarded us an option to buy forty-nine per cent of Noble Air at cost price.

Tourism was not the only busy and successful side of Noble Raredon. Fehim had a hectic year after the Gnome take-over developing trade in Poland. He had several friends and business contacts in the Eastern Bloc country and had been dealing there for eight years since Wearwell days. He visited frequently and on occasion I would go with him. We had both come to love the country and its people. As Poland began to emerge from the shadow of communism, we were struck forcibly by the many and varied needs there which could be met by businesses like ours. In Warsaw, the shops were virtually empty and there was scope for dealing in pretty well any consumer goods.

In a hangover from the Wearwell days, Tri-Sun Textiles was already making low-cost high fashion clothes for Poland. They were sold to Pevex - one of the country's two main duty-free organisations - which had about 1,000 outlets across the country. We knew, though, that we had to spread our net far wider if we were to take advantage of the spectacular opportunities presenting themselves. Though our trading links with the Poles long pre-dated the fall of communism, the rest of Europe - urged by then-President Lech Walesa - was beginning to catch on to the country's potential and we were anxious not to be overtaken in the rush to invest. We were waiting in the wings at just the right moment, and with wages even lower in Poland than they were in the Mediterranean, at an average ten dollars a month, we knew we could be just as successful with ventures there as we had been in Cyprus.

Tri-Sun Trading, under Fehim, began to branch out steadily from the clothing side. During his years of contacts there, Fehim had made firm friends with a Polish buyer, Ewa Donde, and her family. When we decided it would be best for us to open an office in Warsaw, to seek out new business and liaise with South Audley Street, we asked her to take charge there. She agreed, and the office was launched in September 1988. Ewa quickly found more customers willing to take our clothes. She also discovered that there was a huge but largely unmet demand for training shoes. Via the South Korean Embassy in London and the Board of Trade, Fehim located a major training shoe manufacturer in South Korea and soon Tri-Sun Trading was buying tens of thousands of pairs of sports shoes a month and exporting them to Poland. Business at Tri-Sun Trading and Textiles was beginning to take off just as surely as Mosaic Holidays and Noble Air had done.

Our first year at Noble Raredon also saw us laying the foundations for major future investments. On the tourism side, I took the first steps towards my dream of establishing an international hotel group - and thereby creating a vertically integrated tourism business in which we could manage every link in the chain, from the tour operator, through the airline, to the holiday accommodation and services. In the latter part of 1988, when Fehim, Trevor and I had visited North Cyprus to contract the hotels there for our Mosaic customers the following summer, Trevor had commented that there were not enough good quality hotels in the country to meet the demand for package holidays. We decided there and then that the only way for us to be sure of the quality we needed for our clients was to build and run our own hotel.

One sunny afternoon, Fehim and I drove Trevor up into the foothills of the Kyrenia mountains, about five miles east of the resort town. We drove up about a mile and a half from the main coast road, through narrow twisting lanes which led between huddles of whitewashed houses in the village of Çatalköy. A few hundred yards above the village, in a quiet spot below the pine-clad crags, we stopped the car and got out. "What do you think of building a holiday village here?" I asked Trevor, gesturing towards a wide stretch of scrubland, dotted with carob and olive trees. Trevor stood for a few moments, taking in the mountain backdrop and the view over the village to the blue sea beyond. "Fantastic!" was his response. The land we stood on already belonged to Fehim, who had inherited it from his grandfather, twenty years before. By the time the three of us flew back to Britain from that trip to Cyprus, we were already planning the development we could build on the plot. In January 1989, Noble Raredon purchased the land for £100,000. Two months later, we announced a two-for-seven share rights issue to raise £4.16 million for new projects. Of this, half was to fund the construction of the North Cyprus holiday village. We had already decided to call it The Olive Tree, in reference to the traditional Cypriot trees which abounded on the site. I was to get the shock of my life when I revisited the area soon after the builders moved in, and found they had left hardly any of the original trees standing.

Part of the cash raised from the rights issue was also earmarked for a similar holiday complex on Turkey's Aegean coast. A few months earlier, we had discovered the part-built Sunset Holiday Village in a idyllic setting at the popular mainland resort area of Kusadasi. Construction had ground to a halt because of a disagreement between the nine partners who had set out to establish the village, so part shares in the project were up for sale. It was a superb opportunity. As soon as the rights issue had taken place, Noble Raredon paid £1.7 million for a controlling fifty-one per cent stake in the 380-bed complex, setting aside a further £300,000 for its share of the remaining development costs. The cash injection made it possible for the holiday village to be completed. We appointed a hotel management expert, Terry Causer-Rees, to oversee the final stages and put her at the helm of our newest subsidiary, Noble Hotels. Under Terry's eagle eye, Sunset opened for a short trial period on the 8th July 1989. It proved such a success that it was soon fully booked for the summer of 1990. Within months of that trial opening, we were planning with Sunset's minority partners to expand capacity to 650 beds.

As our first tourism season drew to a close in autumn 1989, repeated complaints about the hotels from Mosaic's North Cyprus clients drove it home to us that we would have to bring that area under our control urgently if we were to maintain high standards. While Sunset Village was already built, by that stage the proposed Olive Tree was little more than a sea of rough walls, dust and concrete-filled foundations. It was imperative, though, that the North Cyprus holiday village should be ready for the 1990 season. Ever-optimistic, I set a 1st May deadline for the opening and published an artist's impression of the complex in Mosaic's 1990 brochure. By the end of 1989, bookings for the 210-bed Olive Tree were already strong. It would simply have to be finished on time.

That Christmas, I looked back on what had been an immensely busy year - not just for Noble Raredon but also for the family. That February, we had celebrated Tijen's twenty-first birthday. Then, little more than eighteen months after her wedding, there was more romance in the air with Levent's engagement to a young Turkish Cypriot musician. Rüya Taner, a pianist, had been living in London for several years with her parents. Her father, also a musician, was cultural attaché to the TRNC Representative Office in the capital and we knew the family from Cyprus days. Rüya and Levent had been friends for some time, but I had not realised how close they had grown until the late summer, when they announced to me and Rüya's mother, Sifa, that they wished to get engaged. They wanted to go out together on their own, and in Turkish society it was frowned upon for young people to "date" unchaperoned unless they were engaged.

I was quite taken aback. It all seemed very sudden and Levent was still young. On the other hand, I thought a sensitive musician might just be the perfect match for my rather shy elder son, so I did not lodge any instant objections. Sifa and I agreed to talk it over with the children's fathers. After discussion, we concluded that Levent and Rüya seemed well matched, so perhaps their union would be a good idea. In keeping with Turkish custom, we arranged to pay an official visit on the Taner family in September. Although the occasion was not too formal or serious because we all knew each other already, we were determined to act in accordance with tradition. Our two families sat opposite each other while Rüya served us cups of Turkish coffee - traditionally a sign that the prospective bride is willing, provided the coffee she makes is sweet. Rüya's coffee was suitably sugary. My mother, who was on holiday from Cyprus, was eager to play the role of head of the family for the occasion - something she had missed out on when her own son's engagement was agreed in Istanbul. Her duty for Levent was to speak the time-honoured Turkish words which translate roughly as: "In the name of God and Prophet Muhammed, we wish your daughter to agree to marry our son." There was delight all round when, as expected, Rüya's father Yilmaz gave his consent and the two youngsters were officially declared *sözlü* - promised. Their engagement took place three months later.

The lowest point of that year had been the death of Auntie Finney on Valentine's Day - an event which, looking back, I would come to regard as a harbinger of all that was to follow, somehow marking a downturn in our fortunes. She had been ill for some months and when she became too sick to stay at home and had to be hospitalised, I used to visit her every day on my way home from work. One evening, I called in quickly to see her and Auntie Finney implored me to stay longer, adding, "I won't be here tomorrow." I dismissed her words as being merely a ploy to persuade me to stay, but sat a while anyway to keep her company. I would always be thankful that I had not rushed away from her bedside. Early the next morning, we had a telephone call to tell us that Auntie Finney had died in the night. At her funeral, we shed as many tears of grief as her own children and grandchildren, so close had we grown to Auntie Finney during the twenty-one years we had known her. It seemed like the end of an era.

As the 1990s dawned, Fehim and I saw ahead of us a new decade ripe to receive Noble Raredon's enthusiasm and initiatives. During 1989, we had seen our already modest profits plummet, but we were not worried - profits were bound to be depressed as we ploughed more and more resources into starting the new businesses which would take the company forwards. When Noble Raredon's annual report was published at the end of October 1989, the continuing heavy start-up costs had pushed pre-tax profits down to £48,000 over the preceding seventeen months. Turnover was up to £11.3 million for the seventeen months, though, and the group's assets had increased in value from £745,000 at the time of our take-over to a staggering £9.57 million.

We entered the new decade in the same entrepreneurial vein. While I focused my energies on bringing the tourism projects along, Fehim was hatching plans in Poland - plans which seemed somehow very familiar. Political events in the country were providing a catalyst for his ambitions there and he was eager to exploit the moment. For some time, he had been aware of the problems that the lack of adequate packaging facilities had caused for Polish agriculture. Now his investigations into how to solve the difficulties were beginning to point in certain directions. Fehim was sure that the same kind of cardboard box plant which had launched Polly Peck on the road to international success nine years earlier could prove the key to development in Poland.

During the early weeks of 1990, he and Ewa Donde set out to find the right site for an Eastern European version of North Cyprus's Uni-Pac Packaging. By the spring, Ewa had come across a perfect industrial location - complete with its own small railway system - at a town called Torun, 350 kilometres north-west of Warsaw. Tri-Sun Trading made out an initial letter of intent to embark upon a joint venture with the local municipal authorities, who would hand over the land on a leasehold basis. All that remained to be done was to secure the funding, order the machinery for the plant and begin work.

At the same time, the more Fehim delved into Polish manufacturing industry, the more trading potential he uncovered. Though he discovered many needs in the country which could only be fulfilled from abroad, he also began to encounter home-produced goods which cried out to be exported. The quest for the cardboard box factory coincidentally flushed out a source of cheaper, but better quality, paper products which could replace the raw materials then being used at Uni-Pac, in Famagusta. A source of cheap newsprint also emerged, which could be tapped for the newspaper industry in Turkey and North Cyprus. Even Polish-made bicycles were found to be so low in price that they could profitably be exported to Turkey.

Poland, too, would provide a unifying link between the Eastern Bloc trading field and my dreams of tourism luxury. The more Fehim and I spent time in the country, the more we saw the desperate need for good quality hotels if the international business and travelling community was to be adequately served. The Japanese and Americans, in particular, were already starting to flock to Poland to set up their ventures, but they were plainly disgruntled by the primitive accommodation they found. Among the beautiful old-style buildings of Warsaw, Fehim and I one day stumbled across two very shabby hotels which were housed in such fine premises that we knew they could be transformed into high-class establishments. As I looked at the Saski and the Polonya Hotels, with their grand architecture subdued under an aura of depressing tattiness, I saw in them the next two Noble Hotels. In the spring of 1990, we recruited architects in London to draw up plans to revamp the two hotels and submitted tenders for consideration of the Polish government.

May 1990 proved a crucial month in many ways for Noble Raredon. Within the first week, we announced a rights issue to raise £5.2 million. The lion's share of the cash - £4 million - was to finance the Polish cardboard box factory and £900,000 would buy out the minority interest in Turkey's Sunset Holiday Village, leaving £300,000 to boost the group's working capital. Eighty per cent of the offer was taken up. In North Cyprus, the Olive Tree had opened its doors just in time for the first visitors who had booked with Mosaic. Fehim and I were too busy with the rights issue to fly out for the 1st May opening. In the event, it was touch-and-go whether everything would be completed in time. Less than twenty-four hours before the first plane-load of guests was due to touch down at Ercan Airport, the builders were still in, putting the finishing touches. With only about three hours to go, Terry Causer-Rees, Noble Hotels' marketing executive, Sabina Shaida, and operations executive, Colette Langan, were still down on their hands and knees sweeping brick-dust from the floors and scrubbing down the tiled reception area. I telephoned from London just as the guests were due to walk in at about eleven o'clock that night and Terry told me she had only just had time to change her clothes before having to step out with a smile to welcome the holidaymakers.

In all the excitement, we still did not forget the Gnome Photographic business, renamed Elite Optics. That May, we announced that the business would move to a new Welsh Development Agency site at Llantrisant, a few miles from its original premises in Cardiff. Elite Optics, which by then had joint managing directors in Roy Phillips and Michael Eccleshall since James Hallsworth's retirement in August 1989, received a regional aid package of about £1 million to secure the move, planned for the second of July 1990.

That May and the busy weeks which followed came as a kind of crowning glory on all our efforts so far. Future projects were well advanced and new businesses like Sunset Holiday Village, Mosaic and Noble Air were poised for rewarding second seasons. We saw the coming months as the time Noble Raredon would reap the rewards of its investments - the time when, with everything seemingly going our way, we would build on the foundations we had laid.

That July, we decided to capitalise on our growing good fortune by taking a health hydro holiday in St Lucia - ten days together for Fehim and I, Tijen and Rifat, Levent, Rüya and Irfan. It was a holiday to remember - a rare opportunity for us all to relax as a family, but still my brain was programmed to business - every morning at six o'clock, I would stroll the sands barefoot with Fehim, planning how we might launch a similar all-inclusive "body holiday" in North Cyprus. I was also taken by our hotel's piano bar, which featured as its centrepiece a grand piano-shaped bar fashioned from marble, beneath which sat the real instrument played by the resident entertainer. Years later, I would incorporate a similar "piano bar" into our Olive Tree hotel. I still treasure a photo of us all sitting in the piano bar at St Lucia - on the last happy holiday we had together.

CHAPTER SIX

Polly Peck Goes Public

My business parting of the ways from Asil had coincided with a push by my brother to further expand and diversify the business at Polly Peck. Firmly settled now in the splendour of 42 Berkeley Square, Asil was establishing the working pattern which would see him through a period of enormous expansion within Polly Peck. Ensconced at his desk in his beautifully furnished office, he would spend long hours considering the company's future and its next moves. He was free now, too, to concentrate on long-term strategy, appointing Anthony Reading as group managing director to handle the day-to-day running of PPI.

Throughout the late 1980s, Asil was frequently in the office seven days a week - New Year's Day was the only day he was guaranteed to take off. Most days he would come in early, often at eight o'clock, and would study the Reuters screens and press cuttings before turning to the day's other matters. During the day, he would drink instant coffee and mint tea and snack on cereal or toast and olives. Lunch would be from a tray on his knee. Ihsan, his valet, would bring in a huge solid silver tray, which had to be arranged just so with a beautiful lawn tray cloth, silver cutlery, white china plate with gold rim and individual bowls of food - often melon, cheese and yoghurt. He never drank at lunch-time and rarely went out to business lunches. If he had a guest to lunch in his office a bottle of chilled, white Montrachet would come out. Always immaculately turned out when he arrived in the morning, as the work progressed, his tie would come off. The shirt would be unbuttoned at the neck by the end of a particularly taxing day. Once the shares had closed for the day he would sit in the office for a couple of hours winding down with whoever had stayed behind, sipping champagne or whisky on the rocks and nibbling lettuce leaves splashed with lemon juice.

Aisling Daly, as Asil's new PA, had been briefed to keep the world at bay. She had to learn, my brother said, who to let in and out of his office. As they established a close working relationship, the two of them devised a procedure by which Aisling would inspect new visitors in one

131

room before going through to Asil's office to warn him what to expect - whether someone seemed pleasant or whether they had a weak handshake. Aisling found it hard to adapt to working in the rarified, yet rather impractical, antique setting - while Asil was away she took the opportunity to move Jean Thomas's modern office furniture from Commercial Road as a surprise. Asil made little comment on his return, but when Aisling got to work the next Monday, he had had all the office furniture moved out and the antiques reinstated over the weekend. Finally they settled on a compromise - the installation of some reproduction cabinets, which Asil disliked but accepted.

My brother was a PA's nightmare - he would make private appointments with people who appeared at the top of the stairs unannounced and had to be fitted in to any existing schedule. A diary was made for him with details of the day's programme, but Asil would scribble diagonally across it or use it for doodling. He never wrote down any of the appointments he arranged personally, priding himself that he always remembered them. His desk, with its parade of miniature bronze and gold turtles, was a continual chaos of paperwork. Whenever Asil went out to the bathroom, Aisling would take the opportunity to race into his office and gather up documents from the desk, which she would then sort through and return in orderly piles. The middle drawer of his desk was Asil's sacrosanct territory - there he would keep his private papers, letters from lawyers and accountants, even his set of worry beads. Any letters he did not wish to reply to immediately would be slipped into the middle drawer, to be dealt with at a later date.

Asil's executives found their boss sometimes frustrating to deal with, reluctant to delegate, yet with a powerful magnetism. "Charisma filled his room," said one employee. Ordinary staff members found him awe-inspiring and a little terrifying. He could be moody and often grew exasperated with his directors, some of whom he felt had been foisted on him by the City. Asil would sometimes take advantage of the absence of executives to organise things as he thought they should be - most notably during the 1989 Windsor Horse Trials, of which PPI was a sponsor, when he bounced into the office one morning and called the personnel manager in with the pay-roll. The personnel manager emerged white-faced with a list of seven underlined names to be sacked. Asil, meanwhile, remained in his office, sitting back with his feet on the desk, grinning broadly and announcing, "I think we're going to have some fun."

Among those to go were David Fawcus's secretary and a financial controller brought in by Anthony Reading. Fawcus and Reading were at Windsor and heard of the sackings via a telephone call from North Cyprus to their mobile phone during lunch. Furious, they both stormed from the party and headed back to Berkeley Square for a meeting with Asil - which failed to get all but one person reinstated. Reading resigned soon afterwards. Fawcus remained, but would be moved sideways the following year to the post of deputy chief executive, making way for Reg Mogg as finance director.

Still, everybody wanted to be part of this business which was exploding - wanted to prove what they could do. From 1987 onwards there was a mounting level of excitement throughout the building. Everyone in PPI recognised what Asil had achieved and believed he had a plan for the company that was attainable only by him. Asil's intention during the mid-1980s was to make Polly Peck a truly international business, supplying high quality goods all year round at prices affordable by the mass market. To do so, he judged, certain strategies were needed. One was to widen the existing network of sources so that the company could be assured of a consistent supply of goods at competitive prices. The other was to broaden the scope of the existing businesses, so that PPI could extend its control to include manufacture, distribution and marketing. His primary aim was to throw the Polly Peck net wider in three key regions - Europe, including the Near and Middle East; the Americas and the Far East. By expanding geographically, he felt the company would be less exposed to the dangers of depending too heavily on any one area.

In line with this policy of diversification, 1987 was a year of major investments and acquisitions. The push for new opportunities was concentrated in two major directions, into businesses in the Far East and in the fast-growing consumer electronics market, which dovetailed in the year's major coup that October - the £20 million purchase of the Taiwan-based Capetronic Group, which virtually trebled the size of PPI's consumer electronics division overnight. The purchase not only gave PPI a major presence in the Far East, but also a significant role in the consumer electronics market world-wide. Capetronic, with four Taiwanese factories and one in Hong Kong making household electrical goods, computer monitors and audio systems, had an international staff of more than 4,000. It was a major player in the field and had extensive contracts to manufacture goods for brand name customers in the US, Europe and Japan. Asil was very excited about the take-over. He was convinced the acquisition of Capetronic would provide mutual benefits throughout PPI, with the expertise in Taiwan aiding the group's existing production and the manufacturing capacity at Vestel providing a boost for Capetronic.

Far Eastern activity was not confined solely to the electronics field. Asil had that year recruited a new management team to supervise the priority developments in the region. Headed by British businessman

Barry Buttifant, the group became official offshoot Polly Peck International (HK) Ltd, a local holding company, and set about seeking new outlets for all the group's activities. Hong Kong-based Impact Textiles Group, bought in October 1986, and PPI's other textile concern in the colony, the majority-owned Shui Hing Knitting Factory, were the oriental reflection of a new trend in Polly Peck's textiles division. After Fehim and I left, the traditional marketing and manufacturing base in Britain, Turkey, North Cyprus and the Middle East had been all but phased out. Now the division was looking to new areas altogether - Portugal, America and the United Arab Emirates. Broader foreign connections also figured greatly in PPI's other core operation - food and agriculture. Europe, the Near and Middle East remained the main focus, with storage and packing facilities being bettered and the European distribution and marketing network expanded. By tapping into new and far-flung markets in the Far East and Latin America, though, the division was able to seek out exotic produce and to establish a cycle of year-round supplies. From Thailand came enchantingly-titled mangosteens and rambutans; from Indonesia were brought sweet pineapples; from Uruguay, oranges; from Mexico, avocados and mangoes. Pakistan and the Philippines too became the providers of unusual fresh fruits and vegetables. Following on from production, new inroads were made into marketing and distribution, taking PPI closer to its goal of being a fully integrated business growing, purchasing, packing and selling fruit and vegetable-related produce of all kinds.

The following year, 1988, was another period of growth and also one of accolades and recognition which Asil felt were long overdue. In June, *Management Today* magazine placed PPI top of its growth league for Britain's 250 biggest companies. Two months later, PPI was accorded alpha stock status on the London Stock Exchange, being admitted to a select club of some 145 companies granted such a classification. After two solid years of investment and purchases, PPI was reaping the rewards. In his annual message to shareholders that year, Asil reported a warm reception for the company in the financial markets and a growing confidence in the group's policies among investors and bankers. That confidence was put to the test in October 1988 when a new subsidiary - Polly Peck Far East Limited - was floated on the Hong Kong Stock Exchange. PPI retained seventy per cent of shares in the company, which held most of the group's textiles interests and was to spearhead the further drive into the Far East.

Within weeks of my departure from Polly Peck, Asil had gone public with PPI's intentions to go into the leisure business. A prospectus had been released detailing plans for the luxury hotel at Antalya: 404 double bedrooms and twelve suites, each with spectacular views over the bay and the mountains beyond; restaurants, shops, bars, an international casino and - to attract the sought-after lucrative business market - modern conference facilities. A completion date of late 1989 was announced for the eight-storey hotel. In fact, it would only be finished precisely one year later, in September 1990, by which time circumstances would ensure that its launch was not to be quite the glorious moment Asil dreamed of.

That new leisure branch proved to be a major growth area during 1988, sign-posting the direction in which Asil was keen to take the group. North Cyprus was the scene of considerable activity. Work was well under way on several hotel properties - refurbishing the 114-bedroom Palm Beach Hotel at Famagusta; completing and fitting out the Jasmine Court complex of 143 holiday apartments with hotel facilities on the western fringe of Kyrenia; and the half-built Zephiros site six miles further along the coast - now known as Crystal Cove - which Asil planned as the TRNC's first five-star hotel. In Turkey, meanwhile, the contractors were still busy on the luxury hotel at Antalya. By now, a management agreement had been signed with the Sheraton Overseas Management Corporation and the hotel, once completed, was to be known as the Voyager Antalya Sheraton.

Polly Peck's quest for expansion reached its peak in 1989. The major commercial milestones of the year - indeed of the decade - were achievements which, Asil felt, marked a coming of age for the company. On too many occasions during its ten-year existence, he believed, PPI had been the object of City scepticism. Now its long-awaited maturity was acknowledged with the group's admission to the *Financial Times* Stock Exchange 100 share index - a grouping of the City's leading public companies. In the late summer, the buzz of excitement which had been building up inside the Berkeley Square offices reached fever pitch as the company achieved, in quick succession, two of its most acclaimed moves. In August, following days of speculation that a massive deal was afoot, Asil announced the £557 million purchase of the tropical fruit division of the Del Monte Corporation; seven weeks later, the group paid 15.6 billion Yen (£68.7 million) for a fifty-one per cent controlling interest in well-known Japanese audio and consumer electronics firm Sansui.

The acquisition of Del Monte, announced on the 7th September and completed in December, aroused virtually unanimous approval within the City. The deal, sealed by Asil with a trip to the United States, followed three months of talks involving Mark Ellis and Anil Doshi in America and Asil on the other end of a trans-Atlantic telephone line. Del Monte was acknowledged as the biggest brand name in the industry and it had an extremely healthy trading profit to show during 1988. With one stroke, PPI became one of the world's largest suppliers of fresh fruit and vegetables. The group also took a two per cent stake in the sister Del Monte processed food business, which Asil had initially been keen to buy alongside the tropical fruit business, but had been forced to abandon as too costly. Del Monte's key value lay in its internationally-known brand name. Ownership of the familiar label - respected for its high quality produce - would give PPI greater purchasing power and would also maximise the profits the group could make on the sale of its fresh produce. The take-over also brought with it a fleet of thirty-nine cargo ships, giving PPI's world-wide transport links an enormous fillip. The Del Monte purchase was financed partially by a rights issue, partly by term loans and partly out of working capital reserves. Unusually, the banks providing the extra finance insisted on a "ring fence" agreement, which meant PPI would have no access to Del Monte's funds until all the loans used to purchase it had been repaid.

The Del Monte deal was the subject of considerable merriment in our house. For some time, the fruit company had been running television commercials featuring a man who rode around on a horse, wearing a big Stetson hat, checking out the orchards - his signal that the fruit was perfect for picking would send up the shout "the man from Del Monte says yes". In our family, it had been a standing joke that my father, whose favourite job in North Cyprus was supervising the citrus groves and deciding when to harvest, was the real-life "man from Del Monte". In early September 1988, my brother had been sitting with us in the garden at South Woodford having lunch. On the table was a selection of fruit bearing the Del Monte label and Asil had picked up a pineapple to take a closer look. Someone took a photograph, joking, "Mr Nadir says yes." Exactly one year later, on a Sunday, Asil arrived at our house to tell us he had finally clinched the Del Monte purchase - that Mr Nadir had indeed said "yes". Quick as a flash, one of the boys ran upstairs and fetched a white ten-gallon hat which they had bought for Fehim during a family holiday in Las Vegas years earlier. "Now you really are the man from Del Monte," was the cry as the huge hat was plonked on Asil's head.

The acquisition of Sansui Electric Company, revealed in October and brought to fruition during the early days of 1990, was scarcely less spectacular than that of Del Monte. Though a far smaller take-over, it nonetheless brought with it similar advantages for PPI. Asil flew out to Tokyo to sign the deal and was given the kind of reception a visiting royal might have expected. He had never been to Japan before and when he got back he told me how impressed he was with their manners and how he admired their efficiency. "If I was starting my business life over again, Bilge, I would definitely use Japan as a base," he said. Ownership of Sansui gave the group a brand name of international standing and access to world-renowned engineering, design and research capabilities and to a licence for manufacturing video cassette recorders. It also gave PPI an increased share of the Japanese market and a greater public profile within Japan. Moreover, it was something to be proud of, since it was only the third-ever foreign take-over of a quoted Japanese company.

As 1989 faded, PPI was set to enter the nineties with a newly defined focus, having shed the textiles division following a board decision in November to concentrate solely on the three key divisions of electronics, food and leisure. In the summer of 1990, the board would take another strategy decision, this time resolving to move away from the leisure industry. It was a resolution which did not square with Asil's vision of where PPI was heading in the nineties. His plan was partially to off-load the company's agricultural and electronics interests through flotations in New York, Tokyo and Istanbul. This, he intended, would leave PPI cash rich for the first time and free to concentrate on leisure, which would in turn benefit Turkey and North Cyprus.

In the event, only one of the talked-of flotations ever took place. In June 1990, soon after PPI's share price hit what would prove to be its highest-ever level, 462p, the manufacturing and exporting operations of Vestel were sold in an Istanbul Stock Exchange flotation which raised $90 million. Asil had expected the forty-nine per cent flotation of PPI Del Monte in New York, which had been on the agenda since 1989, to take place in May or June of 1990. But it failed to materialise. The first stage of the flotation was an "initial placement offer" of shares, about which there was supposed to be total secrecy. Somehow word spread, though, prompting a message to Berkeley Square from the US corporate lawyers dealing with the placement that everybody "from the tea boy to the chairman" should observe the necessary silence. The markets were already full of the news, though, and a reproof followed from the New York Stock Exchange. From then on, the flotation seemed to slip further and further from PPI's grasp. Later, a senior member of the Greek Cypriot administration would boast that they had played a major part in scuppering it.

It was a supremely optimistic and purposeful Asil who set his sights on the 1990s, determined to consolidate the achievements of the decade past. He vowed to shareholders to continue the unbroken record of growth and profitability "into the 1990s and beyond" and to ensure the company's share price reflected the true value of its businesses. Signing off his message in the annual report issued in April 1990, Asil proclaimed: "I am confident that 1990 will be an exciting start to a second decade of growth for the group, and that the strategy we develop in the 1990s will be as successful as that implemented during the 1980s." The irony of that sanguine prediction lies heavy on my heart.

———————

As Asil's business empire grew, so his life became more complex. In 1989, advised that he was a potential terrorist target, he took on a team of bodyguards to protect him in London and on business travels abroad. Since his earliest involvement in Polly Peck, Asil had grown used to being on the receiving end of a steady trickle of Greek and Greek Cypriot threats. For all those years, he had simply dismissed the attempts at intimidation and had got into the habit of merely answering abusive telephone calls with a few choice remarks before putting the phone down and getting on with his work. The threats did not worry him greatly - he was convinced the Greeks would be too afraid of reprisals from the Turkish community to risk trying to harm him physically in London. And the evidence thus far had seemed to back up that assumption - since the early eighties, his Greek enemies had concentrated their energies on political, economic and propaganda attacks in preference to any physical assault. In late 1989, however, it seemed that the situation had become more serious. Asil was approached by the Metropolitan Police's Anti-Terrorist Squad, which warned him they had information that, as a high-profile leading businessman, he was a potential target for terrorist activists either from the Greek community or from the PKK - the separatist Kurdistan Workers' Party, outlawed in Turkey and waging a bloody campaign since 1984 for an independent Kurdish homeland in the Turkish south-east. The PKK, which formed a kind of unholy alliance with the Greeks in its fervent anti-Turkish sentiment, had sworn to mount attacks against economic targets within Turkey. For the Greek Cypriots, Polly Peck and its Turkish Cypriot chairman were still "public enemy number one" for their activities bolstering the economy in the north of Cyprus, which they considered had been snatched from them unlawfully. For either faction, then, Asil could be a prime target.

The approach from the anti-terrorist officers alarmed me and convinced Asil that the time had come to take the threats against him more seriously. He put the officers in touch with Çavlan Süerdem - a man whose father had been in the military and who Asil had taken on as his personal adviser the previous year. Süerdem had been an adviser to Turkish Cypriot President Denktas and had good connections in both North Cyprus and Turkey. He was working from an office in Polly

Peck, liaising on Asil's behalf over business prospects in the region. On the anti-terrorist officers' advice, Süerdem got in touch with a security recruitment agency run by a Mrs McMurray, the wife of a senior police officer, Chief Superintendent Colin McMurray. It was Isabel McMurray who recruited Asil's first three bodyguards, Dave, Alan and Sandy. All three were ex-SAS and Alan had also been a police officer. From that moment on, in early 1990, Asil never went anywhere during the day without at least one of the armed trio. Whenever he was in his car - he used a Bentley or a Ferrari - one bodyguard would travel with him, while another often led the way or followed in another vehicle. While he was at the office, they would wait downstairs. Only at night did Asil relax the security cordon around him. When he got home from the office in the evenings, the bodyguards would leave for the night. Still Asil did not drop his guard completely, though. He had a gun licence and kept a revolver in the cabinet beside his bed.

Asil's private life took on a chaotic note, too, during the latter 1980s. In 1988 he started seeing a new woman - Abide Gönültas, a German-born twenty-three-year-old of Turkish origin who had been a secretary at the Vestel factory in Manisa, outside Izmir. She and Asil had met when Abide looked after him and his guests on my brother's occasional visits to Vestel - Abide quaking in her shoes at being under the boss's scrutiny - and had formed a relationship after Abide came on holiday to London in May 1988, staying on to work at PPI. I felt very concerned for Abide since Asil was still living with Joanne - after all, Abide was new to England and was barely older than Tijen. I felt she ought to be told that Asil was already living with another woman; that he had been married before, had family commitments and if she thought things would change quickly, she would be disappointed. One day, I took her to one side and explained the situation. Abide looked me in the eye and said, "But I love him. I want to be with him." It was clear there was no way of deflecting Abide. She was a very determined young woman. In fact, despite her youth, I was amazed later by how well she handled the difficult days; how she stood by my brother when he needed someone most.

Later, my brother's love affairs became even more entangled, until at one stage there were five women in his life. It was our mother's dearest wish that Asil would find a good Turkish Cypriot wife and settle down. After Tijen's wedding, she kept asking him how was it that her granddaughter had got married, but her son had still to find a wife who could look after him properly? My mother knew Narin Ferdi and felt that she would make Asil the perfect bride - she was intelligent, educated at London University, from a good family and was by then a judge in North Cyprus. In traditional Turkish style, my mother arranged for Asil and Narin to meet and they hit it off. Asil told her he would marry Narin and they announced their engagement.

The problem was, though, that Asil's life in the late eighties had become so hectic on the business front. He was travelling around the world all the time and really did not have the time to devote to his new fiancée, who came to London to see him and stayed at the Ritz. At that stage, he felt he should try to tidy his life up - but he abhorred confrontation and could never bear to hurt the women in his life. The press would later portray him as a latter-day Sultan with his harem, but in truth, he simply collected more and more women because he found it impossible to break a relationship off. He could not cope with the tears. By the end of the decade, he was divorcing Aysegül for the second time and Lesley was living apart from him with their two children. Joanne was with him at the house they now shared in Aldford Street and every few days he would see Abide, who was sharing a flat with a friend. It was after Asil had travelled to New York to finalise the Del Monte purchase that he realised it would take time to sort out his affairs and it would be unfair on Narin to keep her waiting. He told me one day how upset he was about the difficulty, because he liked Narin very much. They decided it would be best for her to go back to North Cyprus. I know Narin was upset, but she never held it against Asil.

The end of their relationship broke my mother's heart, and Asil was distressed to have disappointed her. He and my mother have a very close bond - at particularly busy times or moments of crisis within PPI, he would give instructions that he was to receive no calls "from anyone except my mother". When, in his mid-forties, Asil returned to Istanbul to sit his final university exams - turning down the offer of an honorary degree - he asked the Dean at the graduation ceremony to hand the certificate to my mother, saying, "I did it for her."

Our whole family was aware of the tangles in Asil's love life and it sometimes made for tricky moments as we tried to be discreet. As a family, we decided that Asil had the right to be with anyone he chose, so we would just accept whoever he turned up with on a given day. After all, they were all aware of each other. Even the children - Irfan was only in his teens at the time - grew up with the kind of diplomacy where their *dayi* (uncle) was concerned which is seldom seen in youngsters of their age.

Looking back on Asil's chequered emotional past, it is clear to me that my brother emerged scarred from his marriage to Aysegül, who managed to maintain a hold over him for years after their relationship had run its course. He was always looking for a deep attachment - he admires other people who do find emotional happiness, and is envious of their success. What Asil needed was a woman who accepted that she would always play second fiddle to his business activities. "Nobody ever understood that Polly Peck was my life," he has been heard to comment sadly.

Asil's mood of acquisition during the late 1980s infected his private business life too. His private holdings were concentrated on two fields, newspapers and banks. Through the press, he believed he could educate people and positively influence public opinion on Cyprus. Banks were a natural business progression. In North Cyprus, he already had the Kibris Endüstri Bankasi- Cyprus Industrial Bank - which our father had founded and in the middle of the decade he bought the Impex Bank in Turkey, an institution specialising in foreign trade finance and investment advice. Later, Asil would hand over control of Impex Bank to Bülent Semiler, a Turkish Cypriot adviser to the Turkish President. Asil thought of Semiler as a friend - indeed he had once given his private plane to fly Semiler's mother for urgent medical treatment - and when he left Turkey for the last time in December 1990, anticipating his arrest, he agreed to sell Semiler his Impex Bank share-holding for $27 million, with the option to buy back. In the event, Semiler transferred the shares into his own name but, despite claims to the contrary, never paid the two agreed instalments - no doubt taking advantage of the fact that my brother was unable to leave Britain to pursue the debt. The situation resulted in Asil having to fight for months in court to prove to his creditors that he had not sold the bank and pocketed the proceeds. It would also leave him feeling badly let down by a man he had trusted.

By the end of the 1980s, Asil had turned himself into one of the major figures in Turkish publishing - and the most influential newspaper proprietor in North Cyprus. In 1988, he bought the mainland daily *Günaydin*, acquiring with it another national daily, six regional papers and nineteen publishing houses. Early 1989 saw another major publishing purchase in Turkey: this time it was Gelisim Yayinlari, a group producing eleven magazine titles including popular political weekly, *Nokta*. In the autumn of that year, Asil took over loss-making middle-market newspaper *Günes*, and during its first year under his stewardship it carved a niche for itself as one of the country's main quality dailies. After the troubles of 1990, when Asil's personal wealth was badly hit, the Turkish publishing ventures would become one of the first casualties, *Günes* closed down and *Günaydin* taken over by its staff. Asil's newspaper interests in North Cyprus proved more hardy. In 1988, he set up his own company, A-N Graphics, to undertake commercial printing and newspaper publishing, and plans were formulated to launch both a

Turkish-language daily newspaper and a weekly in English which would be able to promote the TRNC. A well-known Turkish Cypriot journalist, Mehmet Ali Akpinar, took charge of the daily, which was to be called *Kibris* - Turkish for "Cyprus". Printed on state-of-the-art presses, the colourful *Kibris* hit the streets of North Cyprus for the first time in July 1989, becoming instantly the country's biggest-selling daily by a huge margin. It would prove itself a useful ally of the ruling National Unity Party (UBP), rankling with the country's other political parties, whose own papers could command nowhere near the same readership. Asil mopped up a little of the remaining market by establishing another daily, *Yeni Gün*, and a weekly, *Bozkurt.* Key editorial staff were recruited from Britain to produce the English-language weekly, *Cyprus Times* - launched soon after *Kibris* in the autumn of 1989. A glossy quarterly magazine in English, *Turquoise*, reflecting the cultural life and heritage of Turkey and North Cyprus, was also produced from the A-N Graphics offices in a residential suburb of Nicosia. When the bad times hit, in the latter months of 1990, dozens of people would lose their jobs. *Yeni Gün*, *Bozkurt* and *Cyprus Times* would be closed down, the staff of *Kibris* sharply reduced and *Turquoise* would simply fade away.

Business purchases were not the only items on Asil's agenda during those years. At the end of the decade, he bought Zeytin Adasi (Isle of Olives), a tiny island in the Gulf of Fethiye on Turkey's Aegean coast for $1 million. Back in England, he had bought two grand country houses - Baggrave Hall in Leicestershire and Burley-on-the-Hill in Rutland - but his business life had by then become so hectic that he hardly ever had the chance to visit them and he showed little interest. Elizabeth Forsyth, however, thought they would be good investments.

Burley-on-the-Hill was a commercial proposition. The idea was to turn it into a residential conference and training centre - complete with its own golf course - which would eventually be injected into Polly Peck. Planning permission was later turned down, however, and the house would be sold soon after the Polly Peck troubles of 1990. Baggrave Hall, which was being restored, was a stately home set in rich agricultural land. It had a farm attached and a herd of prize cattle was established there. Elizabeth Forsyth enjoyed the challenge of organising the refurbishment work - she selected the renovation team, decorators and landscapers and even travelled to Scotland to select the cattle for the Baggrave herd. Asil's idea was that the house would be somewhere for all the family to go at weekends. I think he was becoming aware that, with him so very busy at work, a gap had developed between him and the rest of us. He thought that at Baggrave he could recreate the kind of relaxed atmosphere we had enjoyed at his first country home in East Grinstead a decade earlier. We were all going to have our own apartments at Baggrave - Asil's, of course, would include an office where he could carry on working during his stays. I remember Elizabeth coming to ask me how I would like mine decorated. I saw the plans and the colour schemes from the interior designers, but never got to see the house itself. Asil saw it once before he bought it but I think he only ever spent a handful of nights there in one of the cottages that had been done up. Baggrave Hall, too, would be an early casualty of the subsequent financial crisis.

At one point, Asil had half a dozen racehorses - I think Elizabeth thought it was a good diversion for him and she had plenty of contacts with the "horsy set". She knew our family had loved horse racing, too, from way back in our Cyprus days. The best known of Asil's horses - which had cost anywhere between £10,000 and £30,000 each - was Golden Freeze. I remember going with Asil and Meral's family to see it run in the Cheltenham Gold Cup. We were all very excited - we had lunch in the owners' enclosure and our horse was tipped to win. Jenny Pitman was the trainer and her son Mark was the jockey. What a let-down it was! Golden Freeze was several lengths ahead of the field when suddenly the jockey fell off and we watched, stunned, as the horse charged down the course on its own. Asil was disgusted. When he got back to the office, he announced that he was fed-up with the horses. "I'm going to sell the bloody lot," he stormed.

Though my brother was busy building up a rapidly expanding corporate and private empire, he was swift to ensure it was not all a one-way traffic. He felt PPI should be responsible for putting something back into the communities within which it operated. In Britain, this involved considerable donations to charity - £476,000 between 1985 and 1988, mostly for chronically sick or underprivileged children. By 1989, charitable contributions had been stepped up to £485,000. One project, budgeted at some £80,000 a year, provided scholarships for Turkish Cypriot students to be educated in the UK and America - students who, Asil hoped, might eventually benefit PPI by bringing their expertise into the company. Another £75,000 would be set aside to pay for employees or their relatives who fell ill to receive the best medical attention. Asil also paid personally for many more such cases. Cultural causes were also high on the list for aid, including a programme of exchange visits between the UK and the eastern Mediterranean. For several years, PPI paid air fares, hotel expenses and pocket money for a group of Dr Barnardo's children and their teachers to visit North Cyprus, where they embarked on community projects including beach clearing and helping to spruce up the grounds of Kyrenia castle. The company was also wooed by Sir Alex Alexander to provide sponsorship for a ballet at the Royal Opera House and a cheque for £500,000 was handed over shortly before the troubles hit in 1990. When the ballet was performed that autumn, however, PPI's name was not on the list of sponsors. I presume the cheque must have been returned.

Asil was always prepared to dig into his own pocket to help the needy. On one occasion in 1989, he arrived in the office saying he had been moved to tears by a television programme the previous evening about the work of a Spastics Society centre for disturbed children. PPI went by the board that morning as Aisling Daly was detailed to track down a Spastics Society representative for my brother to speak to. A meeting was arranged with the society's director, at which it was agreed that Asil should give £1 million towards the £5 million development of a second such centre planned for the Milton Keynes area. Asil's contribution was to come from his own Nadir Cultural Trust which Elizabeth Forsyth was instructed to set up. In the end, Asil's financial troubles prevented him from giving his promised support. Even after his arrest in 1990, when money was running short, Asil was still generous. Once, I remember, Turkish Cypriot well-wishers had collected several thousand pounds to meet his legal bills - but my brother gave a lot of it instead to a visitor whose daughter was in danger of going blind because he could not afford to pay for vital surgery.

Sometimes the hypocrisy of the charity celebrity circuit would get to Asil. PPI actively supported the World Wide Fund for Nature's efforts to preserve endangered species and their habitats and I remember once they sponsored a dinner for the charity at Hampton Court Palace. Asil was at the table next to Prince Philip, the fund's president. At that time, Asil was incensed that turtle soup, containing chunks of turtle meat, was on sale in the shops while turtles were an endangered species. It was a subject particularly close to his heart - North Cyprus is fortunate to have some of the few beaches where the threatened sea turtles come to lay their eggs each year. Before this dinner began, Asil put a can of turtle soup at the royal guest's place, hidden by the menu. When Prince Philip picked the menu up and saw the can, he was furious, Asil told me later. Afterwards, the prince talked privately to Asil - I expect this was supposed to be an honour, a thank-you for PPI's sponsorship, but the two men had little to say to each other.

Asil's financial support was not limited to charities. For many years, he made numerous donations to the Conservative Party, building up a network of influential contacts through the party, ever eager to exploit his commercial knowledge and Polly Peck's healthy finances. When information about Asil's links with the Tory party and the scale of those political gifts hit the newspaper headlines in 1993, it would cause a furore which I find hard to understand. Everybody who was seen to make money and be successful was heavily courted by the Tory party fund-raisers sooner or later and Asil - as one of the most spectacular success stories, the epitome of the hard-working entrepreneur beloved of Margaret Thatcher - was no exception. Indeed, during the Thatcher era of the 1980s, I believe there was a particular effort to "flirt" with businessmen from ethnic minorities, so I suppose Asil was a very obvious target for them. As far as he was concerned, it was important to become part of the society in which he lived and worked - not to adopt a "ghetto" mentality. We had, after all, been brought up in Cyprus to admire the British way of life. When Asil was first contacted by people from Conservative Central Office in the early eighties, he didn't see it as part of a process of "social climbing" - rather, because of his position as the best-known Turkish Cypriot in Britain, he felt he had a duty to respond and saw it might be an opportunity to explain the position of North Cyprus.

At one time or another during those years, Asil met virtually every minister. Often, he would attend Conservative Industrial Fund lunches, where a minister would be a guest speaker. At other times there would be twice-yearly drinks parties with the Prime Minister at No 10 Downing Street. The object of the three-monthly Industrial Fund lunches, attended by all kinds of prominent industrialists and bankers, seemed to be chiefly fund-raising. All kinds of issues were brought up, though, including taxation and economic policy, and Asil considered them a useful forum for the exchange of ideas. He would not go to all of them - in fact, he often disliked the idea of attending and forced himself to go, as he put it, "to keep the peace". Generally, he only went if the speaker was to be someone he admired. Whenever he decided to go, the organisers would ring up in advance to double- and treble-check that he would be there. Afterwards, he would come back to the office brimming with boyish excitement and brandishing the seating plan. Almost invariably, the table arrangements put him on the right-hand side of the main speaker. Aisling Daly came to realise that each of Asil's Industrial Fund lunches would be followed by a call from a Colonel Aylmer, requesting an appointment to see Asil. The colonel's visits would be very brief, arranged by Asil at the very beginning or end of the day, and he would leave with a cheque. Once, in February 1990, Asil attended a Tory lunch at which he was asked to a private meeting with Kenneth Baker to discuss the Conservative Party's image and ideas for its economic policy. The meeting was arranged for a Thursday morning the following month at the party's Smith Square headquarters. Economic issues were very close to Asil's heart - he often commented that the Conservatives "didn't have a clue" what they were doing.

Whether these invitations were just made to flatter the donors into thinking they were near the centre of power, or whether genuine attention was paid to what they said, I don't know. But once Asil was "in" this circle, he met dozens of politically prominent people, Mrs Thatcher included. Just before Mrs Thatcher visited Turkey, he was asked to come to the Department of Trade to see Alan Clark, then a DTI minister. They spent time talking about how she might present herself there and what her speeches should contain. Because Polly Peck and Asil did business in parts of the world of which British business had little experience, his views were often sought. The huge construction firm, Trafalgar House, for instance, consulted him when they were pitching for the contract to build the new Bosphorus Bridge. The contact was apparently made through the British government, which was understandably keen to see major UK companies succeeding. This was the kind of "networking" of which Asil had become a part.

In fact, Labour's Peter Shore had been one of the first British politicians Asil ever met, in the late 1970s when we were running Wearwell and the socialists were in power. My brother was never particularly political - he simply wished to be well connected with whichever government was in office. During the mid-eighties, I remember Michael Heseltine coming to lunch at our headquarters in Commercial road. Similarly, Asil met Lord McAlpine, then treasurer of the Tory party, several times. On one occasion, he had lunch with him at McAlpine's shop just round the corner from Savile Row. Asil knew McAlpine not just because of being one of the largest donors to the Conservative Party but also through Ayşegül. She was a keen connoisseur and collector of antiques and antiquities - as was McAlpine - and they traded together for many years. Ayşegül would be one of the first people to tell Asil about Michael Heseltine's heart attack in Venice in June 1993. She was in Venice that weekend and had been socialising with McAlpine. Heseltine had had an enormous row with McAlpine - no-one knows what it was about or why Heseltine had decided to take a trip to Venice to see McAlpine. Was it something to do with Tory party funding and the storm brewing over Asil's donations? McAlpine denied that he and Heseltine had talked about Asil - but then, he also denied publicly any recollection of ever having lunch with Asil.

While a figure of £400,000 would come to be bandied about in the press, the fact is that over the years, from the mid-1980s onwards, he gave far more. All these payments except two were made to the Conservative Industrial Fund - the total was well over £1 million - and most were paid with cheques drawn on Uni-Pac's Jersey subsidiary. Since Uni-Pac was not a UK company, it was perfectly legal not to declare the payments in the accounts, and I think Asil was also reluctant to irritate

Labour-controlled Tower Hamlets borough, where he had a number of building projects in the offing. There was, however, nothing to stop the Conservative Party declaring the donations if it had chosen to - the truth is that the secrecy element comes from the party itself, which chooses not to disclose details of its funding. When news about Polly Peck's donations started to make headlines in the summer of 1993, it would be made to look as though he had paid them under the table out of some kind of slush fund, since by then it would be known that Asil had approached several politicians, some of them ministers, with his complaints about the bizarre events surrounding his prosecution. What I resent about the political donations is the hypocrisy of the Conservatives in accepting all that money from a company registered in North Cyprus...while their government still refused to recognise the country.

Claims that Asil donated to the Conservative Party in order to secure a knighthood for himself would also become common media currency, but I do not believe that was his main motivation in responding to the overtures of the Tory fund-raisers - nor, I know, am I alone in this judgement. Asil really rather despised the "clubby" circles he felt obliged to move in, yet he would say that he had to be seen to "play the game". But I am sure, too, that at the back of his mind was a sneaking feeling that being awarded a knighthood would, at last, show his detractors that he, an immigrant from a former British colony, had "made it". During the late 1980s, there was at least one occasion on which it was intimated to him that a knighthood might come his way and he thought it might prove useful in future. "It would be nice, wouldn't it?" he remarked casually when he returned to the office one such day. During the Thatcher years, a large number of prominent businessmen were honoured. They had trodden the same path as Asil - the political flirting; the receptions at No 10 Downing Street; the meetings with ministers; the involvement with charities - it was a familiar circle for those who wanted entry to the Establishment. Asil was such a major contributor to Tory party funds that it would be astonishing if the subject had never been brought up, but when it was mentioned, he never took the idea forward. His rather unusual marital and domestic arrangements could have meant a problem of who would become "Lady Nadir" - sorting that out was the kind of complication my brother simply could not have dealt with on top of his business.

Above all, I know Asil regarded the political donations and his own high-profile position as a good thing for North Cyprus. His Tory contacts gave him the chance to put the country's case to those at the highest level when the occasion arose. Asil once said he had discussed North Cyprus with Margaret Thatcher. While he maintained his political contacts the possibility always existed to raise the issue - a possibility which aroused considerable alarm in Greek Cypriot circles, where it was acknowledged that there was no South Cyprus representative of similar standing.

During those years, Asil also built up his friendship with Turkish Prime Minister Turgut Özal - later to be elected to the presidency in 1989. The two men met frequently, finding they were of like mind on economic and business issues. Özal had worked at the World Bank in Washington and his economic ideas - his pursuit of a free-market economy and the privatisation of monolithic state industries - had more than a little in common with the Britain of Margaret Thatcher. In Asil, he found just the kind of businessman he admired and wished to encourage, attracting foreign investment to his country.

Turkey was a key player in diplomatic manoeuvring on the Cyprus issue and Asil would often discuss the issue with Özal during their meetings. On one occasion, Fehim and I had travelled out to Cyprus with Asil for an Easter break and were about to leave Cyprus for the return journey to Britain when Asil received a telephone call from a diplomatic source to say that Turkey was on the verge of serious talks with America on the Cyprus situation. He sprang into action immediately, calling Turgut Özal and arranging to see him later that day.

We altered our flight plan to the UK to go via Ankara and set off that afternoon in Asil's private plane. We checked in at our hotel in the Turkish capital and Asil waited in his room for the summons from Özal. The call came after eleven o'clock that night. At about half past eleven, Asil set off for a midnight meeting at the Çankaya - the Turkish Presidential Palace. Fehim and I, intrigued to learn what was discussed, sat up waiting for him to get back. It was two o'clock in the morning when Asil returned. He reported to us that he had urged Özal not to agree to US demands, and had appealed to him to give North Cyprus more time to build up a sound economic footing before a Cyprus deal was struck. Just how much my brother's words affected Özal's stance is impossible to judge, but when the US-Turkish talks on Cyprus subsequently took place, they did not bring the political progress the Americans desired. Asil's involvement cannot have gone unnoticed.

While Asil was making friends in the upper echelons of Ankara's political world, he was undoubtedly treading on toes in the country's business community. His Polly Peck flew in like a whirlwind to hit at the heart of the industrial sector, headed by the empires built up over generations by a handful of families. PPI introduced direct competition through Vestel and also threatened to make inroads into Turkey's domestic car market when it launched talks with Peugeot and Çukurova in 1990 to make cars in a joint Franco-Turkish venture. Asil's arrival bred resentment within the commercial dynasties.

During those years of expansion, I am convinced my brother also ruffled feathers much further afield with his visionary and highly nationalistic views - often publicly expressed - of what the future might hold for the Turkish region. One example in particular sticks in my mind - a speech he delivered to industrialists and politicians in Izmir in 1988 at the foundation-laying ceremony for a new trade centre. At that time, the Soviet Union had not yet begun to break up into individual states and Turkey was trying to join the European Community. When I read the speech Asil had prepared, I was amazed - and a little worried. He was predicting that the Turkish-speaking areas of the USSR would one day become independent republics. He envisaged a union of these Turkic states with Turkey that would create a huge political and economic bloc stretching from Europe to the frontiers of China. Asil appeared to be suggesting that Turkey's future lay there, rather than with the EC. When I read the words, I asked Asil whether it was wise to be proposing such an idea which could dramatically tip the regional balance of power. "Bilge, one day, no power will be able to stop the Turkish nation," was his reply. I feel sure that ideas like that, coupled with Asil's position in relation to North Cyprus, set alarm bells ringing in international political and diplomatic circles.

CHAPTER SEVEN

The Taxman Cometh

By that time, behind-the-scenes wheels were already in motion which would lead to Asil's downfall, and with it my own. It was in 1989 that rogue tax-man, Michael Allcock, first took an interest in my brother's affairs - and within just a few years he was boasting that he was the man who, single-handedly, brought down Polly Peck International. At the time, of course, we had no inkling of just how crucial would be the involvement of Allcock - later disgraced and jailed on corruption charges. But looking back now it is possible to piece together the trail of destruction that began with a straightforward tax inquiry and ended with the ruin of two public limited companies and criminal charges against the head of one, my brother. And the devastating chain of events prompts questions in my mind - and, I know, in the minds of many others - about the actions and motives of the investigating authorities.

Michael Allcock, a former small-time tax-man from Colchester, had had a meteoric rise to success, becoming the head of the Inland Revenue's Special Office Two, a section nicknamed the "Ghostbusters" for its investigations of wealthy foreign businessmen. By 1989, he had become a Revenue legend after bringing in a record £100 million during three years in charge of the department. But he had also acquired a reputation as a bully and was rumoured to be open to "sweeteners" from his tax probe targets - precisely the flaw which, in February 1997, would see him jailed for accepting bribes worth more than £150,000 from an Arab businessman.

When Allcock decided Asil was to be his next big quarry and asked for a meeting, it was alarm bells over the tax-man's conduct which prompted Asil's advisers to warn him against agreeing. It was to prove a costly refusal. A frustrated Allcock and his team scattered "Section 20" notices willy-nilly around the City, demanding information about dealings in Polly Peck shares. At one point, Allcock was said to have threatened to turn up on the steps of PPI's Berkeley Square offices. The intimidatory tactics infuriated Asil's tax advisers, Coopers & Lybrand. So much so that a senior Coopers partner even wrote to Sir

Anthony Battishill, chairman of the board of the Inland Revenue, threatening to suspend all co-operation with the Revenue unless the "irregularities" ceased. One stockbroker - Jonathan Bekhor, whose firm had handled share purchases in the past for our family trusts - later revealed that, after months of threat and pressure, he had been coerced by Allcock into naming both Asil and Conservative politician, Michael Heseltine, as the beneficiaries of trading in Polly Peck shares through offshore companies, even though he had already told the Revenue that he had no idea who was behind the firms. The involvement of Heseltine, against whom there has never been any evidence of impropriety, seemed bizarre. But *Business Age* magazine, reporting the tale almost six years later, summed up my own thoughts when it commented that "…one intriguing possibility lies in the timing." In 1990, when Bekhor said he felt the Revenue was "out to disgrace" Heseltine, the MP was preparing to quit the back benches after five years in the political wilderness and challenge for the leadership of the Tory party.

By the time Asil first knew of Allcock's interest, early in 1990, the investigation was already beginning to focus on South Audley Management, where Allcock thought he had established links to overseas company "fronts" for substantial dealings by my brother in PPI shares. He was wrong - some of the companies identified by the tax-men were totally unrelated, while others concerned legitimate family shareholdings. But when a series of leaked stories about the Revenue's "findings" appeared in the British press in August that year, it would prove absolutely devastating. The stories would unnerve investors and worry the banks, setting in train a crippling loss of confidence eventually leading to the destruction of PPI. The killer blow to investors' nerve, in the form of a highly publicised raid on South Audley Management, would come from the Serious Fraud Office - enticed into action, I believe, by the tantalising bait of the leaked tax investigation and, we would later learn, by tip-offs from Allcock himself.

I have never been able to satisfy myself about the motivation behind the Inland Revenue's investigation. Was the Inland Revenue responding to pressure from other quarters to unsettle Asil? Or did he simply fall foul of a corrupt tax man? And if he had played along with Allcock, would his company - and mine - still be alive today? Asil believes the Greek Cypriots were behind the inquiries from the very outset, and I have seen evidence that this may be so. Whatever sparked the Revenue's activities off, one thing seems clear: the internal considerations of the government department in relation to my brother's - or any individual's - tax affairs should not have become public knowledge. In the British financial world, where a company may be made or broken by rumour, suspicion and confidence or lack of it, the publicity about the tax investigation was to set in motion an ultimately cataclysmic chain of events.

In fact, the Inland Revenue's own investigations were settled amicably. After an original tax demand of £22.75 million - and speculation in the press that Asil's liability might run to more than £100 million - the Revenue would settle for a hugely reduced sum of £5 million. This was no more than Asil would have expected to pay, and the tax authority added a rider which stated that there had been "no criminality on the part of Nadir against the Inland Revenue". Vindication indeed...but by then the damage had been done.

Though the Inland Revenue inquiry itself would end in agreement, the ripples which spread from it proved devastating. For the Greek Cypriot government in South Nicosia, it came as a golden opportunity to cause trouble for their old adversary, Asil Nadir. Ever since the orchestrated campaign which nearly toppled Polly Peck in 1983, the Greek Cypriots had been engaged in a war of attrition against Asil and Polly Peck. By means of propaganda bombardment - rumour, false information and innuendo delivered to the ears of the financial and legal institutions of London and New York - the South Cyprus authorities hoped to deal a killer blow to the empire of their "public enemy number one", and thereby dent the slowly blossoming economy in the North of the island. According to journalist, David Barchard, "...every journalist or broadcaster who uttered a word in defence of the Turkish Cypriot point of view could be sure of a barrage of angry letters to his editor."

The British press scoffed when it was suggested that the Greek Cypriots had had some involvement in the downfall of Polly Peck and Asil Nadir - but the truth of the claim would later be confirmed by some of the most senior members of the Greek Cypriot government at the time. One of the key players was Yiorgios Iacovou - Greek Cypriot Foreign Minister between 1983 and 1993 and our former Famagusta playmate. George Vassiliou, who was South Cyprus President from 1988 to 1993, was also closely involved. Both men were to reveal the extent of Greek Cypriot behind-the-scenes opposition to Asil and Polly Peck during questioning by a British journalist in 1993. In his interview, Iacovou would describe how the South Nicosia regime commissioned a team of accountants and advisers to study Polly Peck's activities in depth and obtained a full list of the company's investors, who at the time included among their ranks the then-Master of the Rolls, Lord Denning, and one prominent Greek Cypriot. The information the Greeks received back from their team was that no firm could possibly achieve the sort of spectacular growth recorded by Polly Peck. The advisers claimed there had been an "amazing exaggeration of profits", while intelligence reports from North Cyprus alleged that Polly Peck was claiming to have assets which did not exist. What those bogus assets were supposed to be was never revealed. Thus armed, according to Iacovou, the Greek Cypriots "mounted an assault", leaking their "information" to newspapers - specifically *The Observer* - and to the Board of Trade, the Institute of Chartered Accountants, Rothschilds Bank and the Stock Exchange regulatory body. Iacovou would later admit that they also passed "a lot of information" to the Serious Fraud Office.

However damning the Greek Cypriots considered their evidence, for years it had borne no fruit and was generally dismissed as anti-Turkish propaganda. Moreover, it had landed them in hot water on several occasions. According to Iacovou, the United Nations' "quiet pressure" to "lay off Nadir" in 1983 was a warning echoed over the following years as intercommunal talks aimed at bringing about a political settlement in Cyprus resumed sporadically. On Iacovou's own admission, the UN, in those days headed by Secretary-General Perez de Cuellar, often cited anti-Nadir activities as being "liable to disrupt the talks". On at least one occasion, Turkish Cypriot leader Rauf Denktas complained to the UN about the "hard time" the Greeks were giving the company which was North Cyprus's biggest economic force - this incident revealed in an interview with George Vassiliou. Vassiliou himself showed concern about the disinformation campaign being waged against Polly Peck, urging the Greek Cypriot Anti-Nadir Committee not to rock the boat. Vassiliou had restarted intercommunal talks after being elected to the presidency in 1988 and warned the activists that they risked the talks being broken off. When the drip-feed of "information" from South Nicosia failed to have the desired effect over the years, the Greeks adopted a change of tactics. According to Iacovou, they decided to sit back, gather their information and wait for the "right time to attack". That time came at the end of the decade.

As the 1980s drew to a close with Polly Peck's triumphant acquisition of Del Monte Fresh Fruit, the Greek Cypriots began to panic that Asil was becoming virtually untouchable. "He could not be stopped," Iacovou would recall in 1993. The scale of his donations to the Conservative Party led South Nicosia to fear Asil might be in line for a knighthood. According to Iacovou, the Greek Cypriots saw him in a position to start influencing the British government. With no Greek Cypriot of equal status to counterbalance him, they feared he might be able to affect Westminster's Cyprus policy, creating an atmosphere more favourable to the Turkish side.

There was fear in South Nicosia, too, that Asil's power in North Cyprus was also on the increase, rendering him and his economic influence an ever-greater obstacle to the political union which the Greek Cypriots sought on the island. From across the Green Line, they eyed with concern an increasingly close relationship between Asil and the leader of the North's ruling National Unity Party (UBP), Prime Minister Dervis Eroglu. Eroglu's party took a hard-line approach which resisted any suggestion of an agreement with the South. Greek Cypriot opinion was that the Premier was proving "more fanatical" than President Denktas, who had held out against a settlement for a decade and a half. South Nicosia feared the mutual support between Asil and Eroglu would further erode any hopes of a Cyprus solution. In Iacovou's own words, Asil was a "dangerous" man for the Greek Cypriots. While South Cyprus had been alerting the British authorities about Polly Peck and Asil for years, Iacovou would comment, "everybody was giving him protection". The Inland Revenue probe into Asil's tax affairs made a chink in that protective armour which the Greek Cypriots were eager to exploit.

It was the end of 1989 when the Anti-Nadir Committee met and decided to move again against Asil and Polly Peck, this time targeting Britain's Serious Fraud Office through Interpol. According to George Vassiliou, the approach to the SFO was made after the Greek Cypriots had got wind of the Inland Revenue's inquiries. Among the tip-offs they passed on was a claim that, according to Iacovou, money was being siphoned off by Asil into the Cayman Islands and Liechtenstein. Money was indeed held in the Caymans, in legitimate family trusts. There was no connection with Liechtenstein, but this allegation was to resurface much later from the lips of the Serious Fraud Office.

Events in 1990 added further impetus to the Greek Cypriot campaign. Early in the year, George Vassiliou would recall, a "well-placed intelligence source" disclosed that Asil was hatching plans to inject new life into Varosha - the Famagusta suburb close to where we had once lived, which had stood abandoned since the end of the 1974 war. Predominantly Greek Cypriot in its heyday, Varosha had stood idle under Turkish military control for sixteen years, largely maintained as a Turkish Cypriot bargaining counter to bring to the negotiating table. As Vassiliou would explain, the Greek Cypriots knew that redevelopment of even a small part of Varosha would constitute a serious obstacle to the continuation of the Cyprus talks. The plan they learned of in 1990 shook them to the core - Asil had held secret talks with the Trust House Forte hotel chain with a view to a venture involving the Golden Sands Hotel, in which THF had a majority stake. The hotel, on the southern edge of Varosha, overlooking the sweeping east-facing bay, had been opened with great ceremony by Archbishop Makarios in 1974, just weeks before the outbreak of war had forced the evacuation of its holidaymakers and shut its doors for good. Some fifteen years later, the Golden Sands was a forlorn sight on the southern fringe of Varosha, just one of about 7,000 derelict hotels, restaurants, bars, offices, shops and houses which make up the "ghost town". On this occasion, the Greek Cypriots' information was correct. So highly sensitive was the nature of the scheme that only a handful of people apart from Asil had known of his discussions. Not only would the proposal have stirred up a political hornets' nest; it would also have sparked fury within Polly Peck itself, where the board had just voted for a move away from the leisure industry.

It was at about the same time that the Greeks became aware of the plans to float PPI Del Monte in New York. Buoyed by the success of a case they had brought in the American courts, claiming Greek Cypriot ownership of some mosaics which had ended up in the US, they decided to try their luck against Polly Peck in the States. Through the Greek Cypriot office in New York, they scored "some success" by intimating to US financial institutions that the firm had built itself on a foundation of "phantom profits". There was little need for documentation, commented a top level Greek Cypriot source: "It was sufficient just to cause trouble behind the scenes to stop the flotation." Not content with merely blocking the Del Monte flotation, the Greek Cypriots also congratulated themselves that - in the words of another source involved at the time - the thwarted Wall Street flotation "had a knock-on effect on the instability of Polly Peck shares in London that summer, which may have accelerated Nadir's demise".

Still rubbing their hands with glee over the Del Monte flotation, the Greek Cypriots went on to play a shadowy role in the shattering events which unfolded in Britain in the latter months of 1990. According to Iacovou, they passed on "one serious informant" about Asil - a man living in North Cyprus - to the UK authorities, but the SFO seemed to have "scared him off". Whatever else it did, Iacovou was satisfied that the Greek campaign had "rocked the Nadir empire". And he would comment: "When the bubble burst, we co-operated to expose him."

The behind-the-scenes activities were reflected in the Greek and Greek Cypriot media. In July 1990, the Greek-language newspaper, *Simerini* remarked on a "comprehensive plan to curb the activities of Asil Nadir". On 30th August, the Cyprus Broadcasting Corporation would report that a "negative atmosphere" had been created against Asil in the British press and on the London Stock Exchange. The next day, Greek Cypriot Deputy Chief Prosecutor, Luka Loukaides, would confirm to the South Cyprus House of Representatives that the Foreign

Affairs Committee had been co-ordinating all anti-Nadir activities in conjunction with Athens. *Simerini* would report the speech, adding the exhortation: "Let us all attack Asil Nadir. It is inevitable now to shoot him. In the past he was very powerful, but not now."

While Greek Cypriot concerns over Asil's activities were predictable, his blatant economic support for North Cyprus was also breeding resentment in a quite different - and much more powerful - quarter. The New York-based United Nations had seen fit to tell Asil's Greek opponents to "lay off" Polly Peck, but I suspect the US administration in Washington took a far dimmer view of what the company and its chairman were doing.

By the 1980s, continuing the US's decades-old interest in Cyprus and its effect on regional stability, Washington had become heavily involved in promoting talks between the island's Greek Cypriot and Turkish Cypriot communities. When George Vassiliou had come to power as South Cyprus president in 1988, the Americans had begun to take a tougher line with Turkey. In Vassiliou, they recognised someone with whom they could deal - a pragmatic businessman rather than a purveyor of idealistic political rhetoric. Vassiliou, finding American government ears open to him, had succeeded in painting a clear picture of Turkish Cypriot intransigence alone blocking the way to a Cyprus solution. While the White House was delighted to be discovering a potential new ally in the modern Turkey led by Turgut Özal, the US administration knew it must walk a fine line between encouraging Ankara and pacifying America's large and vociferous Greek lobby. US opinion was that the best way to bring the Turkish Cypriots to heel was through pressure from Ankara - an influence which could be instigated in turn by pressure from Washington. Yet with Dervis Eroglu's anti-negotiation National Unity Party ruling in North Nicosia and Rauf Denktas as President, the picture was not quite so straightforward. While they were in power, there would be little hope of a settlement except on terms which gave the Turkish Cypriots at least partial self-determination in their own territory. What was needed, in American eyes, was a more amenable hand on the tiller of North Cyprus. At first glance, the answer seemed obvious. Asil Nadir was a powerful figure, university-educated, business-minded, from a family well-respected and deeply rooted in Turkish Cypriot culture, yet with a clear bent towards Western European ideas and manners.

In the late autumn of 1989, the US Embassy in London made contact with Çavlan Süerdem, requesting that Asil meet Nelson Ledsky - the US State Department's Special Cyprus Co-ordinator who was at the time actively involved in negotiations on the island. At first dubious, Asil immediately consulted Ankara and the TRNC government before agreeing to see Ledsky. In fact, it was not the first time that a government had made contact with him about the Cyprus issue - during previous discussions with British officials, it had even been suggested to him that the authorities could offer him access to "some other island" in the world, if only he would withdraw his business influence from Cyprus. The discussion with Ledsky, however, was to be his first - and last - with United States authorities.

The meeting took place in Polly Peck's Berkeley Square offices on the afternoon of 14th December 1989, with Çavlan Süerdem present throughout, and went on for two and a half hours. Though couching his thoughts in diplomatic terminology, Ledsky made no pretence of the fact that he was dissatisfied with the attitude of Rauf Denktas. He criticised Denktas as unreasonable, but was full of praise for George Vassiliou. Curious about why Ledsky had asked for this meeting, Asil pointed out to the US envoy that he was an industrialist, not a politician. Ledsky's response was that Vassiliou too was a businessman of a similar background, adding: "Between us, we can solve this problem." Asil explained that the Greek Cypriots were very hostile to him personally, citing a number of recent newspaper attacks. Ledsky answered that he would "ensure that Vassiliou says something positive about you". True to his word, Vassiliou would subsequently make a public statement praising Asil during Ledsky's next visit to Cyprus…though he would go back on the attack as soon as the envoy had left the island. As the Berkeley Square meeting reached its conclusion, Ledsky spelt out the reason for the visit - Asil should meet Vassiliou, he said, and together they would be able to help solve the Cyprus problem. It was a clear invitation to my brother to usurp the elected TRNC president's role. Asil was non-committal in his immediate response and Ledsky left saying he wished to leave open the lines of communication between them. Asil emerged from the talks outraged by what he considered the American's cheek at trying to use him to undermine the Turkish Cypriot President and vowing that Ledsky would not be entertained in the building in future. Later his views on the issue, which followed the official Turkish Cypriot line, were set out in a paper to the US State Department.

Within a matter of weeks, North Cyprus was in the run-up to a general election and Asil became more heavily involved than ever. With TRNC President Denktas throwing his weight behind the incumbent National Unity Party (UBP), lending his personal popularity and credibility to the party he had founded, opposition politicians decided their only hope of winning office was to join forces. They formed an opposition coalition and mounted their campaign against Dervis Eroglu and UBP.

As the clock ticked away towards the election, set for May 1990, it was a neck-and-neck race. Rumour was rife in North Cyprus that considerable outside funding was being poured into the opposition campaign. The left-wing Republican Turkish Party - led by Özker Özgür - was known to have links with the Greek Cypriot communist party, Akel, and to have well-established contacts with the Soviet Union.

The prospect of an opposition victory was viewed with alarm by many. The coalition - a bizarre set of bedfellows comprising the far left, the religious right and the Social Democrats - was committed to seeking a settlement with the Greek Cypriots and a speedy end to the sixteen-year-old partition of the island. Though he was not averse to the principle of a settlement with the South, Asil was determined that it should not happen before a few more years had elapsed - years in which the Turkish Cypriot economy, with his continued commercial assistance, could develop and become self-sufficient. He could not sit back and watch a reportedly internationally-bankrolled opposition snatch power…only to give up hard-won independence in the haste to strike a political deal. Asil used his newly-launched newspaper, *Kibris*, then selling some 6,000 copies a day and the run-away market leader, in a bid to thwart the opposition's quest for power. The paper lent its own voice to promoting the UBP anti-settlement stance - a stance which said that early settlement would mean risking the end of the physical security obtained during the 1974 war. Asil's printing facilities in North Cyprus were also used to help publish UBP election material and helped fund campaigning. Asil had supported UBP in the 1985 general election, but this time, through his newspaper, he was in a real position to influence the outcome.

From my own back-seat viewpoint, I was very worried to see Asil take such a prominent part in the electoral process. It was plain that his influence in North Cyprus was such that if he threw his weight behind one party it would almost certainly win. I begged Asil not to get involved, but he refused to be swayed. His aims for that election campaign went far beyond mere domestic politics. He wanted to see North Cyprus on the international map - a force to be reckoned with economically - and he believed passionately that the only way to achieve that was to keep the pro-settlement lobby out of office. "If we want North Cyprus to survive, Bilge, and be able stand up to the other side," he would tell me over and over again, "we need the time to get on our feet and be able to stand up as economic equals to the Greek Cypriots."

Asil's unequivocal support for UBP made him a lot of foes within the other Turkish Cypriot political parties. Rauf Denktas understood

159

and endorsed his actions as a means to the end they both sought. The two men met and discussed the situation. Dervis Eroglu and his party were left with no illusions about the reason behind Asil's backing. In exchange for his considerable assistance, Eroglu agreed to support Rauf Denktas in the presidential election that was to follow. The general public, meanwhile, was largely unaware of the discussions behind the scenes. When UBP eventually emerged as the election winners, taking fifty-four per cent of the vote and a landslide thirty-four out of fifty seats in Parliament, just as I had feared, Asil acquired a great many enemies who resented his interference.

Nor would resentment over that election have been confined to the shores of Cyprus. Thousands of miles away, in Washington, UBP's victory must have left the US administration fuming, its hopes of a less hard-line TRNC administration effectively outmanoeuvred by one man. The seriousness with which they viewed the situation was reflected in a confidential message purportedly sent at around the time of the election by the American Ambassador in Ankara to the Turkish government. Revealed in a *New Statesman* article by former British Labour MP, Christopher Price, the communication was quoted as saying: "Turkey and the US should enter into closer relations. Our wish is to offer you support, but there is a Greek lobby in the USA. You know their influence. If they get angry, they withdraw their vote support from the US Congress. First we have to silence them. This will be achieved through a solution to the Cyprus problem. As for Denktash remaining in his armchair, this is impossible. Denktash and the National Unity Party should be ousted from the administration. But if this is to materialise, Nadir, who is their most important supporter, should be neutralised."

That May general election must have been the last straw for a US administration already irritated to see that Asil also had the ear of the Turkish president, Turgut Özal - not only on economic matters, in which they had a very good understanding, but also on the politics of Cyprus. Reading between the lines of the evidence we have - and a veil of official US secrecy drawn over other information - I believe the Americans, having been rebuffed in their diplomatic overtures to Asil, sought a direct approach. If Polly Peck could not be deflected from supporting North Cyprus, then the firm and its chairman would simply have to be put out of action. As the Greek Cypriots acknowledge, their back-room "stirring" had failed, over seven years from 1983, to penetrate what they described as a ring of "protection" around Asil and Polly Peck. PPI was hailed as the best-performing share of the 1980s on the London Stock Exchange and its chairman, designated the thirty-seventh wealthiest man in Britain, was the very epitome of the Thatcher era which had spawned his commercial success - hard-working, self-made

160

and unafraid to take risks in the pursuit of enterprise. But the United States, with its then much-vaunted "special relationship" with Britain, was one power which could have had the protection breached. A coded message sent through diplomatic channels from the US State Department to Britain's Foreign and Commonwealth Office at that time cautioned that Polly Peck and its chairman had become an "impediment" to a Cyprus solution. They must have been well pleased by the events which followed.

Was there an officially-sanctioned campaign to do away with that "impediment"? Some, I know, would ridicule such a suggestion. But there are certainly those - some highly placed in the British Establishment and privy to its inner workings - who believe there was. The volume of evidence uncovered in the intervening years, some of which has yet to be made public, leads even me - not by nature a conspiracy theorist - to feel sure that there was more to my brother's commercial demise than the public has been given to understand.

Undoubtedly, it was a complex international backdrop against which would be played out the final months of Polly Peck - the puzzling months in which our family life was turned upside down.

For some, there seemed to be signals of what was to come. The first indication of trouble brewing came in the autumn of 1989, when Asil received a message from an official within the Turkish Foreign Ministry in Ankara, warning him to expect an attack. It was not the first time that there had been such alerts, and since there was no indication from which quarter the assault would come, there was little prospect of anticipating it. But Asil did try to cover himself against the obvious avenues of attack. He guessed that the Greek Cypriots might make an attempt to frame him by smuggling guns or drugs on to the PPI cargo fleet, so he issued an order that every ship should be searched from top to bottom - including by sniffer dogs - before each sailing.

At about the time of Nelson Ledsky's visit, Citibank, our family's bankers and trustees, hired a commercial investigation agency to make inquiries into PPI. The agency they chose was Kroll Associates, which has also been used by the American secret service, the Central Intelligence Agency. At the same time, Citibank's London representative also approached Elizabeth Forsyth, asking her about drugs and arms-dealing rumours involving Asil which had reached the bank's ears in the US. When Elizabeth looked shocked and categorically rejected the suggestions, the Citibank representative apologised, saying he was under pressure from the US on the issue. In July 1990, weeks before the Polly Peck troubles began, Citibank wrote a "put option" on 7.9 million PPI shares. The terms of this "put option" were that the bank would sell the shares once their price on the Stock Exchange reached 200p. It seemed a very strange move. At that time, Polly Peck shares were trading at more than 450p and there seemed no indication that their value was likely to be more than halved. What prompted Citibank to write that pessimistic "put option" while the shares were riding high, we will never know for sure. We can only speculate that the bank may have been alarmed by someone or something.

During the early summer of 1990, Asil became aware that the steady flow of dinner and discussion invitations from the Conservative Party appeared to be drying up. At about that time, he had lunch with Sir Peter Blaker, chairman of the Conservative Industrial Fund, and Brendan Bruce, the Tory party's communications director, at which they talked of the government's economic and regional policies. The meeting finished on a friendly note, but it was to prove the last. Asil thought little of the sudden hiatus, becoming preoccupied with more pressing concerns as the year wore on. But he was to be reminded of it in a very disturbing manner when, by chance, he ran into Brendan Bruce in Partridge's delicatessen in Sloane Street the following year. Bruce said that what he described as a "high powered delegation" of two men from the security services had visited him and questioned him about his discussions with Asil. They had told him that Asil was "one of the most dangerous men in the world" and that upcoming events would be "embarrassing to the British government". "They warned me off in no uncertain manner," Asil later recalled a "terrified" Bruce telling him that day.

For us there were no such warning signals; no alarm bells ringing. Just as we thought we were riding the crest of a wave, almost overnight it seemed that we found ourselves floundering in a financial and emotional whirlpool. Normal life ended in August 1990. On the 2nd August, Saddam Hussein's Iraqi troops invaded Kuwait and the whole world was suddenly on war alert. Polly Peck, with its heavy involvement in Turkey and North Cyprus on the fringe of the Middle East, was hit immediately by fears of a wider conflict, its shares falling 43p to 410p in a matter of days. Noble Air soon felt the effects of the sharp increase in fuel prices which followed and began to lose money. World-wide fear of air travel, too, would quickly knock Noble Raredon's core holiday business.

By the end of the first week in August, when the first newspaper article appeared linking Michael Allcock's tax probe to dealings in Polly Peck shares, some £200 million was wiped off the value of PPI. Over the following weeks, there was to be a deluge of similar articles. The timing was critical. Polly Peck had always operated with a high proportion of short-term borrowings - using a large number of lenders so that one single source of finance would not become too dominant. This now made the company vulnerable to any loss of confidence. PPI had some loans that needed to be renewed in the autumn and doubts aroused by what was to be virtually a daily dose of "revelations" in the press now made the banks nervous about renewing facilities that they had been happy to lend in the past.

Fehim and I had gone to Poland on business almost immediately after our St Lucia holiday. We went to view the site for the cardboard box factory for the last time before giving the green light for construction to begin. We also wanted to look again at the two hotels for which we had put in refurbishment tenders. On the night of Saturday, 11th August we were in our Warsaw hotel room when Tijen phoned from London, where she had got the early editions of the Sunday papers. She said Noble Raredon's public relations consultant had alerted her that morning to the fact that there were going to be knocking articles about Polly Peck in the newspapers the next morning. The stories would also mention South Audley Management and Noble Raredon. On the Friday, August 10th, we discovered later, Asil's PR man, William Grosvenor, had taken a call from Dominic Prince of *The Sunday Times*, asking to talk to my brother about illegal share trading allegations. Virtually simultaneously, Elizabeth Forsyth's secretary at SAM had answered the telephone to Michael Gillard of *The Observer*, who was making inquiries along the same lines. Elizabeth was in Switzerland with Asil, discussing private financial matters with a series of bankers. Neither she nor Asil responded to the inquiries. Elizabeth would comment later that, because everyone involved knew the media's information to be "radically flawed", they did not give the issue the priority it required, feeling sure the truth would eventually emerge.

The Observer of Sunday, 12th August came out with a story headlined "Polly Peck share deals: Tax probe", while *The Sunday Times* blared "Swiss link in Polly Peck dealings probed". Both articles said the Inland Revenue was investigating deals in Polly Peck shares by a number of Swiss "letterbox" companies - firms registered to a Swiss address, usually for tax purposes. Companies called Tristan, Gateway and Riverbridge were named and a link was drawn between them and South Audley Management. I had never heard of any of the companies, and when I asked Asil he, too, was puzzled. Later, however, we learned that Tristan was a company owned by a family trust and legitimately managed by Confidas, an arm of Citibank - the three firms shared the same address, hence the purported link between them. David Fawcus had told *The Observer* he was not aware of any Inland Revenue investigation and that it had nothing to do with Polly Peck. William Grosvenor told *The Sunday*

Times: "There is no connection between Gateway, Riverbridge, Tristan and Polly Peck or between them and Asil Nadir." In fact, the tax investigators and the other authorities they contacted believed wrongly they had found a link between all three companies and my brother. Any suspect share dealings were nothing to do with Asil or South Audley Management - and indeed no charges have ever been made regarding this.

Unfavourable publicity about Polly Peck had been a regular feature in the columns of *The Observer* for almost a decade, but to see similar information in two separate newspapers made me instantly suspicious that information was being leaked by an official source, and that this time the position could be serious. Even more alarming for me was the fact that both stories mentioned me and Noble Raredon - by implication, it seemed to me, suggesting that we, too, might be party to any supposed wrongdoing. *The Observer* highlighted the fact that Arseven Gümüs, a director of Noble Raredon, had been a founding director of SAM from 1987 until his resignation the previous year. *The Sunday Times* went further, pointing out that SAM and Noble Raredon had both been registered at the same address in South Audley Street until the 18th of May 1988 - the day Fehim and I had taken over Gnome Photographic Products. It said the three "letterbox" companies named had traded in Noble Raredon shares as well as Polly Peck's and also commented that Tristan had the same address in Switzerland as Fairweather Investments, the family trust which held the controlling stake in Noble Raredon on behalf of my family.

I was very angry and bewildered by the allegations and worried for both Asil and myself. On the Sunday the stories appeared, I telephoned Asil, now back in London, and found him in his office. He sounded very upbeat and told me not to worry about what had been written. Then he told me that he was to approach the PPI board that afternoon and put to them a plan to make Polly Peck private. Though the press would later portray the buy-out as a shock move prompted by the weekend's bad publicity, it was nothing new to those who knew Asil well and had heard him talk of going private for several years. When I had left PPI three years earlier, I had explained to Asil how I felt the company no longer had a family atmosphere and he had agreed. "One day, we will run it again as a family," he often used to say as we reminisced over the old times. On occasion, he had grown depressed about the "rat race" into which he felt the demands of the City had increasingly forced himself and PPI. While Asil's gut feeling and vision had made Polly Peck a success story, he was frustrated at having to make more and more appointments to the board in order to satisfy City opinion. He felt his own power to make snap, instinctive decisions to take advantage of good opportunities was being whittled away and resented what he saw as the erosion of his control over the company. In truth, I have always felt Asil had completely the wrong temperament to run a public company, and as that clash became more trying, he would tell how he dreamed of selling his shareholding, taking a boat and sailing off to an island in the Caribbean, where he could while away the days sitting under a tree with family and friends, sipping good wine and eating cheese and olives. But, however low he felt, he would force himself to go on, refusing to be beaten by the Establishment's pressure. By 1990, though, he had decided to take up Swiss residency for tax reasons and was already laying plans to take PPI private by the end of the year - floating off the electronics and agriculture sides - and move its head office to Geneva where he could concentrate on the leisure operations, focusing on Turkey and North Cyprus. There, he had had his eye for several months on a beautiful lakeside house. A few months before, he had shown me photographs of the pink villa set in splendid gardens overlooking Lake Geneva. Not only would this solve his long-running debate with the Inland Revenue about his tax status, but it would be an ideal base from which to run the global empire he had been building.

So the news of the proposed buy-out came as no surprise to me that mid-August weekend. In my heart, though, I wondered whether the timing was right. What concerned me, too, was whether he had secured the financing for what would be a very costly purchase. Asil told me he had and assured me that everything was "under control", but I put the receiver down with a vague sense of disquiet. I knew my brother well - he was such an optimist that, sometimes, if he got a positive response to initial discussions on a given topic, he would consider it as good as done. I crossed my fingers that it was not the case this time.

The fact was, though, that when Asil had travelled back to London that weekend, infuriated by what he saw as a continued negative press attitude and vowing to do something to stop this once and for all, he was heading for disaster. His arrival in Berkeley Square on the Saturday afternoon was likened to the roaring of a maddened lion, as he stormed into his first-floor room, flung his jacket across a chair and slammed his briefcase on the desk, announcing that he was going to bring his buy-out plans forward. "I've had enough of them all. I'm going to do what I want to do and I'm going to take this company private," he said. When Aisling Daly suggested hesitantly that this might lead people to believe that there was some truth in what the newspapers said, he answered back: "They can believe what the hell they like. If it goes private, there'll be no need to worry about share prices rising or falling on rumours." That afternoon was spent drafting, amending and reprinting the wording of Asil's letter to the board and trying to contact board members to call them to a meeting the following day - Mark Ellis was on a touring holiday in Italy and could not be reached; Radar Reshad was in Cyprus; Del Monte chief executive, Brian Haycox, was found on a boat in Miami and flew to London immediately.

It was a group of nervous and shocked executives who gathered at PPI at noon the next day. Asil went down to the board room at half past two when the meeting began, put his letter to the directors and left them to their discussions after half an hour, returning to his room and closing the door behind him. Some forty-five minutes later, David Fawcus joined Asil briefly and then they returned together to the meeting. Soon afterwards, Asil emerged again, mounting the stairs to his room with the directors behind him firing questions. Asil's letter had advised the board that he was giving them advance notice of his *intention* to make an offer for the company, provided the financing was in place. But the statement which the board sent to the Stock Exchange announced that he *had* made an offer to purchase the shares.

Over the next few days, Asil and his advisers sought to finalise the funding needed to make the offer for Polly Peck. Asil believed it would cost around £2 billion for the shares, but he would also have to refinance the company's debts, which were then about £1 billion. Now it seemed vital to be able to proceed, to counter suggestion that Asil had simply stage-managed a bid, then a withdrawal, to deflect attention from PPI's bad press. As the week progressed, and each new avenue was closed off, Asil grew more and more down, as I noticed when I called to see him most evenings after work. Towards the end of the week, he commented to one member of staff: "Next time I wake up with a stupid idea, don't let me do it, will you?"

My worst fears were realised on Friday the 17th, when Asil announced that the bid was off. It was one of the most damaging events in Polly Peck's history - the shares plunged, the Stock Exchange launched an investigation and even the company's most stalwart supporters were bewildered by the turn of events. Why did my brother withdraw his offer? He has always said that certain institutional shareholders had made it clear to him that they would not sell, meaning that he could not have secured the ninety per cent voting rights he required. He also believed many shareholders were looking for a higher offer than he had calculated on making. Some press reports referred to a minimum price of £5 a share - the price had fallen to under £4 just before his offer - others put the value at £6 or more. It made the bid too expensive. I feel sure Asil had the facilities to buy, but not at the price he felt was now expected.

———————

The Nadir family, Cyprus, 1948

Left, 1951: a birthday party for Asil and Bilge

Below, 1953: Asil and his mother in front of the Europa Grocery Shop, Cyprus

Left, 1973: Wearwell goes public — Asil Nadir, Irfan Nadir, Fehim Nevzat, Güner Kasif, Johnny Holder & Jean Thomas

Above, 1983: Asil and Levent in St Tropez
Below left, 1988: Bilge with Asil at Tijen & Rifat's wedding
Below right, 1987: Asil with President Denktas in Cyprus

Above, 1988: At home after the wedding of Tijen & Rifat — Bilge and Asil's mother with seven of her grandchildren
Below, 1988: A reception in Loch Manor in Cyprus to celebrate the marriage alon
with Bilge's & Fehim's twenty-fifth wedding anniversary

Above, September 1989 — "Del Monte"

Above, 1984: Asil with Princess Anne

Middle, 1992: Michael Mates — his gift of a watch to Asil was grossly distorted by the media

Below, 1990: After the opening of the Antalya Sheraton, from left to right — Tijen, Bilge, Asil, Safiye & Meral

Above, 1991: Lonely days in London — Bilge and Sunny

Below, 1997: Elizabeth Forsyth, the former head of South Audley Management — conviction for handling stolen funds quashed

*Left, 1993: Bilge & Fehim i
Cyprus*

*Below, 10th May, 1993: As
back in Cyprus — "the big bir
is back!"*

Though we did not know it then, that weekend sent Polly Peck slithering towards disaster. As August wore on, events went from bad to worse, accompanied by one unfavourable newspaper article after another. The press continued to focus on South Audley Management and the position of Jason Davies, a former stockbroker friend of Asil's eldest son, Birol, and a one-time director of SAM. There was also close interest in the Swiss companies. By then, we knew of Tristan's legitimate operations, but the others were still a mystery.

For all the bad publicity engendered by the speculation over the share probe, at no time was my brother ever linked to these dealings. He was never questioned about them and no charges have ever been brought against him in relation to them. Nor, even, were there any charges relating to South Audley Management, which had been so conspicuously linked to the share allegations. But the damage was being done - not just to Polly Peck as a company, but to Asil personally. Like many entrepreneurs, his wealth was completely bound up with his share-holding in the firm he had created. He had borrowed against the value of his shares - not excessively - but as the implications of what was happening hit him, I believe he began to worry that what appeared to be a concerted attack on the company was aimed, at least in part, at undermining his personal financial position. To my mind, that was one reason why he had decided to bring forward his plans to take the company private.

Despite the unabated onslaught in the press, Asil still believed he could restore confidence in Polly Peck. The share price perked up a little when the company's interim results were announced early as a damage limitation exercise and showed pre-tax profits up seventy-two per cent. Asil was busy trying to get the company's loans renewed and find fresh sources of finance - not easy in the aftermath of what would later prove to have been a devastating turning-point in PPI's fortunes. He never gave me the impression of being desperately worried. Far from it. He was preparing himself and all of us for the opening of PPI's luxurious Voyager Antalya Sheraton hotel - the jewel in the company's leisure crown on the Mediterranean coast of Turkey, just forty miles across the water from North Cyprus. Asil refused to listen to suggestions from some quarters that the launch party should be put off - his only concession was to agree that the guest list should be whittled down. By then, PPI's share price had dropped to 243p, but there was Asil, asking us what we were going to wear to the grand opening.

The hotel launch was set for Saturday, 15th September and I had long been looking forward to it. For Asil, the long-dreamed-of launch of his own top hotel - rated by the Sheraton group which managed it as one of their best three hotels in the world - would boost his slightly battered commercial image and turn the spotlight away from the reported boardroom disagreements within Polly Peck and the bad publicity surrounding the firm. For his sake alone, it was an occasion we were all determined to enjoy. When we flew out to Antalya on the Friday afternoon we were not to be disappointed by the spectacular that had been laid on. Though a team of interior designers had been hired to decorate and furnish the hotel, Asil had insisted on being personally involved throughout, choosing fabrics, furniture and colour schemes for all the rooms and judging the final effect from a series of artists' impressions. Several times, he had shown me various coloured sketches, but this was my first glimpse of the real thing. When I walked through the doors, the scene took my breath away. Once inside, it was as if a slice of sophisticated America had been transported to the southern shores of Turkey. On the uppermost floor, Asil had had the Sultan's Suite built for his own personal use. It had a magnificent view, lavish accommodation and its own roof-top swimming pool.

More than 100 guests, including investors and journalists, were invited from London for the two days of festivities and were brought out on a Noble Air plane from Stansted to Antalya - two hours late because of a Greek air traffic control strike. There were influential members of the Turkish business community flown in from Istanbul and Ankara and the guest of honour was the Turkish Tourism Minister. More guests flew over from North Cyprus with my mother, among them TRNC President, Rauf Denktas. Tour operators from several different countries were also invited to come and see the hotel for themselves. The weekend began with a banquet for 1,000 on the Friday night and there was a buzz among the waiting bankers, brokers and journalists when Asil failed to appear at the start. Popular Turkish singer, Sezen Aksu - the entertainer that evening - was part-way through her act when Asil stepped into the banqueting hall and took his seat beside the Tourism Minister and President Denktas.

The second evening - the launch night itself - was a glitzy black tie affair in the hotel gardens. An enormous reception was laid on inside the hotel and then bedazzled guests were led outside to dinner in a fantasy setting. The entire hotel blazed with light and the gardens, perched high on the cliff-top above the sea, were illuminated by flickering candles. American singer, Randy Crawford, led the entertainment and a magnificent fireworks display lit up the night sky. There was a speech by the Mayor of Antalya and Asil gave a speech too as he symbolically handed over the hotel keys to its Sheraton management.

Lavishly perfect though the occasion was, however, I was aware of an undercurrent of tension. The press contingent spent the weekend watching Asil's every move, following him around the hotel and grounds and taking every opportunity to ask him the as-yet-unanswered questions hovering around PPI and the share dealing allegations. The close scrutiny made Asil highly uncomfortable and he spent most of that weekend in his rooms upstairs. During the Saturday, he was visited there by Turgut Özal, who came to wish him well with the new venture. I felt sure Asil could find out who was behind the share dealings and begged him to act to expose whoever was involved. I even asked a mutual friend to do what he could to persuade Asil to take swift steps to clear his name. The friend - who would afterwards describe it as the worst weekend of his life - urged my brother that unless he answered the share dealing question it would be very damaging to Polly Peck and might even ruin the company. But Asil was adamant. "As long as my conscience is clear - which it is - there is no need to worry," was all he would say.

As Fehim and I relaxed in our suite after the events of the Saturday night, we agreed it had been a superb weekend, but I could not shake off a worrying sense that something was not right - I had a real premonition that something bad was about to happen. It had been an extravagant two days and I felt a twinge of resentment over some of the people who were there to enjoy the hospitality - important business people who carped about my brother behind his back out of jealousy of his success; journalists who were taking every opportunity to quiz him about Polly Peck and its problems. Just as we were thinking of going to bed, at about one o'clock, there was a knock on the door. It was one of my brother's bodyguards to say that Asil wanted us and my mother to come up to his suite. The three of us took the lift up to the seventh floor, where we found Asil sitting beside the pool in the Sultan's Suite with Abide, Çavlan Süerdem and PPI architect, Armagan Tekvar. As we sat and chatted about the previous two days over a pot of tea, I got the distinct impression that Asil was disturbed. The conversation never veered from mundane topics and reassurances over how well everything had gone, yet by the time we said goodnight I was certain my brother shared my own feelings of unease. Although he did not mention anything, I realised afterwards that he must by then have received faxed copies of articles which were to appear in the next day's British Sunday newspapers. Among the continued bad press was a story which raised questions over Asil's contacts with Isabel McMurray, the senior policeman's wife who had set up his team of bodyguards. My brother was furious at the innuendo of impropriety, knowing as he did that it had been the police themselves who had suggested Mrs McMurray's recruitment agency to him. I think that new barrage of publicity brought it home to him that the relentless press campaign would not let up.

169

Looking back, that weekend was the beginning of the end for Polly Peck and for our happiness. For more than a month, Asil had been able to put up a "business as usual" front to hide the deep troubles surrounding his company. Within days, that facade would be ripped away.

———

Three days after we returned from Antalya, the Serious Fraud Office raided South Audley Management, confirming my fears over Asil's refusal to try to scotch the share dealing innuendo. As Michael Gillard wrote in *The Observer* the following weekend, the SFO team was investigating allegations of illegal trading in shares and claims that the Polly Peck share price had been manipulated. According to press reports, the then newly-appointed SFO director, Barbara Mills, and a team of seven SFO investigators were on the doorstep at half past eight on the morning of 19th September. All the people working at SAM - about fifteen in total - were refused immediate entry to the premises and were asked to supply their names and home addresses. Elizabeth Forsyth, holidaying in Switzerland, learned of the raid in her routine daily call to the office that morning. She immediately informed solicitors, Vizards, and notified Asil that the raid was taking place. On legal advice, Elizabeth would remain out of Britain for nearly four months until agreement was reached for her to return for questioning by the SFO. She would subsequently live in self-imposed "exile" in North Cyprus until returning for further questioning in September 1994.

I did not discover what had taken place until that afternoon. Looking back, the raid was clearly a critical point in the chain of events, but at the time I did not foresee how it would have the effect of hitting at Polly Peck through the "back door". Had the Serious Fraud Office raided PPI directly, they would probably have had to get the shares suspended in advance. But by targeting South Audley Management they were under no such obligation, even though SAM was by that point closely associated with Asil because of the press reports. The impact on Polly Peck was devastating.

The morning after the raid, PPI shares opened trading at 243p, but as rumours began leaking into the market, the share price took a spectacular dive. One rumour was of the SFO's raid on South Audley Management the previous day - a claim which was easily proved when, according to journalists, press callers to the SFO received confirmation that it had indeed taken place. According to writer, Tim Hindle, a banker in the City of London received confirmation early that day that Asil was to be questioned by the SFO that afternoon - an interview which had, in fact, been arranged voluntarily by Asil in a bid to resolve the deteriorating situation. The Stock Exchange jitters were further fuelled by a series of bizarre allegations surfacing through news agencies: first Asil had been assassinated by a Middle East hit-man; then he had committed suicide in Hong Kong; then he had been arrested; finally, the stories went, Polly Peck had lost money in Turkish bonds. At Polly Peck, the switchboard was jammed by anxious investors and journalists trying to get at the truth. Round the corner in South Audley Street, I was at my desk that morning when one of my PR men rang to say he had "heard the bad news" and to give me his condolences. I asked him what he meant and he said he had heard that Asil was dead. Fortunately, I had only just spoken to my brother ten minutes previously and knew him to be safely at his desk in Berkeley Square, so I was able to dismiss that rumour straight away.

On the Stock Exchange, nobody wanted to risk waiting to find out if any of the rumours were true. The stampede to unload PPI shares hit the price hard, with evidence of the share slump prompting other investors to join the rush to sell. Asil acted the instant he got wind of the panic. At half past eight that morning, he called his brokers and asked for PPI's shares to be suspended immediately. He could see a false market had been created and knew a share suspension would give PPI the time it needed to clarify its position. His appeal went unheeded. Shearson Lehman and BZW went on trading and as the price plummeted further, banks which had held Asil's PPI shares as security against personal loans also began to off-load the holding in a bid to get some cash return. At twenty minutes past ten, when the shares reached 210p, Citibank exercised its option to sell 7.9 million shares.

It was about half past eleven when I went round to Asil's office to talk to him about the previous day's raid. I had never seen him so angry and upset. Normally, he would stand up and give me a kiss in greeting. This day, he was far too preoccupied. He was pacing around his desk, alternately sitting and standing, shouting into the telephone receiver which was clamped against one ear. "They've got to suspend the shares," I heard him bellow before he slammed the phone down and let rip with a volley of swearing. Naively, at the time I could not really understand why he was quite so enraged - after all, we had seen and survived major share fluctuations at Polly Peck before. It was only later that day that I realised what had happened - not only had the plummeting shares devastated the company's value, but because Asil's personal borrowings were secured against his share-holding, he was being pushed closer and closer to financial ruin.

Finally, at twenty-five past two that afternoon, the shares were suspended at 108p at the third time of asking, some five and a half hours after Asil's initial request. By then, more than thirty million Polly

Peck shares had changed hands that day and the value of Asil's personal stake in the company had fallen by a staggering £160 million.

As we watched the dust settle, there was shocked disbelief at what had happened. Journalists would later describe the events of 20th September as the most dramatic corporate collapse ever seen in Britain. For us - and for thousands of stunned PPI investors - it was hard to comprehend how a corporation like Polly Peck could have been reduced to rubble in a single day by largely inaccurate rumour-mongering. A month earlier, Polly Peck's market value had stood at £1.5 billion. Yet the business itself was still as sound and as profitable as it had been the month, even the day, before, and there had been no suggestion to the contrary. As *The Financial Times* Lex column commented: "The shares plunged so fast, and in circumstances so bizarre that Polly Peck's market price has lost all contact with fundamentals." Lex went on to comment that, at 108p, the share price had, "...a deathbed rating that companies reach only when nearly bust", adding: "But that surely is not Polly Peck's position." The share price collapse had been brought about solely by news of the raid on South Audley Management - which was no evidence of any wrongdoing - and the totally unfounded scare stories about Asil. Moreover, it had been compounded by the failure of the Stock Exchange to suspend Polly Peck's share trading until the third time of asking. Had trading been halted at the first or second request, the position would have been much different. Why had the Stock Exchange dragged its heels? What gain could it possibly perceive in allowing a major corporation to be brought to its knees - dragging 23,000 shareholders down with it?

That afternoon, Asil went voluntarily to the Serious Fraud Office headquarters in Elm Street. There, he was served with a Section 2 notice, depriving him of the right to silence. In a three-hour interview with an SFO accountant, David Morrison, and solicitor, Robert Wardle, Asil was asked about a wide range of companies and individuals. In front of them, the SFO had a number of documents. When Asil asked where they had come from, he was told they had been handed over by the Finnish bank, KOP. KOP would later strenuously deny having given any documents to the SFO at that time, although they did hand over notes and documents much later, at the end of December 1990. In fact, the documents concerned were identical to papers which had much earlier been in the possession of the Inland Revenue. Their presence on that desk at the SFO seemed to be clear evidence that the SFO and Inland Revenue had indeed been working together, despite protestations to the contrary by Special Office Two's crooked tax-man, Michael Allcock.

The day after the share collapse, Allcock and his deputy, Richard Cook, went to the solicitors, Vizards, who were dealing with the Inland Revenue on Asil's behalf. They were clearly alarmed at the way the tax investigation had culminated in the collapse of PPI and at pains to dissociate themselves from the SFO's activities. They pointed out that they had not leaked any information, either to the press or to any other regulatory body. When Asil told me about this visit, I wondered who was going to pay for the huge losses suffered by Polly Peck shareholders. Later, in 1993, Allcock's own solicitor would reveal that his client had indeed passed information about Asil's affairs to the London Stock Exchange and had been "instrumental" in the referral of them to the Serious Fraud Office. Allcock had breached his own rules, for the Inland Revenue is prevented by law from disclosing information on tax-payers' affairs to third parties, including the police. And, in Asil's case, the information they relayed had been misinterpreted. Also forbidden by law is the kind of collaboration which clearly took place between the Revenue, SFO and Stock Exchange. As Allcock himself would later admit, in an interview for a *Panorama* programme that was never broadcast: "If it wasn't for the relationship I had with the Stock Exchange in that last few years, which was all totally unofficial, incidentally, Polly Peck would never have been broken."

During the meeting at Vizards, Allcock handed over a note of a telephone conversation which had taken place the previous month between a Mr Parrott, a senior Inland Revenue official, and Michael Chance, a deputy director of the SFO. According to the note, Chance had telephoned Parrott on Tuesday, 21st August and had invited the Revenue to a meeting two days later to exchange information which might assist the SFO's inquiries into Asil, Polly Peck and South Audley Management. The meeting was to be between the SFO and the Department of Trade and Industry, with a member of the Metropolitan Police present. Parrott declined the invitation, saying the Revenue could see no purpose being served by it, and was said to have told Chance that he regarded the SFO as "being on a fishing expedition led on by newspaper articles", adding that the SFO had "nothing to go on" and was unlikely to find anything. According to Parrott's note of the conversation, Chance agreed that this was the case. Allcock's opinion of the SAM raid, recorded by Vizards, was that the SFO "had acted badly and the SFO would succeed whichever way - that either way they would find something or they would have destroyed the company". Events would bear that judgement out.

Allcock and Cook were not the only people concerned at the way the SFO had conducted itself. There was press criticism of the high-profile raid on SAM. As a report in the *Financial Times* a month later stated, the SFO was now under pressure to justify its actions. The article concluded: "…unless it [the SFO] can carry its investigation forward, its part in the demise of Polly Peck will continue to haunt it."

When Asil emerged from Elm Street, it was to a barrage of publicity. Though the pavement outside had been deserted when he arrived, by the time he left it was swarming with reporters, camera-men and photographers. Television lights blazed, flash-bulbs went off and microphones and tape-recorders were thrust in front of him as he ducked into his car amid a bombardment of shouted questions. It would later emerge that a news agency had been tipped off by the SFO that Asil was attending Elm Street for interview - just one of a series of leaks from that quarter which would later prompt a magistrate to insist that leaks from the SFO must stop.

The raid on SAM and the share collapse it precipitated set in train a three-month nightmare, likened by one member of staff at PPI to a house of cards falling one by one. Throughout, though, Asil would never publicly lose his cool or his confidence. When one door closed, he would simply move on to another. Looking back, I cannot believe just how calm he appeared. If the banks had been nervous about extending facilities to Polly Peck since the share dealing allegations had surfaced in August, now they were panicking. Asil knew he must find new sources of cash if the company were to survive. Amid talk of replacing him as PPI chairman and more innuendo in the press, Asil flew to New York on 28th September to talk to Turkish President Turgut Özal, who was in the US for an International Monetary Fund conference. He flew back with a promise from Özal that he would help by arranging a facility for him in Turkey. On 1st October, PPI issued a statement saying it was seeking an answer to its liquidity problems but could not provide sufficient information for trading in its shares to resume. "The chairman has been in contact with the government of Turkey and the board draws considerable encouragement from the degree of interest shown by that government," the statement added. Four days later, a meeting of PPI's creditor banks agreed to give the company another week's grace to find the cash it needed.

In the event, the Polly Peck board's faith in assistance from Turkey proved misplaced. True to his word, Turgut Özal returned to Ankara and raised the question of a financial lifeline to PPI. But we were told his efforts to help were blocked by Minister for Economic Affairs, Günes Taner, a former Citibank executive in Istanbul. Why Taner put the brakes on, we have never been entirely clear. Journalist David Barchard's suggestion was a lingering resentment on Taner's part over being stood

174

up for lunch by Asil in the past. The explanation I consider nearer the mark is that the "old guard" of Turkish industry had grown to resent Asil as a newcomer who had shaken up their cosy monopolies. They brought their own pressure to bear on Özal through Taner. If PPI was given state aid by Turkey, they would pull all their cash out of the Turkish banks, draining the country's financial system dry. It was a powerful threat and Asil quickly realised his hopes of a bail-out from Ankara were at an end. Banks in Turkey did offer to put up £100 million as a loan, but Asil felt they were asking for too many assets as security - including the newly-opened £60 million Antalya hotel - and he refused to accept. "I'm not going to give in to blackmail," he told me angrily. Asil was hurt and disappointed, I am sure, by the reaction from a country in which he so strongly believed, yet he still managed to hide his feelings. Only once, when I walked into his office to find him giving Günes Taner a piece of his mind over the telephone, did I detect how angry he must have been.

For the rest of October and November, Asil embarked on an exhausting round of shuttling between London, Istanbul and North Cyprus. On 12th October, the creditor banks met again and - fearing any hasty action on their part might make it impossible to recoup their debts - agreed to give PPI further time to come up with a financial solution. One member of Polly Peck's staff was upset to hear the bankers sniggering behind closed doors after the PPI contingent had been asked to leave the meeting. Only a few months earlier, those same bankers had been falling over themselves to lend Asil money.

By this time, Polly Peck was in dire straits, but I felt confident that when Asil went to North Cyprus he would, as a last resort, return with money to prop up the company. Yet he came back empty-handed - something many people still speculate about whenever the demise of Polly Peck is discussed. Day after day when he was in Cyprus, Asil would go and sit on the sun-warmed rocks on the shoreline below the Crystal Cove Hotel site, staring out across the Mediterranean towards Turkey while he wrestled with his thoughts. Finally, towards the end of October, he came to what was probably the most momentous decision of his life - he would not bring the cash back to the UK. To bring back money from North Cyprus, he knew, would have meant draining the companies there, severing their vital cash flow, and disrupting the entire Turkish Cypriot economy. As he remarked to one member of staff, when it was suggested he might pacify the banks by bringing some cash back from the island: "I am not releasing a penny out of that country because those bastards intend to get me one way or another."

Many people wondered why Asil did not just produce the money shown as "cash and bank balances" in the last set of Polly Peck accounts, dated December 1989. But it was not that simple. Between then and the following summer, though, a great deal of that money had been spent on developments in Turkey and in North Cyprus and by the autumn the advance payments to the fruit growers had also been made. There were also substantial funds on deposit in North Cyprus, and Asil knew they were crucial to the country's foreign exchange reserves.

Asil's decision was one which few people outside North Cyprus or the wider Turkish Cypriot community would be able to understand. Even I found his determination hard to swallow. During the years to come, on occasions when we were all scratching around for cash, I would snap at Asil, "You just had to be a hero, didn't you?" Now that I have returned to live on the island, though, I accept that he saw then, more clearly than I, just how ruinous a wholesale cash drainage operation would have been. At that stage, more than one in five families in the TRNC depended upon Asil, either through the Polly Peck companies or his private banking and newspaper interests. He had brought much-needed foreign capital and investments to a country that had been starved of them. To have removed the money would have given victory to the enemies encircling him. Among ordinary Turkish Cypriots, Asil had acquired a saviour status which he valued more than his own wealth. He was not prepared to sacrifice that trust and respect. Asil had not lived in Cyprus since his teens and had been too busy even to visit for twenty years until leading the first trip by investors in 1981. But he had seen through my father's eyes just how important their state was to Turkish Cypriots, giving them a place to belong and to feel safe after all the suffering and violence of the previous decades. Through our father, too, Asil had understood the importance of Polly Peck to that independent state. It had been the first company to bring hope to North Cyprus in the first grim years following the 1974 war and it had afforded the country the chance of continued survival, in spite of the world's refusal to recognise its existence.

The death knell for Polly Peck sounded on 24th October when Asil, for once showing the strain, arrived back at Berkeley Square for a board meeting which concluded that there was no option but to call in administrators. Asil begged the rest of the board to give him just a little more time, but they refused. They had been advised that PPI was trading insolvently, they argued. It was a plainly shocked and exhausted Asil who was seen to mount the stairs to his office, almost in tears as he remarked, half to himself, "They simply don't understand me." It was one of our worst-ever days. For me, it brought flooding back all the memories, stretching back more than a quarter of a century, of how we had built up Wearwell and then Polly Peck; how hard we had all worked to create a thriving business. I felt particularly for Asil - I knew how much he cared about the company which had been his life for a decade. To Asil, Polly Peck was like an adored child. Indeed, over the years, he had devoted far more of his time and energies to PPI than to his human offspring. The night after the board meeting, when I called to see him at home, he still tried to keep up a brave face. He believed the company was still fundamentally sound and, ever the optimist, assured me the appointment of administrators would be "only temporary" until the financing could be put on to an even keel. "It has been a rotten day. I am going to have a hot bath and relax," was his comment that night to journalists.

Administrators are court-appointed officials, usually accountants, who give a troubled firm relief from its creditors and time to reorganise in the hopes of surviving. In Polly Peck's case, the three men named the next day by Mr Justice Morritt to try and steer the company through turbulent waters were Michael Jordan and Richard Stone, both of the Cork Gully insolvency branch of accountants, Coopers & Lybrand, and Christopher Morris, from accountants, Touche Ross. The latter's task was to represent the PPI shareholders and to investigate whether they might have any claim against the company's directors. Asil agreed to remain as chairman and work alongside the administrators, giving them what assistance he could - particularly in relation to the Turkish and North Cyprus businesses - to get the company back on its feet.

Asil established a good relationship with Richard Stone. Nevertheless, he felt unable to put his faith in the administrators. He lost patience with them when Stone and Jordan, against Asil's advice, announced themselves in North Cyprus as being from Cork Gully - something guaranteed to upset the whole community, which feared they had come to sell assets and close the companies. After their appointment, as he still pursued his quest for financing, he reconsidered his decision not to retrieve the money from North Cyprus. But hours more thought on the Cypriot seashore during his visits made him more convinced of his strategy. He was determined that, for the sake of the country and the companies operating there, the administrators should never be able to seize any of the resources held in the country. Asil knew he would have to face the music for his actions. But he never envisaged just how serious the repercussions would be.

As the new administrators got down to work at Berkeley Square, a team of accountants from Peat Marwick McLintock had been allowed to operate in a basement office for three weeks, methodically going through the company's books for the Serious Fraud Office. On Tuesday, 30th October, however, that orderly pattern of working was destroyed by what I can only term a piece of pure theatre on the part of the SFO. That day, at eight o'clock in the morning, SFO investigators descended on PPI's offices in spectacular fashion. Staff arriving for work were searched and sent home, while the sixteen investigators enlisted the help of a locksmith to force open drawers and cupboards. They took no documents from the building, though, when they left late that night. The raid attracted considerable press attention. One journalist who turned up at the office on a quite separate mission soon after the raid began found his way barred by policemen. When he returned to his car, he heard a local radio station broadcasting news of the raid on one of its early-morning bulletins. Abide Gönültas discovered the raid in progress when she turned up for work as usual. As soon as she realised what was happening she retreated, telling the policemen standing guard that she had come to visit a friend but would return another time. As soon as she was out of sight of the building, Abide raced to the nearest telephone box and called Asil at home. When I heard the news from David Heaton, my finance director, I raced round to Asil's house in Aldford Street to comfort him. I found him sitting in the living room, calmly sipping a cup of tea and showing no visible sign of emotion. When I asked him what was going on, he remarked: "They were already in there. I don't know what they're after - they're just putting on a show." When I passed PPI's offices at seven o'clock that evening on my way home, there was still a police car outside and a swarm of journalists on the pavement. Given that the SFO's representatives already had a presence in 42 Berkeley Square, there was no need for the high drama of the raid that day. More than a month after its disastrous raid on South Audley Management which had precipitated the Polly Peck share crash, I believe the SFO was under pressure to come up with charges to justify its actions and was determined to find some basis to prosecute. If no charges were forthcoming there would be tough questions to answer over who was to blame for the company's collapse.

Two days after the raid, it seemed there was a slight upturn in Asil fortunes. His lawyers were granted leave by the High Court for a judicial review to examine the Serious Fraud Office's conduct. The whole family was hopeful that the SFO would be told to "put up or shut up" on the issue of the share dealings probe. Our hopes would be dashed the following month when Asil was arrested before he had the chance to make the appeal.

While I was deeply afraid for my brother through all this, at the outset I had had little suspicion that his predicament would have a knock-on effect on Noble Raredon. I knew the business press had always drawn a connection between Asil and me as his "little sister" - sometimes dubbing Noble Raredon "little Polly" - but it was quite clear that in reality there was no link whatsoever between our two companies. Asil had no stake in Noble Raredon and the only common ground between us in terms of business was through Asil's Noble Air. As September turned into October, though, I had begun to realise that, regardless of logic or justice, I too was being sucked into the controversy which raged on in the newspapers. As Asil's sister and close working colleague for so many years, there seemed no way of extracting myself from the mire into which my brother's company was sinking. And when I saw how Asil was suffering as he tried desperately to save PPI, the last thing I wanted to do was put distance between us. In the good days, I had been happy for people to make the connection between us; maybe bask a little in Asil's reflected glory. Now the going was tough, but I was determined to give my brother all the support I could - risking whatever fall-out might come my way.

The first article to bring home to me the serious possibility of Noble Raredon taking a knock in the wake of the South Audley Management raid appeared in *The Financial Times* on Saturday, 29th September. The story told how our family kept corporate shareholdings "disguised" by nominees and trust companies in offshore centres such as the Isle of Man, Jersey and the Cayman islands. It was accompanied by an illustration which mentioned me, Fehim, Fairweather Investments, the trust of which we were beneficiaries, and Noble Raredon. It clearly linked us to South Audley Management through the fact that SAM had once shared our offices and through Arseven Gümüs's former directorship at SAM. A very similar chart appeared in *The Guardian* a few days later, this time mentioning us under the heading of "Asil Nadir's international network".

Far worse was to come. Noble Raredon had agreed overdraft facilities with two British banks - up to £2.5 million with the Midland and £2 million with the National Westminster. In the second week of October, we needed to send some money to Poland, but when we tried to do so, the Midland Bank informed us that our facilities had been withdrawn. As soon as I heard this, I rang the branch and asked to see the manager straight away. He came to our offices that day. I was armed with all my figures and projections, had with me Noble Raredon's finance director, and was psyched up for a financial tussle. I was stunned to be told baldly by the bank manager that the facilities had been withdrawn "because you are Asil Nadir's sister and you have lost your credibility". I just looked at him, trying to digest his words and racking my brain to think what I had done wrong. For a few seconds I was not certain I had heard him properly. Then the initial shock gave way to fury - how could this man sit there and tell me there was nothing wrong with the company, nothing wrong with the projects, but that it was me that was the problem…and not even me as a person, but because my brother was Asil Nadir? True enough, Asil had been interviewed - voluntarily - by the Serious Fraud Office, but I had always supposed that the principle of justice was to believe in someone's innocence until they had been proven guilty. Moreover, even if Asil had been guilty, how could they suggest that his situation in any way tarnished my "credibility" just because we were related. "What kind of age are we living in?" I burst out angrily. "Are these the Dark Ages, that you can sit there and say you are punishing me because I am from a certain family?" As the manager, full of apologies, again reiterated the Midland's stance, I mentally faded out his voice, concentrating furiously instead on what the next course of action should be. We were coolly polite as we said our goodbyes. A few days later, the NatWest called us to a meeting. Having heard of the Midland's action, they said, they had decided that they too should withdraw their facilities. This time I did not even bother trying to argue it out with them. I could see there was no point.

Clearly, we would have to approach other banks to try and establish the vital credit lines we needed to continue the business. As one newspaper at the time put it, the banks had "pulled the rug from under the feet" of Noble Raredon. But there was too much at stake simply to give up - we had spent more than two years establishing the foundations for profitable and varied businesses; now there was everything to play for and I was determined not to let these two banks' unjust and short-sighted behaviour stand in our way. I realised how right my decision was when, a few days later, I received a fax from the management and staff at the Olive Tree Hotel in North Cyprus. They said they had heard about our difficulties and offered to work without pay if they had to, to keep the business going. The selfless offer gave me the will to fight on.

First, though, we had to take stock. For weeks, although hardly any Noble Raredon shares were changing hands, we had noticed a steady decline in the price. In early August, the shares had stood at 93p - a price which was only slightly down on the year's high of 102p and valued the company's market capitalisation at £23 million. Within three weeks of the first newspaper reports of the Polly Peck shares probe, the shares were down to 67p. By 18th October the share price had slumped to 26p - an alarming two-thirds reduction over a period of less than two months, which gave the company a market value of just £5 million. That day, the directors agreed at an emergency meeting that we should request a suspension of Noble Raredon shares on the Stock Exchange while we sought new sources of funding. We knew the sharply reduced share price in no way represented the position or prospects of Noble Raredon. The company's assets were valued at £11.5 million and debts totalled £2.5 million - £1.8 million on loan from the Turkish Tourism

Incentive Bank, secured on the Sunset Holiday Village, and the remainder in the form of an overdraft. The meeting was unanimously of the opinion that the share price had been affected, as we announced in the public statement released later that day, "entirely due to market sentiment following the suspension of dealings in Polly Peck International Plc and as a result of the family relationship between the chairman of Noble Raredon…and her brother".

The Noble Raredon share suspension hit the headlines in all the newspapers the following morning. Several papers described it as a "new knock" for the Nadir family. *Today* saw it as the "£10m disaster for Polly Peck tycoon's sister" and another edition of the same paper announced that "the curse of Polly Peck" had spread. There was little time to dwell on what had happened, though. The biggest task ahead of us was to find new banks willing to extend credit facilities. Almost every day for the rest of October and into November, I filled my briefcase with details of our projects, targets and feasibility studies and did the rounds of the banks. Every one of them turned us down, refusing even to open an account in the name of Noble Raredon.

As I began to run out of British banks to approach, determined not to be beaten, I set my sights on continental institutions with branches in London, still with no success. My next strategy was to try a Turkish bank. I approached a London branch of the Cyprus Credit Bank, where Tri-Sun Travel already had an account, and asked for credit facilities to be extended. The manager there, Hüseyin Evren, said he would check with the head office in North Cyprus and I was delighted when, a few days later, he told me he had been given the go-ahead. Now, it seemed, we could get back to work.

My happiness was to be short-lived. A couple of days after that confirmation, Mr Evren came to visit me with his assistant, Sonay Yahyalar. The manager came straight to the point: he was very sorry, but feared that if he gave me the facility he had promised, he might have difficulty in keeping the London branch open. Mr Evren was unwilling to discuss the matter, but when I pressed him he told me his fears stemmed from a visit by Bank of England officials that day. They had asked to see the Tri-Sun Travel accounts and were handed the file which included a letter detailing the proposed credit facility. Mr Evren said the officials had told him they were "disappointed" to see the bank still handling Nadir family business accounts. Then they had turned away and remarked casually that the branch's computer system was not up to scratch, so it might have trouble renewing its operating licence the following year. To Mr Evren's ears, those few comments contained an obvious warning. I had to agree with him. As soon as I heard the story, I gave up on attempts to find finance in Britain. For the next twenty months, I would try my luck with banks in Istanbul, Switzerland and Germany…growing steadily more disillusioned with each new rebuff.

In the meantime, we had some tough decisions to take within Noble Raredon. Our first move was to halt all proposed new investments. All the Polish projects, including the cardboard box factory and the hotel refurbishment, were put on ice. To rub salt in our wounds, we would discover several months later that our Warsaw hotels tender had been judged the best submitted - by that time, however, we would be in no position to go ahead with it. The credit squeeze meant some projects ground to a halt part-way through. Only those operations already up and running - Mosaic Holidays, The Olive Tree and Sunset holiday complexes, Tri-Sun Travel and Elite Optics - were able to continue functioning because they could generate their own day-to-day cash flow.

During the first weeks following the share suspension, I began to receive a string of rather odd callers. Public knowledge that we were in difficulties seemed somehow to attract the most unsavoury characters to our door, either in South Audley Street or at home. They all wanted to seize ownership of Noble Raredon on the cheap, but I was in no mood to relinquish control. My fighting spirit was intact then and I still had so many plans to see through. As far as I was concerned, Asil's problems were no more than a temporary hiccup. As soon as he was able to get back on his feet and prove himself in business again, our situation too would be righted. The first caller that autumn offered me 30p a share for our 14 million shares, meaning I would be selling our stake in the company for just £4.2 million - a stake which just weeks earlier had been worth more than £13 million. I laughed at the offer and then showed our visitor the door, as I would terminate every similar offer during the weeks to come.

As the stress mounted, cracks began to appear in the unity of the Noble Raredon directors. Trevor Davies had already resigned in September, but I asked him to stay with us as a non-executive director and he agreed, attending only for board meetings once a week. The remaining directors began to get the jitters that we might be trading illegally now our source of funds had been withdrawn. They wanted to call in the administrators, but I vetoed that plan - with £11.5 million in assets and only £2.5 million in debts, the company was sound financially. Instead, lawyers were summoned to confirm the legal position for the directors, who did not wish to be held responsible. Another suggestion was that Noble Raredon might be able to secure new funding if I stood down as chairman. With the benefit of hindsight, maybe this was the only way we could have saved the company. At the time, though, it was something I refused to countenance. My resignation would have been as good as admitting there was something wrong with the company or its investments, while it was obvious the only "fault" lay in my being a Nadir. I had always been proud of my name - of my family - and it hurt me more than anything else that it should now be the cause of so many problems.

CHAPTER EIGHT

The Turquoise Conspiracy

By the end of the year, Asil's predicament took an alarming new twist which, for the time being at least, deflected my attention from the dilemma at Noble Raredon. For a month during late November and early December, he had been in Turkey and North Cyprus, lobbying hard for the financial backing Polly Peck needed. While he was away, he received a message from the administrators, asking him to come to a meeting with them. The meeting was fixed for Sunday, 16th December at Polly Peck's offices and Asil announced that he would fly back from Turkey the day before.

As the meeting drew closer, I began to be more and more uneasy about the prospect of Asil returning to London. To me, it seemed strange that the administrators were asking to meet on a Sunday. For a week beforehand, close friends and business associates began ringing to warn me that my brother would be arrested the moment he set foot in Britain. The meeting with the administrators was merely a ruse to lure Asil back into the arms of the Serious Fraud Office, they cautioned. One caller implored me to tell Asil to challenge the administrators to meet him in Turkey if they were serious about wishing to talk. Alarmed, I telephoned Asil in his room at the Sheraton Hotel in Istanbul and begged him not to make the journey. My call met a frosty response. Asil, I discovered later, had received similar warnings from other people and was quite irate by now, snapping, "Why shouldn't I come back? I've done nothing wrong. If they are going to question me, let them. I am going to come back."

Desperate to make him realise how worried I was, I again dialled Istanbul, this time to speak to Fehim, who was with Asil at the Sheraton. I urged him to talk to my brother and try to make him change his mind. Fehim was no more successful, though. When he broached the subject over dinner in the Sheraton that night, Asil told him matter-of-factly, "If you're concerned about coming back with me, go on another airline." Buoyed then by Asil's confidence, Fehim countered, "If you're going, I will be with you."

By the time that Saturday arrived, I felt weighed down by a heavy sensation of dread, sure that something terrible was going to happen. From the outside, it seemed just another normal day, and as I made myself a cup of tea that morning and sat down with it at the kitchen table, I gave myself a mental shake. Asil was sure everything would be all right, I told myself, and I was simply allowing silly worries to get the better of me. I was determined to conjure up a light-hearted mood, to try and act as if there was nothing wrong, if only for the children's sake. Levent had his final university examination that morning and Irfan was in the midst of studying for mock A-levels coming up soon at school. Tijen and I spent the day Christmas shopping and it was three o'clock by the time we got home, laden with bags and exhausted from battling the Saturday crowds. The outing had left me in a slightly happier frame of mind. Asil and Fehim were due to land in two hours and we were expecting them home soon after six o'clock, so Tijen and I settled down for the wait.

At half past four, a telephone call shattered our quiet hopes that the travellers would be home soon. It was Hasan, Asil's chauffeur, who had driven to Stansted airport to meet him, only to be told the jet had been diverted to Heathrow because of fog. He was on his way to Heathrow and would call again. As I put the receiver down, I looked out of the window and felt a twinge of that morning's fears - in South Woodford, just forty miles from Stansted, the sky was perfectly clear. Later, I would learn something even more alarming. Hasan had been shadowed all that day by an unmarked car, which reappeared twice even when he lost it in traffic.

On Asil's private jet 434AN, meanwhile, there was some consternation. The plane had taken off without a hitch at half past two Istanbul time and was cruising smoothly above Paris, heading for Stansted, when captain David Dahl contacted London for permission to land. Behind him, the other travellers - Asil, Fehim, architect, Çetin Kursat, Alan, one of Asil's three bodyguards, and David's wife, Jo-Rae, who was the plane's stewardess - were in relaxed and jovial mood. Over the radio came the reply that Stansted was fog-bound, so the flight was to be diverted to Heathrow. David radioed back: was it possible to land at Luton instead? The answer was negative again. Luton was fog-bound, so was Gatwick and the only place to land was Heathrow. David was immediately suspicious. He turned to Asil, sitting beside Fehim, and said, "There's something funny going on. Let's go back to Paris, land there and see what's happening." Asil shook his head: "No, we'll go on to Heathrow if that's what they say."

186

Almost as soon as the wheels touched down at Heathrow, the entire plane could sense that this was no ordinary landing. Outside in the falling dusk, on the secluded area of tarmac where David was being instructed to taxi, stood row upon row of police cars - eight or nine squad cars, Transit vans, uniformed officers with flak jackets and machine guns, others holding large police dogs on leashes. As Asil would remark afterwards, it was like a scene from *The Untouchables*. David, an American ex-Vietnam fighter pilot used to split-second decisions and hasty get-aways, offered Asil one more chance. "It looks like we've got a welcoming party," he called back over his shoulder. "Just say the word and we can take off again for Paris or somewhere else if you don't want to be welcomed." Again Asil refused, telling David simply to go where he was told. As David pulled up a few moments later in front of the police and cut the engines, Asil looked round at the others and saw the waxen pallor of Fehim's and Çetin Kursat's faces. "Don't worry," he tried to reassure them with a smile. "It's me they've come for." It was just after five o'clock.

The calm was shattered the instant the plane door opened. In seconds, several policemen had charged on to the aircraft, shouting, "You're all under arrest," in a chorus which sounded to Asil like a battle cry. Yet he would describe later how, as he watched all the police activity inside the plane and outside, he felt a serene detachment creep over him. One of the officers shouted, "Who's Nadir?"

Asil countered swiftly. "I am - and it's *Mr* Nadir to you." Then he turned to Fehim and said, in Turkish, "When you get home, try to contact my lawyers."

Immediately one of the policemen barked, "No talking Turkish. You have to speak English."

A senior officer boarded the jet a few moments later. He went up to Asil and said, "Mr Nadir, you are under arrest. Would you follow me?"

Fehim and the others, told to stay in their seats, watched aghast as Asil was led down the steps. Several policemen remained on board. One went up to Jo-Rae Dahl - a plainly Western-looking woman with bright auburn hair - and said, "You must be Miss Gönültas." When she said she was not, he looked around suspiciously and asked, "Where is Miss Gönültas?" apparently disbelieving when he was told that Abide was not on board. Meanwhile, another officer went straight to the back of the plane and started knocking on all the wooden cabinets where food and emergency equipment was kept, as if looking for a secret compartment hiding something...or someone. This zealous persistence perplexed the travellers at first. Only later would we discover that rumours had been put about saying that there was a huge cache of drugs on board Asil's jet. Nothing, of course, was found. We would also

187

learn that informants in Turkey had provided the UK authorities with the names of all those who had arrived at Istanbul's Atatürk Airport for the flight that afternoon. Abide had, indeed, been with the party, as reported, but she had gone along merely to see them off and had afterwards returned to the city.

Asil was led out of the plane and driven to the police station inside Heathrow. He was allowed to make one telephone call. Then he was taken to a cell and told he would have to stay there before being taken to London for questioning. He looked around the Spartan cell and then lay down on the wooden bench, shut his eyes, and waited. The cell door remained open.

Meanwhile, Fehim and the others were being taken from the aeroplane. They were told to leave their bags behind and a police minibus ferried them to the airport police station. As he walked through the door into the small waiting area at about six o'clock, Fehim noticed the two cells at the end of the room. Both doors were open and through one he caught sight of a man's legs and feet lying along a bench. He recognised the shoes and trousers instantly. As he walked closer and peered further into the cell, he saw Asil stretched out, with his arms across his face.

Jo-Rae Dahl noticed Fehim's glance and joined him near the cell. "That's Asil!" she said in a shocked tone. At that moment, one of the policemen noticed where they were looking, strode across and pushed the heavy cell door to. It swung shut with a resounding metallic thud. The noise would haunt Fehim's nightmares for months to come.

For three-quarters of an hour, the group sat there, waiting to find out what would happen to them. The mid-December evening had brought with it a fierce chill and they were all bitterly cold, unable to get at the warmer clothes in their baggage. Fehim, chain-smoking all the while, chatted quietly in Turkish with Çetin Kursat. Around them, the others sat mostly in silence. Eventually, they were asked to identify their luggage and a passport controller arrived to check the travel documents. She was shown into the cell to check Asil's passport. When she had finished, Asil was called from the cell. Fehim and the others turned to look at him as he walked through the room behind a policeman, with a proud posture and a broad smile on his face, before disappearing out of the front door and into a police car. Fehim felt a surge of confidence - he could tell his brother-in-law was in fighting mood. A few minutes later, the other travellers were allowed to leave.

The first firm information I received was at six o'clock, when Asil telephoned me from the police station at Heathrow. I snatched up the receiver, hoping for some good news. I was stunned to hear a very serious-sounding Asil on the end of the line. "Bilge, listen to me very carefully," he said in Turkish. "I am OK. Don't worry. We have been met and I am told I am being taken to Holborn police station. Find Peter Knight or Robert Burrows and get one of them to meet me there."

I could tell he was trying to keep the conversation short, so I merely answered, "All right, I'll do that." I felt sick as I replaced the receiver, shaking my head in disbelief. Peter Knight and Robert Burrows were both solicitors, so I knew the situation must be serious. For a few minutes, Tijen and I panicked. Had it been a weekday, we would easily have been able to contact the two solicitors through their offices - Peter Knight at Vizards and Robert Burrows at S J Berwin. But this was after six o'clock on a Saturday evening and all our efforts to find either man drew a blank. I was pacing around, frantically trying to think of a way to reach them, when Abide called from Istanbul. She had been anxious about Asil since seeing him off that afternoon, but when I relayed the news to her, she took it very calmly - she knew Asil had left her behind that day because he was half-expecting to be arrested. She gave me Peter Knight's number and at about seven o'clock I was finally able to get through to the solicitor, who assured me he would either go to Holborn himself or send a colleague. By the time Robert Burrows called me a few minutes later, the cold reality of the situation was beginning to sink in - what I had dreaded for so many days had now happened. I had no idea what I should do. Should I go to Holborn myself? If I did, would I be allowed to see Asil?

"Stay at home and stay by the telephone," was Robert Burrows's advice. He promised to keep me in touch.

At about nine o'clock, the doorbell rang. Tijen ran to open the front door to Fehim, Alan and Dave, another bodyguard. All three seemed shell-shocked. They just looked at me and shook their heads as if hardly able to comprehend what had happened. Fehim's face was ghostly white and he looked as if he might faint at any moment. Dave and Alan left after a few moments and I tried to make Fehim comfortable, offering him soup or a cup of tea. By this time, Irfan and Levent had both learnt of the afternoon's events and they, too, tried to lighten the atmosphere. But Fehim was completely closed off from us, wrapped up in his own experiences, and, try as we might, we could not get through to him. He refused all offers of food or drink and just sat cross-legged on the settee, staring ahead sightlessly while we all fussed around and repeating over and over: "They put him in a cell and shut the door." He was plainly in a state of shock and it frightened me to see him that way. As the evening progressed, he became able to explain to us, in halting sentences, exactly what had happened.

Half an hour after Fehim got home we caught a news-flash on the television which said Asil Nadir had been arrested and taken to Holborn police station for questioning. They showed a photograph of him on screen - suddenly it all seemed very real. From that moment on, the telephone scarcely stopped ringing as relatives and friends heard the news and wanted to find out more. Every hour, too, Asil's solicitors rang from the police station to keep us up to date. The press had also been kept well informed - Hasan told us that the pavement outside the police station was packed with waiting journalists by the time Asil got to Holborn. At my request, Hasan spent the evening outside in the car, waiting in case Asil was released and needed to be taken home. It would prove to be a vain wait. Shortly before midnight, our telephone rang for the last time that evening. It was Asil. He could not talk for long, but told me the police wanted to question him and insisted on keeping him overnight.

Knowing there was nothing more to be done until the next day, we decided to try and get some rest. Sleep escaped us, though. As I tossed and turned between the sheets, I thought of Asil lying alone in a police cell. Then I thought of my mother, and Meral, who was visiting Cyprus, unaware of Asil's arrest. By the time we had received definite news from Asil, it had been too late to call them. I prayed that they would not find out from the newspapers or television before I had a chance to break the news myself the following morning. I shed silent tears in the dark. Beside me, Fehim wrestled with his own nightmare thoughts, shivering occasionally as time and time again he heard that cell door clang shut in the back of his mind.

At Holborn police station, it was proving a long and frustrating evening for Asil. He had arrived there at about eight o'clock and, after fighting through the press crowds, had found his lawyer, Martin Lewis of Vizards, waiting for him. After he had emptied his pockets and handed over his passport, he was asked if he was ready to answer questions and he replied that he was. He waited and waited, only to be told then that he should have twenty minutes to talk to his lawyers first. "But I'm ready now," said Asil.

Twenty minutes came and went. Eventually another policeman emerged and informed him that he was to be kept at the station overnight because he should rest for eight hours before being questioned. Asil and his lawyers were incensed. Martin Lewis argued strenuously that Asil should be allowed home - he pointed out that his passport had been taken away and assured the officer that Asil would report to the station voluntarily the next morning for questioning. Asil watched as a heated debate went on for a few minutes, but to no avail. Finally, he told us later, the exasperated officer put his hands over his face and said, through his fingers, "Look, I have been instructed from above to hold him, and that's exactly what I'm going to do."

Lewis insisted on a note being made on the custody record that he had lodged an objection on the grounds of unlawful imprisonment.

It was very late by the time Asil was led to his cell. First he had been allowed to call me, and he had also sent a message to Hasan, asking him to bring his shaving kit and a cardigan to the police station. He said later he could not believe what he saw when he stepped through the cell door. As the door was swung shut behind him, he stood motionless in the middle of the tiny room and looked about. The space was little more than four paces long, with a wooden bench and an open box which, on closer inspection, turned out to be a makeshift toilet. The air was stale and rank-smelling. Everything looked filthy. On the walls could be seen smeared traces of excrement. A piece of blue plastic lay on the bench and he picked it up gingerly by one corner to discover it was a very thin and grubby mattress. It was a long way from Berkeley Square or the Voyager Antalya Sheraton.

Moving back towards the door, as distant from the stinking "toilet" as he could get, Asil slipped off his shoes and sat on the bench in a cross-legged Buddha pose. For several hours, he remained like that, calmly trying to absent his mind from that dirty cell. Reality refused to go away, though. All around him raged the customary uproar of a Saturday night in the Holborn police station lock-up. All night long came the shouts and screams of the drunks, brawlers and prostitutes being held in the other cells. In Asil's own cell, every twenty minutes the metal sheet covering a small barred opening in the door slid noisily open and someone looked in before sliding it shut again. At one point, Asil asked the mystery observer for a glass of water. A few moments later the cell door opened slightly and a white plastic cup of water was slid through the gap. When Asil picked it up, he told me afterwards he winced to see the word "prisoner" written around the cup in felt tip pen. After three o'clock had passed, Asil felt weary and decided to try and get some sleep. He reached out to the light switch on the wall and turned the dimmer control, but nothing happened. For most of the night he sat bolt upright in the bright light - shivering because the cardigan Hasan brought from his home never reached him.

A habitual early-riser, Asil was fully awake and ready to face the day by about half past five. He was tired from the lack of sleep, but felt calm and had been brought his shaving kit, together with a bowl of water and a mirror. It was another four hours, though, before anything began to happen. Asil's lawyers arrived at half past nine and soon afterwards they were all led upstairs and into an interview room at the Serious Fraud Office headquarters which, though officially in nearby Elm Street, adjoin Holborn police station.

Asil sat facing the interviewing officers across a broad table. Behind him sat Peter Knight and Robert Burrows. The SFO men reached into the files and pulled out a sheaf of documents which they spread on the table in front of them. Picking up the one of the documents, the SFO interviewer held it out for Asil to look at. Then he said, "I put it to you that you stole this money."

Asil looked at him. "This is a PPI transfer document and the transfer of money is to Uni-Pac Packaging, a wholly owned subsidiary of PPI. How can I have stolen this money?" he replied.

Without a word, the interviewer picked up another document - again a transfer of funds to Uni-Pac - and repeated the same allegation. Asil looked at the document and gave him the same answer. After more than three hours of this verbal to-ing and fro-ing, Asil asked to be allowed to see his lawyers alone. The request was granted and the three were led back downstairs to the cell. There, Asil told his lawyers: "These documents are just one half of the equation. In Turkey and North Cyprus there are documents which show where the money went. If they were to go to Turkey and North Cyprus they could see the evidence for themselves and we could get this matter cleared up quickly."

When the three of them trooped back upstairs, Peter Knight put this suggestion to the SFO men. It was immediately rejected. "If there is such information, give it to us now," insisted the interviewer. Asil explained that, as the chairman of a major multi-national corporation, he was not able to carry with him details of every single financial transaction. The interview ended in stalemate late that Sunday afternoon.

Asil was taken back to his cell. His lawyers advised him that he would have to be charged by about five o'clock or else released - by then, it would be twenty-four hours since his arrest, and under British law only terrorism suspects may be held for longer than that without charge and without a magistrate granting a further period of custody. While the lawyers went to get something to eat, Asil listened intently to catch parts of a dispute outside between what seemed to be one of the SFO men and the female custody officer in charge of the cells. From what he overheard, the SFO wanted to keep him for a further twelve hours for more questioning, but the custody officer was adamant that Asil would have to be released by ten past five unless he was charged. "We're already in deep water over this," she told the other officer. "Either charge him by ten past five or he will go free." As the argument went on, the custody officer gradually softened, until eventually a compromise was agreed: Asil would be held for a further six hours, until eleven o'clock, and then he would be released if no charges were brought.

When his lawyers returned, Asil told them what he had overheard. As the three of them sat in the cell and waited, Peter Knight tried to comfort Asil by saying there was no way he could be charged - the SFO had not revealed any grounds to do so. But at about quarter to eleven there was a sudden commotion outside, the cell door opened and Asil was summoned. As he walked out, he came face to face with about a dozen police officers standing round. Among them was Lorna Harris, the SFO officer who would be in charge of his case. Asil would say later that the atmosphere was as if he was a wild animal that they had just trapped. Lorna Harris stepped forward and informed Asil that he was charged with eighteen counts of theft and false accounting - charges involving a total of £25 million. He was photographed and his fingerprints were taken. From respected chairman of a high-flying conglomerate to suspected criminal held in a police cell in just a matter of weeks…he found it hard to comprehend.

After another sleepless night in the cell at Holborn, Asil was again clean-shaven and waiting by about six o'clock. He had been told that he would be taken early that Monday morning to Bow Street Magistrates for a bail hearing. At eight o'clock he was hustled, handcuffed, from a police van into the court building and taken straight to the basement cells. The hearing did not begin until eleven o'clock and the wait was to prove a bizarre few hours. The first news came from his lawyers, who told him that the prosecution would be vehemently opposing bail.

As he sat, contemplating his situation, another man approached the cell and asked Asil to come forward to the small grille in the door. He did as he was asked and the man pushed a document through the bars into his hand, saying quickly, "I am from the Inland Revenue and this is for you."

Asil looked at the paper which he had involuntarily reached up to take. It was a tax demand for £600,000. "You bastard," was all he managed to say to the other man, who was retreating hastily. He discovered later that the man was Richard Cook, Michael Allcock's deputy at the Inland Revenue. When one of lawyers returned to the cell later, Asil asked how Cook had been allowed to come and hand over the demand. "While I was going up there to be hanged, they were allowed to come and give me a parking ticket?" he queried in amazement. He told me afterwards, sarcastically, that he had found the Inland Revenue's humanity very touching.

193

At South Woodford, we had spent the Sunday in an agony, wondering what was happening to Asil and expecting all the time to hear that he had been released. Again, the lawyers kept up their regular bulletins and we raced to the telephone every time it rang, hoping to hear good news. I got up at six o'clock and sat down to telephone my mother in Cyprus. I had hoped to speak to Meral, but found my mother alone. I did all I could to play the situation down, keeping the conversation short and just saying Asil had been taken in to answer a few questions.

That day seemed one of the longest we had ever lived through. As the evening arrived, our spirits rose a little - we were counting down the minutes, knowing that Asil had not been charged and would soon have to be freed. We sat around in the house, trying to act as if it was a normal Sunday, but inevitably the conversation kept returning to Asil. The telephone did not stop ringing with friends and relatives saying their thoughts were with us. A television news-flash late that night fulfilled our worst fears. It said Asil had been charged and would appear the following morning at Bow Street Magistrates Court. As we stared at the screen in stunned disbelief, the telephone sounded. It was Robert Burrows confirming what we had just heard. I was frantic - what on earth should we do now, I asked the solicitor? He urged me to stay calm and arranged to meet us the following morning before the court hearing. He said the court was sure to set a substantial sum as bail and suggested I should start contacting people who might be willing to stand as sureties.

For half an hour, we racked our brains to think of suitable people who would put up money to secure Asil's bail. Any one of us was willing, yet with business so precarious at Noble Raredon our personal financial position was difficult too. There was only person I could think of immediately who had both the means and the emotional involvement to help out - Aysegül. Though we had had our differences in the past, I was desperate to do anything I could to help Asil. In law, at least, she was still Asil's wife and we had all remained on cordial terms, largely for the sake of their two children. Without a second thought, I picked up the telephone and dialled Aysegül at her Eaton Square flat. She agreed instantly to stand as a surety. We chatted for a few minutes about all that had happened in the last few days and arranged to meet each other at court the next morning.

Monday morning dawned after another restless night. Fehim drove Tijen and me to court on his way to another appointment. As we motored towards the city, Irfan rang on the car phone and said Asil had just called our house, sounding calm and saying he was fine. Poor Irfan hadn't known quite what to say to this wealthy entrepreneur uncle who had just spent a night in a cell, so he asked how it had been. "Well it's not The Olive Tree," was Asil's retort. Asil had given Irfan the names of some of his contacts who might be able to help with the bail money. Tijen and I met Robert Burrows at Middle Temple. He introduced us to a barrister who would be handling Asil's case, Edward Jenkins. Later, Asil would choose his own QC, Anthony Scrivener. Robert Burrows was very kind to us, explaining all that might happen. The barrister, though, seemed detached and businesslike. To me and Tijen, scared, very emotional and coming up against the law for the first time, the meeting was cold and clinical. We chatted nervously as the four of us made the fifteen-minute walk from Middle Temple to Bow Street. We arrived to find Aysegül already there and hurried into the court-room, pushing our way through the crowds of journalists and photographers outside. The court-room too was packed.

If I had expected Asil to show signs of the strain of being arrested and held in custody for two nights, I should have known better. He was as well turned-out as ever when he emerged through a door on the right-hand side of the room, flanked by two policemen, clean shaven and dressed in a suit and tie. As he walked into the dock, he turned towards us, sitting in the front row of the public gallery, and smiled. I felt the tears rising, but blinked them back as I managed a faint smile in return. As he looked across the room at us, I saw something else in his expression which at the time I could not place. Afterwards, he would chide me for coming to court looking "wan and miserable" and without any make-up. As far as he was concerned, we were engaged in a battle of nerves and we must always make sure we looked good and never showed any public sign of weakness.

Asil stood and listened as the court clerk read out the list of charges - a list which seemed formidable enough to me, but which Lorna Harris said were only "specimen charges". She announced that the SFO was opposed to bail and requested that Asil be remanded in custody. Asil's barrister stood up and said there was no reason to object to bail. He pointed out to the presiding magistrate - Chief Metropolitan Magistrate Sir David Hopkin - that Asil lived in London, had done so for almost thirty years, and that virtually all of his family was in Britain, so there was no risk that he would abscond. As the SFO argued back, the barrister beckoned me to one side. I followed him outside the court-room and he told me quietly that if we could offer a large sum of money as security, the SFO might agree to bail.

"Just get him out, however you can," I pleaded.

"How much can you raise?" the barrister asked.

"I don't know," I answered, feeling tears of helplessness rise again. "Just do your best and we will accept whatever you say."

I had virtually given the barrister a blank cheque to secure Asil's freedom - yet the amount of bail fixed still came as an enormous shock. As the magistrate announced that he would remand Asil on bail, I felt a wave of relief pass over me. But the relief was cut short as I listened to the conditions he imposed: Asil was to live at his home in Aldford Street, to surrender all his passports and to report to Savile Row police station every day between seven o'clock and nine o'clock in the evening. In addition, he was not to have any contact, including even messages through third parties, with anyone who worked, or had ever worked, for Polly Peck or any of its subsidiaries. There was a gasp in the court-room as the final condition was read out - that the sum of £2 million should be lodged with Asil's solicitors, S J Berwin, as an irrevocable deposit, and that there should be up to five further sureties totalling £1.5 million. The room swam around me as I tried to take the figures in. As Asil was led away through the side door, there was a hubbub on the press bench as reporters scrambled out to go and send their stories - stories which would reveal the following day that the £3.5 million bail was the highest ever imposed in Britain. We sat in shock alongside Aysegül for a few seconds as the court-room emptied around us.

By now it was lunch-time and the court offices were closed. While we waited for them to re-open at three o'clock, Tijen and I sat in Robert Burrows's office ringing everyone we could think of to raise the bail. We had arranged to meet Aysegül back at Bow Street at three o'clock and gave the same message to anybody who offered to help. We also asked them to bring other friends with them, in case some were rejected as sureties. I felt sick as I dialled number after number, only to be told bluntly by the person at the other end that they did not want to get involved. Some even refused to come to the telephone, no doubt guessing from what they had heard on the news why I was ringing. Others said they would call back - of course, they never did. These were people we had thought of as friends; some were business associates whom Asil had helped a lot. Radar Reshad, a Turkish Cypriot and a member of the Polly Peck board, had started his share-holding with gifts of Polly Peck shares from Asil and had worked alongside my brother as he built the company up - just months earlier, he had sold his shares for several hundred thousand pounds, but now, approached by Aisling Daly, he declined to help. Then there were high-powered individuals who had been only too keen to be associated with Asil just a few months earlier...but now he was down on his luck they just did not want to know. They opened my eyes to the duplicity of human nature.

When we arrived back at Bow Street just before three o'clock, though, we were greeted by a reception which did a lot to restore my battered faith. Milling around in the foyer of the court building were dozens of

Turkish Cypriots we had never seen before, most of them young men. They had heard about the bail conditions on the news and had simply come down to do what they could. One offered his factory as security, others were willing to pledge their homes and several said they had no cash with them, but would come back with money the next day. One young man thrust an envelope into my hand containing £1,000 which he had saved up washing cars and doing weekend odd jobs. He said to me, "Your brother is the reason we can hold our heads up high in this country and say we are Turkish Cypriots - we're proud of him."

The tears rolled down my cheeks as I looked at all these warm-hearted people, who were willing to pledge what little they had for Asil's sake, even though they did not know him. We took no money from them, but collected the names and addresses of everybody there, explaining the very large sureties we needed and promising to contact them again if they could be of assistance. It was a scene I will remember for the rest of my life. I was overwhelmed by their kindness, which struck me even more deeply when I searched the foyer with my eyes and saw that not one of the so-called friends I had approached had even turned up. And they were the sort of wealthy sureties - some of whom could even pledge the entire £3.5 million alone - which we desperately needed. In the midst of all this, Aysegül walked in. She must have seen the misery on my face, for she put her arm around my shoulders. It was a simple gesture which showed me a hitherto unseen softer side to my sister-in-law and would alter my feelings towards her, introducing a note of genuine warmth into our relationship. From that day on, I saw Aysegül in a different light and was prepared to admit that I had misjudged her. In future, when we spoke, it would be as two mature women, accepting each other as the very different people we were. Whatever had gone before, during the often stormy twenty-nine years that she had been part of our family, when we were in trouble, she was the first to offer help. For that, I would always be grateful to her.

As soon as the court offices opened, Robert Burrows and Martin Lewis took us upstairs to begin the process of swearing in sureties. Aysegül went first and her £500,000 pledge was accepted. I wanted to stand as a surety too, but Robert Burrows advised me not even to attempt it. I was sure to be rejected since I was Asil's sister, he said, and the courts would not accept immediate family as sureties. Tijen was ruled out too - as was Necat Ugursal, who had been a very close friend of my father and offered £1 million-worth of his property in London; Asil's former secretary, Jean Thomas, and her brother; and a friend of Aisling Daly who offered to mortgage her house. By now, time was running out that day and we were advised to come back to court only when we had all the money and the sureties arranged. We left Bow Street in dispirited mood, feeling we had failed - we had been unable to spare Asil from another night's detention and it was obviously going to be an enormous task to secure his release. In fact, it would be more than two frantic days before he went free.

During those hectic days, Asil found himself caught up in the grinding wheels of the prison system. Having appeared in court, he could no longer stay in the police station cell but would have to be despatched elsewhere as a remand prisoner. Nor was there any longer the "luxury" of police car transportation - as Fehim and I watched unaware, he left Bow Street under our very noses in the back of a van, sitting hunched up in one of a row of metal cages. The van took Asil and other prisoners from Bow Street across the Thames to a Central Distribution Depot where they would be allocated to a particular jail or remand centre. Asil and the others from Bow Street were herded into a huge room. The first thing that struck him, he said afterwards, was the filth. He estimated there were about 100 men in the room. At one side stood a toilet, without any door, brim-full of excrement. Everyone turned to stare at Asil as he walked in. Feeling conspicuous in his navy Bijan suit, white shirt and tie among the casual jeans, denim jackets, jumpers and leathers, he tried not to attract any more attention to himself during the one and a half hours it took to be "distributed". Each man had been given a number, with which they were summoned to be taken elsewhere. Asil's number was the last to be called. For the second time, he ducked his head to climb into the back of a van. As he pulled his legs in to allow the door of his cage to be locked, a thought struck him: there he was - he told me afterwards - a person who had only just been charged, experiencing how he would be treated if he had committed murder.

The destination was Wormwood Scrubs, B Wing. All the new arrivals were gathered in one reception room, where they were served with bread and soup which Asil found inedible. One by one, each man was called through to another room, where they had to empty their pockets, strip off, take a shower and then dress in regulation prison gear of striped blue and white shirt and jeans. Belts and shoelaces were taken away. When Asil's turn came, he emptied his pockets and started to undo his belt when the warder stopped him, telling him he could keep his belt and his own clothes. Asil came away feeling uneasy - he wanted to look the same as all the other inmates, instead of standing out as the only prisoner in an expensive suit, and did not like the fact that he, alone, had been allowed to keep his belt. As they waited again, the men were split into twos to share cells. Asil found himself paired up with a tall, black youth called Anthony, who was in custody accused of stealing a £16 belt. After brief medicals, they were taken to the cell and the door was closed behind them.

Asil looked around. In the grimy room, about four strides long, stood two narrow beds and two chairs. At the far end was a shelf and two buckets - the only toilet they could use during the twenty-three hours a day they were shut in the cell. Above the shelf was a high, barred window giving the only natural light in the room. Alone in the cell with Anthony, Asil felt a twinge of alarm - he wanted to shrink back from his cell-mate, whom he noticed almost constantly talking to himself as he paced restlessly up and down. Instead, Asil decided to begin a conversation with the youngster, in the hope of establishing some friendly bond between them. He started by asking Anthony about himself and his family and the talk soon turned to reminiscences of Jamaica, where Anthony was born and where Asil had holidayed. By the time Asil came to leave, Anthony would weep at losing his new-found prison pal. He had given Asil the name and address of his sister in London and later, when Anthony was released, Asil would contact the young man's sister and send them two air tickets to Jamaica.

This was not the only rapport Asil struck up during his days at "The Scrubs". That first evening, when the cell doors were briefly open, he received a deputation of three prisoners. The spokesman for the trio told Asil they were "in charge of" B Wing. "We know who you are and we are sorry you are here. We're at your service. Anything you need, we can get for you, food, drinks, whatever," he said. Asil asked if they could get a radio - the following morning it was brought to the cell and he was able to hear the news about himself on the local Greek radio station, while Anthony later tuned in to a reggae channel and began dancing around the cell. Later, there would be deliveries of sweets, cigarettes and drinks. Jokingly, he asked the B Wing providers whether they could get him a small colour television.

"Yes, just give us a few days, guv," came the prompt reply.

From the moment Asil entered the jail, he would tell us later, in his own mind he felt in danger. Despite the blue suit which set him apart, he had no safety worries about his fellow-inmates, who would bang their tin cups on the table noisily whenever he came into the canteen at meal-times - a demonstration of support in the enclosed prison world. But he determined to be on his guard - against just what, he was not sure - and devised his own daily routine. He and Anthony would take it in turns to stay awake throughout the night. Once dawn had broken and they had done the early morning routine of "slopping out" the buckets from the cell, Asil would start to feel safer. Sometimes, he would doze a little. Occasionally there would be the few officially-sanctioned visitors - his lawyers, or the Turkish Consul-General in London, Dogan Alpan. At other times, he would sit crouched on his bed, his body still in the cell, he said later, but his mind floating far away, imagining the most vivid green fields in Tibet so clearly that he could almost see himself sitting there. Throughout, he felt very distant, as if he was watching it all happen to someone else. One morning, as the sun was rising, he found himself looking at what to him summed up in one image both freedom and captivity. As he lay on his bed, staring at the wall opposite, the shadow created by the barred window caught his eye. Between the shadow bars, he saw the shadow of a bird perched on the window sill outside. He listened quietly to the bird's song, then watched its shadow take wing into the sky.

Prison life had its lighter side, too, Asil told us later. On his second morning at Wormwood Scrubs, he heard a commotion outside and the cell door was flung open. Stepping out on to the landing to investigate, Asil asked another inmate standing nearby what was happening. "It's shopping time," he was told. Asil, who had not realised there was a prison shop, was delighted. He had been given the HM Government weekly allowance of £1.40 when he entered the jail and decided this would be a good opportunity to spend it. He took the money and went down the corridor where he was directed. He waited in a queue outside the shop then, when his turn came, stepped up to the counter. Behind it was a coloured female prison officer who seemed in a chirpy mood. Asil greeted her and then started giving his order - two packets of cigarettes, a box of matches, some chocolate, crisps and a can of Pepsi-Cola.

As he reeled off the items, he was slightly nonplussed to see the woman behind the counter begin giggling. By the time he had finished speaking, she was bent double with hysterical laughter, finding only enough breath to gasp: "Man, where do you think you are?" before dissolving into fresh guffaws.

"What's so funny?" asked Asil, as the laughter continued.

When the woman had calmed down enough, she told him: "You can't have all that - you've only got £1.40."

"OK," said Asil, slapping his money down on the counter, "there's all my capital - what *can* I get for it?" At the end, he was faced with a choice: fourteen cigarettes, or thirteen cigarettes and two sweets. He chose the latter and realised he had better try to make the goodies last.

His prison shopping trip is a story he loved to tell afterwards, complete with all the actions, and it earned him much light-hearted teasing from those of us who knew him well. We all realised that Asil had no idea of modern prices, having long since given up the habit of carrying money with him - for years, small purchases like cigarettes had been made for him by staff, while larger outgoings had been dealt with by account or credit card.

For Tijen and me, it was a race against time to organise Asil's bail money. From the Monday when the £3.5 million was set to the following Thursday, 20th December, we did not set foot inside the Noble Raredon offices while we made our ever-more-desperate round of telephone pleas for help. The lawyers had warned us that the courts would close for Christmas at lunch-time on 21st December. If everything was not officially signed and sealed by then, it would mean Asil certainly spending another ten days in custody, over Christmas and New Year, until the courts re-opened after the break. It was a prospect I tried not to think about, but as the days went by with only painfully slow success, it began to look increasingly likely.

When we arrived home dejectedly in South Woodford on the Monday evening, we had only secured one surety of £500,000 - Aysegül's - and still had £3 million left to find. All that night I spent on the telephone, talking to Turkish Cypriots who I hoped might help us. Eventually I struck lucky. Ramadan Güney, owner of what he claimed to be Europe's largest cemetery at Brookwood, in Surrey, had been a good friend of my father. Out of respect for that old friendship, he agreed to put up a £1 million guarantee. On the following afternoon, he met us at Bow Street Magistrates Court and was duly accepted as a surety. By the afternoon of Tuesday, 18th December, then, we had all £1.5 million of sureties in place. But we still had to secure the £2 million irrevocable deposit.

During Tuesday night and Wednesday morning, we managed to secure a few offers of cash from friends - many of them in Turkey - but there was still a problem. Most of the donors wanted to remain anonymous, and the lawyers advised us that the courts would never accept that. The breakthrough we had longed for came early on the Wednesday afternoon and, ironically, we suddenly ended up with more than we needed. Almost simultaneously, we had two separate offers of £2 million. One was from Sezai Türkes, a friend from Istanbul who had known my father and had made his fortune in the construction industry. The other came through Gülten Ahmet, a friend in Istanbul. Scarcely daring to believe our luck, we gratefully accepted both offers to start with. Later that day, we returned Sezai Türkes's money - with our faith in humanity restored a little. But hurry as we might, by the time we could chivvy the banks to transfer the money to Berwin's account, it was too late for the solicitors to go to court and confirm that the deposit had been paid. So near...but yet so far. We trailed home that Wednesday night elated by our achievement, but disappointed that our efforts had still failed to spare Asil another night of incarceration.

On the morning of Thursday, 20th December, knowing we had done all we needed to, we went back to work. I could hardly concentrate. Every time the phone rang on my desk, I grabbed the receiver, expecting to hear news of Asil. It was not until nearly three o'clock that Robert Burrows called. First, he told me that Asil was about to be released. But then he followed up with one of the bitterest blows of all, reminding me of Asil's bail condition, that he must not have any contact, direct or indirect, with anyone who might be called as a witness by the SFO, specifically all existing and former employees of Polly Peck or of any subsidiary company. The implications of this were enormous. It put some 20,000 people world-wide into the category of "banned" contacts as far as Asil was concerned. And, most importantly, because of the way our family had worked, among them were most of his close relatives and many of his best friends. The immediate effect was that Asil would have to go home in a minicab and must not be picked up by Hasan - officially employed as a Polly Peck driver. In addition, Asil's girlfriend Joanne Mackey - formerly a designer with the Inter-City subsidiary - would have to move out of the home she and Asil shared in Aldford Street before he could enter it. Worse still for me was the fact that I too, along with Fehim and my mother, was prohibited from seeing my own brother. Under the terms of the bail, I could not even telephone him, write him a letter, or send a message through anyone else. I was stunned into fury - how could it be right for the court to order someone to sever links with virtually all their closest family and friends, particularly when they had not been convicted of any offence, merely accused? I may have managed to secure Asil's freedom, but what kind of freedom was it to be?

Asil had almost given up hope of getting home for Christmas when he heard the news of his impending freedom from fellow-inmates at Wormwood Scrubs, who said they had seen the official release papers. That Thursday afternoon, he said goodbye to Anthony, both of them with tears in their eyes. Just after three o'clock, Asil was ushered out of the prison through a side door and into a waiting minicab. He directed it to Aldford Street and settled back to enjoy his first taste of liberty for five and a half days. As they were about to round the corner from Grosvenor Street into Aldford Street, Asil sat bolt upright in the back seat and told the driver to stop. Obviously, word of his release had quickly spread. Ahead of them, a hundred yards round the corner, was a horde of press men and women, right outside his door and spilling over from the pavement into the street. Asil took a split-second to decide - he wanted to look his best before facing the press, so told the minicab driver to reverse back round the corner out of sight. The next destination was Lesley's house in Chester Square. There, he took a leisurely half-hour wash and shave and stepped out of the door looking his usual pristine self - not like a man who had just spent five nights in a dirty cell.

By the time Asil got back to Aldford Street, imaginations were running riot among the press corps. The news was that Asil had left Wormwood Scrubs at three o'clock and he should have arrived at least half an hour ago. What could have delayed him? Perhaps something had happened to him? Could he have gone somewhere else instead? Asil ordered the minicab driver to pull in at the far end of Aldford Street, some way from the crush outside his door. Arriving from the opposite end of the road, he was able to walk unseen most of the way. It was only when he was about twenty-five yards from home that a couple of photographers turned and spotted him. The shout went up: "Here he is."

Within a matter of moments he found himself engulfed in a mass of microphones and cameras. He pressed on through the surging crowd, smiling broadly, and managed to gain the doorstep. As he walked up the steps to the front door, he felt himself tread on someone who had stumbled in the crush. Looking down, he told me afterwards, he saw the face of one of his lawyers looking back up at him from the ground. On the top step, Asil turned to the press below with a smile and told them, "I'm sorry it's so cold and raining on you. I wish everyone a happy Christmas." Then he stepped into the house. Unseen hands firmly shut the green front door behind him. Later, Asil would go out himself to serve cups of tea to the waiting crowd of press.

Inside the house, Tijen was waiting with Aysegül and Asil's lawyers. There were tearful greetings all round, but for Asil it was to prove a bittersweet homecoming, as Robert Burrows explained to him that he was barred from seeing some of the people most dear to him. As he digested the news, he told the lawyer, "If I can't see my family or talk to my mother, I'm going to be a prisoner in my own home - tell them I want to go back to jail."

For me, that night was more difficult to bear than the five that had gone before. Now I knew he was home, my fingers itched to pick up the telephone, just to find out how he was, but I fought the temptation. I did not want him to end up back in prison for disobeying the bail conditions. It was another sleepless night and a busy day ahead. With news of Asil's arrest, the banks had stopped their credit to Noble Air, putting it in serious operating difficulty, so Fehim spent that Friday trying to find new lines of credit to keep the airline in business. That afternoon was the Noble Raredon Christmas party - a rather subdued affair this year. In previous years, Fehim and I had taken all the staff out to lunch at a restaurant. This time, nobody felt much Christmas spirit, but we were determined to have a few drinks in the office just to keep up traditions. It was half past one and I was just going down to the party when Irfan burst through the door, dripping with rain and out of breath. "Come on, mum! Quick! They've said you can see Uncle Asil now!" he yelled.

A few minutes earlier, Irfan had been with Tijen and Asil in Aldford Street when a telephone call had come for Robert Burrows, who was also there. The caller was lawyer, Peter Knight, who said he had obtained special permission from the court to relax Asil's bail conditions and allow him contact with both me and our mother. Asil's reaction to the news was a simple, heartfelt "Brilliant!" While he was called to the telephone, an impatient Tijen, catching sight of Irfan in the doorway, had told him to run and fetch me from my office, which was just round the corner.

I jumped out of my chair and tore after Irfan down the stairs into the street, not even pausing to grab my coat or umbrella. Ignoring the rain which soaked me almost instantly, I raced after Irfan along South Audley Street and into Aldford Street, dodging round a couple of bewildered passers-by who turned to stare. On the pavement outside Asil's house, a group of press photographers huddled by the black railings hoping to snatch a shot. I pushed past them, through the green door and up the stairs to the living room.

Asil was still on the telephone when I raced through the door, struggling in vain to regain a little composure.

"I don't believe it! She's here already," I heard him say before he let the receiver fall and strode round the table to meet me. I ran into his arms, hardly seeing where I was going through a haze of tears. We clung to each other, both weeping, for minutes before Asil pulled away slightly. Looking down at me, he chided: "I've kept my cool until today - now just look at me!"

I smiled at him through my tears and laughed as we hugged again. I felt as if I would burst with joy and relief to see him again. Beside us, Tijen and Irfan both sobbed. Even Asil's two bodyguards furtively wiped their eyes. A tiny voice reached us faintly from the telephone receiver, which still dangled, forgotten. The sheer emotion of that reunion still makes me cry whenever I think about even now - none of us in the room that afternoon will ever forget it.

Over the next few days, I visited Asil regularly. We would sit in the evenings drinking tea and he would tell me all about his experiences in jail. Once, when I asked him anxiously how he had been treated by his fellow prisoners, he assured me, "Don't worry about that, Bilge. I was treated better inside than I was by the authorities outside."

There was one question I knew I had to ask him - about the charges that had been brought against him - but it was hard for me to find the right words. I did not want to be blunt and hurt him any further by making it look as if I had no faith in his integrity. Finally, while we were talking one day about the latest stories in the newspapers, I asked, "Did you really do anything against the law?"

Asil has never lied to me, but on the odd occasion that he has tried to skirt round an issue and avoid telling me the entire truth, I have always been able to see through him straight away - at those moments, his normally firm gaze falters and he tries to avoid eye contact with me. This day, though, he turned to me and looked me straight in the eye as he said, "Bilge, don't worry about it. All you need to know is that I have not stolen any money. I did not break the law."

Although special permission had been granted for Asil to be able to have contact with me and my mother, the stringent bail conditions remained hard to bear. While Asil could visit our house and see me and the children, he was still barred from seeing Fehim - in fact, although the bail conditions were relaxed at a subsequent hearing, Asil and Fehim would not meet or speak to each other again for more than a year. Almost the whole family was similarly affected, since at one point or another so many of us had worked together. When the courts re-opened in January, a special application was granted that the bail conditions should not include Asil's family and others like Joanne and Abide.

In the long run, his personal life would not be the only victim of Asil's bail - his business interests would suffer badly too. Prohibited from travelling outside the UK, he could no longer maintain proper control over his private concerns in Turkey and North Cyprus and there were those who would take advantage of his absence. While there were a few days in store for Asil and the rest of us when we could barely scrape together the money to pay the milk bill, some abroad were growing fat at his expense.

Despite all the difficulties, though, there was no doubt then in Asil's mind that he would see the case through. He watched as the pillars of his private business empire were laid waste far beyond his control in the Mediterranean, never for an instant considering skipping Britain to go and lead a salvage operation himself, even though the temptation was put in his way. In those very early days, there was at least one offer to smuggle him over to North Cyprus. By the time Asil was told of the plan, the escape was organised and a private jet already chartered. In

North Cyprus, a state unrecognised by any country except Turkey, he knew he would have been outside the reach of UK law, yet he refused point-blank to go. At that early stage of proceedings, his belief in British justice was still intact and he was determined to fight the charges, sure that he could prove his innocence in court. It was a belief which would take twenty-eight months to be destroyed.

The Tuesday after Asil's release from prison was Christmas Day, but we all felt little cause for merriment. The next morning, Fehim and I flew out to North Cyprus with the children. We all badly needed a break from London, and with Asil safely out of custody we decided it would be good to be with my mother when she celebrated her seventieth birthday on New Year's Eve. At the end of our holiday, Fehim and I flew to Istanbul to talk to a friend who we hoped might help us find a way out of our own business troubles. The children were flying on to London, so we kissed them goodbye when we landed at Istanbul, saying we would see them at home in a few days. We spent the day in Turkey before flying back to North Cyprus to tie up some remaining loose ends there. Two days later, on 12th January, our seats were booked to fly back to London. The evening before our departure, I was packing the suitcases in our bedroom when Fehim came in, took my hand, led me across to the bed and sat me down. "I'm not coming back with you," he announced.

The news hit me like a slap - I knew he had been very distressed to witness Asil's arrest almost a month earlier, but I had no idea just how deeply the experience had affected him. As we talked then, I learned that he had been quietly brooding over the incident and had grown more and more suspicious of the police's behaviour that day at Heathrow. He had thought their actions grossly out of proportion to the situation and now he was convinced that something similar might happen to me when we flew in this time. During our stay in Cyprus, his fears had been fuelled by the information that a Greek reporter had telephoned a friend of ours in Istanbul and had warned that I would get "the same reception" when I returned to Britain. Sitting on the edge of the bed, Fehim begged me not to fly back the next morning, but to stay a while in Cyprus with him and think the situation through first. I, in my turn, took no notice of the warning, which I thought was simply meant to frighten me. I tried to persuade Fehim to come back with me, but it was no use: I was determined to go back and fight to save Noble Raredon; Fehim was equally determined not to go and said he would resign from the company. Finally, we reached a kind of compromise. I would go back as planned the next morning, but to soothe Fehim I allowed him to telephone the Turkish Consul General in London, Dogan Alpan, and ask him to meet me at Heathrow - that way, he would be on hand to help if anything did happen. Fehim, we agreed, would spend a few weeks in North Cyprus before rejoining us in South Woodford. I had no idea then that it would be eighteen months before he set foot in Britain again, but still it seemed the blackest New Year ever.

CHAPTER NINE

Beware of Strangers

If any good could be said to have come out of all our troubles, it was that, in some ways, they brought the family closer together than ever before. For me, it was a bittersweet realisation to see that, through adversity, I had regained the old Asil - the brother I had known so well. During the previous few years, I had begun to discover that Asil's success had a price in personal terms - that as a well-known public figure there were many more people besides his family who had a claim to his attention. Though I would still have gone to him if I was concerned about something at Noble Raredon, and though I knew he had still valued me as the one person who would tell him what I saw as the truth instead of simply saying what would keep him happy, our once-daily contact had dwindled. Both of us had been too busy with our own business concerns to recognise the distance opening up between us. Only occasionally, if I had sat down to think about it, had I been uneasily aware of Asil gradually growing away from us all, so wrapped up was I in Noble Raredon and he in Polly Peck and in a private life to which we had little connection.

Suddenly, he was back with us. In those dreadful closing months of 1990, I had begun to feel a rekindling of the old intimacy between us. When he had been arrested and needed help, his only telephone call had been to me. Now, barred by his bail conditions from seeing many of his friends, he relied on our family totally to give him the support and comfort he needed. Almost instantly, he dropped the image which had begun to accompany him as "Asil Nadir, global business chief", becoming once again just a part of the family. And from having become a rare and fleeting visitor to family occasions, Asil's presence was now the norm at least every Sunday at our traditional weekly get-together. That first winter, we would get a log fire going and all sit round it together after lunch. As the weather improved, we would light a barbecue outside in the garden and cook kebabs. Most weekends, we would amuse ourselves playing cards, sitting around the coffee table in our living room. We played ten-card rummy and, with money in short supply, it was agreed we should draw up a running "tab" for our debts to each other, which would be paid off once the troubles were over. Levent designed a debts sheet on his computer and during the months that followed, as the case dragged on from one appearance to the next, the tab would mount up and up. Asil always liked to win at cards, but in two years of these Sunday games, he would amass the biggest single debt of all, owing £275 to Irfan. By then, he had been declared bankrupt and he would delight in telling Irfan, "I'm sorry, I won't be able to pay you - I'm bankrupt!"

Those Sundays became the one time that, whatever brave face I had had to put on for the outside world while I battled the troubles engulfing us, I could just be myself. I missed Fehim desperately, and longed for him to be with me in London, but as spring 1991 arrived and he had not come back for either Tijen's birthday in February or Irfan's in March, I realised that it would be a long time before he felt able to return. I was too busy fighting to save Noble Raredon and trying to look after my brother, though, to spend time moping.

However dispiriting a week Asil had had, too, he would make the effort to join us. For that one day at least, we would make sure he knew he was not alone. He, in turn, would almost always try to put up a cheerful front. If he saw we were miserable, he would often stand up and lead us in a rendition of rousing Turkish battle songs, or grab me by the hand and pull me up for some energetic Turkish dancing. Sometimes, I would catch sight of the children's faces and could tell from their expression that they privately thought we had gone quite crazy. Each weekend, Asil would arrive at our house with his arms full of heavenly-smelling flowers which he would help me arrange in vases. As the months wore on, I knew how difficult things were for him and had on occasion given him money to help him pay his bills. One day, as we arranged the customary flowers alone in the kitchen, I said to him, "Asil, you don't have to bring so many flowers - one or two bunches will do."

He turned to me, his hands full of daffodils, and said, "When we are short of money, Bilge, I would rather eat less food and still have flowers around me."

Those family Sundays brought a new closeness between Asil and my children. To Tijen, Levent and Irfan, their adored "dayi" (uncle) had been a flamboyant and impressive figure, with a complex and high-powered jet-set lifestyle, whom they would see in the press and who would appear from time to time in person, armed with flowers and gifts, like an exciting whirlwind blowing in from another world. Since the death of their grandfather, too, they had looked up to him even more as the head of our family and were horrified and bewildered by what had happened to him. Now they were seeing a very different side of him - a side which they saw as sensitive, vulnerable and, despite his efforts to appear sanguine, sometimes deeply unhappy. They had the time, too, to get to know him better, and each one of them set aside their Sundays to spend with "dayi". In time, they would be able to read his thoughts almost as well as I could. And while Fehim was away, they began to look on Asil as a father figure.

In so many ways, for all of us, those light-hearted Sundays were therapeutic - it was a great comfort to know that, however bad things became, the family was still there in the background. Without that solidarity, I'm not sure now how we would have survived. All of us had to find our own way of coping with this new and frightening situation. Meral, shocked and troubled by what had happened, tried to comfort her own family - sons Tolga, now twenty-seven, Tunç, who was three years younger, and baby of the family Evren, just ten. Her husband, Güner, took the situation badly. He had remained at Polly Peck after the share collapse, only to be made redundant when the administrators took control. Now he was out of work and concerned for his family's welfare. For months, it seemed, I hardly saw him or heard him speak a word. The shock-waves of distress even spread as far as North Cyprus. There, Fehim's brother, Ilker, had found himself depressed by Asil's arrest and unable to cope with the strain of trying to run the companies after the administrators took over in London. He quit his job, retreated to his house in the tiny mountainside village of Ozanköy, east of Kyrenia, and was scarcely seen to venture outside his front door for the next year.

It pained me too, to see how upset Asil was that he did not have a close and loving family of his own to help him over the time of crisis. I knew he dearly wanted to have a stable home life like mine, but though I sympathised with his distress, I could see that his ambitions to build his business had left him no time to work at creating a happy family. Instead of spending time with his children, he had put in long hours tied to the business, lavishing the boys with the best he could buy them. In a heart-to-heart one day, I told him this. "But I did it all for them - for the family," Asil replied in hurt tones. I felt that his time - not material possessions - was the most important gift he could have given his children. Asil's sons by Lesley, Giles and Eren, had still not reached their teens, yet virtually all their lives he had been a part-time father to them, conducting an on-off live-in relationship with their mother, which must have been confusing for the youngsters. The two elder sons, too, were products of a twice-broken marriage, brought up in a frequently stormy household. Serhan, born to Asil and Aysegül in the mid-1970s when Asil had started to become very successful in commerce, would want for nothing. Asil was determined he should have the best of everything - not least the best public school education, for by then he had realised his own disadvantage within business circles through not having an "old school tie" - so Serhan was sent to Eton College. Asil's oldest son, Birol, twenty-six years old by the time the troubles struck, had turned out a mixed-up young man, brought up mostly by nannies and struggling to find his own identity in the shadow of a wealthy and highly successful father. Birol was working in the City as a stockbroker, and like all sons of exceptional men, he found it an uphill struggle to make his own mark on the world.

While we battled our problems in London, thousands of miles away Fehim and my mother struggled with their own. Already shocked and depressed by what had happened, my mother now found herself deluged with visits and telephone calls from people involved in the North Cyprus Polly Peck businesses and in my brother's private concerns. Unable to contact Asil for guidance, they were suddenly like fish out of water and turned to my mother as the person closest to him who was available to them. Weighed down by her own worries, and with little in the way of practical help to offer, my mother could do nothing but sit and listen to all their troubles - the last thing she needed at the age of seventy. Whenever I spoke to her on the telephone, she would be in floods of tears and it distressed me to see how she was suffering.

Fehim was plunged into fear and suspicion over what was happening to us in Britain and frustration at his own inability to do anything to help. For months, he shut himself in our Kyrenia flat day and night, eating and drinking little, smoking constantly and praying for us all, in self-imposed solitary confinement. At night he was still plagued by the recurrent nightmare of the cell door clanging shut with Asil inside. Fehim ventured out little, only occasionally going to the Olive Tree to check how business was doing there. He saw virtually no-one, apart from an occasional visit by my mother or Rüya's parents. His brother, Ahmet, and sister-in-law, Yazgan, had moved to North Cyprus by then and they tried to help, encouraging him to leave the flat when they could and trying to enfold him back into a family atmosphere. Whenever they saw him they were shocked to see the amount of weight he had lost. He barely saw his other brother, Ilker, living his own personal crisis a few miles down the road. Meetings with my mother helped neither of them - they were both so depressed that they would just sit together and talk about what was happening in London.

With every downturn in London - each new charge brought against Asil; each obstacle in the way of him proving his innocence; each new blow to Noble Raredon in Britain or in North Cyprus - it seemed to Fehim the knife was being twisted a little more. As the months passed, he would phone frequently, trying to persuade me to abandon what little we had left in the UK and fly out to join him. But I still had my combative spirit intact and refused to concede defeat when I had done nothing wrong and our company was sound. Tijen, in turn, would phone him from South Woodford begging him to come home and telling him how much we needed him by our side. In the long, dark nights, tormented by what he saw as his own uselessness and unable to sleep, Fehim would sit alone in the flat and weep. On several occasions, he contemplated suicide, mentally rehearsing how he would go to the bathroom cabinet, take down a bottle of sleeping tablets and end everything by swallowing a handful. Only the knowledge of how his actions would pile even more misery on to us all kept him from harm.

At those moments, Fehim thought - as I did thousands of miles away from him - that our situation could get no worse. We were wrong. Throughout 1991 and 1992, it seems a plot was being hatched which would involve not just Asil but also me in a serious criminal investigation and would prove the final spur to drive me from my home for good. Just what was being schemed for us, we would not fully realise for almost two years. The story which follows has been constructed from the sworn affidavits of two key protagonists, Michael Francis and Wendy Welsher, who claim they were put up to the entire fabrication by the British authorities early in 1991. The authorities, for their part, say they knew nothing of it until around the middle of 1992, when, they say, Francis approached them with his and Welsher's supposed "evidence" against us. Although Michael Francis is not the most trustworthy of witnesses and I can never find any sympathy in my heart for either him or Wendy Welsher, I feel inclined to believe their shocking version of events. And even if the official version is to be believed, clearly the police, too, found Francis and Welsher's tale of entrapment credible. For on the basis of their promised "evidence" they would arrest me and my brother and would raise in court the potentially trial-derailing spectre of a supposed plot to bribe Asil's trial judge. Francis and Welsher's story may seem far-fetched, but it is supported by the affidavit of another witness - a business studies graduate with no criminal record - who claims he acted as a messenger between them and their police contacts. His story places Francis and the Serious Fraud Office in contact as early as January 1991. There are also travel tickets, hotel reservations and tape-recorded telephone conversations between Francis and the police contacts - whose names and even telephone numbers are detailed in the affidavits - which seem to back up what Francis and Welsher have to say. My italicised account of their tale places the alleged plot against us in chronological context, but was unknown to us at the time. Only in the summer of 1993 would we learn what sordid machinations had apparently taken place.

In January 1991, Michael Francis was living under the assumed name of David Kent. A repeated offender who had collaborated with the police since 1980 as an agent provocateur and informant, he was in breach of two police bails. That month - just weeks after Asil Nadir's arrest - Francis says he was approached out of the blue by the Serious Fraud Office, via an officer he had known for several years. The two arranged to meet at half past ten the following morning, in the Grosvenor Hotel at Victoria Station. Francis asked another man - the subsequent "third witness" - to accompany him. According to Francis, the officer knew he had jumped bail and was wanted by police. He had a proposition for Francis, which the latter would later describe as "the most amazing" he had ever heard: in effect, Francis claimed, it was a proposition to entrap Asil Nadir. Francis was to approach Nadir and offer, for the sum of £3.5 million, to get him his passport back and help his case by getting reporting restrictions lifted. If he succeeded, Francis was told he would be paid £500,000 and criminal charges outstanding against him would be dropped. Francis says the reason given for the proposal was that Asil Nadir was standing in the way of certain political issues and that, although the Serious Fraud Office's action had brought about the collapse of PPI, they could not substantiate the charges they had brought and feared being cited in legal action by Nadir. Francis's participation would enable Nadir to leave the country and the ensuing scandal would deflect attention from an embarrassing matter, allowing it to be brushed aside, he claims to have been told.

Francis says he was wary, particularly in view of the sum of money on offer which he felt was unusually large, but was in no position to argue. When he voiced his reluctance, it was hinted that, if he did not co-operate, he would be "put away for years". Francis requested additional confirmation of the details from a higher authority and a meeting allegedly took place at the SFO's Elm Street headquarters the next day at which all the details were confirmed, including the £500,000 pay-out if Francis accomplished the job.

Francis says he decided he would need assistance with the scheme and, with the SFO's agreement, he contacted a long-standing business acquaintance, Wendy Welsher. Welsher had known Francis under one of his many aliases - Michael Adams - since the mid 1980s while both were involved in timeshare projects in Spain. Francis knew that Welsher had been extensively connected with similar developments in Turkey too. Francis says his SFO masters agreed that, given the Nadir family's close interest in leisure and tourism, she was the ideal candidate to make the initial approach. Francis explained a diluted version of the scheme to Welsher. She says she thought the entire scheme very odd, but that Francis persuaded her that she would be working for the police and would be doing both the British government and Asil Nadir a great favour. Welsher, too, says she asked for confirmation and Francis arranged a meeting with his SFO contact - Welsher was satisfied that the proposal was above board when the officer showed her his warrant card. He led her to understand that the SFO had run into difficulties with the case and needed her help. The idea of the plan, she claims to have been told, was for the Nadir family to be embraced in business deals, through which the proposition could be put for the return of Asil Nadir's passport, either to Nadir himself or to any other member of his family. The return of his passport, Welsher says she was told, would enable Asil Nadir to remove himself from Britain and pursue his businesses elsewhere.

In February 1991, Welsher says she travelled to Istanbul to try to establish contact with the Nadir family via the mainland, where she was already involved in a £140 million timeshare development. After three or four days, she travelled back to Britain having been unable to secure an introduction. On her return to London, however, one of her Turkish associates telephoned and gave her the name of a "Mr Mustafa" who had a connection with one of the family companies.

Towards the end of March 1991, Noble Air's London manager, Mustafa Ebgü, told me a woman had called trying to get in touch with me or my mother about a potential project in North Cyprus. She had described herself as a businesswoman who had been involved in a holiday complex in Spain and was considering a similar investment in North Cyprus. She had said she would soon be visiting the island. My initial reaction was to brush the inquiry aside. It was a hard time for Noble Air, which had been experiencing financial difficulties since Asil's arrest and I was still extremely busy running around from one bank to another trying to raise the vital cash to keep both the airline and Noble Raredon afloat. But I did not wish to seem rude, so I asked Mustafa to tell the woman, if she called again, to visit my mother once she got to Cyprus and discuss the scheme with her. I thought no more of the matter.

Wendy Welsher made arrangements to visit North Cyprus. By then, she had met "Mr Mustafa" in London and had convinced him she had a very good business proposition to put to the Nadir family. He in turn had given her details of how to find the family in Cyprus. Welsher says her SFO contact arranged for her accommodation and flight costs to be met and, before she set off, she was asked to a meeting with a senior officer who again confirmed her instructions and coached her on what she should say at the meeting in Cyprus. She was to use her own initiative and, if it seemed appropriate, was to suggest the £3.5 million passport scheme. If not, she was to start by suggesting simply joint participation in a holiday village project. Welsher was booked on to a flight that March, with a room reserved at a hotel in Kyrenia.

I had hoped to be reunited with Fehim that Easter, taking my usual holiday in Cyprus with the children, but by then the crisis at Noble Raredon had reached such a pitch that I was unable to go. While I remained in London, the unknown woman who had telephoned Noble Air called on my mother at her home in Kyrenia and introduced herself as Wendy Welsher. She said she had been involved in a holiday development in Turkey, as well as the one in Spain, and was keen to embark on a similar project in north Cyprus. It was common knowledge on the island that my mother owned land, and Wendy said the site for the proposed development could be part of her contribution to the North Cyprus scheme. Wendy, meanwhile, would use the contacts she said she had in Europe to raise the necessary finance - which she put at £3 to £4 million - from the banks. She would also take care of all the groundwork, including carrying out feasibility studies and getting plans drawn up. The work would be put out to tender.

My mother was impressed. Wendy seemed a pleasant, friendly woman, impeccably turned out as befitted her image. My mother was also won over by her toddler daughter, Claire Louise, and the fact that Wendy spoke some Turkish. This eased their conversations, since my mother - even after eighteen years in Britain - had never felt really at home speaking English. The suggested project was also a big attraction. My mother was all too painfully aware of the problems both Asil and I were battling in London, so she was drawn to the idea of a tourism-related business which she could start off herself and which might prove a help to her children. She thought she could surprise us all by having the project completed - at a site she owned between Lapta and Kyrenia - by the time Asil's troubles were over. Moreover, it was a project in which her proposed partner seemed willing to take on the lion's share of the effort. It was a chance for her to carry on the kind of commercial activities my father, Asil and myself were so keen on and simply appeared, at first sight, too good an opportunity to miss.

My mother told Wendy Welsher she was very interested in principle but asked her to make contact with me in London and explain the scheme again. She was too wary of possible language misunderstandings to commit herself there and then, but told her visitor, "If my daughter says it is all right, then I am willing to join you."

Wendy Welsher returned to the UK and a further meeting with her alleged SFO contacts. Privately, she had deemed Safiye Nadir to be "too honest and too serious" to be able to broach the passport proposition, but she says she kept that judgement from the policemen, telling them that the holiday village development approach had gone well and that she would continue to work for them. Later, Welsher says she confided in Francis her concern that it would not be possible to approach the Nadirs about the passport. He told her just to go along with the SFO.

Wendy Welsher rang me at home soon after her return from Cyprus. She said she brought news of my mother, so I invited her round to South Woodford for tea. Like my mother, I found her very friendly and we got on well. I was far from certain that the holiday projects she spoke of would work out, but through my telephone contacts with Cyprus I was very pleased to see how much enthusiasm the idea seemed to have aroused in my mother. I had been very worried about the effect that our troubles had been having on her - it was hard for her, at the age of seventy, to stand by helplessly 3,000 miles away and watch two of her children go through the biggest crisis of their lives. If she was keen to pursue this project, then what harm could it do? The land was available and if Wendy was willing to look after the organisational side, why not go along with it? She seemed a sensible person.

I gave Wendy the green light for the scheme and she went away to start arranging the studies which would be needed to raise the finance. From time to time, she would come to see me at home, bringing her daughter, who quite melted my heart. Soon, because of these visits, we had established a closer relationship than usual for a business contact. Wendy seemed genuinely sympathetic to the position we were in. She frequently telephoned my mother, inquiring after her health and asking how she was coping.

> *There allegedly followed several meetings between Welsher and two SFO contacts who told her to continue talking to the family about timeshares and impressed upon her that if she received any documentation from the Nadir family - particularly if it bore the signature of Asil Nadir - she should pass it straight to them. "Little did they know that I had not, and had never in all my time and association with the Nadir family or with Mr Nadir himself, spoken about the £3.5 million for the return of his passport," Welsher would say later, adding, "At no time at any meetings, or [in] documents that I received from the Nadir family, has there been a document with Mr Nadir's name on." Meanwhile, Michael Francis discussed Wendy Welsher's progress at a meeting with SFO members at the Grosvenor Hotel in Victoria. Under their instructions, Francis says, he flew to Zurich and opened a Swiss bank account in preparation for the money Welsher was expected to receive.*

By July that year, Wendy told me all the plans needed for the holiday village were arranged and needed to be executed in order to approach the banks for funding. The sum of £100,000 was needed to pay for the studies and she said my mother had agreed to pay that as an advance, which would be reimbursed once the financing was secured. If that was what my mother had agreed, I told Wendy, then that was fine by me.

This conversation coincided with plans I was making for a family trip to Paris. I had promised Irfan I would take him there for a weekend as a reward for working so hard towards his A-Levels despite all the distractions of the past year. Irfan was anxiously awaiting his results and I was on edge too, knowing how much the outcome might affect his entire future. I felt the trip abroad would do us both good. It was also an ideal opportunity for us to be reunited with Fehim, whom we had not seen since Christmas. Sensing how down he seemed, I had persuaded him to meet us. I booked us rooms at the Hotel Scribe, near the Opera House. I must have mentioned our plans to Wendy. She quickly suggested that we should meet in Paris to conclude the arrangements for the Cyprus project - an idea which seemed sensible, since there would be tax advantages from not striking the deal in the UK. When I told her I was hoping to meet Fehim there too, she seized on this as a good means for my mother to send the money.

It was a warm Thursday afternoon when Irfan and I flew into Paris from Heathrow. We checked into our rooms at the hotel and walked round the corner to a bistro for dinner, while we waited for Fehim who was coming on a later flight from Turkey. Afterwards, we returned to the hotel to find Fehim there. It was a tearful, yet joyous reunion. The three of us sat up for hours, catching up on each other's news and relishing being back together again for the first time in seven months. We were all determined to make this a weekend where we could leave our troubles behind.

The following morning, Wendy arrived at the hotel. She had with her an agreement which my mother - again cautious of misunderstanding English - wanted me to sign as well as her. Wendy, too, was adamant that I should sign - she said she was concerned that, since North Cyprus was an unrecognised country, there should be another party on our side of the deal who lived outside the island. I read it quickly, signed beside my mother, and thought little more of it. I handed over the £100,000 which Fehim had bought from my mother in Cyprus and Wendy left soon afterwards. Fehim was worried for her safety, carrying such a large amount of cash round Paris, but Wendy declined his offer to accompany her. "It's OK," she told us, "I've got some friends waiting for me." Fehim, Irfan and I toured the sights of Paris that afternoon and enjoyed a cosy dinner - trying to act as if we had not a care in the world. As we flew back to London the next afternoon, leaving Fehim to wait until Sunday morning for his flight to Turkey, I had no idea of the supposed trap into which I had just walked.

Wendy Welsher, who claims her trip had been funded by the SFO, walked straight round the corner from the Nevzats' hotel to the George V Hotel, where two SFO men were supposedly waiting for her. She says she handed over to them the £100,000 and the joint co-operation agreement signed by Bilge Nevzat, which had been drafted by the SFO. A few days later, Michael Francis says he kept a pre-arranged meeting in Zurich with one of the SFO pair, who deposited £100,000 from his briefcase into a bank.

During the coming months, Francis and Welsher say they had several conversations with the SFO. Each time, Welsher says she was given notes explaining the information she was to pass on to the Nadirs. In October, she says she was told to set up a Swiss bank account to receive the £3.5 million the authorities were expecting. It was to be an escrow account - an account requiring joint authorisation for every transaction - between her and Bilge Nevzat, and Welsher was to persuade Bilge Nevzat to meet her in Geneva for this purpose. Once the arrangements were in hand, the SFO allegedly gave her a ticket to Switzerland. Michael Francis says he, too, went to Geneva at the same time with an SFO contact.

As 1991 progressed, I saw Wendy several times, mostly meeting at Noble Raredon's offices, in a restaurant nearby or sometimes at the Grosvenor House Hotel. I found her easy to get on with and was delighted by the friendship she seemed to have struck up with my mother. She often came to court when Asil was due to appear, saying she was there to lend us moral support. On a number of occasions, she met Asil, sometimes bumping into him at my office, or when she visited us at home in South Woodford. I introduced her to Asil as a friend of our mother and their contact was purely social - they chatted about mutual acquaintances in North Cyprus or about business ideas such as the timeshare concept with which Wendy was involved.

Seeing how desperate I was to keep my company afloat, Wendy advised me on converting the Sunset village at Kusadasi into timeshare apartments. On one occasion, she brought to me a wealthy-looking woman whom she introduced as "Mrs Oliver", who had connections in South Africa and Holland and who might be able to help me find financing. Mrs Oliver told me I might be able to use the Sunset village as collateral against a loan and asked me a lot of questions about the complex. Though nothing ever came of that discussion, I was grateful to Wendy for trying to help.

By the autumn, Wendy had still not produced any of the studies paid for with my mother's £100,000, but the reasons she gave for the delay always seemed plausible. She assured me every time we spoke that she would give the documents to my mother as soon as they were finished. Frankly, with Noble Raredon under ever greater pressure and Asil's troubles mounting by the day, I had little attention to spare for the Cyprus project.

That October, Wendy said we should go to Switzerland to open a joint bank account to receive the funds for the holiday village. Since it was a mere formality, involving no money exchange, I agreed to go along, spotting the chance, at the same time, to approach the Swiss banks for the finance needed by Noble Raredon. I flew to Geneva that month and was met at the airport by Wendy, who had gone on ahead. With her was a man she introduced as a colleague and friend, "Mr Adams". It would be more than a year before I realised that this was just one of several pseudonyms used by Michael Francis - jailbird, police supergrass, and the man who would later say he was hired to frame us for an alleged bribery plot. That day in Switzerland, he simply seemed a normal businessman, conservatively dressed in a smart navy blue suit. The three of us had coffee together at the airport and then took a taxi into the city. On the way, we dropped "Mr Adams" off at his hotel, where he said he had friends waiting. It was my last sight of him for many months.

Wendy and I quickly opened our joint account, but my approach for Noble Raredon finances proved less successful. Though we had achieved our main object in Geneva, I felt nonetheless defeated and distracted as we headed back to the airport. On the way, Wendy stopped the taxi briefly at the hotel where "Mr Adams" was staying, saying she wanted to speak to him. We travelled back to London on the same plane, but sitting separately, and spoke briefly while we waited for our luggage, before going our separate ways. Nothing at all in our contacts thus far had seemed abnormal. Stupidly, perhaps, I had no suspicions.

Throughout Wendy Welsher's "courtship" of myself and my mother, as a family we were experiencing one blow after another. Devastated though they were to see what was happening to us all, the children coped magnificently. Looking back, I do not know how I could have pulled through without them. From somewhere, they found new reserves of courage and maturity and they simply refused to stand by and let us all sink into despair. Throughout those difficult months, with Fehim away, they were unfailingly beside me. Most of my energies were taken up with the continuing fight to save Noble Raredon - a battle which was falling increasingly on to the shoulders of an ever-smaller group of staff. In January 1991, Corporate Development Director, Arseven Gümüs - also our company secretary - had announced that he, like Fehim, would be resigning. I had appointed Tijen as company secretary in place of Arseven Gümüs and made Terry Causer-Rees a director. Finance Director, David Heaton volunteered to go to South Wales and run the Elite Optics division - Noble Raredon's only profit-maker. I sent Sabina out to North Cyprus to oversee the months-old Olive Tree Hotel. One by one, the directors and some key staff members began to dive off the sinking ship. Other staff, I reluctantly had to let go. Day after day, Tijen and I would travel to South Audley Street with Levent, who had joined the firm shortly after Asil's arrest. We would sit at our desks and try to act as if there was nothing wrong, shoring up what little of Noble Raredon's business was left intact and racking our brains for new ways to try and salvage what could still be rescued.

Still reeling from Asil's arrest and the ripples of the Polly Peck crisis, our shares still suspended nearly four months on, international events that February dealt us another cruel blow. Six months after the Iraqi annexation of Kuwait, the Western allies had laid down a February deadline for Saddam Hussein to withdraw his invading forces. When he failed to comply, the Gulf War was declared, with the West launching a series of devastating air strikes against Baghdad and other targets within Iraq. Ill-equipped to hit back at the attacking Western jets, the Iraqis retaliated with missile assaults on Israel. There were threats that civilian targets in the West - including passenger aircraft - would be a focus for terrorist activities. The warning sounded loud and clear for the flying public, which still had very vivid memories of the Lockerbie bombing a year earlier and the ordeal of passengers held as Saddam Hussein's human shields after their plane touched down in Kuwait on the day it was invaded. Travellers cancelled their plans by the hundred thousand, sending the airline industry into a global tailspin from which it would take more than a year to recover.

North Cyprus felt the repercussions of the war particularly acutely. For while people the world over were scared off air travel in general, destinations perceived as being within the Gulf danger zone lost out the most. Turkey, sharing a border with Iraq and placing itself in the front line by shutting off a crucial oil pipeline and allowing air raids to be launched from its American air bases, seemed a risky place to visit. Cyprus - just sixty miles off the coast of Syria - was judged by many to be too close for comfort, while the siting of two major British bases in the south of the island gave would-be holidaymakers added cause for concern. In the days leading up to United Nations' February deadline, flights out of North Cyprus were packed as many residents with links abroad chose to sit the war out at a safer distance. Incoming flights were far less popular and many were cancelled because there simply were not enough passengers to make economic sense.

The longer-term implications were equally devastating. January, February and March should have been, as usual, the peak months for holiday bookings, but trade slumped. Even late bookings from April onwards failed to save the summer from disaster. North Cyprus had been expecting a boom season but, in the event, the number of visitors dropped dramatically. It would take years to get the fledgling tourist industry back on course.

For us, the setback could not have come at a worse moment. Noble Air was hit on several fronts. Already facing serious cash difficulties because of Asil's troubles, its bookings dropped off dramatically at the same time as the cost of aviation fuel soared with the outbreak of war. It was to prove a lethal combination of circumstances. The airline struggled on until early 1992, when it was finally forced to cease operating. Able to finance itself through holiday bookings, Mosaic Holidays had been one part of the company still able to function despite the banking blocks placed on its parent company. Yet as the tourism slump began to bite and its sole source of income all but dried up, it too found itself on ever shakier ground. In retrospect, I feel sure the businesses would have been able to pull through the crisis, had the

Gulf War, crucially coupled with the banks shutting off their credit facilities, not dealt them a fatal blow.

By the latter part of 1991, I became extremely concerned about the performance of our German subsidiary, Mosaic Reisen. Under German law, the local management had full executive responsibility for the company, but it had lost a million Deutschmarks in the preceding year and looked in dire trouble. In the end, we were forced to conclude that there was no hope and put it into voluntary liquidation.

The Sunset Holiday Village at Kusadasi was suffering badly too. I had had hopes of keeping the business going, but late in 1991 I was forced to sell our stake in Sunset at a much reduced price when one of our lender banks in Turkey demanded repayment of a $500,000 loan secured by the holiday complex. Ironically, it was my brother's former Impex Bank - now in the hands of Bülent Semiler - which forced our hand. Fortunately, however, the proceeds from the sale paid off most of Noble Raredon's debts in Britain.

Asil, meanwhile, was fighting legal and commercial battles on several fronts. Whenever we thought progress was being made, however small, some new twist would emerge to dash our hopes again. His primary fight lay in the criminal courts. In January 1991, Asil was charged with a further eighteen counts of theft and false accounting, bringing to thirty-six the number of charges he faced. The prosecution indicated that more might well follow. That September, he was arrested again and questioned twice. No new charges were brought until the next month when, after voluntarily attending Holborn police station, he was charged with a further fifty-eight counts of theft totalling £130 million - seventy-six counts in all. The introduction of new charges provoked concern among Asil's legal team over its effect of delaying the transfer of the case to the Crown Court. That November, the expected transfer again failed to take place, with the SFO winning a delay in which to consider new evidence. By then, PPI's former group chief accountant, John Turner, stood in the dock alongside Asil, charged with ten counts of false accounting.

The proceedings at that time were often quite farcical. At one early appearance, I recall Asil asked for his passport back, and DCI Dave Watson of the SFO argued against it, suggesting that Asil would go to North Cyprus and never come back. Waving around a small thin book, Watson claimed Asil was giving money to President Denktas. To make his point, the policeman produced a Turkish newspaper which he claimed demonstrated the danger - Asil was very powerful over there, he said, and he had just bought a gunboat. We were all astonished, including the magistrate. Asked if he understood Turkish, Watson admitted he did not, but he had been assured it was definitely a gunboat.

They all took a closer look at the photograph. Asil's QC, Anthony Scrivener, said it looked more like a police launch to him. Eventually it was established that it was a lifeboat, that had been a charitable donation. The little book that Watson was brandishing was in fact a building society pass book in the name of President Denktas's son, also with the initial "R", and showed the princely sum of £40. Asil had been the young man's guardian some years ago while he was studying in Britain. He had since died in a car accident and Asil had kept the book as a memento. It had disappeared in one of the police raids. This was the "evidence" that Asil was paying Denktas. I didn't know whether to laugh or cry, it was so absurd. But maybe it hinted at just how desperate the SFO appeared to be.

For four months after his arrest, Asil's bail was tightly controlled. In April 1991, Bow Street Magistrates' Court agreed to some relaxation of the bail conditions, allowing him to report to police weekly, instead of daily, and to spend nights away from home, provided he told police three days in advance where he was going and how long he would be away. A further application for variation of bail conditions that August, however, brought into focus the difficulties created for Asil by the North Cyprus dimension to his case. It also highlighted a major rift between the three administrators now in charge of PPI. The application, which sought to enable Asil could travel to North Cyprus with the administrators, was turned down. It was later revealed that, while Richard Stone and Michael Jordan had supported the move, feeling Asil's presence with them on the island was critical to their success, it had been opposed by Christopher Morris.

It was not the only occasion when the North Cyprus connection had far-reaching ramifications. In July that year, Asil's lawyer in North Cyprus invited the SFO - with the sanction of the Turkish Cypriot government - to visit the TRNC as part of their investigations. The SFO at first agreed to go, although citing "considerable practical difficulties" because North Cyprus was unrecognised by Britain, and told Asil's UK lawyers they were making arrangements. Later, they changed their minds. Though North Cyprus is not recognised by the UK government, other British police operations have taken place before and since in conjunction with the TRNC's own authorities. The SFO claimed afterwards that such co-operation had been only on an informal basis, but that a more formal approach was now being demanded.

The SFO's refusal to travel to Cyprus led to an evidential stalemate. Asil argued in his own defence that any transfers from PPI which were the substance of the theft charges against him were only half the equation. The counter-transactions, in which corresponding amounts were paid into the Cypriot subsidiaries, were all documented in North

Cyprus - a point which Asil had made to the police when he was first arrested. He also explained that PPI had operated a kind of "secondary banking" system on the island, with locals exchanging Turkish lira for "hard" currency - the firm profiting on each transaction. The SFO demanded that the paperwork should be sent to the UK for them to examine and when it was told that TRNC law prohibited this, refused to go and look at it in North Cyprus. In a bid to get round this stand-off, Asil took the highly unusual step of furnishing his own evidence. He commissioned an independent report on the books by accountants Binder Hamlyn. A forensic report by British experts was also carried out on the documentation studied, to try and allay any fears of deception. The results of all these studies were sent to the SFO and copies went to the PPI administrators. The documents were ignored.

At Polly Peck, the administrators seemed in disarray and there emerged clear evidence of a split between the three - Jordan and Stone appointed to try and salvage the company, and Morris appointed to flush out any misdemeanours by its directors or auditors. Michael Jordan had told the BBC in January 1991 he hoped to come up with a scheme to relaunch the company within the next few months. Two days later the administrators confirmed they were planning to sell all the firm's assets in the United States apart from PPI-Del Monte. That April, Russell Hobbs Tower was sold to Pifco Holdings for £7.785 million. Some journalists said the deal had been made "on the cheap". Five months later, the German fresh fruit distributing subsidiary Früco Früchtehandel was sold for 36 million Deutschmarks - 11.5 million Deutschmarks less than PPI had paid for it in 1989. The courts in North Cyprus had effected and upheld an injunction denying access by any of the three administrators to Polly Peck subsidiaries there. At the end of April, it was reported that Jordan and Stone were planning to hand control of PPI's Mediterranean operations back to Asil. The proposal was staunchly opposed by Morris.

Autumn 1991 saw Morris make a surprise new move which again set him apart from his fellow-administrators. In October, he sought, and won, a High Court injunction freezing the assets of some North Cyprus and family-related companies and individuals, saying the administrators were attempting to recover more than £500 million. Among the companies and individuals affected was the Central Bank of the Turkish Republic of Northern Cyprus, which found itself unable to move foreign exchange reserves held in banks in England and Wales. The departure aroused immediate hostility in North Cyprus and had the effect of involving in the action thousands of people totally unconnected with PPI. Turkish Cypriot Prime Minister, Dr Dervis Eroglu, denounced the action as "an extraordinarily serious mistake". Morris's injunction drove another wedge between the two camps of administrators. Michael Jordan said the court order would further delay the administrators' attempts to gain control of the Polly Peck assets in North Cyprus. Richard Stone said it "must put in doubt" the inclusion of those assets in any PPI reconstruction plan. Asil publicly attacked the proceedings as misguided, saying they would be no benefit to PPI, its creditors or shareholders and would only "divert essential resources to speculative litigation". It would be five months before the injunction relating to the Central Bank was overturned. Touche Ross eventually agreed to pay legal costs for the bank of some £800,000 and issued the following statement: "Christopher Morris accordingly apologises to the governor and the board of the Central Bank for the allegations of fraud and money laundering which were made in the course of proceedings." The cost of the first seven months of PPI's administration was revealed at £8.4 million - a £5.9 million charge by Coopers & Lybrand and a £2.5 million bill from Touche Ross, which included £56,000 for "communication with Coopers". The total cost worked out at well over £35,000 a day.

Asil was also fighting actions by his personal creditors. In August 1991, the creditors launched an attempt to have him jailed by the High Court for contempt of court, claiming he had breached previous arrangements through the sale of Impex Bank. Asil argued that, had he received the due payment for the bank - which, in fact, he had not - the proceeds would have been channelled to the creditors. His QC accused the creditors of trying to "terrorise" him. That October, the judge cleared the way for the creditors to apply for Asil's committal to prison, dismissing defence arguments that the proceedings should be struck out. The case would rumble on in the courts until July 1992, when the creditors finally agreed to withdraw.

26th November that year brought two bitter personal blows for Asil. That day, he lost his year-long fight to stave off personal bankruptcy. In a surprise initial action, Den Norske Bank lodged a petition for repayment of a £1.5 million loan Asil had personally guaranteed. Other creditors jumped on the bandwagon and Asil was declared bankrupt with debts totalling more than £90 million. The effect of the bankruptcy was to strip Asil of his personal directorships. Since PPI had gone into administration, he had been a nominal director and chairman of the company. Now he lost even the title. On the same day, he was replaced as a director of Vestel by administrator Richard Stone - Asil's position complicated by the fact that he had been unable, since losing his passport, to attend any board meetings in the previous year, as required by Turkish law.

More injury was to follow as news of the bankruptcy spread. Later that day, I was sitting with Asil in his Berkeley Square office when the fax machine began to churn out page after page. Asil walked over to it and picked up the first couple of sheets. He read for a moment and then put them down again with a shrug. He said nothing about the contents of the message, but I could tell from his face that something had upset him. A few minutes later, he pushed the faxed documents across the desk to me. They were divorce papers which Asil had years earlier sent to Aysegül, but she had refused to sign. Now she was sending them from Istanbul, all signed as required. We looked at each other without a word.

The following morning, Asil and I were both working in South Audley Street when one of my Noble Raredon employees, Sacit Danish, asked me if my brother was moving house - he had noticed a big removal van outside the Aldford Street house. Without telling Asil, I walked straight round to see what was happening and found a bewildered Joanne Mackey sitting in an empty home. The bailiffs had been in, stripping every stick of furniture barring the bed and two cream-coloured sofas. Pictures and ornaments had also been taken, including even several knickknacks which were of purely sentimental value and worth virtually nothing. I was horrified. I knew Asil would be devastated if he saw his home like that. Quickly, I arranged for a few bits of furniture to be brought from our house in South Woodford - these pieces of mine would also be taken away in a later raid. Meanwhile, I sent Joanne out to buy as many flowers as she could find. She arrived back with an armful of blooms which we arranged as best we could round the house. By the time Asil returned from the office, Joanne and I had made the place look as homely as possible. Typically, my brother tried not to show that he was upset at losing so many of his personal possessions. "The flowers are beautiful," he kept telling us as he looked around. In fact, Asil spent most of the evening trying to comfort me, recounting tales of all the wealthy and successful people he knew of who had once been bankrupts. Soon afterwards, Asil would also lose the lease on the house and would move into the flat in Eaton Square which Aysegül had vacated when she moved to Istanbul a few months earlier.

In December 1991 I met Wendy Welsher again. This time, she had persuaded my mother that, because North Cyprus was not recognised internationally, she would need some guarantee from outside the island as collateral for financing the holiday village scheme. My mother could not think of how to provide the necessary security. Then she remembered that Aysegül had left some of her antiques behind in

London and decided to ask her if she would put up one item as security for the loan. Over the telephone from Istanbul, Aysegül agreed to put up one of her paintings - *Sisters*, by Lord Frederick Leighton, valued at about £500,000. Aysegül had left the painting for safe-keeping at South Audley Management's offices and she had given Abide power of attorney to handle it under her instructions. I happened to be visiting the day Wendy came to collect the painting, and watched as Abide handed the work of art to her, along with the official documentation. One of Asil's bodyguards helped Wendy to carry the bulky painting out to her car and we all watched as she drove off, we thought to deposit the painting safely for the bank - although, much later, Wendy would claim to have handed it immediately to the SFO, on whose instructions she said she was acting. As that winter turned into spring, I hardly saw Wendy and began to grow concerned that no plans had yet been forthcoming and no bank facility had been arranged. My patience was beginning to wear thin, but I was anxious not to upset my mother by calling the entire project off - after all, it was really her initiative and Wendy had been in constant touch with her, assuring that all was well despite the delays. In retrospect, I wish I had pressed her more to produce some results. At the time, though, I had too many worries already to want to add to them.

In April 1992, I went to Cyprus for Easter with the children. The day before we were due to leave again, I was at Jasmine Court Hotel when I heard someone calling my name. I was surprised to see Wendy Welsher sitting on one of the balconies overlooking the swimming pool - I had had no idea she was there. Wendy said she wanted to see me and we arranged for her to come to our flat the following morning, 19th April. I was getting ready to go to the airport that afternoon and the flat was full of people who had come to say goodbye. I took her through to the other room and there Wendy told me that we needed to sign another co-operation agreement since the first one, signed the previous year, was now out-of-date. The second agreement was more detailed than the first, and specified that the payment we were to make would go to a man called David Kent - Wendy said he was the person who would be overseeing the raising of finances for the holiday village. Once the finances were in place, the agreement that she produced gave me a week in which to travel from London and check, on my mother's behalf, that everything seemed in order before authorising the deal to continue. I glanced at the document and signed where Wendy pointed to - I should have paid far closer attention to the wording, but I was in a hurry to get the business dealt with and knew, after all, that I was merely giving my signature for my mother's benefit. I would come to regret my haste. Wendy now alleges the document had been drawn up and given to her by the SFO. Months later, it would be shown to me again, altered to impart a much more sinister meaning.

Within weeks of my return from North Cyprus that Easter came an event which gave me one of the best tonics I could have hoped for - Fehim came home. He had been at a low ebb throughout the early months of 1992, battling a bout of bronchial pneumonia and shuttling between North Cyprus and Poland in the hope - still repeatedly thwarted by the lack of available finance - of drumming up some valuable business. In May that year, he spent seven weeks sleeping night after night on a settee in the Warsaw office, cutting his own costs while he tried to secure a trade deal on behalf of contacts in Iran. One weekend, when the deal seemed to have hit a sticky patch, Fehim was sitting alone in the office when the telephone rang. It was Tijen, calling from London in another attempt to persuade him to come home. This time, she sounded more desperate than ever. "Dad, you must come home. Mum isn't feeling well and none of us are the same without you. Without you here to support us, I think we'll all crack up," she pleaded tearfully.

For the next few hours, Fehim brooded over everything in the office, wrestling with his fears. By the time Tijen telephoned again later as arranged, he had made up his mind to fly home. He booked his ticket for 27th June - exactly eighteen months from when he had left Britain.

27th June was a Saturday. At Fehim's request, Tijen had kept the news of his return a secret, telling only her aunt Sidika - Fehim's sister - who she asked to come with her to the airport. As the aeroplane descended into Heathrow, Fehim saw flashbacks of his last landing in Britain, seeing over and over the police storming the private jet and arresting Asil. For the minutes that it took to leave the plane and negotiate passport control and customs, he felt as if he was on a knife edge, waiting for something to happen. Only when he emerged safely through customs to find Tijen and Sidika waiting was he able to relax. Unsure whether to laugh or cry, the three of them embraced across the barrier amid the airport crowds, smiling at each other with tear-streaked faces, hardly able to believe they were reunited. By the time the trio reached South Woodford, I had gone shopping with Levent. When Irfan opened the door to see Fehim standing there, his jaw fell open and it was a moment before he could move from the spot to hug his father. They held each other tightly while our two dogs leapt around their legs, yapping frantically. It was another half an hour before Levent and I got home. I will never forget the scene when Fehim opened the front door to us. It was as if we were watching a film and someone had pressed the "freeze frame" button, as Levent and I stood there, carrier bags still in our hands, face to face with the moment we had longed for.

I tried a couple of times to speak, but the words just would not come. Then, all in one movement, I let go of the bags I was carrying, hardly bothering to check that nothing was broken, and stepped forward into Fehim's arms, tears streaming unchecked down my cheeks. It was a dream come true.

Having Fehim back gave me an enormous boost. For a few exciting days, we were almost able to forget about our problems as we welcomed him back into the family. The day after his return dawned bright and summery and we all celebrated in the garden together, drinking vodka and eating caviar that Fehim had brought with him from Poland. Asil arrived to see his brother-in-law for the first time in eighteen months, bearing huge bunches of flowers and helium-filled balloons emblazoned with the word "welcome". Suddenly, my flagging spirit was renewed. I felt new zest for the battle as I set off for work each morning with Tijen and Levent. Fehim took on the running of the house and it again became a loving haven to return to at the end of each difficult day.

> *During the early summer of 1992 - in June or July - Michael Francis again claims to have met in Zurich an SFO contact, who had with him some prepared statements for Francis to read. Allegedly on the officer's instructions, Francis made a series of telephone calls to John Knox at the SFO - Francis says he was told that Knox's superior, SFO director George Staple, was on holiday at the time. The calls to Knox were devised to incriminate Asil Nadir, Francis says, and to suggest that this was Francis's first approach to the SFO - some seventeen months after he claims to have been recruited. The calls named Nadir, his QC Anthony Scrivener, his trial judge, Mr Justice Tucker, and Metropolitan Police Assistant Commissioner, Wyn Jones, as co-conspirators in a plot to pervert the course of justice. Francis's SFO contact listened in to every conversation and Francis says he got the impression that he had two motives for being there: firstly to ensure the calls were conducted properly and secondly to ascertain that they were not being recorded by Francis. Francis had already hinted to the SFO that he had incriminating recordings of conversations between them. In fact, he says he did then have recordings, but subsequently handed them over to the SFO.*

> *Soon afterwards, in July 1992, Wendy Welsher says she received a call from the SFO, who wanted her to have the painting Sisters valued by fine arts auctioneers, Bonhams, with a view to entering it in an sale. Welsher says two officers met her outside the auction*

house and handed back to her the painting, which she had last seen after collecting it from Berkeley Square the previous December. On their instructions, she says she took the painting into the auction house and kept an appointment they had made for her with a member of the auction house's staff. Bonhams were extremely interested in Sisters, she claims, and she left the work of art there. Soon afterwards, Welsher claims Michael Francis told her to get the painting back from Bonhams as a matter of urgency and bring it to him at an hotel near Charles de Gaulle Airport, Paris - an instruction she says was confirmed to her by the SFO. She says she collected the painting from Bonhams, put it in the boot of her car and drove through British and French customs and passport control without being stopped. Francis was waiting for her at the hotel and she says she handed the painting to him. Francis claims to have taken the painting to Switzerland and left it in a bank safety deposit box. Two days later, the administrators of Polly Peck International, believing there was a legal query over the ownership of the Frederick Leighton painting, Sisters, placed the painting on the UK's Stolen Arts Register. In October 1992, Wendy Welsher would be sought and questioned at length about the painting by the administrators. She claims she was given advance warning of the interview by the SFO, and alleges they made up a story for her to tell. During a couple of meetings with the administrators, she says she made out an affidavit relaying the fictitious information. She never signed the affidavit.

In August 1992, Levent was married in Cyprus. That New Year, when he and Rüya had first announced their intention to get married that summer I had suggested to Asil that, to make sure he could attend, we ought to arrange the wedding in London. Optimistic as ever, though, he would not hear of it. He told me he was "100 per cent sure" his legal troubles would be over by then. We went ahead with the wedding plans, but as the day drew nearer it became abundantly clear that Asil would not be among the guests. Five hundred people toasted the young couple in the grounds of Loch Manor - again, a magical setting as it had been for Tijen's wedding four years earlier - but it was a poignant night for all our immediate family because Asil was the only person missing on what should have been a purely joyous occasion. Right until the last minute, I kept hoping against hope that - I did not know how - Asil would suddenly arrive at the party. Just at the instant when the band struck up Turkish bridal music and the young couple walked in, the telephone on a table in the front garden jangled into life. I answered to hear Asil's voice on the end of the line. As I gripped the receiver, overwhelmed by sadness, he told me, "Look up into that tree outside and you will see me there - I'm with you all, watching." I rejoined the reception with tears in my eyes.

It was later that month that I saw Wendy Welsher again - the first time I had come across her since our meeting in Cyprus in April. At the end of August, my mother sent £11,000 to me in London and asked me to pass it on to Wendy. The extra cash was supposedly needed to finalise the long-awaited plans and feasibility studies - Wendy, though, would later claim to have handed it over at Zurich airport to Michael Francis and an SFO contact, who allegedly paid it into a Swiss bank. I was very wary by this stage and called my mother, warning her to be careful. Nonetheless, on her instructions, I arranged to meet Wendy and gave her the money. Although I had serious doubts by now, I was still reluctant to call a halt to the negotiations; to me, this was no ordinary business deal - I was pursuing it as a lifeline for my mother. During the two years since Asil's troubles had begun, and particularly since his arrest, I had seen my mother slide into a mental and physical decline. As the months dragged on into years, there were moments when I feared she would not survive to see her son a free man. Now, though, this project had given her new enthusiasm to battle on behalf of the family and she seemed to be coping better with everything. I could hear the excitement in her voice over the telephone and whenever we met I could see new light in her eyes. Whatever my misgivings, I mentally thanked Wendy Welsher for giving my mother this new hope. Even if nothing ever came of the project, the £111,000 that had been handed over seemed a small price to pay for my mother's life.

That meeting with Wendy was to prove one of the last times I would see her. By then, I had little energy for anything but trying to save Noble Raredon, and I quickly forgot her. My other major preoccupation was Asil who, for a time during the preceding months, had seemed to be making some headway in his legal battles. After a rap from the Chief Magistrate about the length of time the case was already taking, Asil and John Turner had been committed for trial at the Old Bailey. Asil faced sixty-nine charges, involving sums totalling £149 million, and his co-accused ten false accounting charges amounting to £7.4 million. The case was not expected to be heard before the start of 1993.

That February had also seen the collapse of the second Guinness trial - a serious embarrassment to the Serious Fraud Office which had prompted an judicial statement appealing for reform to complex fraud trials. Within days of the collapse of "Guinness II", six out of ten defendants had been convicted for their part in the Blue Arrow fraud over raising funds for a take-over bid. Just four months later, four of the convictions were overturned by appeal judges who said the case - the culmination of a reported £35 million-plus SFO inquiry - was unfair in its complexity. The third Guinness trial would never take place. At the first pre-trial hearing into my brother's case, Mr Justice Tucker had insisted that Asil's trial should be short and straightforward, centring on no more than ten charges. "If you can't get convictions on ten charges, you won't be able to get convictions on twenty," he told prosecuting counsel. Four months later, on 8th June, Mr Justice Tucker ruled at Birmingham Crown Court in favour of an application by my brother to have forty-six of the charges against him dropped. The charges involved the transfer of £119 million from PPI's accounts to Uni-Pac and the Kibris Endüstri Bankasi and the judge disagreed with the prosecution case that these transactions could be deemed thefts. The ruling undoubtedly irked the SFO, who applied to the High Court and, at the end of July, won leave to challenge the dismissal of the charges. Further action was adjourned pending a House of Lords ruling on a similar issue in another case.

By the end of July 1992, Michael Francis says he was starting to get cold feet about the complex plot in which he had been embroiled. Supposedly deciding to have no further involvement in the affair, he took off for Istanbul and Europe at the beginning of August, eventually returning to Britain via the cross-Channel port of Dover. On 22nd August, Francis was arrested at the Gatwick Penta Hotel and taken to Gatwick police station for questioning. In his briefcase, police found a brochure showing arms for sale and he was detained under the Prevention of Terrorism Act. Three or four hours after his initial arrest, anti-terrorist branch officers questioned him. Midway through the interview, says Francis, one of his senior SFO contacts arrived and told him that any possible charges would be dropped if he continued to co-operate. If not, he would be "put away" for at least fifteen years. Francis says he agreed to co-operate and was left with the anti-terrorist officers to concoct a story explaining away the arms brochure and enabling the matter to be referred back to Sussex police. The tale he says they came up with was that the weapons were not in Britain, but were going to be transported from North Cyprus to southern Ireland. The following Monday, Francis was brought before Crawley Magistrates' Court and remanded in custody at Lewes Prison on charges relating to a false passport and false driving licence.

Wendy Welsher says she was informed of Francis's detention early in September by a police officer who allegedly asked her to persuade

Asil Nadir to travel down to Lewes to visit Michael Francis in jail. Welsher never mentioned the proposal to Nadir, knowing he would be nonplussed by it, but says she reported back to police that she had broached the subject of the journey and that Nadir had refused to go. The same officer then asked her to arrange an introduction for him to Asil Nadir. A few days later, Welsher says she took him to Nadir's office in South Audley Street, introducing him under an assumed name as a friend who wanted advice on doing business in Turkey and North Cyprus. Nadir agreed to see the visitor and they talked for a while. Nadir would later describe the meeting as "weird", reporting that his visitor said little at first, but then went on to tell how he wanted to start a business in the Mediterranean producing electrical components. Nadir would say that that day was the first time he had any doubts about Welsher - the biggest thing that struck him about the mystery visitor, he would tell his family, was that he had on "policeman's shoes".

Shortly after that meeting, on 29th September, Michael Francis claims to have been told that, in return for his co-operation, no charges would be pressed against him other than the minor passport and driving licence irregularities. On 1st October, he says he was strip-searched by two prison officers, then escorted from jail by the SFO and taken to Crawley police station. There, he says he went over several ready-prepared statements with his SFO contacts and made a tape-recorded statement from one of the scripts accusing Asil Nadir of having "salted away" 750 million Deutschmarks and of being involved in arms and drug dealing. The statement cited Mr Justice Tucker, Anthony Scrivener and Wyn Jones as co-conspirators with Nadir in a plot to pervert the course of justice. Francis says he was shown a photocopy of a document signed by Bilge Nevzat and Safiye Nadir - in fact the second timeshare co-operation agreement signed six months earlier. The recorded statement said Francis had the original of the document - a move which he would later describe as a "very big blunder" on the part of the authorities. The original was in fact in the possession of the SFO and would be handed over to Francis more than three weeks later. On the basis of Francis's alleged statement and the photocopied document, the Lord Chief Justice sent an urgent message that day - 1st October - to Mr Justice Tucker, advising him not to attend court for the Nadir case the following day.

During September 1992, Asil's lawyers had given notice that they would seek to have the terms of his bail varied, so that he could travel to North Cyprus with his solicitor to help prepare his defence. The hearing of the application had been set for 2nd October. But when the day came and we waited in court, Mr Justice Tucker inexplicably failed to turn up for the session. Inquiries by QC Anthony Scrivener's PA revealed him to be in good health in his chambers, but to have been detained for "urgent administrative reasons". It would not be until a rearranged hearing date in November that we would discover the real reason for the judge's absence.

During the remaining weeks of October, Francis was taken to a special unit at South Woodford Police Station, where further tape-recordings were made. Wendy Welsher says she was also involved, as the SFO team put together a web of allegations, and says she was helped to come up with a story about a supposed 750 million Deutschmark account in the name of Asil Nadir. She also says she was given a special telephone number for Francis, who was being held at South Woodford. She was instructed to call Francis and to make sure she mentioned the name of Mr Justice Tucker during the course of the telephone conversation, which was recorded. Another couple were also said to have become involved at that stage. They were said to have rung Francis and, in another taped call, claimed that they had been asked by Asil Nadir to move 750 million Deutschmarks from an account in Liechtenstein.

Now it was Wendy Welsher's turn to worry about what she had got herself into. By that October, she claims she was thoroughly fed up with all she was being asked to do. Moreover, during recent conversations with her contact officers, she says she had discovered for the first time that, through her actions, Bilge Nevzat and her mother would also be implicated in the purported plot to change the course of the Nadir trial. The knowledge of what she was doing to the two women, with whom she had become very friendly, sickened her, and she sensed too that the authorities had detected her growing reluctance. Towards the end of the month, she claims to have received a late-night telephone call from a man clearly close to the investigation who threatened that her own life and her daughter's would be in danger unless she went along with the SFO. Frantic with worry, Welsher says there was only one course of action she could think of. She grabbed handfuls of clothes from the wardrobes and threw them into a suitcase, waking her daughter, and dressing her hastily. Soon after the call, Welsher drove away from her house in north-west London. The next morning, she and her daughter caught a flight to see Safiye Nadir in North Cyprus.

Michael Francis, meanwhile, says he was closely involved with the SFO. On 23rd October 1992, he was brought before Crawley Magistrates Court, in Surrey, and bailed on condition, among other stipulations, that he did not leave the country. Three days later, on SFO orders, he went to Gatwick Airport, where he joined a contact on a flight to Switzerland. Once in Zurich, Francis did as he said he had been told and handed over to the officer a series of incriminating taped conversations between the two of them, plus other similar recordings. By now, Francis would say later, he was simply playing the SFO along. He claims he lied to the officer that he also had tapes which would incriminate Asil Nadir and, apparently happy that Francis was co-operating, the SFO man handed Francis a brown A4 envelope containing the original co-operation agreement - now doctored - signed by Bilge Nevzat and her mother. Francis agreed to place the envelope in a safety deposit box. The SFO man's plan was said to be that he and Francis would return to Zurich the following week, as soon as Francis's case had been wound up in the British courts. They would then collect the painting, Sisters, the signed document and the supposed tapes of Asil Nadir and would take them back to London, bringing them in through the "red channel" so that the items' arrival in the country would be logged officially.

Francis appeared again before Crawley magistrates on 29th October, emerging from the court-room with a fine and a statement by the Crown Prosecution Service that there were no more charges outstanding against him. The morning after the hearing, Francis was travelling again, this time to Zurich with two men from the SFO. Apparently flying high as the end of the scheme drew near, Francis says the three of them journeyed out of Gatwick in Elite Class seats and tucked into a champagne breakfast on the way to Switzerland. Francis claims to have taken his contacts straight from the airport to a Zurich bar called the James Joyce and told them to wait there while he went to collect the painting, tapes and document. It was, he says, a stalling tactic. Some time later, Francis returned to the bar and told the SFO men he had been unable to retrieve the items, but would get them to the SFO as soon as he could. Incredibly, Francis says the SFO men flew back to London on the half past four flight out of Zurich that afternoon. During the next five days, Francis says he spoke to them several times on the telephone, repeatedly assuring them that he would be back soon with the required items and documentation. On Wednesday 4th

November, Francis called and said he would be flying back to the UK at one o'clock the next day. Francis says they seemed convinced he was telling the truth.

Around the end of October I received a bizarre telephone call from my mother in Cyprus. She sounded extremely agitated. She said Wendy had been to see her that day and had asked her to pass on an urgent message to me. The message was that Asil and I were in danger and that we should both leave the country immediately. I was very annoyed by this dramatic "warning", which had clearly put my mother into a state of great alarm. For nearly two years since Asil's arrest, friends in the legal world had advised him to be very careful - they feared that, with Polly Peck having collapsed but the authorities still floundering in their attempts to bring my brother's case to trial, his life could be in danger from those who might want to bring this embarrassing charade to a very final conclusion. I was sure this was what Wendy meant, and was irritated that she had approached my mother in such an alarmist manner. As for us leaving Britain - I had a family and a business there to consider and there was no way Asil could travel without his passport. I did my best to reassure my mother, telling her not to listen to anything Wendy said. I too dismissed Wendy's words from my mind...but I was to get a sharp reminder a few days later.

CHAPTER TEN

End of a Dream

"Remember, remember, the fifth of November" goes the childhood Guy Fawkes rhyme...but I will always have cause to recall Thursday 5th November 1992 for a quite different reason. At seven o'clock that morning, I was just getting up to go to work and Fehim had gone downstairs when I heard the dogs start barking furiously. I pulled on my dressing gown and peered through the curtains. In the road were three or four unmarked cars and about a dozen men in civilian clothes were walking across the front lawn. I recognised the man leading them as Detective Chief Inspector David Watson, whom I had seen in court at every one of Asil's appearances. It had to be a raid, I knew, but I felt quite calm - in a way, it was something I had been expecting for some time. By then, Asil had experienced several raids and I was slightly surprised they had never been round to us too. I had no idea then that simultaneous raids were being launched next door at Tijen's house, at Asil's home in Eaton Square and at the Noble Raredon offices.

As I turned away from the window, I heard Fehim shout to me from downstairs, "It's the SFO."

"I know," I shouted back. "Go and open the door."

I pushed open the curtains and was standing at the top of the stairs when Fehim unlocked the front door. I heard DCI Watson tell him, "We are the police," as he showed him his identity card. Then I heard him say: "Is Mrs Nevzat in?" Fehim nodded and the chief inspector went on, "We are here with a warrant to arrest Mrs Nevzat and we have a court order to come in and search your house."

I felt an astonishing calm.

Quickly, I woke Levent, Rüya and Irfan. Then, as if in a dream, I walked downstairs. In the hall at the bottom of the stairs was a crowd of about eight men. I walked up to DCI Watson and said, "Good morning."

He answered, "Mrs Nevzat, we have a court order for your arrest and to search the house."

"Why?" was all I could reply.

239

"For conspiracy to pervert the course of justice and for helping Asil Nadir in moving Polly Peck assets amounting to 750 million Deutschmarks," came the response.

The words hit me like a physical blow. I hardly heard a thing through my daze as the officer read me my rights.

Trying to gather my thoughts, I told DCI Watson I wanted to shower and get dressed. At first, he was reluctant to allow me to do that, saying I would have to wait until they could summon a policewoman from the local station to come and sit in with me, but I showed them the en suite shower room and managed to convince them there was no way I could escape or get up to anything there. One of the policemen sat outside while I went in. As I stood under the jet of water, I felt numb with shock but still very calm.

By the time I dressed and went downstairs, the search had begun. I called John Elgar, our company lawyer, and asked him to get in touch with Monty Raphael, a well-known criminal lawyer. The eight officers had been joined now by a local policewoman and they were spread out around the house, opening cupboards, pulling out drawers, sifting through papers, even through clothes and underwear, studying closely any document they came across. They also paid close attention to all the paintings hung on the walls. Every so often, one of them would take something to DCI Watson to look at. Wherever I went, one of the officers would shadow me. At one point, a policeman picked up from a drawer the running "tab" from our Sunday card games, which showed Asil's £275 debt to Irfan, and peered at it for several minutes. Irfan explained what it was, but the officer still continued examining it for some time before putting it down, as if undecided whether to believe him.

I was more concerned for the others than for myself. Fehim was very pale and quiet - a sure sign to me that he was deeply shocked by what was happening and a painful reminder to me of the day he had witnessed Asil's arrest. Irfan and Levent were just standing around, unsure what to do or say. Oddly, it was Rüya who proved to be a tower of strength - I had thought that as a physically very slight, sensitive musician, she would be the least able to cope with such events. But it was she who remained calm and capable, brewing tea for the police officers and consoling the rest of the family in the hours that followed. Tijen arrived just as the police had begun putting paperwork and address books into plastic bags to take away. As soon as she came through the door, I could see that she had on what I called her "business face". She instantly took charge of the situation. She took the names of all the officers there and then announced that none of them were to go into any of the rooms without one of the family going with them. Then she insisted that they open up the plastic bags so that she could see what they had put inside them. Switching to Turkish, she told us, "Don't let them go into any of the rooms alone because you never know what they might put into your drawers."

An irritated DCI Watson rapped, "No Turkish."

As the search continued, I had several telephone calls. The first was from my Uncle Selçuk, who had rushed to a call box to tell me he had seen official-looking men going into our offices. I told him we too had a "visit" and to telephone Asil urgently. Soon afterwards came a call from Abide, by now living with Asil, who said she understood we had "guests" and wanted to know if I needed help to try and find a lawyer. Another SFO team was at that moment raiding Asil's home. Fortunately, Abide did not reveal this - had I known, I would have been worried for Asil as well as for myself. Soon afterwards, Sabina rang from Noble Raredon's offices in South Audley Street to say the SFO were there too and to ask what they should do. "Let them look round the building and do what they want," I told Sabina. I knew I had no reason for concern. During the next few hours, the officers would go through every drawer and filing cabinet, making a hostile Terry and Sabina go through the computer records and quizzing them about certain names. They were particularly interested in anyone with the name "Michael" - when I heard this, it made no sense, but I would later make the connection. My fourth caller that morning was Monty Raphael. I had been told that I would be taken to Holborn Police Station, so I asked him to meet me there at eleven o'clock.

When the search was over and the time came for us to leave for the police station, Tijen refused to let me go alone. I was told I would have to go in one of the police cars and Tijen was adamant that she would come with me. As we walked out and got into the police car, I tried to behave as though I was totally unconcerned. I felt sure that if the others detected any weakness in me, they would all break down. As if performing in a play, I smiled and tried to hide my feelings, while inside I was in a turmoil of shock and bewilderment. I thought I had succeeded, but Irfan told me afterwards they could see right through my "act". I walked past Fehim, Rüya, Irfan and Levent, who were all too stunned to say anything and told them, "Don't worry, I'll be back soon." On the far side of the garden, I could see our neighbours looking on in concern - by now, the whole neighbourhood knew something was going on. I waved at them as I walked by. As we drove away, I turned for one last look at Fehim and the youngsters lined up in the drive. The instant we pulled away, Fehim collapsed on the doorstep. The boys helped him inside and called Rifat to see to him.

The half-hour journey to Holborn seemed to take forever. I was very glad of Tijen's company as she held my hand to comfort me. At one point she fished a packet of sweets from her pocket, offering them to me and the two policemen with us as if to try to inject an atmosphere of normality into the drama. All kinds of thoughts and worries were passing through my mind. Suddenly, I had a vivid flashback to thirty-one years ago, when we had driven the same streets on my first day in Britain - now I was shocked and ashamed to be taking that route through the City in a police car. I had always thought of myself as so law-abiding that I never for a moment imagined that I would experience being arrested. Nor had I ever thought I would set foot inside Holborn Police Station - the place our family had christened the "KGB headquarters" after listening to my brother's descriptions. Now, as the realisation slowly sunk in that that was where I, too, was being taken, I began to feel a growing sense of horror. I held tighter to Tijen's hand and blinked back the tears. I willed the driver to go slowly and prayed for traffic to hold us up - yet at the same time I wanted the whole thing over with as quickly as possible.

All too soon, we arrived. It was nearly eleven o'clock. We were led in through a side door and along a corridor until we reached a point where Tijen was told she would have to go through to the main police station reception. We looked at each other. Tijen squeezed my hand one more time and said, "I'll be out there the whole time," before going through the door they had pointed out. I was marched along the corridor towards another door, trying hard to keep up with the striding officers who were walking one in front of me and two behind. Suddenly I felt very, very alone.

We walked through a door into the detention area of the police station. In the middle of a square, flanked by about half a dozen cells, stood a desk and a few chairs. The officers told me I was to be interviewed later and asked me a few questions while they filled in a form with my personal details. Afterwards, I went to sit down on one of the chairs but was told to "come this way".

As they led me to one of the cells and opened the door, I shrank back. "Do you mind if I wait out here? I'm still waiting for my lawyer," I asked, gesturing towards the chairs in the middle.

"No, you'll have to wait in there," came the firm reply. I walked inside and the door was swung closed behind me. Though Asil had already described his own experiences to me, nothing could have prepared me for the shock of seeing the inside of a police cell for myself. It seemed to be about eight feet long and six feet wide. Everything was dirty and dusty and it was very gloomy. There were no windows - just the small opening in the wooden door and a glass-paned grille high up in the far wall. I had the impression we were in a basement, although I realised later it was actually the ground floor. I looked

242

around, taking in the wooden bench, plastic mattress and stinking, open "toilet", just as he had described.

The few minutes that I waited there for Monty Raphael stretched out like an eternity. I was relieved to hear the door being unlocked and see him walk in with a young assistant whom he introduced as Elaine. The two of them sat down and Monty explained that I would be taken to an interview room for questioning. "It is obviously up to you, but as a lawyer I would recommend that you don't answer any of their questions," he said.

I was horrified. "But if I don't answer any questions, they will keep me here. Why shouldn't I answer?—I've got nothing to hide."

After about half an hour's debate on the issue, Monty realised how determined I was and we agreed that I would answer questions. It was another two hours before I had the chance to do so.

As we waited, John Elgar joined us. I was glad to see a familiar face. I almost ran to him as he walked in. "John, I don't want to stay here. Why are they keeping us waiting? Do what you can to get me out of here."

It was John who told me the worst - it was possible that if the police wanted to keep me for further questioning, I might have to spend the night in the cell. At that point, my world began to collapse. I looked round the cell at the blue mattress - how could I sleep on that? As for the "toilet", there was no way on earth I could use that box. As a hundred thoughts went through my mind, I became conscious of a gnawing pain in my stomach from the ulcer I had developed some ten years earlier. I explained to Monty that I needed something to eat - I had had nothing since a bowl of cereal early that morning. Elaine went out to get some food and came back with a sandwich, a cup of tea and a Kit-Kat which Tijen had sent. I could hardly swallow the sandwich. It kept sticking in my throat. I drank the tea but, I think, for the first time ever, could not face the chocolate. Monty suggested that I see a doctor. He called a policeman over and I was allowed out to another room which was equipped like a small surgery. There, the doctor gave me two tablets to take with a small plastic cup of water. Then I was led back to my cell and the door closed behind me again.

For another hour, the four of us sat in that cell. I was pacing up and down, trying to think of anything but the situation I found myself in, when from outside I heard the faint noise of a man's cough. It was a sound I recognised instantly. I turned to Monty and told him, "That's my brother."

Almost at that moment, the cell door opened and in the doorway I caught sight of DCI Watson, Asil and two policemen. Oblivious to everyone else, Asil walked straight towards me as I stood in the middle of that tiny room. We kissed briefly on both cheeks and in Turkish he said to me quietly, "It's OK. Don't worry." As one of the policemen commanded, "No Turkish", Asil added in English, "You'll be out of here soon."

As he was ordered out of the cell, Asil's eyes were ablaze. I had never before seen such a look of anger on his face as, in front of the closing cell door, he turned to face DCI Watson and rapped, "Get her out of here. You have no right to do this." For himself, Asil could find the strength to face whatever allegations were flung at him and the hardships that went with them. But it was unbearable to him to see his family suffer too.

It was another hour before I was summoned for questioning - an hour during which I worried about Asil; why he was here; and listened to him coughing in the distance, in his own cell. It was about three o'clock in the afternoon when the door opened and we were told to come upstairs to the interview room. On the way, we passed a ladies' toilet and I asked Elaine if it would be all right for me to go in. Our police escort said it was, as long as Elaine came in with me. It was a comfort to me to be able to wash my hands after sitting in that grimy cell for more than three hours. After only such a short time "inside" even that seemed like a real luxury.

Inside the interview room, my heart was pounding as I sat down at the table. DCI Watson and two policemen sat opposite me, while the lawyers sat behind me. I waited apprehensively as they explained the procedure and started up a tape recorder, giving details of the date, time, my name and theirs. Then the questioning began.

The first question took me by surprise: "Do you know Wendy Welsher?"

"Yes," I answered, wondering why on earth they wanted to know that.

Then they fired the names of several men at me, none of which I had heard before. I found out afterwards that these were all aliases of one man - the mysterious "Mr Adams" to whom I had been introduced by Wendy in Geneva. Then I was asked to explain how I had first met Wendy Welsher. I was shown too, a document bearing my signature and asked if I recognised it. I told them it was familiar - it was the paper Wendy had given me to sign for the holiday village scheme seven months earlier, but it was a photocopy and several parts had been altered by hand since I had seen it. As I looked at it, I realised that Asil's name had been added to the document, lending what had been perfectly innocent a potentially far more sinister implication. I sensed there was something serious afoot, but was still totally perplexed by the line of questioning. Of what interest to them could Wendy Welsher be? Or the strangely altered agreement we had made? Even more oddly, it seemed at the time, I was then shown pictures of some famous paintings and asked if I had seen any of them before. I told them that I recognised one - it was a work of art which belonged to Aysegül but Asil had had it in his office for a while. In fact it was the painting, *Sisters*, which had been given to Wendy Welsher as security for the holiday complex financing. As they asked these strange questions, my mind was in a whirl. I could make no sense of any of it, but one thing struck home - I recalled Wendy Welsher's strange warning days before, which I had dismissed at the time as crazy. Now I was suddenly certain that Wendy had been aware that I was going to be arrested. But how did she know? Was there a connection between Wendy, the police and the SFO? Everything they asked seemed to revolve round her.

Through the turmoil inside my head, I was dumbfounded to hear DCI Watson say the police had been told I was helping my brother to move paintings and other Polly Peck assets to the tune of 750 million Deutschmarks. He said they had information that there were funds in Liechtenstein which we had taken from Polly Peck. It was curiously like listening to the plot of a fantasy film.

The interview went on for about forty minutes before I was told I could go back downstairs, but might be needed for further questioning. As we filed our way back from the interview room, the thought suddenly flashed through my mind that this might mean me spending the night in a cell. I was panic-stricken. I kept telling John Elgar: "You've got to get me out of here. I can't stay the night in that cell. It's so stuffy. I won't be able to breathe. There's no shower. What if I need to use the toilet? There's not even any water or toilet roll."

Back in the cell, I waited and waited. The lawyers painted a bleak picture. I would either be released at about seven o'clock or the police would apply to hold me for a further few hours, until the following morning. I tried to stay calm. Unable to fathom out the reasons behind the questions I had been asked, I gave little thought to my legal position. My biggest and most immediate dread was that I might have to face a night alone in the cell. As the others talked around me, I prayed hard for release, my fingers twisting constantly as I paced the floor. At one point, I was left alone while the lawyers went for a late lunch. As the door thudded shut behind them, I felt a frightening blanket of claustrophobia descend. My heart began pounding and I tried to take deep breaths of the stale air, willing myself not to break down. "You must not be weak - stay strong," I repeated over and over in my head as I sat on the wooden bench and tried to relax until the lawyers returned. I was conscious only of the deafening beating of my heart, the strange weight of the atmosphere and the faint sound of Asil coughing somewhere nearby. As the day ebbed away, the lawyers would again leave the cell occasionally, each time returning with gloomy news - the SFO men were still looking at their documents; they had not yet decided on their next course of action. I would only find out much later the sinister supposed reason for the hold-up.

In Switzerland, Michael Francis had done a "bunk". Asil Nadir and his sister had been arrested in anticipation of Francis's promised return on a one o'clock flight from Zurich that afternoon, 5th November. Francis says the SFO knew they could not charge either Nadir or his sister on the basis of uncorroborated evidence and a photocopied document, but he had assured them he would be bringing with him the painting, the supposed tape recordings and the original document signed by Bilge Nevzat. Now, though, it was well after four o'clock and Francis still had not got on to a plane - nor had he any intention of doing so.

During the weeks leading up to this November finale, Francis says, he had grown more and more edgy about his part in framing Nadir. He says he sensed a level of desperation on the part of the authorities and became convinced that his own involvement would put him and his family in danger. Once he had handed over the documents the SFO needed and his usefulness was at an end, Francis felt sure he would be "disposed of" in some way so as to ensure his silence. His fears appeared to be confirmed when, a day after his arrival in Switzerland, he had attempted to reach Welsher by telephone. Getting no reply at a time when Welsher would normally be at home, Francis had called an SFO contact to enquire whether he had seen her. The contact told him casually he had called round to Welsher's home, but had found no sign of life - the burglar alarm was ringing, the doors were all locked and, from what he had glimpsed through the kitchen window, the fridge door was open. As Francis finished the conversation, he thought hard for a few moments then made up his mind. For all he knew, he said later, Welsher might be dead...and unless he acted quickly, the same fate might be in store for him. Over the final couple of days before he was due to return to London, Francis thought out plans for his total "disappearance". On the morning of 5th November, he checked out of the Swiss hotel where he had been staying and vanished into Europe. An international manhunt launched by the British authorities would, Francis says, fail to flush him out for the next three months. And his non-arrival at Heathrow left the SFO without the concocted "evidence" they had been depending on to charge Nadir and his sister. They had no option but to release them.

At about half past seven that evening came the word I had been praying to hear. I was to be allowed to leave. At the desk in the centre of the cells I was formally told I would be released on police bail provided I signed to say I would return for further questioning in thirty days' time. I could hardly sign quickly enough in my desire to get out into the fresh air and back to my family. At that moment, I understood clearly how a suspect might be tempted into falsely confessing a crime he did not commit - so strong is the urge to do anything that will secure freedom and shake off the pressures of confinement.

It was a matter of minutes before I was reunited with Tijen. She had waited all day for me, sitting in the cold and draughty police station reception with nothing to eat or drink, waiting for messages from the lawyers. In my relief to see her there, I was numb to the enormity of all that had happened. We hugged quickly, said our goodbyes to the lawyers, and hurried outside the find a telephone box. I called the office to reassure an anxious Sabina and Terry that it was all right for them to go home for the night and telephoned home to say we were on our way. With no car and a long way to walk to the underground, Tijen and I decided to start off in the direction of South Woodford and hail a taxi on the way. It was bitterly cold and we trudged almost a mile in the dark, arm-in-arm as I recounted the day's events, before we spotted a cab on the opposite side of the road. It was going the wrong way and was already occupied. We were just about to set off walking again when I caught sight of the driver - I could not believe my eyes to see the familiar face of Len Finney, Auntie Finney's son. He shouted across to us to wait where we were and said he would be back in a few minutes after dropping his fare off.

"Now do you believe in God?" I asked Tijen, only half-jokingly, as we waited on the kerbside. Somehow, I felt, Auntie Finney had been watching over us. It was such a comfort to sink back into the safety of Len's taxi as we sped past the lights of London. Half an hour brought us to the door in The Drive, where everyone was standing outside, anxiously scanning the street. We all hugged on the doorstep and for the first time that day, I allowed myself to break down and weep. I was so glad to be home. It was also a huge relief to hear that Abide had called to say that Asil was on his way home too.

Over a pot of tea and hot soup, I was bombarded with questions while Irfan tried to lighten the air by cracking jokes. I was determined to play down the situation. I said I had been questioned, but that night I told no-one that I had been locked up - I could not bear to upset them any further. On the radio news, it was announced that Asil had been arrested that day, but there was no mention of me. *The Evening Standard* reported that Asil and "another party" had been taken to

Holborn police station for questioning, but no names were given. We rang my mother and other relatives in Cyprus to tell them not to worry, in case they heard about the arrests there. Throughout the evening, we took telephone calls from worried neighbours wanting to know if everything was all right. Asil rang too after he arrived home. I knew how distressed he was and reassured him: "It was nothing, really. I'm absolutely fine."

At that moment, I was in shock - numb, yet determined to remain in control. I did know then that, as bad as that day seemed at the time, the days, weeks, months that followed would be far worse. I could not have comprehended that night the far-reaching and shattering effect that a single day could have on my life, my family and even my personality. The next morning, the whole household jumped and everybody rushed out of their bedrooms when the doorbell went at seven o'clock. We tried to laugh when we realised it was only the milkman, but we could find little funny in our nerves. To this day, I still find my heartbeat quickening if anyone comes to the door so early. For a long time afterwards, I felt physically sick at the thought of all those strangers in our house, looking through all our personal possessions. Our home never felt the same again. My bedroom seemed no longer my own. I felt as if it had been raped, defiled. Whenever I opened the door, I would still see in my mind the policemen rummaging through my clothes and my underwear.

The morning after the raid, Asil was due to appear in court. It was an occasion that would set me thinking hard about my interview the previous day. I went to the Old Bailey as usual, expecting the hearing that had been adjourned from 2nd October to consider varying Asil's bail conditions and giving him his passport back. Instead, Mr Justice Tucker and the lawyers discussed a sudden turn of events described as "bizarre" by Asil's lawyer and "unprecedented" by the judge himself. It became clear that an urgent message in relation to this matter from the Lord Chief Justice had been responsible for the judge's failure to attend court as scheduled the previous month. In a document sent to the Lord Chief Justice, the Attorney-General, Mr Justice Tucker and solicitors involved in the case, it was said that the SFO was investigating allegations that Asil, my mother and myself were involved in a £3.5 million plot to bribe the trial judge. Asil was also said to have been instrumental in disposing of assets belonging to the PPI administrators or the trustees in bankruptcy. The SFO's director was said to have received information to this effect on 1st October. The doctored photocopy shown to me by the SFO at my interview the day before was presented as evidence supporting the claims.

During the debate in court that day, it was suggested by the prosecution that the judge might have to reconsider his position in presiding over the trial since it was "probable" that officers looking into the alleged conspiracy would wish to interview him about it - a prospect which Mr Justice Tucker said he viewed with alarm. I will never forget the look of pure shock on his face. The judge had been sitting forward in his seat, listening to counsel for the SFO, Robert Owen QC. When the possibility of him being interviewed by police was raised, he flopped backwards with an amazed "What?". The hearing was adjourned again pending further investigation. The following month, in a discussion in the judge's chambers, Chief Superintendent Thomas Glendenning of Specialist Operations at New Scotland Yard would admit there was no evidence, other than a tip-off, to back up the bribery allegations. Nor, he would say, was there evidence to justify any suggestion that Mr Justice Tucker should be interviewed.

After the 6th November court hearing, Asil and I had our first chance to talk properly since our arrests. The new allegations had left us both in a state of shock, yet even so we would look at each other from time to time and burst out laughing as we echoed, "750 million Deutschmarks!" It just seemed so ludicrous. If I had access to that kind of money, I told Asil over tea, would I really sit back and see my company at rock bottom financially? Would I really be struggling and scratching round to try and pay the wages of my few remaining staff? Would I be defaulting on the mortgage of my own home through lack of cash? Would he be forced to come to me for help when he could not afford to pay a bill? Asil jokingly suggested that we should tell the SFO that if they were able to find this supposed 750 million then they would be welcome to keep it if they would just give us ten per cent!

Behind the humour, though, for me the gravity of the situation was beginning to hit home. The realisation would prove a turning point in my life. As I tried to put two and two together; to work out what was happening; to consider who Wendy Welsher was and how she had been involved, I began to see that I was in a situation which was beyond my control. From my lawyers, I learned that the maximum penalty for conspiracy to pervert the course of justice was life imprisonment; the least fifteen years. They told me, too, that it was possible I might be arrested again. During the weeks that followed, I would wake up as if from a nightmare, only to find that the real nightmare inhabited my waking hours.

The coming days brought a further burden of troubles. On 7th November, we had a telephone call at home from Fehim's brother, Ilker, to say that their father was very ill in hospital in Cyprus. We had known that he was sick, but now it became imperative for us to go and see him - we were told that his death might be only a matter of days away, although in fact he would live for another three months. My passport had been taken during the raid but it was soon returned and the next week we flew out to Cyprus for a ten-day stay. I would return alone.

Immediately after my arrest, my first thought had been to get in touch with Wendy Welsher, to find out what was going on, but I had been warned off in no uncertain terms by my lawyers. Monty Raphael had told me he would refuse to represent me if he found I had even got within two miles of her, so I was horror-struck when the phone rang at our flat a day or two after we got to North Cyprus and Fehim picked it up to hear Wendy on the line. She was still in Cyprus, she told him, and desperately wanted to see me. I shrank away from the telephone and was relieved to hear Fehim tell her firmly, "Bilge has been instructed by her lawyer not to speak to you."

Again, Wendy begged him to put me on the line. "I just want to explain," she implored.

But Fehim was not to be moved. I could hear Wendy still talking in the background as he slowly put the receiver down. It was the last we would hear of her for nine months.

Those few days away in North Cyprus gave me a chance to reflect on what had been a year of growing heartache for all of us. The whole family had reached virtual breaking point. Getting up to face each new day was a fight - financially, emotionally and even physically. My mother's health had begun to be badly affected again by the stress. But one thing still kept us going - our faith that somehow God would help us through. It was a belief which was strengthened for me during that trip to North Cyprus, when I learned for myself how many people there were praying for Asil and the rest of us.

For PPI creditors, it had been a year of disappointment. At a meeting in early June, the administrators - whose services had to date cost the company in excess of £13 million - dashed hopes that investors might get as much as 30p in the pound back, saying they would be lucky to get 11p and might only receive as little as 3p. Michael Jordan blamed the administrators' failure to win control of the North Cyprus assets. Asil blamed the administrators for selling off Polly Peck's assets too cheaply. Assets were being sold off quickly in Turkey at prices which many people thought were much lower than their market value. In 1994, the Istanbul prosecutor would later look into the matter and judge that there was a criminal case for the administrators to answer. By then, the administrators' bill would have reached a staggering £33 million. As if to add insult to injury, Michael Jordan and Richard Stone were each fined £1,000 by the Institute of Chartered Accountants in

October 1992 for breaching ethical guidelines in their administration of PPI. Stone, of Coopers & Lybrand, and Jordan, of the firm's insolvency arm, Cork Gully, had been under investigation for a year on allegations of conflict of interest. Coopers had been Asil's personal tax advisers for many years, successfully fighting his case against the Inland Revenue, and had also been retained by PPI on several feasibility studies.

At Noble Raredon, I had spent the year engaged in a grim damage limitation exercise, realising my only option was to try to raise the cash we needed by selling off assets. I had hoped this would enable us to start again once the situation was resolved. It was in this climate that David Heaton had led a £1.5 million bid to stage a management buy-out of the Elite Optics division - a business we had valued at £2.5-3 million. I was devastated that Heaton, who I had trusted to run the division for the good of our ailing company, had apparently gone behind my back to take over what was now its only thriving asset. I rejected the offer immediately and invited other offers for Elite, but there were no takers. In the aftermath, Heaton came back with a £900,000 buy-out bid. Again I rejected it, this time asking for his resignation from Noble Raredon since there was obviously a conflict of interest. Over the following months, as word spread in the business world that I was under threat from the banks and looking for an urgent sale, various offers of £500,000 to £600,000 came in for Elite. Finally, in desperation, I accepted £650,000 from a consortium which included David Fawcus, the ex-PPI finance director. Within a year, Elite would be sold on again for £3 million.

Even our few remaining businesses that had once been thriving were now suffering badly from the knock-on effects of our situation. I began to realise just what immense problems the North Cyprus businesses were facing, and it made me aware of the downside to my ideal of a vertically integrated holiday business - with unified control of every stage of the booking process, from the agent, through the airline, to the hotel. When times were good, as they had been, this integration was the perfect situation, ensuring a high standard of service and maximising our profits. Now times were bad, it was virtually a death sentence. With Mosaic Holidays still reeling from the crushing effects of the Gulf crisis and war, bookings were thin on the ground. In France and Germany, both foreign arms of Mosaic - Mosaic Reisen and Mosaic Voyages - had ceased to trade. At the end of the chain, in North Cyprus, were handling agents, Tri-Sun Travel, and The Olive Tree Hotel, and our other businesses were simply not in the position to feed custom through to them. Both Cypriot businesses were creditors of the collapsed Mosaic Reisen, but there was no prospect of recouping the money owed. Little by little, through their exclusive reliance on their sister companies,

The Olive Tree and Tri-Sun were being starved of the cash flow they needed to stay alive. Asil's Noble Air, meanwhile, had folded that March.

The situation was particularly dire at The Olive Tree, we discovered during our visit to North Cyprus. With ill-fated timing, the hotel had opened just three months before the 1990 Gulf crisis, and just four months before Noble Raredon had been plunged into difficulties, and it had very quickly found debts mounting up. By the end of 1992, the hotel owed some £1.7 million and as things stood, there seemed no likelihood of its being able to claw its way back from looming insolvency. All the creditors were in North Cyprus and, knowing how our family was in trouble, they had refrained from demanding repayment. While they were willing to hold off, the North Cyprus management had tried to spare us the knowledge of quite how serious the situation was. Now, many of the creditors were becoming understandably restless, and no-one was sure how much longer they could be kept at bay.

During the later months of 1992, we had made attempts to secure the Olive Tree's future by diversifying its business. The first avenue we had explored had been to convert the hotel into a timeshare complex. We had been advised that the timeshare industry had acquired a poor image and was going through a lean time in Europe, so we targeted the Turkish market. It was not a success. Timeshare, we discovered, was too new a concept for Turkey and by the end of that year, we had not one taker. Another salvage idea was put to us by a Turkish leisure group - they would open a casino at The Olive Tree and would pay us rent for use of the premises. The idea did not really appeal to me for The Olive Tree, which I liked to think had a family atmosphere, but I decided I should go along with it if it would save the hotel.

When the time came for us to leave North Cyprus, it came as little surprise to me when Fehim announced that, once again, he would not be returning to London. He said he would stay behind to help sort out the business problems in North Cyprus, so I barely argued against his decision. I knew how deeply he had been affected by events the previous week and since I planned to come back to the Mediterranean for Christmas and New Year, we would see each other again within a short time. I hoped that then he might feel able to come back with me to London.

The temptation to stay with Fehim was strong. The thought of that police cell made me long to remain in Cyprus, yet I knew I must return to answer the bizarre allegations against me, whatever the risk it might entail. My children were all building lives for themselves in the UK and I was not prepared to put myself in the position where, if I were to run away, I would be unable to go and see them there. For myself, though, I had reached the conclusion that there was no future for me in Britain.

The events of 5th November had brought it home to me that whatever I was up against - whatever, whoever, was prepared to see me go to jail for years for something I did not do - I was not strong enough to fight it. If I could be innocent and yet stand accused of serious crime; if the truth could be twisted in such a way; if the "system" had such powers to ruin someone's life - was it worth even trying to fight back? How could I, as an individual, hope to win? From childhood, I had believed in the ideal of British justice. Already dented by watching the long drawn-out proceedings against my brother, now in one day that faith had been smashed.

On 10th December, I went to Holborn Police Station at nine in the morning for my appointment with the SFO. Just outside the reception area, I met up with Asil and one of his lawyers. Trying to relieve the tension, we joked with each other that we must stop meeting in such places! I was called through first, to be told that there were no questions but that I should report there again in three months' time. Asil was given the same message a few minutes later.

The wintry weeks that followed were among the worst of my life. For more than two years, I had been determined to battle to save Noble Raredon - not only for my own sake, but also for the shareholders who had invested their money and trust in it. Even in the darkest times, I had always rushed to work, certain that each new day brought with it fresh hope; praying that something would come along to help us. Now the last surviving part of the business was also threatened. My fighting spirit crushed, too, I sensed I had reached a dead end.

Troubles seemed to hit me from all sides. Not only was the business sinking rapidly, but I had not been able to pay the mortgage on our house since the summer. I had put the house on the market but there were no offers and the building society was getting jumpy, demanding repayment. For more than two years, I had tried to remain calm and optimistic in the face of every adversity for Asil's sake, but now I felt emotionally worn out and demoralised by the slow realisation that, far from drawing to a close, this legal nightmare could go on…and on. As for my children - I had told myself I ought to stay in England for their sake, to be a support to them there at least until Irfan had finished his university studies. Now I knew it would be a kindness to them if I left. I could not face wearing the brightly-coloured clothes in my wardrobe, picking out instead the drab greys and blacks which seemed to suit better my frame of mind. Sapped of all self-confidence, I could no longer drive myself to and from the office but travelled with Tijen and Levent instead. On the way home every night, I would deliberately sit in the back seat so that they did not see the tears which streamed down my face in the dark. I felt I was a liability to my children. While I remained with them in England, each passing day would bring them more heartache - and I would be to blame.

As 1992 waned, my life lay in ruins. Everything I had prided myself on being - businesswoman, wife, mother - I was no longer. It chilled me to think how my own situation now mirrored the predicament my father had faced, back in the 1950s in Cyprus. Three decades earlier, my father had been forced to sell his businesses and our family had fled to Britain in the face of economic and physical persecution by the Greek Cypriot community in my homeland. To run away then and start a new life had been an adventure buoyed by hope. Now, it seemed, I must flee for a second time, hounded out of the Britain I had loved and revered by faceless persecution.

By now, I had sat in on a dozen of Asil's court cases and I had come to realise that, whichever way he tried to turn, he was being slowly encircled. The painful machinations of the legal system seemed to be going on forever, as we passed increasingly bleakly from one court session to another - to Bow Street, Fleet Street, the Old Bailey, even Stafford and Birmingham in the Midlands. Immediately after Asil's arrest, the court-room had been packed with supporters for every hearing, but by about the fifth session only a handful of close friends still turned up. Tijen and I made sure we were always there with Abide. Other friends came along whenever they could. Mostly, those court appearances took us down a relentless spiral of depression. With each new hearing, we would build up hopes only to have them dashed, and by the end of 1992 I was thoroughly disheartened. It seemed the tortuous court processes would go on forever. Sometimes we would go along to the court, only to find that the hearing was to be held in camera and we would not be allowed in. Then, we would go into one of the other court-rooms and listen in on a rape or murder trial to while away the hours until Asil came out. Those days, hearing details of some of the most sickening crimes as we sat side by side with the defendants' friends and family, laid before me the dirty underbelly of society. The contrast to our own lives was more enormous than I had imagined possible.

Events had taken some bizarre turns during those months. Now our lives had been turned upside down, even the oddest twist seemed commonplace - though looking back, I am amazed that we took so many undreamed-of and strange occurrences in our stride. When Michael Mates - a backbench Conservative MP when he first came on the scene, later to be elevated to Northern Ireland Minister - appeared suddenly in our lives it seemed just another chapter in Asil's long-standing links with the Tory party. With hindsight, though, I find it odd that a Member of Parliament should have struck up such a friendship with a man accused of being a criminal. It was an uncanny coincidence, too, that Mates had served with the military in Famagusta during the 1950s and had been instrumental in the capture of Nicos Sampson, the terrorist who had been a regular at my father's patisserie in the town. In fact, Asil's friendship with Michael Mates would have far-reaching consequences for him and us way beyond anything we could have imagined.

It was during 1992 that I first met Michael Mates, but I had heard Asil mention his name for several months previously and knew he had frequently visited my brother at his office. In 1991, Christopher Morgan, a politically well-connected publicist, had offered his public relations services to Asil. Morgan's partner, Mark Rogerson, was a constituent of Mates in East Hampshire and had approached him about Asil's case. Mates had written to the Attorney-General on Asil's behalf in September 1991 and would do so again in December 1992. In all, he would make three such approaches. His letters would highlight the delays in bringing Asil's case to court; an alleged visit by a Serious Fraud Office representative to North Cyprus and the damage done to the case by the alleged plot to bribe the judge.

One Sunday towards the end of 1992, Asil had a bad cold and could not spend the day with us at South Woodford, so the children and I went to visit him in the Eaton Square flat instead. We were just eating lunch when Michael Mates - by then the Northern Ireland Minister - arrived out of the blue and knocked on the door. Asil went and sat with him in the living room and they had a glass of champagne together. Afterwards, Asil showed Mates into the dining room and introduced him to us. I recognised him instantly from having seen him on television. After Mates had left, I asked Asil what he thought of him. I was concerned about Mates's motives and asked Asil, "Do you trust him?"

Asil replied, "Don't worry, he's OK. He works for the government but he is a friend and he is a fair man. He has told me that at least part of this situation is the work of the security services."

I looked at Asil open-mouthed. "Didn't you tape him admitting that?" I asked. Asil just looked at me. Afterwards, I would discover that my suggestion had planted a seed in his mind. Later, Abide would set up a cassette recorder among the pots of flowers in the living room to capture the words of several of my brother's Tory visitors on tape.

Mates was not the only high-ranking Conservative involved at that time, and when the full extent of Asil's Tory connections was revealed in 1993 - coupled with publicity about his considerable donations to the party - it would cause a crisis which threatened to topple John Major's government. Minister Peter Brooke was Asil's constituency MP and Asil went to see him in his "surgery", accompanied by Christopher Morgan.

Brooke shook Asil's hand and said it was an honour and a privilege to meet him. He was one of the first politicians to write to the Attorney-General.

Earlier, Asil had contacted Tory party treasurer, Lord McAlpine, who had visited him in the office at Berkeley Square in 1991. Asil was becoming absolutely furious at the unjust things that were happening to him. But how was he going to make his complaint heard? To whom could he appeal? Naturally, he believed that those who had so assiduously courted his attention in the past might now listen to him. For all his business brain and superficial glamour, Asil was rather naive in some ways - he certainly never understood the British Establishment and the way it worked. It was a shock to him to discover that an "outsider" was there to be wooed when it suited, but dumped as soon as the tide turned. Later McAlpine was to make out in a vicious article that my brother had threatened to reveal details of his donations to the Tories if the case against him was not dropped. But the real reason why Asil revealed some details may have been that he was stung by the remark of a Conservative Central Office aide to *The Guardian* in the middle of a rumpus over political donations. The aide was quoted as saying that at least they hadn't received money from Nadir. Enough was enough.

At their meeting, Asil had complained to McAlpine over the way the police went about their investigations and the rather bullying way they conducted their questioning. Later, Lord McAlpine would write in his regular *Sunday Express* column about what he regarded as his own bad treatment when he was questioned by police, declaring that any abolition of the right to silence - then being widely debated - would lead to injustices for those caught up in police inquiries. Asil, of course, had had no right to silence when questioned by the Serious Fraud Office and this was something he had complained about. When McAlpine told his own sorry tale in the newspaper, a friend faxed Asil a copy from London with the words "poetic justice" written on it.

Gerry Malone, the deputy chairman of the Tory party, was a politician who later became a little confused about whether he had ever met Asil. Although he was not one of those who wrote to the Attorney-General, he called on Asil in December 1992 at the Eaton Square flat - a visit Malone later confirmed, having originally given the impression that he had never met Asil at all. In fact it was a long meeting - more than two hours - between Asil, Malone and Christopher Morgan. Abide recalled that she had never met anyone who could consume so much champagne and caviar at one sitting as Malone.

In 1992, we knew that Michael Mates and others were writing letters to the Attorney-General. Michael Heseltine mentioned the case to him as well and, like all the others, would receive his share of unfair bad publicity as a result. The Attorney-General would later reveal that he had received letters on the issue from seven MPs in total. Foolishly, I believed that, as the figurehead of the British justice system, the Attorney-General would do something about the irregularities of which he was being informed. But Asil and I were disappointed by the tone of the replies. It was clear the Attorney-General, Sir Nicholas Lyell, was determined just to sweep the complaints under the carpet. We began to get desperate because there was no other avenue open to us. Under the law, it was contempt to speak of what was happening in court behind closed doors. We could not go to the press and talk about how Asil was being investigated over allegations that he had conspired to bribe a High Court judge. It would have made sensational reading, but Asil could have been jailed simply for telling the papers about it. We saw the letters to the Attorney-General as being the correct, and indeed the only possible way.

Christmas 1992 proved decisive for me. Fehim wanted me to join him in Cyprus and I wanted to go…yet inside I was torn, reluctant to leave Asil behind at such a bad time, although there was little I could do for him. For days, I agonised over whether to go. In the end, a friend persuaded me that, if I was to carry on helping Asil, I would have to have a break for the sake of my own health and sanity. I paid a brief Christmas visit to Cyprus with the children. During our stay, Fehim laid the future on the line. Far from having overcome his feelings against the British authorities, he had reached a firm decision. As we all sat together in the flat one day, he told us that he could never return to Britain, so distraught was he at all he had witnessed. "I will not be happy in London, nor will I be happy here knowing you are there," he told me. "If you want us to live together, Bilge, you will have to come here, to Cyprus. I know it sounds harsh, but I can't go back with you."

There were tears as the children tried to persuade Fehim to come back to England, but I could see his mind was made up. The next move was up to me. If I wanted our marriage to survive, we could not spend our lives 3,000 miles apart.

It was "do or die" point for the businesses too. That Christmas, I warned The Olive Tree management - including Fehim and Mehmet Ziya Berkman - that they were now on their own. There was no way that Noble Raredon could help them with their financial troubles. Fehim and Mehmet, in turn, impressed upon me that drastic and urgent action was all that would save The Olive Tree. By then some of the more impatient creditors had launched legal proceedings to recover the

257

money owed to them and more would follow suit. To make matters worse, the casino scheme on which survival hopes had rested had fallen through.

The future looked grim everywhere I turned as I flew back to London. Too tired of the struggle to try to keep my head above water, paying off debts one at a time in the vain hope that some miracle would come along, it was a relief to receive a letter from Fehim and Mehmet Ziya, soon after my return, suggesting a management buy-out of The Olive Tree. By taking it over, they could instil new confidence in the creditors, who would realise that the hotel was responsible for all its own debts, rather than an ailing foreign company. They offered to take on The Olive Tree's debts of £1.7 million and to pay an additional £200,000 - enough to pay off Noble Raredon's outstanding debts and pay off the last salaries. I put everything on the table before one of Noble Raredon's auditors, and he advised me to accept the offer. I felt The Olive Tree was worth more than the £1.9 million buy-out bid, but I knew the only alternative would mean the companies going into liquidation. And my experience of the Elite Optics buy-out had taught me that the first offer in such circumstances was likely to be the best.

In what was to be one of my last acts as chairman, I sent a letter to all the Noble Raredon shareholders, spelling out the situation and calling an extraordinary general meeting for 15th February to consider the sale of The Olive Tree. I explained that I would not be voting on the issue, since I was involved in the management of the North Cyprus businesses and was the beneficiary of the main Noble Raredon shareholding. Any decision on the sale would be entirely up to the other shareholders. When 15th February arrived, few of the shareholders turned up at the auditor's offices, most of them preferring to vote by proxy. The meeting was soon over. The shareholders voted overwhelmingly in favour of the buy-out - it seemed they, too, had reached the conclusion that there was no alternative. I felt an immense sadness as I formally brought the meeting to a close.

The Olive Tree sell-off was the final nail in the coffin for Noble Raredon. It also spelt the end of the road for Terry Causer-Rees - as a hotel management expert, there was now no reason for her to stay. It was a sad moment for us all - Terry had been with the company almost from the beginning and during the troubled days I had grown to value her friendship and loyalty even more. She alone of the original board had remained beside me throughout, until there came a time when there were just the ladies left - me, Tijen, Terry and Sabina. It had been a long, depressing struggle for all of us - sometimes the four of us would sit down and cry together; at other times we just had to laugh and try to cheer each other up. It seemed as if we were living a black comedy. At

Christmas 1992, Tijen and Sabina had even set a litany of all our troubles to the tune of *The Twelve Days of Christmas*, and we all sang along at a special lunch. When Terry finally departed, John Honour, the company's long-time personnel adviser, agreed to step in as a director in place of her, so that I could keep Noble Raredon alive - by law, we needed two directors, and with Terry gone there would only have been me left. By keeping the company in existence, I believed that one day something could be done to revive the business and free the shareholders from the limbo in which they found themselves - where there was life, there was still hope, I thought. For now, though, the company was just an empty shell and without it I had no hope of supporting myself in England. With everything gone, it meant the trust fund my father had set aside to secure the future for me and my family - which had grown in value from £5 million to £14 million with the fortunes of Noble Raredon - had finally vanished. I hoped my father could not see how low I had sunk.

I booked my airline seat to Cyprus for 17th February 1993. It was not a one-way ticket - at the request of the SFO, I planned to fly back to London the following month for further questioning. Still the goodbyes were painful. The night before I left, I had said farewell to Meral and Fehim's sister, Sidika. On the morning of my departure, I packed a few last things and looked around the house - not realising then that it would be my last glimpse of the place that had for almost two decades been our home. Fousun, a close friend of Irfan from university, came to pick him up for lectures that day. Irfan and I said our farewells in the hallway, both bursting into tears as we stood with our arms round each other - from the corner of my eye, I caught sight of Fousun and saw that she, too, had tears streaming down her face. We were both still crying as Irfan got into the car. Jill Phelps, who had been working with the family since the children were tiny, was there too and there were more tears as we parted. As we drove away from the house to go to South Audley Street, I felt as if a curtain was falling on the happy family life we had lived for so long.

I took one last look at the Noble Raredon offices where I had nurtured so many dreams, only to see them laid to waste. It hurt to see it as it was now - not a hive of commercial activity, but just a few remaining people simply tying up a few final loose ends. There, I said goodbye to Asil, reassuring him I would be back in a month for my interview. As he put his arms round me in farewell, he said, "By the time you come back, this will all be over." So many times in the last two and a half years I had heard him speak with such optimistic certainty. Now I found it impossible to share his confidence. I just hoped he did not think I was abandoning him.

I parted from Tijen and Levent in the doorway. All three of us clung on to each other and wept. The children wanted to drive me to the airport but I refused, sure that a farewell at departures would be far worse. Instead I asked Sacit Danish to take me on the twenty-minute journey to Heathrow. As we pulled away from the pavement and I looked back at them waving from the doorstep, I asked myself over and over if I was doing the right thing. I fought hard to retain my composure, but, as the car gathered speed, tears began to flow. However I tried, I would be unable to stem the tears all the way to Cyprus. The normally chatty Sacit was virtually silent all the way to the airport. For a second or two, I caught his eye in the rear view mirror. His face was wet with tears.

I sat alone on the front row of the Cyprus Turkish Airlines jet. The dull thud as the wheels left the runway, sending us into the air Izmir-bound, sounded in my heart like the slam of a door. The upward thrust of the aircraft pushed me back into my seat and as I sank against the upholstery, my mind plunged too into my own private thoughts. For nearly six hours as we journeyed to Turkey and then on to Cyprus, visions of my life passed before me. It was as if I had died. And in truth, it was a kind of death. I was forty-six years old and the life I had created for myself was at an end. Always busy and sure of myself, now I had no idea what the future held - except that I would be thousands of miles from so many people I loved, in a country which, although familiar, had not been my home for thirty-one years. The Bilge Nevzat who was met by Fehim in North Cyprus that chilly February night was, in spirit, a person he had never encountered before in twenty-nine years of marriage.

CHAPTER ELEVEN

The Great Escape

For months after I arrived in North Cyprus, my marriage, my health - my whole existence - were at rock bottom. The twenty-eight-month struggle to save my business had culminated in defeat and I had simply lost my will to live. Like a fool, I had believed I was British, but I had been hounded out of the country I considered my home. Now, when I looked around me at North Cyprus, I scarcely recognised it as the place where I had once lived. Suddenly, it seemed, I belonged nowhere. Every morning when I woke I did not want to move; could not see the point in my life, in getting up or getting dressed. When I did, reluctantly, I would go out on to the balcony and sit there all day, just thinking and crying. I missed my children. I realised that my dreams were shattered and the secure life we had enjoyed - with money in a way unimportant because there was plenty of it - was now over. Instead, we were faced with an uphill struggle to pay off debts and rebuild some kind of life in a new country. Often, I would spend hours thinking how easy it would be to end my life. There seemed nothing I could do to revive my spirits. How much better it would be for everyone if I stopped being a burden on them, I thought.

Though I knew my life in England was at an end, I had not yet adjusted to settling in North Cyprus. The bribery plot allegations against me were still outstanding, so I knew I must return to Britain, if only briefly, in order to clear my name. My next interview with the SFO had been fixed for early March. By the end of February, I had provisionally booked my seat on the plane to London and was mentally preparing myself for the journey back when tragedy struck. Fehim's father, who had been ill for months, died at home on 3rd March. I knew I could not leave Cyprus so soon afterwards, so I called Monty Raphael and he arranged for my interview to be postponed. As the time of the delayed session drew near, Monty telephoned me from London to say the SFO had informed him that they did not wish to see me after all, but would let me know if and when they did want to speak to me. I would never hear another word from them and the matter would simply be laid to rest. For me, it was to remain unfinished business.

Throughout those first weeks, plunged into the blackness of my thoughts, I did not recognise the sickness that had invaded my mind. It took outside observation for me to understand that I was ill and needed help. I was introduced to a psychiatrist who was on holiday in North Cyprus. After hearing about my nightmares, insomnia and harrowing flashbacks, he diagnosed depression and prescribed some tablets. I took one or two, but stopped because they made me feel drowsy. The depression put an enormous strain on my relationship with Fehim, who was forever trying to cheer me up or jolly me into going out. Most days, he would go to The Olive Tree to check how business was progressing. I could not bear the thought of leaving the flat, and having to put on a bright face for all the people we would meet outside, but occasionally Fehim would push me into going to the hotel with him. I resented him for what I saw as a bullying determination to stop me hiding away from the world as I wanted. It took me a long time to acknowledge that he was only trying to help - having learned from his own experience that moping in isolation brought no relief.

In the midst of all our other troubles, Fehim and I were forced to come to terms with the fact that we had been irrevocably changed by all that we had gone through. Earlier, we had been too busy to recognise the effect on our characters wrought by events - and particularly by our eighteen months apart. Now, alone together for the first time in years and with little business activity to distract us, we became aware that we had both turned into different people. Where I had been impatient and determined, now I was passive and miserable. The patient Fehim I had always known had lost some of his easy-going nature, and had grown more quick-tempered. The old Bilge and Fehim had gone for good. There was no turning back the clock, and we would have to work hard to try to adapt. It would take us more than three months to begin to feel a little of the old warmth in our feelings for each other. Even now, despite our love, both of us know our relationship has changed. There are some scars which will never heal fully.

Fehim's outlet was his work. With me beside him in North Cyprus, he felt able to devote his attention to setting our businesses there back on a sound footing. It was a demanding task. First, he tackled some of the more urgent debts, selling off property and land he had inherited from his grandfather to raise the cash he needed. But there was still a hefty debt which needed to be addressed. We managed to negotiate new loans and reschedule the existing ones, giving us time to reorganise the business.

What kept me going during those grim spring weeks was concern for my mother and for Asil. He would never admit it, but I had been able to tell for some time that the long drawn-out court proceedings, complicated now by claim and counter-claim relating to the supposed bribery plot, had begun to get him down. More than ever he needed my support, even if it was at a distance. For my mother's sake, too, I needed to try and be strong. She had grown steadily more depressed until now I feared she might not live to see her son again. At the age of seventy-two, the stress of the preceding months had taken their toll on her health and she suffered from heart and blood pressure problems. Her only consolation seemed to lie in prayer. Reversing the trend of a lifetime, she had turned to religion and often sent Asil parcels of olive leaves which she had blessed with a prayer - a traditional Turkish Cypriot token believed to ward off evil spirits and bring good fortune to whoever burns the leaves. Blanking out my own distress, I did all I could to try and cheer her up, telling her everything would turn out for the best. I told Asil about my concerns and he, too, tried to help by keeping my mother's hopes alive. During that March, he told her he aimed to be able to return to North Cyprus for a religious holiday starting on the 23rd of the month. When that date came and went, he said he hoped to be back in time for the annual "mevlit" service to commemorate our father's death on 1st April. Then he expected to join us before our birthday on 1st May. It was innocent talk, designed only to buoy my mother's fading spirit. Whenever any of my mother's visitors asked after Asil, she would tell them what he had said. Inevitably, word of his supposed imminent arrival got back to London. The dramatic effect the news had there, we would discover during the weeks to come.

––––––––––

Asil had begun to see his position as desperately out of control. For the first two years after his arrest, he had radiated confidence that the matter would soon be cleared up and his innocence established, allowing him to return to the world of business that he loved. As details of the alleged plot to bribe the trial judge unfolded, however, it dawned on him that he was under attack from more than one quarter. After the first court session following our arrests the previous November, when the trial judge Mr Justice Tucker had been alarmed to hear he might be interviewed as the target of the suspected bribery attempt, the saga had grown more and more bizarre. At an "in chambers" hearing in December, Chief Superintendent Thomas Glendenning, of Specialist Operations at New Scotland Yard, had admitted there was no evidence to support the allegation. Nor, he admitted under cross-examination, was there any evidence to justify questioning Mr Justice Tucker. By that time, although Asil had twice been summoned to the SFO in relation to the matter, no questions about it had been put to him. On 8th March 1993, the issue took a strange new twist. At another closed hearing, Alun Jones, the Deputy Director of Public Prosecutions, stood up and told the court that the police were investigating claims that Asil had had three co-conspirators. One of them was the judge himself and the others were Asil's QC, Anthony Scrivener, and former Metropolitan Police Assistant Commissioner, Wyn Jones. This announcement set the court-room reeling. "Me?" asked the judge in horror, adding, "Is there anyone else you are going to include?" Asil could not contain himself as he heard the list of names reeled off. "Tell them they've forgotten the Queen," he muttered dryly to Anthony Scrivener. When Mr Justice Tucker complained of being "left in the dark" by the prosecution and asked what the connection was supposed to be between the four named people, he was told the prosecution could reveal nothing "for operational reasons".

Two days after that hearing, at which was raised for the first time the inevitably delaying possibility of the judge having to step down and a replacement being appointed, Asil was arrested when he turned up as arranged at the SFO headquarters. He was interviewed and bailed on the allegation of conspiring to pervert the course of justice, but no charge was brought. His three supposed co-conspirators were never interviewed about the matter. One of them, Wyn Jones, would remain unaware of his inclusion until the allegations became public knowledge several weeks later, when he would comment that he had never met Asil, Anthony Scrivener or Mr Justice Tucker. Eight months on, the prosecution would be forced to concede it had no evidence to support its allegations.

At one stage, there was even the suggestion from the prosecution that Asil might have instigated the "plot" himself to derail the trial. I could scarcely credit someone making such an allegation, but anyone who has not been in the situation in which Asil found himself, can have no idea how ridiculous that idea is. Waiting for trial is purgatory. The one thing he longed to do was to go into court and fight.

On 12th March, Anthony Scrivener made an application on Asil's behalf that Mr Justice Tucker should, in the circumstances, stand down from the trial. When the judge subsequently ruled that he should continue, a defence appeal was lodged at the Court of Appeal on 1st April for a reversal of that decision. It was opposed by the SFO, which submitted that the judge should remain. The appeal judges ruled against the defence, effectively coming down in favour of the prosecution's argument. Strangely, the prosecution immediately requested leave to appeal against that decision to the House of Lords.

The process of the original trial seemed to be becoming more and more bogged down.

As 1993 progressed, the constant mental battle and the prospect of eventual failure slowly wore Asil down. Normally energetic and optimistic, he had grown ever gloomier about his situation. His weight had ballooned by three stones, his face was puffy and to those who knew him he looked years older. He had enormous difficulty in sleeping as he turned everything over in his mind. An old back problem flared up too - brought on, I am sure, by the stress - and on occasion he had to use a stick to get around. Whenever he tried to talk about what was happening, the doctors shook their heads and diagnosed him as depressed and paranoid - it would be hardly surprising if he was.

Asil had long been convinced that his telephone was bugged and had got into the habit of conducting guarded conversations. Occasionally, he would put his theory to the test by saying certain things - and the "news" always seemed to get out. We were certain, too, that his flat was being kept under surveillance - it seemed too fantastic a coincidence that workmen were off and on, for two and a half years, digging up the road outside the flat or any office where he worked. Then he had discovered that his private mail - including legal communications relating to his defence - was being stopped en route, opened and read before being sent on. This he discovered when he questioned the postman about a letter he was awaiting from his lawyers, only to be told that his mail was being delivered separately from the rest of the post in the area. The Post Office admitted, after inquiries by Anthony Scrivener, that it had obtained a court order to stop Asil's mail and divert it. The trustee in bankruptcy said the mail was being diverted to him, but Asil suspected it was being shown to other authorities too.

The pressures of the court hearings and the raids had been building up to an explosive level for more than two years. Time and time again, he had sat in court listening to Mr Justice Tucker pressing the SFO to focus their prosecution on a small number of charges they thought they could prove. Time and time again, they avoided doing this. More than two years after his arrest, my brother could not even be certain what charges he might eventually be called upon to answer.

Now the attacks were coming from fresh and unexpected quarters. The trustee in bankruptcy had demanded that Asil produce receipts for every purchase of £5,000 or more that he had made during the last five years - or face an application to the court that he be held in custody pending his trial. It was a ridiculous request - for a man of Asil's former wealth, a £5,000 purchase was equivalent to £50 for an ordinary working person, and how many people would be able to show receipts for every such sum going back that far? My brother, who had heard of cases where a defendant had spent eight years in jail awaiting trial, was determined not to take the risk of losing his bail. He had also become aware of pressures building up against anyone connected with him. Family and close friends received letters calling on them to declare any presents which Asil had given them during the last five years. Lesley was under threat of losing her house in Chelsea, where she lived with Giles and Eren, because the trustee in bankruptcy suspected Asil had bought it for her. In fact, it had been paid for by my mother, who wanted to make sure her grandchildren were assured a secure home life. On top of all this, Asil was in imminent danger of being evicted from the Eaton Square flat. The lease had run out and there was no way he could afford the several thousand pounds it would have cost to renew.

I was even worried that Asil was in physical danger. The bizarre twist of the "plot to bribe the judge" seemed to demonstrate how desperate someone was to dispose of Asil and the lengths to which they were prepared to go. After all, through the SFO's actions, one of Britain's biggest public companies had been demolished, taking with it the fortunes of 23,000 shareholders and the livelihoods of thousands of workers. Indirectly, too, their actions had wrecked Noble Raredon. If they could not nail criminal charges to Asil - as was abundantly clear from the delaying tactics and continual changes of the indictment against him - the potential bill for damages was astronomical. So demoralised was I by now over the workings of the legal system, I did not find it hard to imagine that Asil could even be killed. I was not alone in thinking that way. Anthony Scrivener warned him to take extra care and to avoid walking in open spaces. It was an alert the barrister would reiterate at dinner in early May 1993 - the last time Asil and he were together in Britain - when he would lean across to Abide and whisper, "You just don't know what these people might do."

It was the raid on his Eaton Square flat at the beginning of April - the last one, as it turned out - that finally convinced Asil he was not going to get a fair trial. He had become used to raids, experiencing more than a dozen in all. Sometimes they had even proved a little black humour, such as the day when the police opened the door of the deep freezer and started peering inside. Abide, watching them, had wondered aloud what they were doing and a normally very serious-minded lawyer with her had quipped back, "It's OK, Abide, they're just looking for frozen assets."

On another occasion, Tijen tried to stop raiders from entering the room where Asil's private legal papers were kept, pointing out that they were privileged documents. She was pushed against the wall by one of the men, who told her, "If you're not careful, young lady, we'll take you in as well." On the last occasion, they even took the watch Asil was wearing from his wrist. The gesture, Asil felt, was symbolic of attitudes towards him.

The raid started at eight in the morning when Abide opened the door to five men and a uniformed police officer who announced that they had come to remove furniture and other items. They were led by a Mr Wright, of Dibb Lupton Broomhead, solicitors to the trustees in bankruptcy. From then until four that afternoon, they worked their way through the flat, taking furniture, paintings and rugs. Some of the things they took were mine, which I had given to Asil to make up for what he had lost in previous raids. As the raid had finished and Mr Wright was making his way to the door, Asil had put out his hand to say goodbye to him. Mr Wright had spotted the watch - "That watch on your wrist, I'll take it." - and Asil had handed it over. Abide had burst into tears. It was the first time she had broken down.

I called Asil from North Cyprus the next day. It was an important time for us, the beginning of April being the anniversary of our father's death, when we would organise prayers for him at the mosque. This year, I told Asil, we had prayed for him too. Asil asked me whether the mimosas were in flower - at that time of the year in northern Cyprus, the golden yellow mimosa blossoms cover the mountains. I said yes, they were in full bloom, but not for long, so he shouldn't miss them. I was only joking, but by that time I believe he was beginning to think seriously of escape.

Despite his protests, the men who carried out that last raid had also removed every one of Asil's defence papers. My brother and his lawyers were horrified but if they expected any recourse to justice to help them, they would be disappointed. On Tuesday, 20th April, when the incident was brought to Mr Justice Tucker's attention, the judge described it as "highly regrettable, to say the least" but said he had no jurisdiction over the behaviour of the trustees in bankruptcy. He added, "It simply surprises me as a common lawyer brought up in the criminal law...to hear that a man's personal papers relating to his criminal defence can be seized by anyone, and once they have been identified as falling into that category, they have not been immediately returned. What else can I say? I do not think I can help you."

Mr Justice Tucker's words infuriated Asil as he thought them over in the taxi on the way home. If he could not turn to a high court judge for protection when his ability to defend himself was undermined, where could he seek help? If he could not trust in justice, then there was no-one who could guarantee him a fair trial. The thought struck him that he was up against an enemy potentially too powerful for him to defeat. There and then, he decided he had no option but to leave Britain. It was, he felt, the only way he could protect himself and find the freedom from harassment to present his defence. As he later explained to me, he knew his departure would let a lot of people down, but in the long run he felt he could make it up to them once he had been able to clear his name. It was a decision that, just four months earlier, he could never have envisaged making.

By nature a hard worker, Asil's obsession until 1990 had been Polly Peck. When the business had been taken from him, he had turned his mental energies to the law, taking an active part in the preparation of his own defence and becoming an untutored expert in the areas of criminal law which affected him. For more than two years, he had had nothing to do but spend his days talking to his lawyers and poring over affidavits and other legal documents. When the authorities took even that occupation away, Asil had to find something else to keep his mind busy. From 20th April, he devoted his visionary capability and organisational skills to devising his own way out of Britain. At first, he decided only that he should leave soon, but not when he should go. The timing would be forced on him within days by a quite different set of developments. Only a few of those directly involved knew what took place and how it was planned, but I was able to piece together the events from what they told me afterwards.

Asil knew he needed to find someone who could help him get out of Britain - and, he decided, he needed to find them quickly. He decided he had to get to North Cyprus, for there - an unrecognised country from which he could not be extradited - he believed he would have the freedom to speak out and to fight back. For the rest of the day after the court case, he racked his brains to think of people he could call on. Two names came to mind - Peter Dimond and David Hamilton. Asil had met Peter sixteen years earlier through the mutual friendship of Lesley Ellwood and Dimond's wife, Hopie. He had seen him from time to time since then and knew Peter had an aeroplane sales and chartering outfit. David Hamilton he had encountered during Noble Air days, when David had a connection with an aircraft engine sales company in Ireland. In conversation, it had emerged that David had a close Turkish Cypriot friend and was interested in doing business with a North Cyprus-linked airline. Asil and he had discovered a mutual interest in private jets and David, who owned a part-share in a private plane, had half-jokingly told Asil, "If ever you want to go on a short trip, I'd be willing to fly you." Asil instinctively felt he could trust Peter and David to help him get away. Whether or not his hunch was right, he had to take the risk.

That night, Asil called Lesley and asked her to invite Peter Dimond and his wife to a party she was holding the following Saturday, 24th April. He told her to make sure Peter would come, saying he needed to speak to him about something very important. Bewildered, Lesley did as she was asked. A rather reluctant Peter, sensing an undertone of urgency in her voice, agreed to come along. While the days ticked away to Saturday, Asil contemplated the best course of action. He lighted on a two-part strategy which seemed to him the most foolproof method. The first stage of the journey would simply take him to France; the second from France to North Cyprus. The beauty of it was that no-one involved in either half of the equation would be aware of the other's existence. Meanwhile, he also planned how to get Abide out of England without arousing suspicion - he knew she would have to go before him, otherwise the authorities would make life very difficult for her if she was left behind after he had vanished.

When Peter Dimond turned up at Lesley Ellwood's party, he was shocked by the change in Asil, whom he had not seen for several years. He walked with a stick and seemed in a terrible state. The sight reminded Peter of a comment of Lesley's, which his wife had relayed to him, that Asil was "going downhill". Soon after Peter arrived, Asil led him out into the garden, saying he wanted to talk to him away from bugging devices he suspected were in the house. Once the two of them were sitting outside, Asil began to tell Peter about the situation he was in. Peter listened as the events of the previous two years poured out higgledy-piggledy - and as he tried to make sense of all Asil was saying, he became certain of one thing: as far as he was concerned, it was unthinkable that Asil had tried to bribe a judge. Peter repeated to Asil the idea he had suggested to his own wife a year earlier, as they had watched Asil's troubles get ever deeper: "Why don't you leave?"

Glancing round, Asil leaned towards Peter, put his arm round his shoulder, and whispered in his ear, "Maybe that's a good idea. Is there anybody you know in the flying business who would be able to help?"

Peter looked at Asil for a few seconds, before replying, "Do you really want to go?"

"Yes," came Asil's response. "I have to go soon - do you know anyone who can arrange it?"

Without hesitating, Peter said, "Yes. I'll do it. I wouldn't trust anybody else."

Asil told Peter he wanted to leave quickly - perhaps over the coming Bank Holiday - then added in a worried tone, "Can you fly?"

"I can get around," was the casual reply from Peter.

"But can you fly across the Channel?" Asil persisted.

Peter reassured him that he had just completed a race, skimming just twenty-five feet above the English Channel.

"I don't think we need to do that," put in Asil quickly.

The two men discussed aeroplanes for a few minutes, Peter explaining that his own single-engine aircraft would not be suitable for the journey and that they would need to hire another. Then he told Asil, "I can't fly you to Cyprus."

"We just need to get out of England...to a field anywhere, as long as we get away from the UK," said Asil.

The two men parted after half an hour, promising to speak again the next day. During the next few days, Asil would have similar contacts with David Hamilton, who also agreed to help.

Peter Dimond knew instantly the person who could help them. Since Asil had no passport, they would have to leave from a private airfield where, under recent European Community legislation, there would be no customs formalities. The morning after Lesley's party, Peter picked up the telephone and dialled Compton Abbas airfield, in rural Dorset, owned by his great friend Clive Hughes. Peter asked Clive if he could help him by flying a businessman over to France, where he was to look at private aeroplanes. He did not give the businessman's name, but said the two of them would return to Compton Abbas together, leaving their passenger behind. He asked Clive if he could do the job some time during the Bank Holiday weekend, but Clive, who was hosting an air show, said it would be impossible until the Tuesday after the Bank Holiday - 4th May - when his Piper Seneka aircraft would be available. Peter promptly booked it. Then he rang Asil and told him everything was going well.

The next morning, Monday, 26th April, Peter drove from his home in Petersfield, Hampshire, to Compton Abbas. There, he and Clive discussed an outline flight plan, working out how long it would take to get across the Channel and how much fuel they would need. Then Peter drove straight from Dorset to meet Asil. It was half past one when he walked into the Japanese restaurant in Kensington High Street where they had arranged to meet. The room was deserted and as he sat waiting for Asil, Peter began to think for the first time about the extraordinary step he was about to take. He shook off the thoughts as Asil walked in, swiftly checking the table for hidden bugs before sitting down.

Over lunch, the two of them discussed what they were to do. "We'll fly from Dorset across the Channel on Tuesday. What will you do then?" said Peter.

Asil replied, "Don't worry, there will be a jet aeroplane there to pick us up."

"Us? Why me too?" came Peter's startled response.

Asil tried to sound soothing. "It's the best way - you can come to Cyprus and see if there are any opportunities for you there. Tell your wife you'll be back in a couple of weeks."

As they talked more about the coming journey, Peter realised Asil was nervous about the flight. It amused him to see how concerned Asil - a poor air passenger at the best of times, used to travelling in large executive jets - was about the size of the plane they would be using to cross the Channel. When Peter explained, however, that the 800-metre grass runway at Compton Abbas was not suitable for a jet aircraft, Asil nodded his acceptance. Peter asked what plans he had made for France. Asil would say only that the second jet was to be at Le Bourget airfield, outside Paris, at noon French time. As they left the restaurant, Asil handed Peter an envelope containing enough money to pay for Clive Hughes's aircraft.

The next morning saw Peter back at Compton Abbas to draw up the final plans for the flight. He told Clive they needed to fly to an airfield north of Paris, from where their passenger would be able to transfer quickly to Le Bourget. The instant they looked at the map, Beauvais airfield leap out at them. It was the obvious choice - an estimated fifteen-minute drive from Le Bourget. The two men worked out that they would need to leave Compton Abbas at about quarter to eleven in the morning to get to Beauvais on time, allowing for the one-hour time difference between England and France and building in a few more minutes as a safety margin. The 450-mile round trip would take a total of three hours, they estimated - about an hour and a half to get there, half an hour on the ground and an hour for the return leg. Clive asked Peter if he would be coming back with him, to which Peter replied thoughtfully that he had not made up his mind. The trip was to cost £750 for the aeroplane hire and the fuel. Peter pulled out Asil's envelope and counted the money out in £50 notes.

When Asil had been trying to cheer my mother by suggesting he would soon return to North Cyprus, Ramadan Güney, the Turkish Cypriot cemetery owner who had stood £1 million surety for my brother's bail, had been visiting the island. Somehow, he got wind of Asil's words. Alarmed at what he heard, Güney telephoned the police as soon as he got back to London, told them he believed Asil was planning to jump bail and gave notice that he wanted to withdraw his surety. In the light of his tip-off, a ports and airports alert was posted in order to stop Asil leaving the country. The police would later admit, however, that they did not take the warning too seriously, since previous similar tip-offs had, on investigation, proved unfounded. The news reached Asil during the early hours of Friday, 30th April. That Thursday night, Asil told me, he had woken at half past one with a deep foreboding that something was very wrong. After a restless night, he went into his study at six o'clock to find a fax had come from his solicitors. The message said Ramadan Güney had written to the courts revoking his surety and that Asil was to appear at the Old Bailey that day so that his fate could be decided. Fearful that he might be remanded in custody that very day, Asil set about trying to find an alternative surety willing to put up £1 million. During the course of several frantic telephone calls, he got in touch with a member of the Turkish Cabinet who had been a great ally in the past. The Turkish minister took matters into his own hands - he rang Ramadan Güney and instructed him that he should not withdraw his bail pledge until a replacement could be secured. That telephone call did the trick. When Asil turned up at the Old Bailey later that morning, Ramadan Güney failed to appear and the hearing of his application to withdraw the surety was put off until the following Thursday, 6th May. The adjournment gave Asil the few days' breathing space he needed. It also focused his mind. It was imperative for him to leave before Thursday, or he would risk being locked up indefinitely while the clumsy legal proceedings rumbled on for months, even years, more.

If Peter had been uncertain about the importance of what he was about to do, he became convinced of it that Friday. He had arranged to meet Asil to finalise their plans, and when Asil turned up two hours late, agitated and very nervous, it was obvious he had had a very bad day. Asil explained how vital it was for him to leave before Thursday and asked anxiously if the journey really would happen on Tuesday and whether it would be safe. "Believe me," he told Peter, "you are not just carrying me with you, but the hopes of the people of North Cyprus."

That was the moment, Peter would recall later, that the joking stopped. From then on, it was no game, but a deadly serious and vitally necessary mission. There would be no more direct contact between Peter and Asil until they met on Tuesday morning.

That evening, Abide and Asil tried to act as if everything was normal, although both were nervous about the coming days. Abide was to leave the next morning, so she had packed a small bag with a few essentials - she knew there was no way of leaving the flat carrying a suitcase without arousing suspicion. The next day was Asil's fifty-second birthday and Michael Mates had arranged with Abide for a small surprise dinner on the Friday night. Asil was amazed when Mates, PR man Christopher Morgan and Anthony Scrivener and his girlfriend turned up on the doorstep to take him out for a Chinese meal. They went to a restaurant near Victoria, popular among the parliamentary community, and toasted Asil's birthday at a large table in the middle of the room. Michael Mates had another surprise for Asil - a wrist watch to replace the one which had been taken during the raid on his flat. As he ceremonially handed the gift over and watched Asil open it at the table, Mates told him to turn the watch over and read the inscription on the back. Asil burst out laughing as soon as he saw the message—"Don't let the buggers get you down"—and strapped the watch on his arm with a big grin. Everyone round the table joked about the apt humour behind the slogan, little suspecting that two months later the casual gift would cost Michael Mates his job as Northern Ireland Minister. Asil and Abide were ill at ease as they drove home. They felt bad for keeping their plans secret from the dinner companions who were trying to cheer them up. Yet they envied the others for being able to go home to an ordinary life. For them, the next few days would hold the key to any hopes of regaining a normal existence.

Abide had to leave the flat at eight o'clock on Saturday, 1st May to be sure of getting her train. Whatever she did, Asil cautioned, she must behave as if there was nothing out of the ordinary. It was Asil's birthday, but any feeling of celebration took second place to steeling the nerves for what lay ahead. Asil gave her the gold ring he had inherited from his father, which he had always considered a lucky charm, to wear on a chain round her neck. Just before eight, Abide and Asil left the flat, Abide carrying her travel bag inside a black dustbin liner so that it would look as if she was just going to drop the rubbish off on the way out. They drove to South Audley Street and Asil got out, saying a quick goodbye to Abide, who pulled off without a backward glance. To an observer, it would seem as if they would see each other as usual that night.

Abide drove straight to Liverpool Street Station, where she met up as arranged with a friend from North Cyprus who had agreed to travel with her. Together, they got on the nine-fifteen boat train to Harwich. On the way, Abide's friend did his best to reassure her. Abide was not scared - she knew she was in no trouble with the authorities. Yet she was keenly aware of how important it was for Asil that she should get away. If she got into any difficulties, it might endanger Asil's own plans.

When the train reached Harwich, Abide felt the first twinge of nerves. At passport control were two lanes. One was manned by a single officer. At the other desk were two men, one of whom was looking at everyone who went through. A third man was sauntering along the queue of travellers. As she waited her turn, clutching her specially-purchased visitor's passport, Abide tried to brush aside the fear that someone might recognise her face. To her relief, the officer at the desk waved her through with the barest of glances. Once on board the ferry, while they waited for the boat to sail, Abide sent her friend to telephone Asil at Eaton Square and wish him a happy birthday. It was a pre-arranged signal which told Asil the first part of the journey had been accomplished.

The ferry took about seven hours to reach the Hook of Holland. As soon as Abide was on Dutch soil, she telephoned her brother who lived in Germany and announced that she was making a surprise visit. She asked him to pick her up at the station in Herford, the town where he lived. Abide and her friend set off on the cross-Europe express as far as Hanover, changing then to a slow train which took an agonising eight hours. It was quarter to three on the Sunday morning when the train finally pulled in at Herford station. That afternoon, Abide's friend got on to a plane home from Hanover. Abide booked herself on to a flight to Istanbul on the Tuesday morning.

Far away in North Cyprus, I had sensed a change of mood in Asil during the previous fortnight. He had told me about his latest legal problems and the news had added to my worries. Yet whenever he spoke to me on the telephone, he sounded strained but cheerful. Several times, he again asked me whether his favourite mimosas were still in bloom and said he would like to be able to see them. During his call the day before our birthday, he had enquired how our business was going and then commented oddly, "There will be a lot of tourists arriving next week." I did not know what to make of his words. Mulling them over, I did not dare think that he might be hinting at his own arrival. Instead, I became worried that the stress of the past two and a half years was beginning to affect him more than ever.

My fears seemed to be confirmed by a telephone call from London that Sunday evening. After I had left, Tijen had taken it upon herself to keep up the traditional weekend family gathering, mainly for the sake of her uncle. Every Sunday since mid-February, just as before, Asil had joined everybody and had seemed as upbeat as ever. This Sunday, though, she had noticed an alarming change in him. He turned up with only Serhan, saying Abide had a bad cold and had stayed in bed at their flat. Very unusually, he brought no flowers. He seemed preoccupied and was walking with a stick - his back problem, which always grew worse with stress, was particularly bad and he was forced to sit in a different chair to usual, finding his normal seat uncomfortable. Tijen had planned a belated birthday celebration - she had baked a cake and there were presents and cards from everybody - but she found Asil's mood hard to lighten. During that afternoon, he revealed the reason for his depression. He had been that morning to visit Ramadan Güney, to try and talk him out of withdrawing his bail surety. He had found Güney in intransigent mood, however, demanding that certain

274

conditions be fulfilled in return for him remaining as surety. Güney had wanted to be given control of all Asil's and my mother's assets in North Cyprus - including the Kibris newspaper - in exchange for his pledged £1 million. When Asil had pointed out that the assets he was demanding were worth far more than the £1 million, Güney had shrugged and replied dismissively, "Freedom doesn't come cheap."

Tijen's disquiet deepened still further when Asil came to leave. He told them he would not be joining them in South Woodford the next day, which was unusual for a Bank Holiday Monday. As he said goodbye to each of the children, he hugged them hard twice. When Tijen went out to his car to see him off, he embraced her again. To her, it seemed like a very final goodbye - and having seen how down he was, her immediate thought was that he might be contemplating suicide. As soon as he drove away, Tijen picked up the telephone and called me. "*Dayi's* not looking at all well and I just don't know what's wrong with him," she told me. Tijen's worries served to strengthen my own concern about Asil. As soon as I finished talking to her, I dialled Asil's number, but there was no reply.

I received one more telephone call in Kyrenia that Sunday night. It was late in the evening when a friend of the family rang. We chatted briefly and then he asked me about my health, and how my ulcer was. Suddenly, the conversation took a bizarre turn. "The pills made in Germany have been posted via Germany," our friend said. "The others will be with you next week."

I was totally nonplussed. I was not expecting any tablets to be sent out, but sensed from our friend's tone, as he quickly moved on to another topic, that I should not question him. My mind was whirling as I put the telephone down. Fehim and I puzzled over the words, trying to decipher their meaning. Knowing that Abide had been born in Germany, there seemed only one interpretation that made any sense - Abide had left Britain and Asil would be following soon. I hardly dared to think my guess might be correct, but that night I determined not to speak to Asil again for the next few days. Suspecting as we all did that his telephone was tapped, I did not want to tempt him into accidentally giving away any plans. I knew, too, how much Asil liked to be able to surprise people - I decided it was best that I did not know what was going through his mind.

On Bank Holiday Monday, 3rd May, Peter Dimond went flying at Compton Abbas and checked with Clive Hughes that the aircraft was still all right for the following day. Clive confirmed their arrangements and asked Peter to call him when he and his passenger were ten minutes from the airfield, so that he could have everything ready and waiting. That night, at home in Petersfield, Peter watched the television news, paying particular attention to the weather forecast. Conditions were set fair for the morning. Afterwards he rang a contact number and relayed the following message: "The weather is fine and everything is OK for Saturday." Saturday was the code Asil and Peter had agreed to mean that Tuesday. A few minutes later, the contact - unaware of the meaning of his message - rang Peter back to say that Asil would be with him at nine o'clock on Saturday morning. It was the final cross-check which meant that there seemed to be no problems and that the journey would take place as planned. That night, Peter told his wife and two younger children that he was going to work for a company in the Mediterranean and would be back home in a few weeks' time. As things would turn out, he would still be in North Cyprus, unable to return to Britain, four years later.

Asil spent the Bank Holiday Monday at home in Eaton Square. That evening, he reported as usual to Savile Row police station at seven o'clock. Pulling up outside, he left his car engine running and the door open as he went into the station - in case the policemen showed any suspicions, he wanted to make sure of a quick get-away. "There was no way I was going to let them put me inside for years while I waited for justice," he said later. By the time he was due to report to Savile Row again, a week later, he aimed to be thousands of miles away in North Cyprus.

It was five o'clock when Asil woke that Tuesday morning, 4th May. He washed and shaved as meticulously as ever, dressing in grey trousers and a striped blue shirt. Asil crossed the hall into the living room, where he was greeted by his housekeeper of three years, Ufuk. As Ufuk disappeared into the kitchen to make a pot of tea, Asil stepped out on to the balcony overlooking Eaton Square. He stood for a few minutes, deep in thought about the day ahead - a day which could prove the most crucial of his life. In twenty-four hours' time, he would either be a free man, reunited with his family or…he stopped short. It was not Asil's style to look on the black side. He viewed the scene around him, taking in the enormous plant-filled balcony, which ran the entire width of the flat, and the tranquil square below. That balcony was Asil's joy - an oasis of foliage to which he loved to retreat. It would be a shame to leave it behind, he thought as he reached out absently to touch the Cypriot olive tree he had nurtured in its huge terracotta pot. Asil took one last look around before stepping back into the living room.

Inside, Ufuk was going through the regular ritual of burning olive leaves. They were the prayer-blessed leaves sent from Cyprus by my mother so that Asil could ward off the evil spirits as he wafted away the smoke. As Ufuk completed the burning, he closed the remaining olive leaves in a tin and placed it in the middle of the coffee table. When the clock on the desk showed seven o'clock, it was time to go. Asil picked up his white cotton Panama hat - an article of clothing which the family would later affectionately dub Asil's "get-away hat" - and Ufuk was just helping him on with his cream-coloured raincoat when the two of them stopped and looked in bewilderment across the room. On the floor beside the coffee table lay the tin of olive leaves, its lid off. It seemed to have been knocked on to the ground, yet neither of them, Asil would tell us afterwards, had been near it. Stranger still, the prayer-blessed leaves were strewn over the carpet, forming a trail which led to the door. For a split second, Asil would say later, he stood motionless as a voice inside his head told him, "This is a sign." He felt overcome by a calm certainty that nothing would go wrong that day. As he said goodbye, he felt a momentary pang of guilt that he could not tell his housekeeper where he was going. He stepped through the door and heard it close it behind him as he walked away. There was no going back now.

Certain the flat was being watched, Asil had planned his route from the building carefully so that he could get away without being seen. Instead of walking out into the street through the main front door, he crossed the communal hallway and slipped into an inner passageway which ran between each of the blocks ringing the square. Quickly, he strode the few yards to the next block where, turning away from the front door, he went down the steps into the covered garage area - obscured from Eaton Square at the back of the apartments. There, he climbed behind the wheel of his car, started the engine and reversed out. He planned to be far away before anyone noticed the car was gone and he was not at home.

The drive to the rendezvous took an hour and a half. Asil had arranged to meet Peter Dimond at his house while Hopie was still out taking the children to school. Peter had agreed to the plan a little reluctantly. He would have preferred Asil to come by train and to have met him at Petersfield station during the morning rush, but Asil had refused, fearing he might be followed or spotted if he used public transport. Peter's own worry was that, if Asil was being kept under close scrutiny by the authorities, he could be tracked by helicopter if he drove. He was relieved when Asil arrived on his doorstep at quarter to nine, having apparently managed to slip away unseen.

As soon as he saw Asil, Peter did a "double take". Like Asil, he too had dressed that morning in grey trousers and a blue striped shirt. Both had black briefcases and a smile crossed Peter's face as he realised that their clothing looked almost identical. He was amused too by the sight of Asil's hat and raincoat…on what was already turning out to be a beautifully sunny day. As soon as Peter opened the door, Asil stepped quickly into the hall, glancing over his shoulder as he went. Peter had calculated that they needed to leave Petersfield at nine o'clock, so they had a few minutes to spare. He offered Asil a cup of tea or coffee, but Asil quipped back that he would rather have a vodka. He settled for a small whisky. At nine on the dot, Asil and Peter emerged from the house and got into Peter's silver-coloured Honda car - a vehicle whose registration number, F 90 POR, would later be the source of much amusement for the press, which nicknamed it "Polly On the Run". They backed out of the drive and set off towards Dorset. Peter had calculated on an easy drive down at an average sixty-five miles an hour. Once they reached the open road, though, he was perturbed to find Asil telling him nervously to "slow down" every time the speedometer needle moved above sixty. Asil knew Peter used to be a racing driver and feared he might try to show off some of his track skills. Peter did his best to distract Asil with light-hearted chatter - they talked about anything but the day ahead as he tried to keep Asil's eyes away from the speed, at the same time surreptitiously putting his foot down to keep them on schedule.

All was well until the reached the Winchester bypass at about half past nine. As they approached Asil froze in mid-sentence. There, at the side of the road ahead of them, was a police Jaguar. Beside it was a BMW police motorbike and the two officers were leaning across talking to each other through the Jaguar's open window. Peter could see they were motorway vehicles, probably taking a break from patrolling nearby. Though even he would admit later that the sight of the policemen had "twitched" him, a glance at his passenger told Peter the most important thing was to reassure Asil and appear unconcerned. Asil looked deadly white. He had been a non-smoker since a bout of bronchitis at New Year. Now, he reached out for Peter's packet of Silk Cut on the dashboard, pulled out a cigarette and lit it - from then on, there would be barely a moment that day when Asil was without a cigarette in his hand. As they drove closer to the roundabout and passed the policemen, Asil eyed the speedometer. "For God's sake, Peter, slow down!" he hissed.

A calm Peter countered, "If I go any slower, they'll definitely stop us. Just sit tight and look normal."

Within seconds of them driving past the motorbike and the Jaguar, both police vehicles began to pull off. Peter watched them anxiously in his overhead mirror while Asil, unable to turn and look, asked frantically what was happening. Moments later, Peter saw the motorbike roar ahead of the patrol car and begin to close on them. He made a split second decision not to go on to the motorway, as he had planned, but to take the cross-country route west. Keeping to his left to take the old Roman road to Salisbury, he heaved a sigh of relief as the police bike sped by on his right and carried on to the motorway junction. As he turned off the roundabout, he watched in his mirror as the patrol car too passed behind them and went on its way. Asil leaned back in his seat with a slightly shaky sigh as Peter told him, "It's OK now. They've gone."

By now, they were slightly behind schedule and Peter knew he would have to speed up if they were to get to Compton Abbas on time. Again Asil told him to slow down. This time, the request was met with a firm, "We can't." Fifteen miles from Compton Abbas, after negotiating Salisbury, Peter decided it was time to put his old racing skills into practice. Asil clutched his seatbelt as Peter took the narrow hedge-lined bends at more than sixty miles an hour. Peter had set his watch five minutes fast, but he had not told his passenger and now Asil, aware of their looming deadline, did not ask him to ease off the accelerator. When Peter judged them to be about ten minutes from Compton Abbas, he pulled into a field gateway and stopped the car. Asil looked around - there was nothing to be seen but green fields and hedgerows. "Where the hell is this airfield?" he asked Peter uneasily. Peter gestured in the direction of a distant hill as he picked up his mobile phone and dialled the airfield number. "Come on in," was all Clive said to him before putting the phone down.

It was exactly quarter to eleven when Peter pulled up at a deserted Compton Abbas airfield. Everything was ready for them. Just ten feet from where he had parked the car, beside the gate into the airfield, stood the Piper Seneka, its door open and the right-hand engine already running. Asil and Peter climbed out of the car and strode over to the plane, where Clive Hughes sat in the pilot's seat with his back to them. As Asil clambered into the plane, Peter followed him, locking the door behind them and calling to the pilot, "Off you go, Clive." Without looking round, Clive Hughes set the plane in motion and turned it towards the grass runway as his passengers strapped themselves into their seats. Within less than a minute of their arrival, the plane was airborne.

Asil sat silent and motionless, gazing through the window as they lurched into the sky above the tiny terminal and Peter's car, which would later confirm to the searching police what route Asil had taken. As the aircraft banked steeply above the fields and then turned south towards the coast, Asil looked down at the countryside below him, bathed in a lush glow by the May sun. Suddenly, the reality of what he was doing hit him. Was this his last sight of Britain, his home for thirty-one years? He felt sure he would one day return. He glanced down at his watch. Remembering Michael Mates's engraved message, "Don't let the buggers get you down", he allowed himself a brief smile as he told himself, "I won't".

279

As the little plane climbed higher, it started bumping around in the clouds. Asil closed his eyes for a second to calm his flying nerves. Peter Dimond leaned across from the right-hand seat and asked, "Everything OK?"

"Not yet," was Asil's reply.

Clive Hughes levelled the plane out and set course for the Sussex coast. From there, they would follow the radar beacons all the way to Beauvais. Asil sipped orange juice and picked at a croissant as Peter pointed out landmarks along the way. He had little enthusiasm for sightseeing that day. "Where's France?" was all he wanted to know.

As they passed above Beachy Head, Peter told him, "That's it - you can say goodbye to England now."

"But are we out of English jurisdiction?" Asil returned. When Peter replied that they were not, Asil commented: "I'm not interested until we are."

They had been in the air for only three-quarters of an hour when Peter looked out of his window and spotted oil coming from the right-hand engine. As a pilot, he knew it was nothing to worry about, but he was anxious that Asil should not see it. He shifted in his seat, positioning himself casually so as to obscure Asil's view through the right-hand window. Shortly afterwards, peering across Clive's shoulder, Peter noticed that the needle on the dial corresponding to the right-hand engine's alternator had fallen dramatically. "Have you got an alternator out?" he asked Clive as he leant forwards.

Clive was busy looking at a map. "Yes," he called over his shoulder, "but don't worry about it."

Peter was not unduly concerned - he knew that they could survive on one alternator; it was only if the one on the left-hand engine went too that they would lose all power and find themselves in serious trouble. Once again, though, he was concerned to keep the problem from Asil. Seeing Asil lean forward to find out what they were discussing, Peter edged quickly over until he was almost in the middle of the seats, blocking both the view of the aircraft control panel and the engine which was still spitting oil. At that moment, Clive provided a diversion by announcing that they had just left British airspace.

"Good," said Asil, settling back into his seat. "Now, where's France?"

The one light-hearted moment of the journey came as the plane crossed on to the land mass of France. Asil had obtained a false passport in case he needed to show any travel documents along the way. The photograph was of him, but showed him with a beard and glasses and made him look completely different. In his briefcase, Asil had brought with him the false beard and moustache he would need to look like the passport photo…but he had not realised how difficult it would prove to stick the whiskers on without a mirror. When he got them out and started trying to put them on, an amazed Peter watched as they went on crooked, first to one side, then to the other. "Don't bother," he advised Asil with a snort of laughter. Asil took one look at Peter's grinning face, then peeled the lopsided beard off and stuffed it back inside his briefcase.

The Piper sped on across France towards Beauvais. Peter leaned towards Clive to give him some last-minute instructions. If anything went wrong, he was to pick the biggest field he could see and land - there was no way they were going to turn back to Britain. When the plane came within radio distance of Beauvais, Clive put his headset on and began trying to make contact, announcing their arrival. For a few minutes, he got no reply. Finally, Beauvais answered, giving clearance for them to land. Clive gave Peter a quick thumbs-up and Peter relayed the confirmation to Asil. As Clive began his descent into Beauvais, Asil reached into his briefcase and pulled out a piece of paper which he handed to Peter - it was a document which would give him a huge shock. The paper contained the registration number of a plane which would be at Beauvais to take them on across Europe. It also gave the instruction that they were not to land at Beauvais if they saw a distress flare go up from the ground - a signal the waiting pilot had been told to send if there were any problems there. Peter had understood that a car would be waiting at Beauvais to take them to the second plane at Le Bourget. He was stunned to hear Asil explain that he had changed his mind - bringing both planes together at the same airport would mean him being able to stay on the "air side" during the change-over, and not having to risk going through customs. Peter understood that it made sense from Asil's point of view, but it was a move which would later allow the British authorities to trace Asil's flight to North Cyprus all the way back to Compton Abbas...and to Peter Dimond, whose car stood outside the airfield.

———————

On the morning of 4th May, I was in the kitchen of the Kyrenia flat making a pot of tea. It had been another sleepless night. For three days, I had scarcely been able to doze at all, my mind too full of hope and fear to rest even for a moment. Fehim had tried to keep me calm, but I knew he had been just as restless as me. I only hoped we were not reading too much into what we had heard, and that we were not building up hopes which would be dashed. The kettle was just coming to the boil when the telephone rang. Instantly alert, I looked down at my watch as I crossed the kitchen to answer it. It was still very early - only half past eight.

On the line was a family friend from London. The message was brief - but to me the simple words spelled out the hope which I had hardly dared allow into my heart during the last few days. "Don't go out today," the caller told me. "Put some mimosas in a vase, put the kettle on, stay at home and wait for a visit." The meaning was clear - Asil was on his way to us. But as my spirits soared, they were almost immediately pulled back down to earth as fresh doubts and fears crept into my mind. How would he get here? When would he get here? How could he do it without his passport? What would they do if they caught him? What would *he* do if they caught him? He had once told me that, if ever he did try to get away, he would die before he allowed them to take him back to Britain. My heart skipped a beat as that memory flashed through my mind.

On the ground at Beauvais, David Hamilton was waiting. It was just after midday and, if all was going according to plan, Asil should get there any moment. Time for action. The faint mist which had earlier clung in the air above Beauvais had lifted and now the sun beat down cleanly on the tarmac. It was a fine day for flying. He leapt up the steps of his private plane to the two pilots already seated in the cockpit and told them to start up the engines. Then he ducked back out of the doorway to scan the cloudless sky. Less than a minute after he heard the engines whine into life, he caught sight of the speck of an approaching plane. In the Piper Seneka, Peter Dimond pointed out another small plane below them, standing beside the control tower. From a distance, he recognised it as a Cessna Citation and guessed it must be the plane that was waiting for them. Clive Hughes made one more cautious circuit of the airport before deciding it was safe to land. As the wheels touched down, he asked the control tower where he should go, and was instructed to taxi over towards the parked Cessna.

The Piper came to a halt beside the bigger aircraft and Peter Dimond was first out of the door as soon as the engines stopped. David Hamilton stepped forward. It was an odd first encounter for Asil's two "lieutenants". The two men greeted each other, David adding, "I'm a friend of your friend."

Asil climbed out of the Piper and walked across to where Peter and David stood, greeting David with a handshake. David made to usher him to the waiting plane but Asil waved him away, saying, "There's something I have to do before we go anywhere."

Peter leaned back inside the Piper and shouted to Clive Hughes, "Thank you very much - one day I'll tell you what you have done."

Clive looked round in his seat for the first time that day and told him, "That's OK - it's enough that I've done something for you." Peter pushed the Piper's door shut and watched for a few seconds as Clive turned it back towards the runway. Less than a minute later, it had left the ground on its way back to Compton Abbas. The first Clive knew of what he had in fact done would be the next morning, when he heard of Asil's departure on breakfast television. His wife was pressing a shirt in one corner of the living room when the news-flash came on. As the newsreader announced that Asil had flown out of Britain from a private airfield, from the corner of his eye Clive saw the iron moving gradually slower and slower. "Has that got anything to do with you, Clive?" asked his wife after a few moments, abandoning the ironing altogether.

"I think it might have," said Clive, without looking round. "Maybe it would be a good idea if you went and stayed with your mother for a few days."

As Peter and David followed Asil across the fifty yards to the terminal, Peter looked round warily. Only then did he register just how quiet the airport was. Later, he would learn that bodyguards had been posted at the connecting entrance between the "ground" and "air" sides of the Beauvais terminal, preventing anyone from passing through during the minutes that Asil was there. Once inside the building, Asil made straight for the telephone. It was only a ten-second call to a friend. "The big bird has flown," were the only words he spoke before replacing the receiver.

Then it was time to get on the plane. Asil, David and Peter strode over to where the Cessna stood, its engines throbbing rhythmically as the pilots waited for take-off. Within moments, they were inside, the door shut and the plane wheeling round towards the runway. At about quarter past twelve, just five minutes after Asil and Peter had landed, the Cessna's tyres left French soil.

Asil felt slightly safer in the six-seater Cessna. As soon as they had reached their cruising altitude of 29,000 feet, David Hamilton brought out trays of salmon sandwiches and orange juice. He also produced a bottle of champagne, which he promised to open once they were over Turkish airspace. As the minutes and miles ticked away towards their next destination - a refuelling stop at Vienna - both Asil and Peter felt the tension twisting their nerves. Asil's mind was focused on the need to get as far away from Britain as possible; away from Europe and into the safety of the Turkish world. For Peter, the thought flashed through his mind that he was speeding away from his home and family, accompanied by one man he knew reasonably well and another he had never met before. There was no way back, he realised.

283

The Cessna was met at Vienna, as David had arranged. Peter stayed with the plane during refuelling and Asil was led away with David and his pilot. A few minutes later, David and the pilot returned alone. They did not know where Asil had gone. Inside the Vienna terminal building, meanwhile, Asil had found a bar. He walked over and ordered a brandy. He climbed on to a stool and sat sipping his drink calmly for a couple of minutes. Then he set the glass down on the bar and stepped into the gents' washroom, where he studied his image in the mirror and combed his hair back into place. Every inch the movie-addict, Asil would say afterwards that he had planned his actions to add a frisson of suspense and some realistic detail to the day...for the sake of the film which would later be made about it. The others, who did not share his dramatic aspirations, were looking anxiously at their watches by the time their passenger reappeared, smiling broadly. Asil, clearly beginning now to relish his starring role, would comment afterwards that he could not understand why David was looking at him "in such a strange way". After three-quarters of an hour in Austria, the Cessna took off for the second time, Istanbul-bound.

Abide had spent an anxious two days at her brother's flat in Germany. She knew she could not telephone Asil, but somehow he would get a message to her. She could do nothing but wait. As first Sunday, then most of Monday passed by without word, she began to fear that something must have gone wrong. She considered what her next move should be. If it seemed anything had happened to upset Asil's plans, she decided, then she would return to London the same way as she had left. By Monday night, she was beginning to feel frantic when the telephone rang at her brother's flat. It was one of the two friends who were going to help them get through Istanbul. The message he gave Abide seemed to make no sense, but she guessed it could mean that Asil was going ahead with his trip as planned. After a sleepless night, she was faced with having to make a swift decision on Tuesday morning. Should she stay put, in case she had misinterpreted the message, or should she go ahead to Istanbul in the hope of meeting Asil later? She hesitated a while before deciding to take a chance and catch the flight she had booked. Making up her mind, she contacted her friends in Istanbul to meet her from the aeroplane, so that she would not have to wait round the airport where she could be recognised. Then she travelled with her brother to Hanover airport.

It was half past two in the afternoon when she landed at Istanbul, and there were several hours to kill before Asil arrived...if, indeed, he did arrive that evening. She hurried through the passport formalities at Atatürk Airport and, without any luggage to wait for, was quickly through customs and out of the sliding glass doors, hoping not to be spotted by anyone who knew her. Her friends were waiting and whisked her by car to a house nearby where she could while away the rest of the day. As the hours dragged past, a call came through to the house to say the first part of Asil's trip had gone smoothly and he had reached France. As Abide and her friends waited nervously, a second call came, this time to say the Cessna had made it to Vienna. A third message said, "We are very thirsty and we will be there at 7.30 - Topkapi." Between them, they decided that the message meant the plane needed fuel and would be at Istanbul - home to the magnificent Topkapi Palace - at half past seven that evening.

It was after half past six in the evening and the sky ahead was just starting to blush with the faintest sunset crimson when the Cessna's pilot turned to Asil with a thumbs-up gesture and told him, "We've just entered Turkish airspace." Asil broke into a smile and shifted slightly in his seat to study the mountainous landscape 29,000 feet below. Almost home. He felt the pull of Cyprus and family like a wrenching pain deep in his stomach. Afterwards, he would tell us how, at that very moment, he felt he could breathe more easily. On board the plane, Peter Dimond noted mentally that Asil suddenly seemed to look five years younger.

Less than thirty minutes later, the pilot was in radio contact with the control tower at Istanbul's Atatürk Airport. Landing permission granted, soon afterwards the Cessna descended through the pall of yellow-tinged smog hanging over the city. It skimmed high above the Bosphorus and touched down on a runway. Under instructions from a friend of Asil, who had organised the Turkish connection, the pilot taxied smoothly past the waiting jets and came to a halt in a remote area of the airport. As the arrangements for refuelling and the onward journey to Cyprus got under way, Asil could do nothing but wait. He felt he could almost see the end of the nightmare, just 500 miles away.

When my telephone rang in Kyrenia at half past four, I was pacing up and down the living room. Fehim was absentmindedly pretending to listen to the television news. Huge vases full of mimosa stood everywhere around the flat. My first thought that morning had been to drive straight to my brother's house ten miles away in Lapta and to make sure it was ready for his arrival. But we had quickly realised that this would alert people to what was happening - and might even jeopardise the entire plan - so instead we had stayed at home all day, trying to keep busy.

Both of us were hungry, yet the thought of food was unappetising. I had lost track of the number of pots of tea we had brewed since the morning. When the call came, Fehim and I both started instantly towards the telephone, the butterflies in my stomach fluttering wildly again. On the line was our family friend in Istanbul, informing us that the plane had left Vienna, but had not yet landed in Turkey. It was due to leave Istanbul for Cyprus at seven o'clock and should arrive at about quarter past eight. "Asil wants to come quietly and without any publicity," had been the closing instruction. "Stay put and we will let you know how and when he will get to you."

We reasoned that we should hear from Istanbul again between seven and half past. When it was nearly eight, I was growing frantic. "I can't take this any more," I told Fehim, wriggling my feet into my shoes and standing up from the chair where I had been sitting. "Come on, let's go to the airport." Hastily, we telephoned Mehmet, the caretaker of our block, and asked him to come and sit in the flat. If our friend called from Istanbul, Mehmet was to tell him we had gone to Ercan. If anyone else telephoned, he did not know where we were.

As we raced along the twisting mountain road to the airport, one thought after another surged through my mind. Maybe something had happened to the aeroplane after it left Vienna. Surely it should have reached Istanbul by now. Maybe it had already landed in Cyprus and something had gone wrong because we were not at the airport to help. What if they had found out something in London and had alerted Interpol to stop the aircraft? If I thought of one grim possibility, Fehim would voice another even worse. When he tried to be reassuring, I would chip in with a gloomy scenario. For almost all of the thirty-five-mile drive, we mentally tortured ourselves and each other. Then, when I caught my first glimpse of the airport in the distance, I suddenly felt an unexplained wave of optimism wash over me. I turned to Fehim and said, "I don't know how, but everything will be OK. He will get here, I am sure."

As soon as we pulled up at the terminal, we raced inside to see our friend Danis Bey, the airport manager. I knew Danis Bey was a great supporter of my brother and had many a time told me how he was looking forward to welcoming him back. As we were shown to his office, I formulated a plan in my mind. I would confide in Danis Bey what was happening and would ask him to make sure the plane landed and taxied with the minimum of fuss, so that we would be able to spirit Asil quietly through a side exit and into the waiting car. I also needed him to help in case there were any problems if my brother had no identification documents with him. When we stepped into Danis Bey's office though, my hopes were dashed. A young female duty officer was working at a desk in one corner of the room. I knew I could not speak out in front of her.

Instead, I tried more devious means to find out what might be happening. I told Danis Bey that Fehim and I had come to meet a friend - a general from the mainland - who was coming from Turkey on a private plane that night and would be staying with us in Kyrenia. Had he had a call to say what time to expect the flight to arrive? Danis Bey rang through to the control tower alongside the runway. Had they heard anything? The answer was negative. All my optimism vanished in an instant. I tried to keep a smile on my face as Fehim and I exchanged a quick glance. We tried to make conversation as we drank the coffee Danis Bey offered, but I was miles away as my mind flew between Vienna, Istanbul and Cyprus, trying to visualise what might have gone wrong. It was quarter to nine. Where was Asil now?

At Istanbul airport, Abide craned forward in the passenger seat as the airport car rolled across the tarmac towards where the Cessna would park. Now out of sight of the terminal, she took off the dark glasses which she had worn ever since arriving at the airport in the hope of avoiding being spotted by any of the journalists who lurked around the building. With her in the car were the friends she had spent the afternoon with and Asil's friend - captain Bilal Basar, a former Turkish Air Force captain - who they hoped would be able to facilitate the onward journey. Already, she had asked him to organise refuelling for the Cessna. Now he was taking her to join the last leg of the flight - something which would not normally have been allowed because the Cessna was strictly only there in transit. As Abide waited, counting down the minutes, she grew more and more excited and eager to see Asil for the first time in almost four days. She was sure he would be under considerable strain from the day's ordeal and was looking forward to a quiet reunion. Asil had·previously told her how he wanted to remain low-profile, with the aim of having a few days' breathing-space before anyone became aware that he had gone. After minutes that seemed like hours, they heard that the plane had landed. Shortly afterwards, Abide could see the lights of the approaching Cessna through the dusk. As the plane neared its allotted space she stepped out of the car and stood on the tarmac, readying herself to race on board.

The plane came to a halt in front of Abide, and as the engines were cut and the door opened, she stared in disbelief. First out the door was Asil, beaming from ear to ear and emerging as if he was treading on air. It was an unexpected moment which Abide would later liken to the appearance of a ballet dancer, seeming to float almost sideways down the steps. "It was as if he was on stage," she would remark afterwards. As Abide remained rooted to the spot, a small crowd of airport workers gathered as if from nowhere and descended on Asil who, clearly euphoric at being on Turkish territory, graciously received kisses and embraces from all directions. It took a few moments for Abide to fight through the welcoming party to deliver her own hug of greeting. She could scarcely see through the tears of relief which flowed unchecked down her face. She was only vaguely aware of the handkerchief which David Hamilton passed her as she climbed into the aircraft.

Peter Dimond and David Hamilton just stood and watched for a few minutes. The previous parts of the journey had been spent communicating in English. Now, suddenly, Turkish had taken over and neither man could understand a word that was being said. But there was no mistaking the sheer joy which greeted their passenger - clearly received as a VIP even in Istanbul. They looked on as Asil followed Abide into the Cessna…to be followed in turn by just some of the horde which had gathered noisily outside. For a few seconds, the plane rocked alarmingly under the sudden commotion.

As this scene was played out, up front in the Cessna tension was beginning to mount. Tiring of the hubbub, Captain Basar ordered all but the crew and passengers off the plane while refuelling got under way. Meanwhile the English pilot, eyeing the suddenly-descending darkness, was getting concerned. He had never landed at Ercan, in North Cyprus, and as the plane sat in Istanbul, he was without either a flight plan or a vital "plate" - a detailed layout of the Cypriot airport. Without them, he told Captain Basar, he could not go to Cyprus. In a distant office in the terminal building, on the instructions of Asil's friend, urgent telephone calls were made, arranging for the "plate" to be sent from Ankara. As this was organised, a fresh problem was emerging. Istanbul airport officials, mindful of the potential security implications, were refusing to issue a permit or flight slot for the Cessna to take off again for North Cyprus until they knew exactly who was on board. Captain Basar was equally adamant that he could not reveal the names of all the passengers, for fear that the information might fall into the wrong hands before Asil reached safe territory. For more than half an hour, the discussions were deadlocked. Finally, a telephone call by Captain Basar to a Turkish government minister saved the situation and the control tower was given orders to issue a slot for take-off. As the minutes ticked away to the allotted time, there was still no "plate" from Ankara. David Hamilton, agreeing with his pilot, said that flight slot or no flight slot, it was impossible for them to take off for an airport whose lay-out they did not know. An urgent call to Ankara requested a copy of the "plate" immediately. When it arrived in Istanbul by fax a few minutes later, and was rushed on to the Cessna, it turned out to be almost completely black. Asil and Abide held their breath as the pilot pored over it with David Hamilton. There was a general sigh of relief when David announced that the fax, though barely decipherable, revealed that there was only one runway at Ercan and seemed to show all the information the pilot needed. Minutes later, the control tower radioed through with clearance for the Cessna to prepare for take-off. It was after nine when the jet eventually soared into the air, heading south above the minarets of Istanbul.

When the Cessna levelled out safely, David Hamilton unstrapped himself from his seat and retrieved the cold bottle of champagne from the on-board fridge. He popped the cork and poured out glasses for Asil, Abide, Peter Dimond and himself. At 29,000 feet, they clinked glasses. Abide picked up the spent champagne cork from the table and slipped it into her pocket to keep as a good luck charm. She leaned across to Asil and said, "Please pinch me so that I know I'm not dreaming." She unfastened the chain from around her neck, retrieved Asil's lucky gold ring and handed it back to him. It had served its purpose.

For three-quarters of an hour, there was chat and laughter as the jet ate up the 800 miles southwards across the mountains of Turkey to Cyprus. But as the Mediterranean drew nearer, and with it the rocky shores of the island, the light-hearted atmosphere gave way to a mounting tension. The pilot, who had never flown into North Cyprus and was approaching almost blind without an on-board radar, was worried about the mountainous approach path. He was also concerned at Ercan Airport's close proximity to the airport in Larnaca, across the border in Greek Cypriot territory. To land at Larnaca by mistake would be a disaster, delivering Asil into hostile hands at the very last moment. Asil, too, was growing panicky over the tricky landing. He worried that the Greek Cypriots might have somehow picked up information about the flight and might try to intercept the Cessna as it passed perilously close to the border to land at Ercan. As the plane came within fifty miles of the airport, the Ercan control tower picked it up on the radar and made its first contact. There was a note of concern in the air traffic controller's inquiries. The Cessna pilot, not wishing to disclose the nature of the flight and its passengers while there was a danger of Greek Cypriot eavesdropping, had not requested permission to land at Ercan. Officially, said the controller, it should not be allowed to land. The negotiations went on over the airwaves as the Cessna hurtled south at 400 miles an hour. "We need to keep speaking to them in Turkish, so that we can be sure we are landing at the right airport," Asil told David Hamilton urgently. "Let me speak to them."

"You can't do that," cut in Abide. "Someone might recognise your voice. Let me speak to them."

With only thirty miles left to Ercan, Abide stepped forward and knelt down between the two pilots' seats, donning the headphones and beginning to relay messages between crew and control tower, speaking alternately in Turkish and English. It was a position she would maintain until the craft touched down. "Go on, go on," she said as the pilot looked at her for confirmation of what they should do.

As she spoke, Asil was looking through the window, trying to spot familiar landmarks. As the lights of Kyrenia came into view, he craned forward in his seat and demanded in alarm: "How high are we?" Just behind Kyrenia, Asil knew, was the craggy 3,000 foot mountain range on which one plane had already come to grief a few years earlier. It was vital that the Cessna should make its initial approach at well over that altitude, losing height only after it had cleared the rocks. As the plane left Kyrenia behind, the altimeter showed 4,000 feet. Abide kept on talking to the control tower to establish the jet's position. But with less than twenty miles of the journey left, there was still no permission to land.

———————

At twenty past nine, the telephone had sounded on the airport manager's desk at Ercan. Danis Bey had picked up the receiver and given me a nod as he listened to the caller. My hopes had risen. Danis Bey had put the phone down after a few seconds and smiled. "That was the control tower. They've just had a message to say a private jet has left Istanbul and is on its way here. They wanted to know how I knew in advance!"

Within minutes, the telephone rang again. This time the control tower had a problem. The private jet had not requested permission to land and for security reasons it should not be allowed to touch down. What was the control tower to do? My mind raced as I heard of this new hitch. I leaned across the desk and implored, "Please tell the control tower I can personally vouch for the fact that the people on this plane are not strangers - they are friends of ours and they must simply have made a mistake in not asking for landing permission. Please let the aircraft land."

I heaved a sigh of relief when I heard Danis Bey tell the air traffic controller: "It's all right. I am assured by Mr and Mrs Nevzat that these people are friends. Please talk to them on the radio to arrange a landing."

My next concern was to try and ensure that Asil could arrive quietly, as he wished, and would get through customs quickly. With the aircraft less than an hour away, I knew I must find a way to confide in Danis Bey. Hitting upon an idea, I started fanning myself furiously with one hand and saying, "It's very hot in here. Let's go for a walk outside before the plane lands and get some fresh air." He agreed. As soon as the office door was safely shut behind us, I turned to our companion and said: "Danis Bey - this plane that is coming…it's my brother." I will never forget the look of pure astonishment on his face. For a full three minutes, he was robbed of speech and could utter only the occasional "Ha!" as I went on to explain: "I know you wanted to give him a big welcome, but he doesn't want that tonight. I'm not sure what papers he has on him, and all we need is for him to be able to get in and leave quietly. Can you help?" I could see Danis Bey mulling over my words. Deep in thought, he muttered, "Yes" several times then led us back into the office.

It was after quarter past ten and the air traffic controllers were on the telephone again. This time they reported having made radio contact with the incoming plane and seemed relieved to find a Turkish speaker - a woman - on board. I asked Danis Bey eagerly, "Please tell the control tower to ask if the person they have been speaking to is called Abide."

He relayed the message then turned to me with a grin, covered the receiver with one hand, and said, "The tower says why don't you go and ask yourself?…the plane has just landed!"

Fehim grabbed my hand and we sprinted together through the office door and out on to the apron.

The Cessna flew over the flat plain of central Cyprus, descending rapidly. Ahead of them lay the lights of Ercan Airport and of Larnaca Airport, less than a dozen miles away across the border in South Cyprus. As the jet came in low across the shadowy fields, pointing for the northernmost set of runway lights, the atmosphere on board seemed almost frozen. The pilot called back across his shoulder to David Hamilton, "Are we going in or not?" David stretched forward across Abide, still kneeling on the floor, and peered through the windshield into the gloom. His concern was that, since the plane was still without landing permission, the Turkish Cypriot authorities might try to prevent touch-down forcibly by placing some obstruction across the runway. Privately, he felt such a course of action unlikely - stiff questioning after landing was more probable, he reckoned - but he wanted to be sure before giving the okay for landing. From a distance of just a few hundred yards, the runway seemed clear.

David gave a quick nod to the pilot and sat back down. "We're going in," came the pilot's announcement.

"Are you sure it's the right airfield?" shouted Asil.

The Cessna seemed to hover briefly above the first sets of runway beacons, then hit the ground with a couple of jolts. In the darkened cabin, Asil gripped the armrest beside him. He seemed to feel an enormous weight lift from his shoulders as the plane hurtled down the long runway, slowing little by little, and he saw the familiar lights of the terminal glide past in the distance. As he studied them, he saw the figure of a woman run from the building and set out through the railings and across the apron towards the runway, a man following a few paces behind. He stared in disbelief and said out loud, "My God. It's her!"

Breathless and already sobbing, I reached the plane within seconds of it coming to a halt at the far side of the apron. As I ran up to it, I felt as if I was watching somebody else in a scene from a film. Through a dream-like haze I saw Asil emerge from the cabin, followed by a weeping Abide. In a kind of slow motion, I ran into Asil's open arms, tears streaming down my cheeks. Although dry-eyed and obviously buoyed by adrenaline and relief, I could tell Asil was deeply moved from the way he hugged me tight against him and stroked my hair. After a few moments, he held me at arm's length and, touching my face with one finger, said softly, "I'm here now. There's no need to cry any more."

A few moments later, Danis Bey joined us and added his own welcome to Asil. I was surprised to see, too, Mehmet Ali Akpinar - from *Kibris* newspaper - with Mustafa Erbilen, a member of the ruling National Unity Party government. Later, I learned that our friend in Istanbul, apparently unable to contact me that evening, had put another call through to Mehmet Ali. He, in his turn, had been worried that he might not be able to get his boss through customs without any fuss, so he had dragged the MP from dinner in a Kyrenia restaurant to come and bring his influence to bear. At that moment, I was so excited that I barely registered their presence. We set off for the terminal. By the time we got there - me asking on the way if there was a chance that Asil might leave quietly through a side door - a small throng had gathered outside the building and moved towards us. It was after half past ten and the airport was virtually deserted. The only flight due in was a Cyprus Turkish Airlines plane, but it had been delayed in Istanbul and was now not scheduled to land before midnight. Still, it seemed word of Asil's unexpected arrival had spread rapidly around the airport. Virtually every member of staff in the building had deserted their post to swarm instead round Asil, hugging him in greeting and wishing him well. At customs, Asil could only laugh out loud when he was asked to show his passport. As a holder of Turkish citizenship, however, he was waved through when he presented his identity card.

As he passed through the turnstile at the head of our small procession, Asil turned slowly and cast a long look around. He told me later how he had felt at that moment - he was there at last...and he had organised it all himself. In his mind's eye, he pictured himself as the George Peppard character in one of his favourite television shows, *The A-Team*, lighting up a cigar at the end of a job well done and pronouncing: "I love it when a plan comes together."

Outside, Fehim, Asil, Abide and I crammed ourselves into my two-seater car. Abide and I folded ourselves into the tiny parcel space at the back, while Fehim drove and Asil took the passenger seat. In exuberant spirits we sped away from Ercan, leaving a rather dazed Peter Dimond, David Hamilton and the crew to tend to the aircraft. Asil had already told them that he would disappear as soon as he had landed, but that he would arrange for them all to be taken to his "little hotel by the sea". Later, after their passports had been checked and handed back, they were startled to be taken by a convoy of taxis to the far-from-little five-star Jasmine Court Hotel in Kyrenia. That night, they drank champagne in the bar, toasting their success and reliving, blow by blow, the almost-incredible events of the day. A stream of people approached them, offering their congratulations and shaking the four newcomers by the hand. Peter Dimond would remark later, "One man came up to me and said 'You have brought back the only man who can save this country.' I didn't realise until then that it was such a deliverance." In their high spirits, none of them noticed the group of Englishmen sitting on the opposite side of the bar, unobtrusively drinking in every word. It was only afterwards that they would learn that the men were a party sent out on behalf of the administrators of Polly Peck. They would check out the next morning.

We made our way to my mother's house close to the centre of Nicosia. As we drove to the residential Kösklüçiftlik district where my mother lived, we discussed the best strategy for breaking gently the news of Asil's arrival. During the previous months, she had suffered from occasional heart trouble and we were all anxious to try and avoid giving her too much of a shock. We decided Fehim and I should go in to the house first to prepare my mother. Then Abide would join us, leaving Asil's appearance until last.

We pulled up in the silent street outside the gate of my mother's yellow stone house. Fehim and I got out and Asil, slipping across to the driver's seat, said he would take the car a little further up the road, out of sight of the door. There was still a light on and my mother came to the door quickly after we rang the bell. As she ushered us in, I told her that we had come with some good news. "Is Asil OK?" was her immediate question.

"Yȩs," I replied.

"Hopefully he will be coming soon."

Then, after a pause, I added, "In fact, we do have good news because Asil has sent someone to see us."

"Who?" asked my mother.

"Abide."

My mother was overjoyed. Fehim, who had remained near the front door, beckoned down the street to Abide and showed her into the kitchen. She and my mother hugged each other warmly.

"How is Asil?" my mother asked Abide after a few moments.

"He's fine and he's going to be coming out too," Abide told her.

"Very soon," I chipped in, trying to prepare the ground.

For about five more minutes, we chatted in the kitchen as my mother busied herself making tea. When I could see that she seemed calm and happy, I gestured to Fehim to go and fetch Asil from the car. After he had disappeared through the door, I told my mother, "Actually, Asil has already come."

She turned to me with wide eyes. After a speechless moment, she managed to ask, "Where?"

Almost immediately, as if on cue, Asil appeared in the doorway. "Mum, it's me," he said simply.

For a full five minutes, my mother could not stop crying. Even Asil was weeping as he hugged her again and again - reunited after two and a half years apart. As they stepped apart and stood looking at each other, my mother kept slapping herself in disbelief. Between her sobs, she repeatedly thanked God for having answered her prayers and brought her son back to her. It was a scene I will never forget. Afterwards, Asil would tell me how shocked he was to see our mother looking much older than he remembered. In the dim light, she looked to him "as if she was crawling towards her grave".

We stayed at my mother's house for about half an hour, chatting over cups of tea. In those thirty minutes, less than an hour after Asil had landed, there were two telephone calls to my mother's house. The first was from Dervis Eroglu, leader of the National Unity Party and Prime Minister at the time, welcoming Asil home. Asil and he spoke for a few minutes. The second call was from Rüya's mother, Sifa Taner, who had been told of the news and was ringing to see if it was true.

Soon after midnight, we left my mother's house, cramming ourselves back into the car for the journey to Asil's house at Lapta. I had half expected he and Abide would spend their first night at our flat in Kyrenia, but Asil was insistent on driving the extra ten miles to Lapta. "During all this time in London, when I dreamt of the day I would return to Cyprus, I dreamt of sitting on the veranda at Lapta," he said.

It was about one o'clock in the morning by the time the car climbed the foothills into Lapta, where the coffee shops were now deserted and firmly shuttered for the night. We pulled up in the narrow sloping side street in front of Asil's low, whitewashed house. We all stood back to let Asil go in first, then waited outside in the garden for him while he made a quick tour of inspection. For more than an hour and a half, the four of us sat talking. Normally early to bed, we sat up long past our usual time for sleep, toasting the past day with a glass of champagne and then going on to drink cup after cup of tea. We sat around a long trestle table on the arched stone veranda, the water supply to the lily pond trickling in the background and the cicadas chirping in the trees on an unusually balmy early May night. Asil could hardly believe he had made it. From time to time, he would leap excitedly from his seat and look around. "Am I really here?" he would say to no-one in particular.

CHAPTER TWELVE

British Justice

The few days after Asil's return sped past in a blur. North Cyprus seemed to take on an immediate carnival spirit. Everywhere we went - but particularly in Lapta - we encountered the same mood of joyous optimism. So many people were convinced that Asil's arrival would somehow turn the clock back almost instantly to the better days before the Polly Peck troubles. The phone never stopped ringing with people congratulating Asil and wishing him well - later the letters would start flooding in too, from Turkey and even from Britain.

At half past seven on my brother's first morning back, the telephone rang in our flat. It was Tijen, who had been woken by Meral, flying through the back garden in London at five in the morning, shouting that everyone should wake up because she had heard about Asil on the television news. They all wanted to know what had happened and were both shocked and relieved to discover that my brother was safe in Lapta. Within twenty-four hours, the first Turkey-based journalists would be standing outside the wooden double doors of the Lapta house, hoping to be the first to interview him.

By the Thursday morning - thirty-six hours after his plane had touched down at Ercan - more than fifty reporters, photographers and cameramen clamoured outside, blocking the streets and whiling away the time at the village coffee shop - a handy vantage point overlooking the unassuming house below. Some of the photographers clambered on to the bonnets of their hired jeeps to try and snatch a shot over the eight-foot-high wall into the garden, but were summoned back down to earth by the policemen overseeing the hordes - later that first day, the wall would be built up by an extra couple of feet to guard against a repetition. Whenever any of us arrived at the house - family, friends, colleagues or lawyers - we would have to run the gauntlet of shouted questions as we pushed through the milling crowd. Every few minutes, a journalist would knock on the door, asking to speak to Asil or handing in a scribbled note to request an exclusive interview for their own paper.

Some of the stories and headlines which appeared in Britain at that time upset me enormously. Asil was portrayed as a "randy crook" and a high-living playboy who, according to one report, never wore the same shirt twice. The extravagant jet-setter they wrote of was not the brother I knew. In the good days, Asil had indulged in his chosen pleasures - luxury cars, fine wines, clothes from the designer Bijan - but he had certainly worked hard enough for them. And the fact is that, such long hours had he spent in the office, he had had little time to enjoy the kind of lifestyle he could have afforded. He had scarcely ever seen the country homes he owned, had rarely taken a holiday, had lunched from a tray in his office and had ordered clothes in bulk every few months because he could not fit a shopping trip into his busy working schedule. One headline in *The Sunday Times* made my blood boil: "Easy come, easy go." Asil's achievements were down to almost three decades of unremitting hard work. As for "easy go", the years after Polly Peck's swift downfall had been a living hell.

As a whole, the press showed a fixation on trivia, ignoring any of the wider issues being raised. A peculiar piece of nonsense about how Asil used to build sand-castles in the Eaton Square flat, lighting candles on each turret to destroy symbolically his enemies, was accorded number one billing in a double-page spread in *Today* newspaper, though without any explanation as to where the sand was supposed to have come from. Anyone less likely to want sand scattered around his home than my very particular brother, I cannot imagine. Another national paper newsdesk, after its reporter had conducted an interview, demanded that the correspondent include a mention of what colour socks Asil was wearing. Asil found all these stories infuriating - when he spoke to reporters later, he would ask each one whether they were really interested in the important issues, like justice and freedom of speech - the very reasons he had decided to leave Britain. What did tickle his sense of humour, though, were the cartoons about him which appeared in most of the papers. He got a friend in London to buy up all the originals for him - now there is a wall in his Lapta house devoted to the treasured collection of framed sketches.

Asil was shocked to see how quickly the press had arrived in Cyprus. He had imagined that his absence would not be noted in Britain until he failed to turn up at court on the Thursday, giving him a couple of days' breathing space to unwind from two and a half years of tension and to consider his next move. He had not bargained for the tip-offs which ensured that news of his journey would be broken in London during the early hours of Wednesday morning. As we sat in the Lapta house hearing the clamour outside, I told him he would have to say something to the media. Christopher Morgan advised him to hold a press conference at which he would read a prepared statement. Asil was unsure - he preferred to meet members of the press in small groups and to talk to them off-the-cuff. Still, I think, in a state of shock, he went along with Morgan's advice, appearing in the doorway on the Thursday afternoon and announcing that he would give a press conference the following day at the Jasmine Court Hotel in Kyrenia. I felt sure it would be a mistake.

That Friday press conference turned into a near scrum. I was there to see Asil virtually engulfed in the crowds of journalists and onlookers as soon as he stepped out of the car at the side entrance to the hotel. And there, in front of him, lay a beribboned ram ready for slaughter - a sight, he told me later, which brought him out in a cold sweat as it revived memories of his experience at Niksar. Realising how the press would seize on the sacrifice, portraying it not as a customary honour but as a piece of Levantine barbarism, he hurriedly passed a message through his aides that the sheep was not to be killed and was relieved to see the animal led safely away. A joke went round among the journalists that the reporter from the *Sun* newspaper - renowned for championing similar causes - had saved the beast's life by buying it. Inside the hotel restaurant, after waiting for a five-minute barrage of camera flashlights to die down, Asil delivered the speech he and Christopher Morgan had prepared. As I had feared, he looked - and felt - very uncomfortable. Asil had said he expected to be at the press conference for about two hours and to answer questions after his statement. When he finished speaking, though, the first question he heard, yelled from the ranks of reporters, was, "Are you a crook, Mr Nadir?"

At that, Asil brought the conference to an early conclusion, telling the assembled journalists that he was not prepared to continue if they could not show any respect. As some of the journalists turned on the first questioner, criticising him for having ruined everyone's chances with his rudeness, Asil walked out of the room with reporters and photographers racing behind him.

He told me later how he had snapped inside when he heard those words. "If they can't even be polite, I don't see why I should answer their questions," he said angrily that evening.

Ironically, the press were not the only interested parties in Cyprus during those first days. Just twenty-five miles from Lapta, over the border in South Cyprus, an international law conference was taking place. Among those attending were British Lord Chancellor, Lord Mackay, Barbara Mills, now Director of Public Prosecutions, and her replacement as head of the Serious Fraud Office, George Staple. It was a coincidence gleefully noted by the newspapers. Within days of Asil's arrival, Lord Mackay had crossed the border into the North to request that my brother be returned. The British High Commissioner would also be despatched to make a similar approach. At a cocktail party for Turkish Cypriot community leaders, Lord Mackay spent most of his time closeted in a side room with President Denktas - the head of a state which Britain refuses to recognise. The President told us afterwards how the Lord Chancellor, when told that the TRNC had no extradition treaty with Britain, had replied that Denktas should "do something". President Denktas, a barrister, made fun of the other man, telling him, "What do you expect me to do? Kidnap him? Apart from that, I can't see any legal way of handing him over - and as a man of the law, you surely can't be asking me to break the law?"

Joking apart, there were real fears for Asil's safety. The authorities warned us of the danger that he might be kidnapped or, even, that an attempt might be made on his life. The discovery of two parachutes in the mountains near Lapta were taken as confirmation of the security threat. So, too, was a conversation in an English pub overheard by a Turkish Cypriot who immediately telephoned a North Cyprus government contact to alert him to a visit by an English man and three "colleagues". The party was kept under surveillance for a few days - during which they wandered around Lapta - until they left the island. The authorities insisted that Asil should be given twenty-four-hour-a-day protection and accorded him six bodyguards who worked round the clock in shifts. Later, Asil would employ them himself. On Asil's first weekend in North Cyprus, he was anxious to go to the sandy "turtle beach" which he had missed seeing for so long. As we all sat on the seashore, I glanced around - and the sight that met my eyes seemed unreal. As if in a scene from a Hollywood movie, everywhere I looked stood an armed man, keeping guard from the rocky headlands and the dunes behind. "Is this really happening?" I whispered to Fehim.

Throughout North Cyprus, there was a buzz of excitement in the air. At our flat and in Lapta, the telephone still never stopped ringing with well-wishers eager to welcome my brother and lend their support. Time and again, Fehim, myself and my mother would be stopped in the street to receive the congratulations of passers-by - some of them we had never met, but they knew who we were. Wherever Asil went during those days and early weeks, children would run out into the street to greet him and bystanders would wave at his car. Asil's house even became part of the sightseeing trail for tourists visiting North Cyprus. In England, one travel agent reported would-be TRNC holidaymakers inquiring about the possibility of meeting Asil during their stay. Suddenly North Cyprus - even insignificant Lapta - had been put firmly on the map.

My mother was delighted, of course, to welcome her son. After that first late-night encounter at her house in Nicosia, it was a day or two before Asil was able to find time for them to sit down together in private and chat. Ray Harris, an old friend who had worked at Wearwell and Tri-Sun Textiles and had since become a customer of my mother's clothing business, was with her at the factory when a call came through from Asil inviting her to tea with him that afternoon. She looked down at the dress she was wearing and then announced that she would simply have to put on another outfit for the visit, but that she did not have time to go home and change. Ray followed as my mother strode purposefully into her office, went straight to one of the myriad cubby-holes there and pulled out a folded piece of material - it was a floral fabric in pinks and blues which, Ray guessed, had probably been there for several years. Quick as a flash, and with no pattern to guide her, she cut out pieces for a dress, deftly shaping the neck and armholes and the flare of the skirt. Then she tossed the pieces to one of the machinists and asked her to stitch them together. No more than twenty minutes from when my mother took the telephone call that spare length of fabric had been turned into a dress fit for a tea date with Asil. "It looked a million dollars!" an astonished Ray told us later.

No sooner had the fuss died down and all the journalists decamped from North Cyprus back to their offices than a fresh wave of sensation hit, this time centring on Michael Mates. On Sunday, 30th May, two British Sunday newspapers splashed stories about a "minister and Nadir". Michael Gillard, in *The Observer's* business section lead, told how the Northern Ireland Minister had "caused surprise and concern at the Serious Fraud Office" by his lobbying on behalf of Asil. The *Mail on Sunday's* front page lead not only told how Mates had sent three letters about Asil's case to the Attorney-General, but also revealed the wristwatch gift that the minister had given my brother for his birthday, just days before he left Britain. The jokey "Don't let the buggers get you down" message sparked a media sensation. No-one knew who had leaked the information to the two papers, although I have my private suspicions.

Asil and I were together at Loch Manor when news reached us by fax of the reports. We were shocked at the level of publicity and Asil - who had told me about what we nicknamed the "buggers' watch" in the days after his arrival - said he felt very sorry for Michael Mates. The minister had simply intervened quite legitimately in the name of justice, had grown to be a friend and had given a humorous present as a gesture to try and cheer Asil up. To me, it was simply the kind of thing a decent person would do. We considered it very unfair for the man to be pilloried for what he had done - and we certainly never imagined the incident would escalate as it did, to end in Mates's resignation. Soon after his arrival that month, Asil had commented to me, "We still have some friends out there who will try and get some justice on our behalf." Though he named no names, I guessed he meant Michael Mates. I know they kept up an indirect line of communication after Asil left Britain, getting in touch occasionally through a third party and passing messages by code. In the days after those first newspaper stories about Mates, Asil sent a message to the minister saying he was sorry the watch affair had been blown up out of all proportion.

During the following week, controversy over the intervention in Asil's case by Michael Mates and other Tory ministers - Michael Heseltine and Peter Brooke - raged on in the pages of the British newspapers. Labour MPs, quick to scent Tory blood, demanded an explanation. Mates remained tight-lipped, on Downing Street's instructions. In North Cyprus, we watched the furore in growing astonishment, receiving faxed instalments every day. When the first journalists had been on the island in pursuit of Asil, my brother had threatened a Watergate-style disclosure including taped evidence of a government minister admitting that the British secret services were behind the collapse of Polly Peck. I had thought Asil a little hasty in announcing his intentions quite so quickly, but I understood that he had been effectively gagged for two and a half years and was relishing the chance to speak freely. And after all it was the press itself which had sought Asil out, not vice versa. By Sunday, 20th June, three weeks after the first stories broke, the *Sunday Express* was reporting that Mates's future "hung by a thread" after suspicions mounted that it was his voice on Asil's tape-recording. Four days later, he quit his ministerial post.

I was shocked that Mates had gone. To this day, I cannot see what he and the other Tories did that was so wrong. I found it interesting that at the "arms-to-Iraq" inquiry many months later, Michael Heseltine, asked by Lord Scott why he had not intervened further when he realised what was happening in the Matrix Churchill prosecution, would answer that the rumpus over the letters written on behalf of Asil had demonstrated how dangerous it was for a minister to intervene. He was right. Michael Mates's pursuit of justice had ended in him being hounded out of office, yet within a few months it would become clear that much of what he said had been correct.

Mates made his resignation speech to MPs on Tuesday, 29th June. We all thought he would simply take the opportunity to defend himself and were intrigued to hear what he had to say. Fehim and I went to The Olive Tree to watch the speech live on BBC World Service television.

Half-way through, the Greek Cypriot-controlled electricity supply was cut off and we endured a frustrating few seconds' wait until the hotel generator cut in. Asil and Abide were listening at home in Lapta. Asil called Irfan in London and they listened to the telephone while Irfan put his receiver close to a television set. When we heard what Michael Mates had to say - cutting across the attempts by Speaker Betty Boothroyd to silence him - we were delighted. Mates told the Commons how Asil's privileged defence documents had been taken from him. He accused the SFO of orchestrating a trial by media, of improper collusion with the Inland Revenue and demanded an independent inquiry into their handling of the case. He talked of the alleged plot to bribe the judge, saying it had been formulated to destabilise the trial and to put improper pressure on the judge. Mates also told how British, American and Greek Cypriot intelligence services had conspired to bring down Asil and Polly Peck in order to force a Cyprus settlement. It was thrilling to hear some of the knowledge we had lived with secretly for months - under threat of contempt even to talk about it - being made public. Without that speech, I wonder whether the situation would ever have been brought to light. As soon as the speech was over, we began to receive a deluge of telephone calls from people in England, commenting on what Mates had said and relieved that the whole issue was in the open at last. We waited eagerly to see what would happen, and how the media would react.

The following day, it became clear that the Attorney-General was determined to ignore the issues. In a rowdy session of Parliament, Sir Nicholas Lyell insisted there was no basis for an independent inquiry into the charges levelled by Michael Mates and told MPs that the alleged conspiracy to bribe the judge was being separately investigated by the police under the supervision of the Director of Public Prosecutions. The inquiries, he said, had revealed "no credible evidence" implicating the judge personally. On the subject of Asil's personal defence papers, Lyell said only that two bags containing privileged legal documents had been "opened in error", but had not been circulated.

On the same day in Parliament, Liberal Democrat veteran, Sir David Steel stood up and revealed that an official at the SFO had forged a letter in his name - Lyell apologised and dismissed it as just an April Fool's joke. That same day, Michael Jones, the solicitor representing tax-man Michael Allcock, admitted the Inland Revenue had given information to the SFO. A day later, on 1st July, the Attorney-General published forty-eight edited pages of a ninety-seven-page file of correspondence between himself and Michael Mates over Asil's case.

I was seething as I listened to Lyell's reply to Michael Mates but I should have known that Mates's stand would not be taken seriously.

Having been driven from office over the trivial matter of the watch, he was now ridiculed for saying what he knew. It would be many months before Sir Nicholas Lyell retracted his immediate dismissal of Michael Mates's claims or before the Serious Fraud Office finally admitted that they had introduced the plot to bribe the judge allegation into my brother's pre-trial hearings without having one shred of evidence. At the time of Michael Mates's speech, we were all still completely in the dark about how the allegation had come about. It was not until October that I would finally be confronted by the two informers in Asil's office in Nicosia.

As the days following Asil's arrival turned into weeks, I found my spirits plummeting from the high of being reunited with him to a frighteningly black depression. The most ludicrous and libellous stories were being bandied around in the press - some aimed, we would be told later, at blackening Asil's name so thoroughly that no-one in Britain would ever believe a word he said. Newspaper reporters, fed unsubstantiated "information", were trying to prove that Asil was involved in cocaine dealing and that he had traded in arms for the terrorist Irish Republican Army. With each fresh accusation, I begged Asil to reveal the evidence he had in his own defence - and incriminating the authorities - so that the entire situation could be resolved and we could get on with our lives again. But Asil told me I had to be patient. He believed the British authorities were running scared because they had no idea what he knew about their activities. As the weeks and months went by, though, I sensed that he was keeping his evidence close to his chest partly because he was beginning to enjoy the cat and mouse game. While it may have seemed like a game at times, though, to me it was one with the highest stakes…all our futures, our sanity, our lives.

Somehow, I had expected Asil's return to Cyprus to signal a change of fortunes, but I quickly realised that, whatever might happen eventually, there was to be no immediate turn-about. The thought nagged continually at the back of my mind that there was still much unfinished business. Yet it seemed there was no way of attending to it immediately and putting it behind us. Where I had hoped we might all be able to restart our lives, I became aware that the burdens of the past would not be shed so easily. All the while, too, pressing business worries were never far from my mind. We were struggling to put the Olive Tree Hotel back on to a solid financial footing, but the high level of borrowings, coupled with the poor state of tourism in the aftermath of the Gulf War, meant our chances of success were slim.

The realisation of just what a bleak position Asil and I were in knocked me sideways. It was the dawning of knowledge which I no doubt should have had much earlier, but for the previous two and a half years I had had other concerns to occupy my mind. First was the long drawn-out struggle for Noble Raredon. Then, with that battle lost, the pressing issue had been to look after my mother and try and keep her going through the crisis. Now, it struck me, my "big brother" was back with us and, as the head of the family, the responsibility was down to him. In an instant, I had nothing more to do. It was an empty, helpless feeling which plunged me back into my depression, this time deeper than before. I craved the shelter of our flat - I could not face going anywhere and had no energy or will to do anything. To the outside world, I knew I had to pretend there was nothing wrong with my life, but it was too painful to try to put on an act every time I ventured from my front door. The very thought of seeing people was agony. Fehim, anxious to pull me out of my depression, bombarded me with unwelcome suggestions of visits and outings. It was at that time that we had some of our fiercest-ever rows. Finally, in desperation, I began taking the abandoned anti-depressant tablets which the psychiatrist had prescribed.

The final strands which would bring home just how much unfinished business still hung over us began to be drawn together in the weeks after Asil's arrival. I had gone to Turkey with Fehim and Tijen to help her contract hotels for her holiday firm brochure during the coming season and Lesley Ellwood was staying at our flat in Kyrenia for a holiday with her children. One night, I rang Lesley from the Turkish tourist resort of Marmaris to hear that a "Mr Adams" had called me in North Cyprus about three times and had eventually asked for Asil's telephone number. He said it was urgent and that he had information which would help clear Asil's name, so Lesley gave him the number. "I hope I wasn't wrong to give it?" queried Lesley.

In my room at Marmaris, I did my best to reassure her while my stomach lurched violently at the mention of the name "Mr Adams". I had only seen the man briefly on one occasion, but I knew him to be an acquaintance of Wendy Welsher. Events since then had demonstrated to me that Wendy Welsher was not what she seemed to be...neither too, it was likely, was this mysterious "Mr Adams". I was not sure I wanted to find out who these people really were. I felt sure any contact with them spelt trouble.

While I was still in Turkey, "Mr Adams" called Asil on the number Lesley had given him. In the meantime, he had also tried to approach Asil through his lawyer in North Cyprus, Ali Riza Görgün. "I would like to speak to you and I think you ought to listen to me," he told Asil enigmatically when he eventually got through, asking if the two of them could meet somewhere.

Asil, immediately scenting a possible trap to lure him away from North Cyprus, replied coolly, "Whatever you have to say, come here and tell me."

"Mr Adams" was reluctant at first and pressed Asil as to whether he could guarantee his safety if he came to North Cyprus. Asil asked him why he thought he might be in danger. Then, intrigued to hear what the man had to say, told him, "If you want to speak to me, you have no need to worry about your safety."

When Asil told me about this conversation, I was very firm with him. I told him what little I knew - that this man was a friend of Wendy Welsher - and that I did not want anything to do with him. "Mr Adams" turned up in North Cyprus and, meeting Asil alone at his office, announced that his real name was Michael Francis. He set forth allegations of how he - and through him, Wendy Welsher - had been recruited by the authorities apparently to help Asil, but how the initial plan to secure his freedom had allegedly turned into a plot to entrap him and his family - a plot Francis claimed he had effectively scuppered by disappearing the very day Asil and I had been arrested, instead of returning with the "evidence" to England. He claimed the plot had had approval in Britain at the highest level, from the police and Serious Fraud Office to MI6 and beyond. To most people, it would have seemed incredible. Suspicious at first, Asil tested Francis by listening in as he called one of his police contacts. The conversation he heard - and tape recorded - was enough to convince my brother. Francis eventually confirmed his version of events in a signed affidavit.

Asil had half expected Francis to ask him for money, but no cash request came. Francis said he sought only protection for himself - and for his wife and three children who were still in London. During a series of meetings with Asil, Francis claimed he was afraid that the police intended to implicate him, too, in the alleged plot, and when he had seen on the news that Asil was in North Cyprus, he had decided to chance his luck and seek refuge there too. Late that summer, Wendy Welsher, too, arrived in North Cyprus - claiming to have been involved by the authorities in a smear campaign against Asil and to have fled a police "safe house" - and gave her own written corroboration of the bizarre story Francis had told.

Although I had been aware since my arrest the previous November that something very strange had gone on involving Wendy Welsher, it was only after she and Michael Francis arrived in North Cyprus that I discovered the full extent of the alleged conspiracy in which they had had a part. Francis and Welsher made a video tape detailing exactly what they claimed they and their contacts within the authorities had done and backed up the taped evidence with their own sworn affidavits. When I heard from Asil about the tale they told, I was horrified that they had dared to show their faces...and still more horrified that Asil was going to look after the two of them and their families. "After what they have tried to do to us, how on earth can you bear to have anything to do with them, let alone keep them?" I asked him, aghast.

"Bilge, I have to look after them - they are the only witnesses I have got who can prove what they tried to do," he told me firmly on more than one occasion. It was one of the few times in our lives when Asil and I simply could not see eye to eye.

My first encounter with Welsher and Francis came in October when I went to Asil's office in Nicosia to view the video tape and see for myself what had gone on. I had tried to steel myself for the occasion and surprised myself and the two friends who came with me by taking it all rather calmly. I realised these people had come to North Cyprus to help by owning up and I had to respect that, at least. But as soon as I walked into the room and saw Welsher, I felt numb inside. She came straight up to me and kept saying over and over how sorry she was, telling me how she had never intended to hurt us. She said she had come to realise that what she was doing was wrong, but that she was by then too deeply enmeshed and too frightened to do anything. I tried to be polite, but I just could not bring myself to speak to her properly - I was in a state of shock to come face to face with this woman who had done us so much harm.

Watching that video tape and discovering how we had been duped had an immediate and shattering effect on me. To hear how those two people had cold-bloodedly tried to frame us, was ghastly. It left me emotionally churned up and feeling physically sick. Before, I had been bewildered. Now we knew at least part of the truth. The weight of evidence they gave convinced me that Welsher and Francis had had contact with the police as they claimed. Even if the two were lying about having been approached by the police, and had in fact gone to the authorities with their own scheme, the fact remained that the police had gone along with the plan to frame us - they had conspired to try to entrap us. While Asil seemed more settled by the knowledge, I was plunged further into depression.

How could anyone be so cruel to another person, to plot to hurt them so badly? I felt disappointed with human behaviour - with the capacity for betrayal - yet angry at myself for being so naive as to be taken in by the yarn that Welsher had spun. When I looked back on my contacts with her, I kicked myself for not questioning her more closely and for never having been suspicious of her overt friendliness to our family. Though she had never met us before, she had seemed truly sympathetic to our plight. But that, I considered afterwards, had been a deliberate ploy to win us round - and her sympathy had touched on my mother's one weak spot...her children's welfare. On a personal level at least, I had always been used to taking people at face value. Never again would I be so trusting. For a long time afterwards, I could not sleep at night, going over the previous two and a half years in my mind and wishing that somehow I could turn the clock back. Day and night, I raged at myself for having been so stupid, so gullible. Perhaps the experience will prove a good thing. Maybe it had made me naive, spending so much of my life never seeing the dark side of humanity. But at the age of forty-seven, the sudden, forced awareness of evil was a very uncomfortable burden to bear. The mental blackness that threatened to engulf me then would prove a frequent companion. Even snatches of family happiness - the birth to Tijen in 1996 of my first grandchild, a little girl named Safiye in honour of her great-grandmother, and Irfan's 1995 marriage to Fousun, the girl who had been at his side as I waved goodbye to him in London - would only serve to drive away the dark clouds for a while.

By the time we watched that sickening video tape, the initial euphoria had already given way to hard work and financial headaches for Asil as he got down to the task of unravelling the effects of his enforced absence from the businesses on the island. As soon as the press interest had died down, he began going into the Polly Peck offices every day to examine the state of affairs. What he found were businesses which, over months of neglect and financial difficulty, had run up enormous debts - including owings amounting to billions of Turkish lira in unpaid tax and social security premiums. He also uncovered many instances where senior staff within the companies had abused their position. Some people were sacked. Others resigned before they could be fired. I know Asil was very disappointed by the breaches of his trust, but typically he insisted in looking on the bright side, telling me, "Bilge, we must not judge this country's people on the three per cent of the population we have misjudged - don't forget, the other ninety-seven per cent are honest and hard-working."

It took several months for him even to get to the bottom of the situation, but it was to be a far longer haul to try and get the companies back on a survival footing. He knew a long, legal fight-back lay ahead for him, during which time cash flow and investment opportunities would be severely restricted, and he wanted to protect both the companies themselves and the jobs of their workers during the difficult times to come. Yet the more he studied the figures, he realised he was to have no option but redundancies. It was ironic. So much of the reason behind all the difficulties he had gone through in England had been because he had avoided making the North Cyprus economy suffer, but now he could see that that was exactly what was going to happen as a result of the action he was to be forced to take. Sometimes, I know, he found it deeply depressing to think that all his struggle had been in vain. He spoke infrequently about his business troubles, but during those days he spent trawling through the books I could see the strain on his face. He sold off some assets to try and bring in a little cash, but it just was not enough. Only tough measures, he knew, coupled with patience, would see the steady climb back to a sound financial footing - not just for his companies, but with them the entire economy. He knew it would be a long haul to whittle down the simply enormous debts he had found, but now he was among his own people and he felt sure they would give him the time he needed to realise the dream they all cherished - a North Cyprus that was economically self-sufficient.

But it seemed time was a luxury he was not to be allowed. The New Year of 1994 saw a new government in North Cyprus after a general election produced a "hung" parliament. Into power came a right-left coalition between the Democrat Party of Hakki Atun, a former leading member of the National Unity Party which Asil had supported at the 1990 polls, and the Republican Turkish Party of Özker Özgür. As months passed under the new administration, Asil found himself under ever-growing pressure from the government to pay off the companies' debts, yet still unable to find any source of finance. In November that year, we heard one day, quite out of the blue, that officials from the Finance and Economy Ministry's tax department had been sent in to take over the management of the Jasmine Court Hotel, in Kyrenia, and the Palm Beach at Famagusta, in order to recoup some of the outstanding amount. Asil was ill in bed that day, and while Fehim and I were visiting him, the news came through in a telephone call from a member of hotel staff. Ministry officials, we learned, had been put in charge of all cash-handling points, under orders to collect what money they could. In fact, over the weeks it would take for Asil to reach an agreement on a debt rescheduling and get the tax men pulled out, the ministry's actions served only to make financial recovery more difficult. While cash was milked out of the businesses, the civil servants, with no idea of the hotel trade, acted wherever they could to try and cut costs, upsetting ordering systems which they patently did not understand and disrupting the internal cash-flow completely. Asil was typically quiet when he learned of the court-sanctioned take-over, but I sensed he was deeply upset. At moments of crisis, I have heard him bawl and swear with the best of them, but this time he was very calm - too calm. He seemed in shock. On reflection, what hurt him - and me - was the realisation of just how great a role personal spite and resentment, even at the highest levels, had played in the authorities' actions. Such heavy-handed tactics had never before been brought to bear on tax debtors, and it was clear that there were some behind the move taking the opportunity to settle old scores against an Asil Nadir now operating from a obviously weakened business power-base.

Political resentment was rife. Kept out of power by Asil's involvement - against my better judgement - in the 1990 general election, the Republican Turkish Party had been brought to unexpected prominence and came to their role complete with a baggage of hostility against my brother which, over the months, crystallised in negative argument behind the scenes of government and even outspoken comment in the British press. Even those who had no personal or political axe to grind - and, indeed, many who had had reason to be grateful for his patronage in the past - built up a wall of indifference against him. Where they had been happy to accept his support as a far-away "captain of industry", now he was no longer safely at arm's length, they didn't want to know. Where they could have used their power to smooth the way as he tried to get the companies back on their feet, they sat back and allowed his enemies to make the running. And where they should have seized the chance to tap into his extensive commercial knowledge for the benefit of economically-ailing North Cyprus, never once did they seek his advice. The truth is that they felt threatened by his evident popularity. But their attitude revealed just how little they understood Asil. He had no interest in their political positions for himself and his hopes and visions lay far beyond the bounds of North Cyprus, with its population of less than 200,000, in the wider world of business.

There was worse still to come. As the winter of 1994 bit hard, with its slack trade and with no let-up in sight to the continuing financial squeeze, managers of both the Sunzest fruit processing plant and the Uni-Pac packaging business found themselves in dire straits. Asil had deliberately channelled what spare funds he could find into Sunzest, banking on pre-election pledges from the new government partners to increase subsidies to the citrus sector. But no subsidies were forthcoming. When Asil challenged one of the left-wing ministers, he received a sneering response: "Surely, Mr Nadir, you don't believe campaign promises?" Now Asil found himself losing more money than ever. It became virtually impossible to find the cash to pay the wages each month. Some of the workers took to the streets, demonstrating outside the Polly Peck building where Asil had his office - he was particularly hurt to see among them some of the citrus growers to whom our father had first given money all those years ago to get their orchards back into production. The fact was that when Asil had first gone over

310

the books, and discovered just what bad shape companies like Sunzest were in, he should have let most of the staff go straight away - yet he had kept them all on the pay-roll for as long as possible, reluctant to make so many unemployed and certain that he would be able to reach some solution with the government. As he explained later, with a wry smile: "The problem has always been that when it comes to Cyprus and Turkey, I don't think with my business brain, but with my heart."

Asil's nationalistic feelings had always been hard even for me to understand - I often told him that where North Cyprus was concerned, he became over-generous, but we could never agree. During those winter months, though, he came close just to giving everything up - he was much lower than I had ever seen him. The pressure from the government and the outcry of his staff seemed the final irony. North Cyprus had been his underlying business raison d'être for so many years, and his close involvement in the country had been the catalyst for the disasters which had befallen him since 1990. Now it seemed as if everything was being flung back in his face. Privately, Asil admitted he felt betrayed. He found himself feeling, more than ever, an outsider in the land he thought of as home. Maybe, he told me, he had been deceiving himself all those years when he thought his countrymen shared his dreams for the future. Suddenly, it seemed to him that his visions, outlook and determination were quite alien to them. Having once thought only the Greek Cypriots' anti-Nadir lobby and the British Establishment were against him, now he could scarcely believe what was happening to him in North Cyprus. I felt for him - he never got angry, but the experience was breaking his heart. The only thing that kept him going through those tough months was his continued faith in Turkish Cypriots as a whole - faith that it was only a very few who seemed set against him.

That December, Asil managed to persuade the TRNC government to give him the time he needed. After a "cards on the table" meeting with the country's ministers and President Rauf Denktas, at which Asil spelt out the stark options - either give him the breathing space to get he businesses back on an even keel and start repaying their debts, or he would have to close the companies down - a schedule of repayment was agreed for the outstanding tax and social security. Asil agreed to it more in hope than expectation of finding new sources of capital to meet the repayments. As the first instalment drew near, he became gradually more desperate to find the cash he needed. Early one morning in February 1995, he telephoned me with a strange request and an even stranger tale. That night, he told me, he had dreamt that he should contact Sidika Atalay, a Turkish-based businesswoman of Cypriot origin, and now he wanted me to call her and arrange a meeting between them. I found it all hard to take in, but he was deadly serious and told me he had a feeling she might be able to help. I was just as serious - Sidika Atalay and Asil had met way back in 1979 in Libya, when both were in textile businesses, and I had heard of her just a few months earlier when she had been in North Cyprus to open her own bank, but I had never met her and did not feel I could ring out of the blue to ask her to help my brother. "Sorry, but you'll have to call her yourself," I told him. I think Asil was quite shocked, but he did, indeed, ring Sidika that day. It was not an easy call for a proud man to make - that he did was a measure of his determination and desperation.

In that call, Asil admitted he needed help and offered Sidika a commercial partnership in return. As a former country girl from Cyprus - now a forty-eight-year-old divorced mother of two sons and a successful businesswoman who had developed one of Istanbul's foremost hotels - Asil felt she might, like him, have her heart in the island and might be open to the idea of doing business in North Cyprus. He was right. As Sidika told us later, she had followed Asil's business progress from a distance for many years since their early meeting and had long admired what he had done to help the Turkish Cypriot economy. She knew, too, how important it was for North Cyprus to keep the Polly Peck businesses going. Sidika agreed to discuss entering into a partnership with Asil and within two days had transferred to North Cyprus sufficient funds to cover the first repayment to the government. A fortnight later, Asil and Sidika met again for the first time in more than fifteen years and discovered themselves to be a good business match. Both successful in their own right, from very similar origins and commercial backgrounds, they shared the same deep belief in the Turkish Cypriot cause and the need to bring investment and prosperity to the TRNC, along with an understanding of all its political and economic problems.

At that time, a new opportunity was presenting itself. The London-based administrators of Polly Peck had been approaching various business-people in North Cyprus, offering to sell the company's assets in the country - predominantly the hotels, Sunzest and Uni-Pac Packaging. Among those who had expressed interest in buying were a financier, Elmas Güzelyurtlu, and his partner, Mehmet Civa. The administrators no doubt thought they would be ideal new owners - they were supporters of Özker Özgür's Republican Turkish Party, which was so hostile to Asil that selling to them, it must have seemed, would effectively put the businesses out of my brother's reach. Unknown to the administrators, however, Güzelyurtlu contacted Asil and it was agreed that he and his partner should be the "front men" for Asil and Sidika in conducting the negotiations. In due course, a deal was struck giving ownership of the businesses to a company called Learned

Limited. After separate negotiations, Learned also agreed to purchase the lease of the half-completed Crystal Cove Hotel. The directors of Learned were, on the face of it, Elmas Güzelyurtlu and Mehmet Civa, but that was later amended to leave Asil and Sidika as sole directors.

What the administrators thought of the outcome of the deal, I don't know, but the evidence of what was to happen was staring them in the face, if only they could have seen it. I remember Asil telling me one day over lunch how "Bilge" was buying the hotels. I could not think what he was getting at, until he reminded me that my name was Turkish for "wise"…or "learned". At that time, the deal had not been finalised, and I was alarmed that the administrators might realise the significance of the name and call it all off. Asil, though, wore a huge grin and thought the whole thing was an enormous piece of fun.

With the legal wrangling settled over the ownership of the businesses - after rumbling on ever since Polly Peck's collapse in 1990 - Asil turned in earnest to pulling the financial threads back together. In the spring of 1995, he struck a deal with the government to hand over Sunzest to the government in lieu of most of the tax and social security debts. Having lost his enthusiasm for saving Uni-Pac after the protests of the previous winter and with no continuing need to make cardboard boxes once Sunzest had gone, he shut the business down. Within a year, under severe pressure over continuing debts, he offloaded, the Jasmine Court Hotel, then sold the Palm Beach and Crystal Cove hotels, while holding on to his private banking and newspaper interests which had weathered the crisis. My mother and I were shaken by the rapid turn of events, which ended the family links with the Polly Peck operations; I was sorry to see Asil forced into hasty action. But he was relieved to see an end to the cash "fight" with the TRNC authorities for which he had never had any appetite. He told me, "I'm not upset, I'm disappointed - disappointed with my own country."

Asil began to look further afield - seriously eyeing Eastern Europe, the Middle East and the Turkic states of Central Asia as the regions for future trading opportunities. And in May 1997 he made his boldest move yet since leaving Britain. Almost four years to the day after his return to North Cyprus, he flew out again by private plane and landed in Istanbul, the commercial capital of Turkey, to embark upon the latest chapter of his business life. I watched him leave his "sanctuary" with trepidation, but my brother assured me that, as a citizen of the Turkish Republic, he could not be extradited to the UK. Indeed, his first official visitor to welcome him to Turkey was a senior government minister - and when British diplomatic staff later came calling on the Ankara authorities, asking them to hand Asil over, they were told in no uncertain terms to drop the matter. I sense in some quarters a guilty feeling that

Turkey needs to make amends for having left Asil in the lurch when Polly Peck's troubles first began in 1990. That echoes a remark that the late President Turgut Özal was said to have made to his son, and which was passed on to us, shortly before his death in the spring of 1993. Özal himself never had the chance to act upon it.

Soon after Asil went to Istanbul, he asked Fehim and me to join him - and by then, there was nothing to hold us back in North Cyprus. After three years of hanging on to the Olive Tree Hotel, hoping for an economic upturn, or a political change enabling us to compete on equal terms in the holiday marketplace, by 1996 I had realised the day was fast approaching when I might no longer have the luxury of choosing whether to keep the hotel or sell - I had to start listening to what the figures were telling me, not what my heart was saying. Matters had come to a head that June - debt repayments were imminent and I had known that if we could not make them, the banks would move in. Anxious not to repeat the experience of the knock-down Elite Optics sale, when desperation had backed me into a financial corner, I had decided to seek a buyer as quickly as possible. It had been one of the hardest decisions I ever made. I had not been the only one in tears when, flanked by Fehim and Mehmet Ziya Berkman, I called in all the senior staff and told them the news. Of all the businesses we had lost, that had been the biggest wrench. Over the three years when we had been concentrating on the Olive Tree, we had got to know all the staff personally, and many of them had been with us from the very start. I only hoped that the wider resources and marketing potential of the new owners - a Turkish hotels chain - would enable the business to prosper. With no business commitments left, Fehim and I flew to Istanbul in the late summer of 1997.

At his office in a converted "yali", or summer house, beside the Bosphorus, we found Asil busy using his knowledge of Western business ways and his enormous range of contacts in the Turkic world to unite East and West in a series of mutually beneficial projects. As word spreads that he is "back in business", many trading partners from the London days are knocking on his door, keen to link up with him again. With all his old enthusiasm back, Asil is more confident and working harder than I have ever seen before. When I comment that he needs to slow down, and not push himself to work seven days a week, he tells me that this is now his number one priority and he has no time to lose if he is to make up in business terms for the last seven lost years. As determined as he is to prove his innocence of the charges that were laid against him, he is equally determined to prove he can rebuild his life despite

314

all the odds. I am glad to see his ambitions are undimmed by all the strain, and, so focused is he on the task in hand, I suspect he is only half joking when he tells me he intends to build up a new business empire which "will make Polly Peck look like a grocer's shop".

Asil's other big priority over the last five years, of course, has been his campaign for justice, with its painstaking search for evidence of just what - and who - was behind the events of 1990. In the immediate aftermath of his return to North Cyprus, a chain of new developments had begun in the British courts, with John Turner, the former chief accountant and company secretary at PPI, being found not guilty of false accounting, which he had denied, when the SFO decided to offer no evidence against him. The case against Asil - at that time thirteen counts of theft involving £30 million - was adjourned indefinitely.

As long ago as mid-November '93, Asil had been officially cleared of the allegations that he had been involved in any conspiracy to bribe Mr Justice Tucker and, in vain, Anthony Scrivener had called for an inquiry into how the claims had been made in the first place. Even at the last minute, the prosecuting authorities had tried to avoid owning up to the fact that there had never been any evidence - as the transcript of the exchange in court made clear:

> "Counsel: The Crown Prosecution from now on will conclude there is no credible evidence.
>
> Judge: I don't like credible. There is NO evidence - now you can't be more cringing than that, can you? Now you've got that noted, haven't you?"

The same month, the SFO had apologised in court to Mr Justice Tucker over the purported plot, saying it now realised the allegations against the judge to be "spurious and groundless".

The next month, at the beginning of December 1993, Sir Nicholas Lyell had finally admitted that he had misled Parliament by denying that many of Asil's privileged documents had indeed been mishandled by the Serious Fraud Office. Two sealed bags of papers had been opened, photocopied and circulated to the prosecution team, he had admitted in a written Commons reply. The reaction - or lack of it - to the Attorney-General's apologetic admission finally convinced me that no-one was interested in the truth. I felt sure we were never going to get justice. Sir Nicholas had picked a good moment to make his announcement - it was the day that the Princess of Wales announced her retirement from public life, and the media went mad. Misleading Parliament is a serious matter, but you would not have thought so from the muted reaction to his statement and its low-key coverage by the royalty-obsessed press. Nonetheless, it was a vindication for Michael Mates, who - long after Asil came to North Cyprus - has continued to write to the Attorney-General about the case. "Hasn't the time now come to abandon the charges against Asil Nadir and instead institute a searching inquiry into the conduct of the Serious Fraud Office...and maybe an inquiry also into the conduct of Sir Nicholas Lyell?" came the lone voice of late John Junor in *The Mail on Sunday*. I could not have agreed more.

Once Asil had been officially cleared, I, too, had joined the legal fight, with lawyers on my behalf issuing a writ claiming damages for my wrongful arrest and unlawful imprisonment. Serving the writ proved a problem. The SFO said it had not arrested me, since the officers involved had been from the Metropolitan Police - although I clearly recalled DCI Watson showing me an identity card declaring him to be from the SFO. The Met denied any responsibility, saying the arresting officers had been seconded at the time to the SFO. In the end, my lawyers served a writ on both authorities, but in July 1996 the case against the SFO was struck out in the High Court, on the grounds that the actions of the Metropolitan Police officers involved were the responsibility of their commissioner, not the SFO. I could not accept this. If the argument was allowed to stand, it meant Elm Street was effectively above the law - the SFO could do as it pleased and wash its hands of all liability. As my lawyer pointed out in the press, the officers who arrested me were working for the SFO, where all the case files were kept, and the Met had no documentation. He told *The Independent* newspaper, "It is important for the SFO to be held accountable for the people working under its direction. If what they say is right, the SFO can never be held accountable for its actions. The law has not caught up with the creation of the SFO."

That trumped-up bribery plot and the manner of my arrest and questioning had changed my life for ever, leaving an indelible black stain. Someone had to be responsible for what had happened to me, but it seemed they were not willing to admit it. We took the case to a higher court, which ruled that the SFO did indeed bear responsibility and that I had the right to sue. I am still considering my next move. To take the case further will require considerable financial outlay, with the risk of nothing in return. But I still want justice, answers to my questions and the opportunity, at last, to lay this unfinished business to rest.

Since that time, evidence has been coming in thick and fast from unexpected quarters, gathering pace as the months and years have gone on and enabling us, piece by piece, to fit the jigsaw together. In many cases, information has come from people who, five years on, are no longer in the same job as they had in 1990, and no longer feel the obligation of loyalty to keep quiet about what they know. By chance, Arseven Gümüs bumped into Trevor Davies, our old Noble Raredon director, at a concert in London and could not resist ticking him off about having left us so quickly after the troubles began. As Arseven reported back to me later, he was taken aback to be told by Trevor that he had been advised by the British Foreign Office to "get out". Other sources have been less forthcoming, though their silence itself seems revealing. In early 1996, my brother's supporters in the United States wrote to their Central Intelligence Agency requesting them to disclose what information they held about Polly Peck International, Del Monte and Asil Nadir. The reply they received was that the CIA could "neither confirm nor deny the existence or non-existence" of records relating to Asil, quoting grounds of "national security", "national defence and foreign policy", and protection of "intelligence sources and methods". Records held on PPI and Del Monte would be forwarded under the Freedom of Information Act, said the CIA's letter in April 1996. US legislation provides for a ten-working-day disclosure deadline in such cases. Two years later, no details have emerged.

A major new turn in Asil's case came in 1996 when the British Court of Appeal was asked to judge whether Ramadan Güney was liable to forfeit any of the million-pound surety he had given for Asil's bail. Mr Justice Tucker had ordered Güney to pay £650,000, but the appeal court ruled that my brother had, in fact, not been on bail at the time he left Britain in 1993, taking the view that Asil had surrendered his bail at his first Old Bailey appearance in 1992, and that the trial judge, Mr Justice Tucker, had not renewed the bail thereafter. The SFO appealed, but in a seven-page judgement released in May 1996, five law lords dismissed their petition unanimously, upholding the lower court's decision that Güney was not liable to pay anything.

The ruling came at a time when Asil's case was already in the legal spotlight. In September 1994 - against Asil's advice but with his blessing - Elizabeth Forsyth, the former head of South Audley Management who had been in North Cyprus since January 1992, had flown back to London to face questioning by the Serious Fraud Office, confident that she could wipe out any slur on her name and, at the same time, blow the Polly Peck case wide open. I had been less confident on her behalf, feeling the SFO would be determined to make a charge "stick" against the woman who had been described in the press as Asil's "Miss

Moneypenny" - if they could not, they would face some very tough questions about their handling of the entire affair, particularly in view of other high-profile prosecution failures. Elizabeth had been charged on two counts of handling funds allegedly stolen from PPI's Uni-Pac subsidiary in North Cyprus, although neither charge related to any transaction over which Asil himself had ever been accused, and our fears that she would be made a "scapegoat" in Asil's absence seemed justified when - after a six-week Old Bailey trial, ironically, presided over by Mr Justice Tucker - she was convicted in March 1996. When she was jailed the next month for a shocking five years, it seemed to us and other observers the action of a judge anxious to get tough with an associate of Asil, "the one that got away".

Several months into her jail term, Elizabeth was granted leave to appeal against both her conviction and sentence, and when the appeal court sat in the last week of January 1997, they had stunning news. Without a word having been said on Elizabeth's behalf, Lord Justice Beldam immediately quashed her sentence, saying he and the other two judges, having read the papers in the case, had deemed it "disproportionate". It was a nerve-racking few weeks until mid-March to hear the judges' all-important verdict on the issue of the conviction itself. In the end, it was all over in just quarter of an hour, when, in a brief statement accompanied by a fifty-page written transcript, the appeal judges said the conviction was unsafe. They ruled that Mr Justice Tucker had "plainly fallen into error" in not allowing my brother to give evidence at the trial via a video link from North Cyprus. Moreover, they said, he had twice misdirected the jury on crucial issues before they reached their verdict.

While we were all relieved for Elizabeth's sake, more significantly, the final stages of her appeal had turned up an important new piece of evidence for Asil's own legal fight. In 1991, the late Dennis Robertson, then a senior partner at PPI's auditor, Stoy Hayward, had made witness statements to the Serious Fraud Office about the company's financial health. The statements he made should have been shown to both Asil and Elizabeth's defence team, but were not revealed by the SFO until after Elizabeth's appeal hearing opened. Crucially, it turned out when the papers finally emerged, Mr Robertson had given the SFO evidence of the bona fide nature of PPI's "secondary banking" operation in North Cyprus - whereby payments were made in "hard currency" from PPI in London, but were always matched by Turkish lira receipts. The belated discovery of these documents was shocking - and their content potentially highly damaging to the already-tarnished credibility of the SFO. Dennis Robertson had told the SFO as long ago as 1991 that he had overseen the auditing of all PPI's books, and in his professional

318

opinion there was nothing wrong. Yet still the investigators had continued to press more and more theft charges against Asil, based on exactly such transfers from PPI's headquarters in London to its outpost in North Cyprus. Mr Robertson's statement was particularly interesting in the light of evidence from one of the most telling witnesses at Elizabeth's original trial, a forensic scientist - veteran of more than eighty cases, including previous work on behalf of the SFO - who had examined Uni-Pac's records in the TRNC and told the jury the books, in which allegedly stolen funds were accounted for, did not appear to have been tampered with. His testimony echoed the Binder Hamlyn report and related forensic testing which Asil's defence team had supplied - also way back in 1991. The SFO had brought all the charges against my brother, and those against Elizabeth, while refusing to view the books themselves in North Cyprus because of its unrecognised status. Of course, a visit in December 1996 by British Foreign Secretary Malcolm Rifkind - who, like the Lord Chancellor before him in 1993, met President Denktas at his offices in Nicosia - had finally exposed their political scruples for the smokescreen they were.

So how could the SFO, who had not bothered to make the same financial inspections in the TRNC themselves, be so certain that what they saw in PPI's London accounts was theft - and not just complex internal transfers of funds? Why were they apparently determined to deny - and, indeed, it seems, cover up - the assurances of a man like Dennis Robertson, backed up as they were then by forensic tests...if not out of blind desperation to shift the focus of blame for Polly Peck's destruction? The ramifications of the auditor's non-disclosed evidence are enormous. It remains to be seen what effect its sudden discovery may have on my brother's case, as he prepares to join battle against the SFO for abuse of the legal process. Asil, as ever, is boundlessly optimistic. I just hope that, at last, justice may prevail.

EPILOGUE

How do I end this story, this tale of an immigrant family which went from rags to riches and then lost virtually everything? And how can I end when the story of which I write - already so long and complex - has still to reach its own conclusion? In the years since we left Britain, I have felt some of our bitterness start to seep away in the warmth of the Cypriot sun. Yet many of the questions which were turning over in my mind on the February afternoon that I left London remain unanswered to this day.

Brought up to revere British justice, it shocked me to realise that the system could be abused. I had always treasured the belief that a person was innocent until proven guilty - yet I look back now and see clearly that events, and people, conspired from the outset to undermine that fundamental principle in my brother's case. What should we make of the SFO's behaviour - the melodramatic style of Asil's arrest; excessive raids and the publicity surrounding them; the removal and copying of vital defence documents; the twenty-nine-month delay in agreeing on what charges should be brought and bringing the case to court, where it could be fought? What of the most bizarre event in this whole peculiar saga - the moment when, we have been told, the Establishment turned on itself blindly and attacked its own sacred principles? To suggest, without evidence, that a senior judge might be party to a conspiracy to pervert the course of justice was in itself a perversion of the course of justice. What was so important about my brother's case that the authorities seemed hell bent on securing a conviction - on whatever grounds they could find - and were even willing to implicate me? These aspects, and more, stand testimony to the fact that my brother could never have had a fair trial in Britain - a judgement in which I am far from alone.

And what of the conduct of the Attorney-General, Sir Nicholas Lyell? How could he admit that he stood up in Parliament and misled MPs, yet still remain in charge of the legal system - figurehead of the law, of truth, of fairness - while Michael Mates lost his job for speaking out on behalf of a man seeking justice? Lyell said there were no grounds for an independent inquiry. But what kind of nation has Britain become if such issues are allowed to rest unquestioned?

321

Almost eight years on from the collapse of PPI and long after Asil's dramatic flight from the injustice he felt closing in on him, so many people are still in limbo - myself, my family, the shareholders and former staff of two companies. North Cyprus too - the country whose problems and hopes have been such an important part of this story - is still spurned by the world. So much in our lives has changed, yet still so much remains unresolved.

When I first sat down to begin this story, the sun was rising over beautiful North Cyprus, appearing on the horizon where the long, narrow peninsula of the Karpaz points like a finger towards Syria. Each evening, after my day's work, the sun would sink, an orange ball, towards the fertile farms and citrus groves of the west. At that hour, the darkening mountains seemed somehow nearer than during the day, as if I could reach out and stroke their craggy faces. Behind me, I could make out the towers of lofty St Hilarion castle perched on the highest peak, sharply defined against the pale sky, while below, shadows of the ancient castle fell across the pretty harbour of Kyrenia. The distant melody of the muezzin would call the faithful to evening prayer from the mosque, bringing me comfort. Somehow, the sound spelt order and safety in our dangerous world and I would wonder how I could go on feeling angry in such a lovely setting. But even the warmth of the Cypriot sun has not been able to melt away all the bitterness, while the beauties, the sights and sounds of that strange-yet-familiar country, where we have tried to build new lives, are not enough to over-ride the questions and heal my wounds. In spirit, I feel like a refugee, belonging nowhere. Sometimes, when my brother drops his guard, I sense that same rootlessness in him too. Not one to dwell on the past, though, he is still strong despite all he has endured. Sitting in the tranquil, almost monastic atmosphere of his walled garden in Lapta, amid jewel-coloured bougainvillaea and the heady scent of jasmine, Asil, the supreme optimist, could find the tiniest trace of hope in even the blackest moments. But I knew not to misread his contentment - within him remains the old restlessness to move on to the next adventure, and it is this that spurs him on.

As I end my story, we are sitting in Istanbul and only now, at last, am I allowing myself to hope that the worst is behind us. Outside the office lap the waters of the Bosphorus, and as huge tankers glide past I know Asil is dreaming of the day when, again, his own "ship will come in". Ever superstitious, he is convinced that life is divided into seven-year cycles and we are just embarking on the next, upward phase after the slump that began in 1990. As I watch him scan the global maps on his wall and plan the next business step as a "citizen of the world", I wonder cautiously if he might be right. Through the office window I see the

Fatih Sultan Mehmet Bridge spanning the busy waterway, literally connecting two continents, and East with West. It seems a metaphor for the link role that Asil has assumed. I sense this move is right for him and I am glad that, after all the adversities, we are all still together.

Belief in the family, with its indomitable spirit, humour, faith and optimism, is the one thing which has helped us to survive. On our last shared birthday, my card from Asil reminded me that we still have the important things in life - liberty and hope that, as he wrote, "the best years are still to come". Yet I still find it hard to believe all that has happened to us, and if I cannot accept the past, how can I be so sure of the future? I often bring to mind a Turkish saying "Her olmayan iste bir hayir var" - "Out of evil, comes good." I can only pray that this is true.